CRITICAL ACCLAIM
FOR *TRAVELERS' TALES*

"I loved *Travelers' Tales Thailand*. It parts the curtain on a country that has long fascinated and mystified me."

—David Lamb, author of *A Sense of Place*

"...The breadth and color of the collective portrait they provide of Thailand is remarkable."

—Colman Andrews, *Los Angeles Times*

"*Travelers' Tales Thailand* provides a rich and varied look at this ancient and exotic nation...[it] showed me parts of Thailand I never would have found with a map and a standard guidebook. Many of these pieces read like short stories and that's the beauty. The places and the people are real; the events could happen to anyone."

—Judge's citation, Society of American Travel Writers Foundation, Lowell Thomas Travel Journalism Awards

"O'Reilly and Habegger have not settled for the obvious.... As a result this anthology offers a comprehensive and fascinating introduction to the 'Land of Smiles.'"

—The Elliot Bay Book Company, Seattle

"For travelers who want a wider introduction to a country and its culture, *Travelers' Tales* is a valuable addition to any pre-departure reading list."

—Tony Wheeler, publisher, Lonely Planet Publications

"[The] essays...compose a highly personal geographical and cultural portrait of Thailand."

—*Travel & Leisure Asiaweek*

"It made me homesick for Thailand."

—Seth Jacobson, Epicurean International, Inc.

T R A V E L E R S' T A L E S

THAILAND

TRAVELERS' TALES

THAILAND

* * *

Collected and Edited by

JAMES O'REILLY AND LARRY HABEGGER

TRAVELERS' TALES

SAN FRANCISCO

ทำดีได้ดี ทำชั่วได้ชั่ว

Tham dii, dâi dii; tham chûa, dâi chûa.

"Do good, get good; do evil, get evil."

— THAI PROVERB

Table of Contents

Part One
ESSENCE OF THAILAND

Part Two
SOME THINGS TO DO

Part Three
GOING YOUR OWN WAY

Part Five
THE LAST WORD

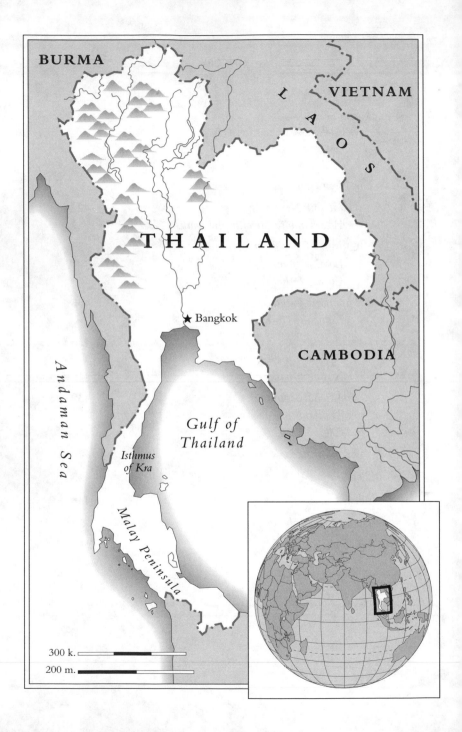

Preface

TRAVELERS' TALES

We are all outsiders when we travel. Whether we go abroad or roam about our own country, we often enter territory so unfamiliar that our frames of reference become sorely inadequate. We need advice not just to avoid offense and danger, but to make our experiences richer, deeper, and more fun.

Traditionally, travel guides have answered the basic questions: what, when, where, how, and how much. A good guidebook is indispensable for all the practical matters that demand attention. More recently, many guidebooks have added cultural and experiential insight to their standard fare, but something important is still missing. Guidebooks don't really prepare *you*, the individual with feelings and fears, hopes and dreams, goals.

This kind of inner preparation is best achieved through travelers' tales, for we get our landmarks more from anecdote than from information. Nothing can replace listening to the experience of others, to the war stories that come out after a few drinks, to the memories that linger and beguile. For millennia it has been this way: at watering holes and wayside inns, the experienced traveler tells those nearby what lies ahead on the ever-mysterious road. Stories stoke the imagination, inspire, frighten, and teach. In stories we see more clearly the urges that bring us to wander, whether it's hunger for change, adventure, self-knowledge, love, curiosity, sorrow, or even something as prosaic as a job assignment or two weeks off.

But travelers' accounts, while profuse, can be hard to track down. Many are simply doomed in a throwaway publishing world. And few of us have the time anyway to read more than one or two books, or the odd pearl found by chance in the Sunday newspaper travel section. Wanderers for years, we've often faced this issue. We've always told ourselves when we got home that we would prepare better for the next trip—read more, study more, talk to more people—but life always seems to interfere and we've rarely managed to do so to our satisfaction. That is one reason for this series. We needed a kind of experiential primer that guidebooks don't offer.

Another path that led us to *Travelers' Tales* has been the enormous change in travel and communications over the last two decades. It is no longer unusual to have ridden a pony across Mongolia, to have celebrated an auspicious birthday on Mt. Kilimanjaro, or honeymooned on the Loire. The one-world monoculture has risen with daunting swiftness, weaving a new cross-cultural rug with it: no longer is it surprising to encounter former headhunters watching *All-Star Wrestling* on their satellite feed, no longer is it shocking to find the last guy at the end of the earth wearing a Harvard t-shirt and asking if you know Michael Jordan. The global village exists in a rudimentary fashion, but it is real.

In 1980, Paul Fussell wrote in *Abroad: British Literary Traveling Between the Wars* a cranky but wonderful epitaph for travel as it was once known, in which he concluded that "we are all tourists now, and there is no escape." It has been projected that by the year 2000, tourism will be the world's largest industry; some say it already is. In either case, this is a horrifying prospect—hordes of us hunting for places that have not been trod on by the rest of us!

Fussell's words have the painful ring of truth, but this is still our world, and it is worth seeing and will be worth seeing next year, or in 50 years, simply because it will always be worth meeting others who continue to see life in different terms than we do, despite the efforts of telecommunication and advertising talents. No amount of creeping homogeneity can quell the endless variation of humanity, and travel in the end is about people, not places. Places only provide different venues, as it were, for life, in which we are all pilgrims who need to talk to each other.

There are also many places around the world where intercultural friction and outright xenophobia are increasing. And the very fact that travel endangers cultures and pristine places more quickly than it used to calls for extraordinary care on the part of today's traveler, a keener sense of personal responsibility. The world is not our private zoo or theme park; we need to be better prepared before we go, so that we might become honored guests and not vilified intruders.

In *Travelers' Tales*, we collect useful and memorable anecdotes by country to produce the kind of sampler we've always wanted to read before setting out. These stories will show you some of the spectrum of experiences to be had or avoided in each country. The authors come from many walks of life: some are teachers, some are musicians, some are entrepreneurs, all are wanderers with a tale to tell. Their stories will help you to deepen and enrich the experiences that you will have as a traveler. Where we've excerpted books, we urge you to go out and read the full work, because no selection can ever do an author justice.

Each *Travelers' Tales* is organized into five simple parts. In the first, we've chosen stories that reflect the ephemeral yet pervasive essence of a country. Part Two contains stories about places and activities that others have found worthwhile. In Part Three, we've chosen stories by people who have made a special connection between their lives and interests and the people and places they visited. Part Four shows some of the struggles and challenges facing a country, and Part Five, "The Last Word," is just that, something of a grace note or harmonic to remind you of the book as a whole.

Our selection of stories in each *Travelers' Tales* is by no means comprehensive, but we are confident it will prime your pump, and make your use of guidebooks more meaningful. *Travelers' Tales* are not meant to replace travel guides, but to accompany them. No longer will you have to go to dozens of sources to map the personal side of your journey. You'll be able to reach for *Travelers' Tales*, and truly prepare yourself before you go.

JAMES O'REILLY AND LARRY HABEGGER

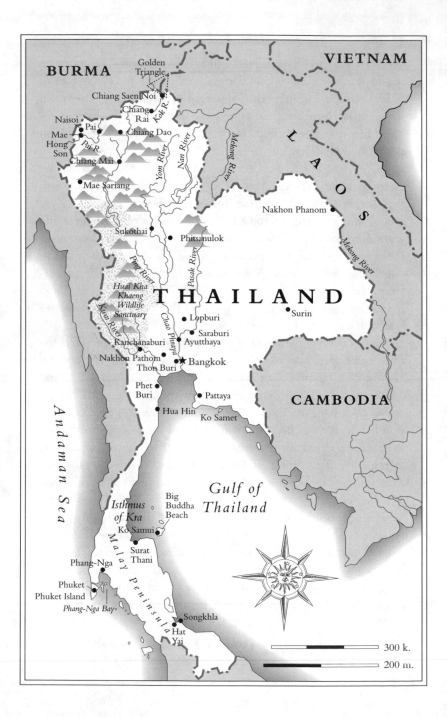

Thailand: An Introduction

Thailand should satisfy just about any traveler's hunger for the exotic, the beautiful, the thrillingly different. But it is a country whose very lure for the foreigner threatens to make it a parody of itself.

It is a country with a deep respect for family and monarchy, and a country with a huge prostitution industry and a corrupt military. It is a thriving place for business, but has serious problems with international copyright and trademark piracy. It is a physically lovely country that is, like many others, being degraded by logging, wildlife exploitation, and overdevelopment. It is a microcosm of all that is right and wrong with tourism, and the traveler's special role as pilgrim, adventurer, and consumer.

But above all Thailand is Buddhist. You'll see evidence of it everywhere, in cities, towns, remote villages, deep in the forest. It influences all segments of society and cuts across all economic levels. Anyone who hopes to gain an understanding of Thailand must understand this. Failure to do so would be like going to Ireland with no appreciation of Catholicism, going to Saudi Arabia thinking Muhammad was just a boxer.

This doesn't mean the country is inaccessible to non–Buddhists. On the contrary, one of the Thais' singular traits is that they don't let religion disturb their lightheartedness and love of life. If eating meat conflicts with the Buddhist tenet proscribing the killing of any creature, never mind, the animal is already dead when the Thai obtains it. Likewise, the killing of insects such as mosquitoes cannot be helped, and the good Thai Buddhist balances such transgressions by "making merit," giving donations of food to monks or gifts to temples. When things go haywire you'll hear the expression *mai pen rai*, or never mind, it doesn't matter. Letting petty matters get in the way of enjoying life just isn't acceptable.

At the same time, Thais take Buddhism seriously. Almost every male spends time as a monk, whether it be a few days or several years. Donning the saffron robe, for whatever period of time, is a highly respected endeavor. Monks are supported by the public, receiving donations of food each day as they wander the streets and byways. This tradition not only provides sustenance for the monks, but also offers a simple way for all to make merit, to learn compassion and generosity, and to enhance their progress with reincarnation.

Thailand, the only country in Southeast Asia never to be colonized, has a long tradition of outsiders in its midst. There is a word to describe foreigners from Europe, America, or Australia: *farang*. It is widely used, often without negative connotation, but some descriptions are indeed unflattering. One states that *farang* are "exceedingly tall, hairy, and evil-smelling." The slang word *kee-nok* likens them to bird dung, something that falls out of the sky. Thais are perplexed by *farang* obsession with time and the future and their apparent disregard for the present. They do not understand Westerners, but for the most part they take us in stride and welcome us with a unique warmth, as we should them, should we have the good fortune to go to this marvelous place.

A Note on Spelling, Meaning, Exchange Rates, and a Warning on Other Matters that Affect the Traveler

As with any tonal language, there are many different ways to spell transliterated Thai words, some of them more correct or less misleading than others. But for the most part we have not tried to be the arbiters of Thai-English spelling, and in most cases have used the spelling our authors chose.

All Thai words are italicized. They are only translated the first time they appear in the text, so for those who dip in and out of the book instead of reading cover to cover, we suggest you turn to the glossary or the index for meaning.

This is not a travel guide in the traditional sense, in which prices and accuracy of exchange rates figure prominently. Consequently, we have not tried to convert figures used by authors to current exchange rates as long as they are in a ballpark with admittedly ill-defined borders.

We are not endorsing products used, trips made, or anything featured in the stories in this book. We urge every traveler to consult not just one, but two or three guidebooks on Thailand, and make careful inquiries about the safety of travel to remote areas. Check with your physician about any health issues that you might face. When in doubt about anything, be a good ambassador.

Above all, talk to people who've been where you want to go or who've done the things you want to do. There is no better source, no travel habit more worth cultivating.

PART ONE

ESSENCE OF THAILAND

* * *

Sixth Sense

Bangkok, for many, has become synonymous with sex.
Robert Sam Anson begs to differ, redefining the
pleasures of the flesh in Thailand's capital.

THE TOURIST BROCHURES WILL TELL YOU THAT BANGKOK IS THE
Venice of the East and that its Thai name translates as City of the
Angels. They will rattle on about the splendor of the Grand Palace,
the awesomeness of the Emerald Buddha, the goldenness of the
sands of Phuket, the magical charms of the hill tribes of the north.
In tones no less rapturous, they will tell you that this improbable,
fairy-tale kingdom—where members of the reigning Chakri dynasty are revered as demigods and where there is a coup attempt,
on average, every three and a half years—is the Land of Smiles.
All of which, more or less, is true.

But that is not why I come here, and—eschewing such worn-
out destinations as Paris, London, and Rome and the whole of the
sun-splashed Caribbean—have been coming here off and on for
nearly twenty years. What brings me to Thailand are reasons far
more basic and far more elusive. It is, you see, the most sensuous
spot on earth.

All right, I know what you are saying. Even from here, in my
orchid-filled aerie high above the Chao Phraya river, with the smell
of cooking curries wafting in and the sun glistening off the spires
of Wat Po—even from here, literally halfway around the world,

where I awake each morning to the sound of crowing cocks and chanting monks, I can see the smirks. "Sensuous, huh? What this guy really means is sexual."

There are three specifically Thai concepts you're bound to come across and which may help you to comprehend a sometimes laissez-faire attitude to delayed buses and other inconveniences. The first, ใจเย็น *jai yen, translates literally as "cool heart" and is something everyone tries to maintain—most Thais hate raised voices, visible irritation and confrontations of any kind. Related to this is the oft-quoted response to a difficulty,* mai pen rai— *"never mind,"* ไม่เป็นไร *"no problem," or "it can't be helped" —the verbal equivalent of an open-handed shoulder shrug which has its base in the Buddhist notion of karma. And then there's* สนุก *sanuk, the wide-reaching philosophy of "fun" which, crass as it sounds, Thais do their best to inject into any situation, even work. Hence the crowds of inebriated Thais who congregate at waterfalls and other beauty spots on public holidays, and the national waterfight which takes place every April on streets right across Thailand.*

—Paul Gray and Lucy Ridout,
The Rough Guide Thailand

You have a point. Pleasures of the flesh there are in Thailand, and in ingenious profusion, as anyone who has been here, including a million or so R&Ring GIs—not to mention innumerable "boom-boom" touring Japanese businessmen—can attest. But though I am informed (secondhand, of course) about these wonders and have had described to me, almost quiveringly, the salubriousness of the Patpong Road-style "body massage" (for a modest fee, an amiable young lady employs hers to rub yours), such is not the stuff I am talking about. By sensuous, I mean just that: having to do with the five senses, to which I would add a sixth, the imagination. In the excitation and stimulation of these, Thailand has no peer.

Given the competition from the likes of, say, pre-hippie-invaded Bali, that is a heady claim. But throughout the years, a lot of others have come to the same conclusion, including a young Polish seaman who put in here a century ago, before taking up his first command. His name was Jozef Teodor Konrad Korzeniowski, and from what he recorded about his arrival in this

"Oriental capital which had yet suffered no white conqueror" (it still hasn't), he seems to have been impressed. "Here and there," he wrote, "towered great piles of masonry, king's palace, temples, gorgeous and dilapidated, crumbling under the vertical sunlight, tremendous, overpowering, almost palpable, which seem to enter one's breast with the breath of one's nostrils and soak into one's limbs through every pore of the skin." Smitten by the sensuality of Bangkok, the seaman was to return here frequently. Later he became a writer and changed his name—called himself Joseph Conrad.

Sometime after Conrad, another writer—this one named Somerset Maugham—came to Thailand, contracted malaria, and nearly died. None of which diminished his enthusiasm for the place. At twilight, he wrote, he would sit on the veranda of his hotel and gaze out across the Chao Phraya at the distant trees, whose lacelike silhouettes reminded him of a Japanese print. One evening, he went on, "a flight of egrets flew down the river, flying low and scattered. They were like a ripple of white notes, sweet and pure and spring-like, which an unseen hand drew forth, like a divine arpeggio from an unseen harp."

By my own first visit to Thailand, as a holidaying war correspondent from Vietnam, the egrets Mr. Maugham had written about had long since departed, casualties of Bangkok's urban sprawl. There were still trees along the Chao Phraya, but fewer of them, because of the apartment buildings that were springing up. The sunlight Conrad had described so vividly remained, of course, as did the crumbling temples and palaces, even if they were becoming soot-stained under the capital's choking pollution. In my hotel room (the same one in which Maugham lay delirious from malaria), I could hear the sounds of the city, though not, I fear, the soft *susurrus* of the casuarinas. Instead, there was the honking of cars, the sputtering of *samlors*, and the cries of hawkers promoting "look-look" shows. Other things were missing as well, including Jim Thompson, the former OSS man and Thai Silk King, who had lately disappeared in Malaysia, the victim, depending on who was telling the tale, of either a tiger or an unnamed intelligence agency. I wondered, on that first brief visit to Thailand, what all the hoo-ha was about.

Later I learned, which is the way it is, both with Thailand and with sensuality. Neither of them immediately smacks you in the face. Rather, the country and the quality unfold: gradually, languorously, like the petals of a water lily at first light.

In short, you can't go looking for sensuousness, here or anywhere else. You have to let it overcome you, and the way to start is by getting hot. For some reason, heat and sensuality go hand in hand (when, for instance, was the last time you heard Siberia described as sensuous?), and the heat in Bangkok, where the Thai start donning sweaters when the temperature drops below 85 degrees, is an extraordinary kind. Five minutes in it and you are drenched to the skin. After an hour, your mind is on its way to being parboiled. It starts playing tricks. The noisy *tuk-tuk*s, which from the tinted-glass windows of the air-conditioned hire-car seemed like so many three-wheeled menaces, take on an inexplicable charm. The street sellers' sweets, which had previously aroused only worries of dysentery, seem indescribably tempting. Even the smell of urine, which permeates many a Bangkok back alley, seems, if not agreeable, pungently natural. The hotter it gets, the longer you stay out in it, the more you find yourself seduced, lured. And then, even without realizing it, you are captured.

Once Bangkok has gotten hold of you, it begins revealing its sensual treats. There is, for starters, the food, which has an effect quite unlike any other on the palate. Thai cuisine is famous—some would say notorious—for being hot, and much of it is. Its spiciness, though, is not of the Mexican or Indian variety. Bite into a *chili relleno* or spoon down a mouthful of no-holds-barred Bengali curry and your taste buds are not so much tickled as bludgeoned into submission. With Thai food, even the brings-tears-to-your-eyes sort, it's different, not in the BTU level but in the kind of warmth it brings to the

Tuk-tuk

tongue. Sample, say, a chicken-in-coconut-milk soup or a fried cat-fish salad, and you find your mouth percolating with the complexity of half a dozen tastes and spices—a little mint here, a little ginger over there, a little cilantro, garlic, and sweet onion somewhere else—all conspiring to bring pleasure. And fiendishly conspiring, at that. For no matter how incendiary the initial experience, how sincere the vows not to tempt gustatory fate again, one finds one-self unable to resist another bite.

At this point in the meal, you are ready to delve into some of the more arcane items on the menu, like serpent's head soup, horse balls (they aren't what you think they are), or, my personal favorite, urgent beef—so named, apparently, because of the urgent need one has for liquid refreshment after consuming it. All notions of dieting (a concept welcomely alien to Thailand) are put aside. The ingredients are healthy and fresh, and besides, the Thai at the next table, none of whom have a millimeter of fat, are shoveling down helpings from eight different dishes. Thus assured, you signal for several more of your own—and after that, dessert. Invariably, it is fruit, except that it doesn't look or taste like fruit. The slices of pineapple, watermelon, papaya, and mango are recognizable enough, as, after a bit of examination, is the tangerine, whose top rind has been quartered and pulled back so that it resembles an oversized camellia. The intensity of their flavor, however, comes as a shock. Even more startling in appearance, texture, and taste are a number of other fruits—mangosteens, Chinese apples, and rambutans—which are all but unavailable in the West. And even they pale in sensual significance next to the appeal of the durian. Supposedly a member of the fruit family, the durian, which resembles a pineapple crossed with an armadillo, has a teeth-chattering sweetness that, by Thai standards, is rather conventional. It is the aroma one never forgets. The best description I have heard of it—from a

Another way to describe the durian experience: "Eating durian is like sitting on the toilet eating your favorite ice cream."

—JO'R and LH

Durian fruit

Singapore hotelier who refuses to allow it on his premises—is "one ton of overripe Limburger cheese, only more so."

The essence of Thailand is simply expressed in its fruits—exotic, sweet to the taste, and almost infinite in variety. Here are some of the common ones:

Durian—the prickly skinned fruit known for its fierce smell has a shell so thick that it is regarded as an offensive weapon in Thailand. Some say it's an acquired taste.

Longan—a relative of the lychee, round, about the size of a large grape, it has a sweet, white flesh.

Mangosteen—its maroon-colored skin reveals delicate white flesh that is a favorite with foreigners.

Pomelo—looks like an oversize orange with a similar, but sweeter taste.

Rambutan—smallish, hairy-looking; appears to be the last thing you would ever want to put in your mouth, but its white fruit is enchantingly sweet.

Also be sure to taste the Thai variants of the banana (kluai), mango (mamuang), papaya (malako), and pineapple (sapparot).

— Gault Millau: The Best of Thailand

Suffice it to say that the food of Thailand, like the country itself, leaves an impression on the senses that lingers long after the experiencing of it is done.

Of course, it never is quite done. The Thai are among the world's great snackers, and they can be found munching day and night. There is much to tempt them, not only in the dozen-per-block food stalls and sidewalk soup kitchens that together give Bangkok the smell of one vast stewing pot but also in pile after shimmering pile of fruit, vegetables, spices, fish, meat, poultry, and condiments of every size, color, manner, and description. And the edibles are only the beginning. Any market of consequence will also be piled high with bunches of fresh-cut orchids, roses, and chrysanthemums (for use at home, or in devotions to Buddha, whose enigmatic image peers down from everywhere), to say nothing of glistening bronze ware, iridescent silks (Thailand's are among the world's finest and are certainly the most acidic in hue), gleaming cutlery, and, in many markets, "never-can-tell, boss" imitations of Calvin Klein jeans, Gucci luggage, Izod shirts, and Rolex and Cartier watches. All of which—

along with puppy dogs, cats, squirrels, goldfish, monkeys, and may-or-may-not-be-real antiques, sapphires, emeralds, rubies, and diamonds—are sold, bartered, hawked, and bargained for to the accompaniment of native and American music turned to ear-splitting volume.

If you keep your head in these places, you can get a good buy. If you keep your eyes and ears open, you can also gain an appreciation of some of Thailand's sensuality. There are, for instance, the colors—a spectacular array of them, from the coolest blues to the deepest crimsons—and the at once chaotic yet ordered way in which goods are displayed. Even the humblest street vendor labors to ensure that his small store of whatever—be it a mound of peppers, a cache of scarlet runner beans (they're like the American variety, only five feet long), a sackful of religious amulets—is arranged to please the eye, his own and those who might chance to buy. Unlike in the West, where so much of what we consume is spread out in prepackaged, flash-frozen, take-it-or-leave-it heaps, in Thailand, presentation is, if not everything, a whole lot of it. You see an item and you instinctively want to touch it, handle it, smell and taste it. After a time, even the cacophony around you makes sense. The music, the saffron-robed monks, the chattering women, the sing-song tonal language, the astonishing natural bounty— it is all part of a piece.

The shards of this piece lie everywhere in Bangkok: in the markets; in the temples (one of which, Wat Trimitr, features a Buddha image constructed from five and a half tons of gold); in the gaily painted *tuk-tuks*; in the sinuous rhythms of classical Thai dance; in the woven lotus necklaces that festoon the rearview mirrors of the taxicabs; in the constant smell of burning charcoal and smoldering joss; in the wind chimes and temple bells that really do tinkle; in the skyful of kites that "fight" over the Grand Palace in February and March; in the candy-colored, ever-pulsating neon lights; in the stylized serpent images that guard the gables of buildings; in the water towers designed to look like flower blossoms; in the palm leaves that are used to wrap purchases, the twisted reed that doubles for rope, and the bamboo that substitutes for metal scaffolding;

in the huge multicolored trucks adorned with flags and beaten-metal Buddha images; in the naked children splashing unself-consciously in the river; in the New Year's custom of laughingly dousing strangers with water bombs; in the sight of an elephant turning up incongruously in a rush-hour traffic jam (and being given the right of way); in the barber who massages your fingers and shoulders after she cuts your hair; in the laundry that comes back gift-wrapped with an orchid attached to it; in the songbirds that are purchased for the express purpose of being set free; in the constant parade of honking, chugging, wheezing traffic up and down the Chao Phraya; in the royal topiary that is clipped, literally, with tweezers; in the torpor of the ceiling fans and the gauziness of the mosquito nets; in the sweet, sugarcane taste of the local whiskey; in the hand-holding habit of male Thai friends; in the eyes of Thai women, who, when you look at them, look right back; in a million other ordinaries that are the stuff and fabric of Thai life.

I have been trying to understand and give in to this life for nearly two decades now, and every day brings a new sensual discovery.

Often, it comes from the unexpected. Like driving to an appointment and finding, on one of Bangkok's busiest street corners, just down the block from McDonald's and a stone's throw from the local VD clinic, a throng of Buddhists paying bowing, joss-burning, gold-leaf-laying homage to a flower-bedecked image of Brahma. As you watch, open-mouthed, the Thai dancers in glittering sequined costumes snaking gracefully through the crowd, it suddenly strikes you: Brahma is a Hindu god. No matter, he is a sensuous, good-hearted fellow, capable of all manner of great deeds, and for the Thai, who are nothing if not catholic in their tastes, that's what seems to count.

In the sensual mélange that is Bangkok, you are always finding things like that, often in the unlikeliest of locales. Go, for instance, to the Rajadamnoen boxing stadium and you witness not just two young pugilists beating each other's brains out with fists, elbows, knees, and feet (everything but biting goes) but almost a ceremony of carefully choreographed aggression, complete with a ringside orchestra of drums, cymbals, and flutes. The protagonists enter the ring dressed in multicolored embroidered robes, bow to each other and to the crowd (which is engaged in a frenzy of betting), then fall on their knees for several minutes, seeking Buddha's intercession ("O Lord, give me a good left hook."). Then, something that can only be described as very Thai happens: the fighters begin to parade around the ring, not so much exercising as dancing, and a very feminine, sensual sort of dance it is. There's nothing in the rules of Thai boxing that requires them to do this, but invariably they do, as if they are proud of their bodies and want to strut their stuff. The fight that follows is nearly as exotic. It's vicious enough—there's no knockout like the one that results from a swift kick to the chin—but in its own peculiar way highly sensual, too, like a confrontation between a mongoose and a cobra. The fighters slowly circle each other, the crowd rhythmically chants, the flutes play and the cymbals chime, and when it is over, everyone—even the poor fellow who picks himself up off the canvas—seems very glad to have been a part of it.

There is a lot of noise at these matches, as there is nearly everywhere in Bangkok. The Thai are mad about sounds, and they like to hear as many of them as possible, preferably several different ones going on at the same time. There is, for instance, the riverboat anchored beneath my balcony, which, before setting out on its evening cruise, honks its whistle—the first stanza of "Oh Susanna." Call the Federal Express office and, when you are put on hold, an electronic tone plays "Home on the Range." Call me and my phone will play you a rendition of "Happy Birthday" followed by "For He's a Jolly Good Fellow." And so it goes, not merely on the phone or in elevators or in markets or in shops, but everywhere. Always the sound of something engaging the ear.

The sounds, the sights, the sensations—the sheer sensuality—are what keep me coming back to Bangkok. And still I am discovering more.

The other afternoon, for instance, I was returning from the Foreign Correspondents Club, where every Saturday a two-week-old edited version of five days' worth of Dan Rather is shown. With satellites, we could no doubt have Rather's revelations the same day, but I, for one, am glad for the delay. It makes what Dan says less ominous, and, no small wonder, Dan himself seems rather funny. In any case, I was coming back the way I always do, which is to say, up the river by longtail boat, then by foot down a little *soi* off one of the main drags. In hardly more than a hundred paces, I had entered a large *wat*, or temple, and an entirely different world. Instead of traffic, car horns, and filth, there was a huge, palm-lined courtyard, where the only sounds were the padding of monks' feet and the occasional screeching of parrots. A pair of ponies ambled by; then a water buffalo; then a brace of bulls, massive and white; and finally an aggregation of dogs, cats, and roosters, off on some mutual adventure. Emerging from the *wat*, I was, in a moment, back in modern Bangkok, where as usual the traffic was snarled, this time by a pair of half-dressed sewer workers who, apparently not having much to do, had curled themselves up, one atop the other, for a midday nap in the middle of a bustling intersection. No one seemed especially bothered by this. At length, I reached my apartment and, following Thai custom, doffed my shoes before walking barefoot across the cool, polished teak floor. It was then that it hit me: not the *wat* or the Rather newscast or the longtail boat or the laborers dozing in the roadway, all of which I was used to by now, but the feel of the floor on my feet. A very small thing, but a way of letting you know that you have entered somewhere different; a way, too, of conveying that, for all the barriers we place against feeling, we are still alive. That, I suppose, is what the sensuality of Thailand comes down to: a constant reaffirmation of the astonishing variety of life.

I'm possessive about this land, but the secret is getting out. Every year, the country fills up with more and more foreigners— *farangs*, the Thai call them, not entirely happily—who, having experienced Thailand's sensuality, find themselves unable to leave. One of them is an 85-year-old Frenchman of my acquaintance, who, having traveled the world over during his long life, came to Bangkok a year or so ago. Seeing the place, tasting its delights, he checked into a hotel suite overlooking the Chao Phraya and informed the management that he would be there until he died. It is a demise that I envy.

Robert Sam Anson has been writing about Southeast Asia since the Vietnam War era. He is the author of War News: A Young Reporter in Indochina, *published by Simon & Schuster.*

★

I climbed to the sun deck to watch Bangkok from the river as I had so often watched the river from Bangkok. The life of Bangkok is on its waters and it was on the river that I had always sensed the real heart of the country. The bulk of the people in Thailand were like the ones who clustered on the banks of the river or who paddled on it in their teak craft and these were the people with whom no *farang* ever talked beyond, perhaps, a few words of bargaining. When any Westerner tells you that he knows the East like a book and pretends to be an authority, beware, for he is lying. Even the Westerners who stay for years rarely penetrate below a certain class in the East. They meet the Westernized, the cultured, and the rich and always behind this shallow façade are the numberless Siamese they cannot begin to comprehend and who are Thailand.

Carol Hollinger, *Mai Pen Pai Means Never Mind*

✦ ✦ ✦

Monk for a Month

The Western overlay in Thailand
is not as thick as it seems.

WITH HIS HIGHTOP TENNIS SHOES, WISHAN SLAPS OUT THE rhythm of a new Madonna track, pulsing through the sound system of the café in southern Thailand where we've met. He talks about Western movies and clothing styles as he leans back in his fashionable jeans, pirated knock-offs of a famous brand, available in any of the street markets of Bangkok. His hair is cut just above his ears, falling to the collar of his polo shirt. This guy could pass for a local anywhere from California to Toronto.

We became acquainted through a translator, his English teacher, over ice cream and *cha yen*, a sweet Thai iced tea with milk. As the conversation winds down, he invites his teacher and me to a party that night. I am all for parties, even parties in Thailand, so it takes me all of an eighth of a second to accept. It is almost as an afterthought that I enquire about the occasion. In the best English he's been able to pull off all morning, Wishan smiles and says, "Tomorrow I will be a monk."

Whoa. A monk? That would certainly be a significant departure for Wishan. I mean, he told me that he owned a nightclub in Bangkok. There were movies and fashion magazines to keep up with. What about his jeans and t-shirt? What about his hair? Aren't monks bald, old men? I had seen plenty. A visit to Thailand is like saffron on parade. Flashes of orange robes worn by the Buddhist monks, the *phikkhu*, are conspicuous throughout the country.

The devotees to the teachings of Buddha are as ubiquitous as the *wats* which they inhabit. So, was this to be some sort of religious transformation? Was he going to ditch his business, and his life, to become one of these?

His answer to me was yes, and no. Yes, Mr. Westernized was about to embark in a spiritual journey into the heart of Thai Buddhism, but no it wouldn't mean permanently forsaking his secular life. As esoteric and incomprehensible as the life of a monk may have seemed to me, I learned that it is a road often taken by the Thai male as a paean to his country's ancient and revered religious heritage in Theravada Buddhism. Traditionally, a young man at the outset of adulthood enrolls in the community of monks, the *sangha*, for anywhere from one to three months—although in many cases he will remain a monk for several years, supporting himself as he pursues an education. Many will even return to the *wats* periodically throughout adulthood.

Wishan seemed eager to continue the tradition by becoming a *phikkhu*, he was following his father and grandfather before him. For the next 30 days, he would be without his Western clothes, without his nightlife, and yes, without his hair. His head would be shaved that very afternoon in the first step of his initiation.

Nakhon Sri Thammarat is a bustling city of more than 100,000 in southeastern Thailand. It was Wishan's hometown, and he had made the eighteen-hour journey from Bangkok by train to serve for a month in a familiar *wat*. Few Westerners are seen there—they are lured either to the beaches of Phuket and Krabi just across the isthmus, or to points farther north. But the Thais are a very friendly people, and Wishan's family had no reservations whatsoever about inviting me, an outsider, to attend the ceremony by which their son would become a monk.

Somerset Maugham described Thailand's temples as being "...like prizes in a shooting gallery at a village fair in the country of the gods." And in the sharp, midday sun, Wat Mahathat was indeed an incredible, spark-ling mosaic of colors and ornamen-tation. I could almost hear the scissors being readied as we arrived at the temple.

*In a temple, don't walk
in front of praying
Thais; walk around them.*

—Elizabeth Devine and
Nancy L. Braganti,
*The Traveler's Guide to Asian
Customs and Manners*

With a relaxing air of infor-mality he was received by the head monk, the *jao-awaht*. They exchanged bows and went into the older man's chamber where they kneeled, facing one another. Outside, we were like kids taking turns peeking through a knot-hole as we clustered around the small door of the darkened room to see what was happening. For a few minutes they remained on their knees in the shadows. The *jao-awaht* chanted quietly as Wishan, still and silent, bowed his head. The monk lifted himself to a chair, took a pinch of Wishan's hair between the thumb and finger of one hand as he lifted a pair of scissors with the other. I held my breath, and cringed a little, imagining my own being shorn away. The others knew, but I didn't, that this part was only to be the symbolic snipping of a single lock from the top of his head. The old monk worked quickly, allowing not a hair to fall to the floor.

But it was to be only a temporary reprieve for Wishan. Across the sandy courtyard sat a single chair with a small pan of water and a safety razor beside it. He was guided from the room to the chair and instructed to remove his shirt. A younger monk then appeared to tend to the tonsorial duties. With little pause for ceremony, he took it straight to Wishan's scalp. His head tugged under the pull of the blade as it began slowly to expose the light skin where his hair had been—first the left side, then the right. Finally, as my friend sat quietly with a lap full of hair, the barber-monk shaved off his eyebrows.

Believe it or not, you would have a great deal of trouble recog-nizing your best friend—even your spouse, after they'd had their eyebrows shaved. It makes for quite a transformation. After just ten minutes he didn't look like Wishan anymore, to say the least. He looked like…well…like a monk.

He was undressed and wrapped in a simple, orange robe by yet another monk. He knelt beside a stone well as a bucket was lowered, filled, and dumped over his body. Seven times the bucket was refilled and poured on him, drenching as it washed away the hairs and any remaining vestige of the guy I had met a few hours before. He stood, beaming. The water seemed to bring him out of the shallow trance he'd been in for a few minutes. For the first time he smiled, and reached up to touch his smooth head.

The party was an elaborate banquet by any standard. With Thai music played by an orchestra of Wishan's friends, we dined from before sunset until late that night. Plates full of standard Thai fare and local specialties weighed down tables set up in the family's courtyard. Thai curried chicken, Thai noodles, shrimp, squid, rice, and Mekong whiskey continued to pour from the kitchen as guests arrived all night long. Although the party was given in his honor, it was Wishan, dressed in a traditional gown of gold and white, who acted as host. He neither ate nor drank, but made sure that everyone's plates and glasses were constantly refilled as the fête went on into the morning.

Wishan was still in the gown at daylight—it was forbidden for him to sleep the night before. The tranquilizing effect of the Mekong whiskey had sent most of us home to bed after one o'clock, so the morning arrived somewhat rudely. The bands, drummers, gongers, and a saxophonist reassembled to lead a parade back to Wat Mahathat with Wishan hoisted aloft to the shoulders of his brothers and father. The morning sun was resplendent on the front of the temple. Wishan, the soon-to-be monk, rode along in silence to the cheers, his eyes closed, his hands pressed together in meditation, shielded from the blinding sun by an ornate parasol.

Wishan's feet didn't touch the ground until he was inside the temple. He walked up to the altar where he was met once again by his old friend the *jao-awaht*. The ensuing litany lasted several hours. We, the faithful, knelt stoically on the ungiving marble floor as the old monk read from the *Tripitaka,* the body of Buddhist scriptures which includes the Vinaya, a set of 227 rules guiding the monastic order. I understood no Thai, but I could tell that all 227 were being read, point-by-point. My knees froze, locked, and began to swell. Hours later, as quietly as it had begun, the ceremony ended. Wishan was a monk.

Wishan the *phikkhu* would be counted among the approximately 250,000 other monks active at any one time in Thailand. Joining early in the spring, he was missing the season of peak enrollment, Pansaa, a religious holiday best described as a sort of Buddhist Lent, which falls during the three months of heaviest monsoon rains. It is thought that during Pansaa one gains more merit by being a monk than at other times in the year. Civil servants wishing to re-robe for this occasion are even granted leaves of absence by the government.

Today, about 60 percent of those eligible to join the *sangha* do so. Considering that the *sangha*, or Buddhist brotherhood, is thought of as having the highest status and prestige of any social group in the country, it is surprising that the numbers have fallen off in recent years—a result of changing economic and social conventions brought about by the Westernization of Thailand and Southeast Asia. But even in light of all this, monks are still being venerated as an integral part of Thai society. They set the standard of behavior in any community. It's believed that by serving, housing, or feeding a monk, a layman gains merit that will elevate his social standing in subsequent incarnations.

Wishan will rise at four o'clock daily to begin his strictly regimented days in the *wat*. Following his morning bath and a period of private morning devotions in his own room, a monk will leave the *wat* at sunrise with a group of others to collect food and offerings from around the community. By 7:30, the monks return to the temple compound for breakfast, usually eaten privately.

The bell is sounded a second time at 8:15 to call the monks into the inner sanctuary of the *wat*, for the commencement of the day's spiritual teaching. After recitation of the morning prayers, the new monks stay behind to receive instructions from the *jao-awaht* before adjourning for the main meal of the day. It must be finished by noon according to strict Buddhist doctrine. No one may eat between midday and breakfast the following morning.

At five o'clock the monks have a second bath before returning for prayers. Evening classes follow, beginning around 7:30. It is during this session that the monks examine one of the four areas most central to the knowledge they will gain while in the monastery: the story of the life of Gautama Buddha; the Dharma, or the philosophy of Buddha; the essays written in discussion of the Dharma; or the Vinaya, the rules governing the *sangha* and by which each monk is expected to conduct himslf.

The monks retire between 10 p.m. and midnight for a night of hungry sleep before the next morning's bell. Wishan may well have decided to remain a *phikkhu* for another thirty days or for a year, or forever. But chances are he is back in Bangkok, back in blue jeans, in the office of his nightclub. Every single day he will encounter at least a few of the monks that populate the numerous *wats* in and around the city. Whether or not he rejoins at some time in the future for a weekend, or for a Pansaa season, he is sure to carry with him a new understanding of the religious and social heritage of his people. And hey—the eyebrows will grow back!

Timothy Fall is a writer and actor who played Chad, the strange comic book artist, on the television series "Bob," starring Bob Newhart. He lives with his wife in Los Angeles.

*

> Let not a man trace back the past
> Or wonder what the future holds:
> The past is but the left-behind,
> The future but the yet-unreached.
> In the present let him see
> With insight each and every instant
> Invincibly, unshakably,
> That can be pierced by practising.
>
>   —Bhaddekarat-tagatha (Verses on a well-spent day),
>   quoted by Tim Ward, in *What the Buddha Never Taught*

✦ ✦ ✦

Love in a Duty-free Zone

*The currency of erotic commerce is emotion
as well as cash, and morality falters
beneath a gentle human touch.*

MY FIRST REACTION TO BANGKOK WAS SHOCK; MY SECOND WAS to know that shock was not right, but I didn't know what was. "Those who go beneath the surface do so at their own peril," wrote Wilde, and the more I looked at the bar scene, the more my vision blurred.

Before very long, in fact, I began to discover that the ubiquitous couple of Bangkok—the pudgy foreigner with the exquisite girleen—was not quite the buyer and seller, the subject and object, I had imagined. In many cases, I was told, the girls did not simply make their bodies available to all while they looked at their watches and counted their money; they chose to offer their admirers their time, their thoughts, even their lives. The couple would sometimes stay together for two weeks, or three, or thirty. They would travel together and live together and think of themselves as lovers. She would show him her country, cook him local delicacies, mend his clothes, even introduce him to her parents and her friends. He would protect her from some parts of the world, teach her about others. For the girl, her Western suitor might prove the mature and sophisticated companion she had always lacked; for the man, his Eastern consort could be the attentive, demure, and sumptuously compliant goddess of his dreams. He would obviously provide material comforts and she physical; but sometimes—in subtler ways—their positions were reversed. And as the months passed, sensations sometimes developed into emotions, passions settled down into feelings. Often, in the end, they would go through a traditional marriage in her village.

Thus my tidy paradigm of West exploiting East began to crumble. Bangkok wasn't dealing only in the clear-cut trade of bodies; it was trafficking also in the altogether murkier exchange of hearts. The East, as Singapore Airlines knows full well, has always been a marketplace for romance. But Thailand was dispensing it on a personal scale, and in heavy doses. It offered love in a duty-free zone: a context in which boy meets girl without having to worry about commitments, obligations, even identities. Love, that is, or something like it.

As I returned to the bars, I steadied myself against their mounting equivocations by noting that at least some of the girls were as hard and fast as their propositions. These creatures of easy virtue were indeed no more than what they seemed: all artifice. Their pleasure was strictly professional, their "darlings" dangled in all the wrong places. They could be touched in any place except inside; they would

As with gambling, the trick is to go to Patpong [the red-light district] in a group—far safer and more enjoyable than wandering around on your own—and to look "poor." I spent five nights researching Patpong's bars and clubs—the first four nights, I dressed casually and received no hassle whatsoever. The last night however, I wore a smart 400B [B denotes baht, Thai currency] shirt, and was bodily assaulted within 30 seconds of arrival. It's generally a good idea to have no more than 500B in your pockets—that way, even if you get talked into trouble (bar girls can be very persuasive), you won't be able to afford it.

—Frank Kusy,
Cadogan Guides: Thailand

extend themselves to any man who entered. When money was mentioned, their soft gaze turned hard; when a fat cat came in, their eyes irresistibly wandered; and when the closing hour finally arrived, they took off their glass slippers and turned off their tricked-up charm. In all of a second, these temptresses could shrug off or reassume their serviceable grace; in a single night, they would sleep with three or four customers. Did she enjoy what she did? "Ah," croaked one husky-voiced young girl who had been dancing with extraordinary abandon. "It's a job."

Kai too was bracing, almost reassuring in her toughness, her freedom from questions and qualms. Managing her life with brisk efficiency, she delivered a breakdown of all the relevant figures—bottom lines, profit curves, spreadsheets, and the rest—with the scrupulous poise of a recent graduate from the Harvard Business School. Her body, she explained, was a worthwhile investment. She made $10 an hour teaching Thai classical dance. By comparison, she took home only $4 an evening from working in the bar, seven hours a day, seven days a week, twenty-eight days a month. But if she managed to snag a partner for the night, she could get $20 at least, more than an average Thai worker makes in a fortnight. And what job offered better perks? She could stay at the finest hotels, learn about—and sometimes travel about—the world, be wined, dined, and fêted, procure free tickets to every disco in town. Bright lights, fast cars, affluent white knights from abroad who were prepared to whisk her hither and thither—she could have them all. In return, she had to do very little. Just dance, flirt, kiss a little, and sleep much of the day. "It's a business," she concluded matter-of-factly. "You understand me, I show you good heart."

All this was simple enough: these girls had no illusions about the trade they were plying, and it was nothing more than a trade, usually of body for money. Yet all too often, the young ladies of the night were not so conveniently transparent: many, in fact, seemed not to be counterfeiting, so much as enjoying—for profit—a kind of frolicsome high spirits that actually came naturally. Their lust for lucre was real, but so was their charm.

Take Nitya, for example, a lovely round-faced minx with hair that fell to her waist and a smile that could stop hearts from beating. That she could support herself just by drinking in the glamour of the big city was such a delight to her that she could not help but chatter uncontrollably. Her English boyfriend, who lived in Saudi Arabia, had been visiting her, she told me, for four years now. He sometimes sent her money and he always brought her presents. "Once," she said, eyes alight with pleasure, "I say I want a video machine." And? "My boyfriend give me it. Otherwise I angry." Wasn't that a little conniving? "Why?" She pouted. "Some man give girl house. Five hundred thousand baht [$20,000]. Video only fifteen thousand baht [$600]. No problem."

A happy incarnation of the imp perverse, Nitya was jubilant at the effects of her appeal, and her appeal was only kindled by her jubilation. Sure, she admitted, she often got her sister to write her letters to her boyfriend. But she knew that he loved her, or needed her, much too much to abandon her. Once he had flown all the way to Bangkok only to find her in a hospital delivering an Arab-featured baby. "He cry, he very angry," she recalled, in the excitable staccato of bar-girl English. "But he cannot go." Once he had visited and found that her passport was filled with recent stamps from Denmark, Sweden, and Germany. "He sad. He ask me why I hurt him," she cheerily reported. "What can I say? I was wrong." He walked out on her. But pretty soon he came back, as she knew he would. In any case, she assured me, she was always kind to her boyfriend when he visited, and she still wrote letters to his 70-year-old mother in Glamorgan. "No problem," bubbled Nitya exultantly. "No problem."

Indeed, for every girl who opened herself up like a cash register, there seemed to be forty others who had about them more curious purity than seemed good or right. These were not the dull-eyed whores or jaded trollops of street corners, but coltish, puckish young kids, blessed often with a friendly, fresh-blown sweetness, sensual but not too far from innocence. And though they might be hardheaded, hardhearted they usually were not. Some, to be sure, were human calculators, some were blazing-eyed tigresses, all were polished charmers. But many, at heart, seemed nothing more than mischievous school girls. When their favorite song came on, they could not help jumping up, singing along, and dancing with their friends. And most of the rest of the time, they were to be found in a slumber party mood, holding hands together, swapping stories about boyfriends, playing children's dice games or chattering on about Mamá and Papá. Many were country girls more pious in their Buddhism than the city's sophisticates, and many brought an uncomplicated zest even to the rigors of the job: one girl showed me the book that she had studied every day for a year in order to learn English, another told me that she had spent three months paying $10 an hour for Japanese lessons after learning that yen flowed more freely than dollars or deutschemark.

So even as they went about their very adult trade, the girls who worked in the bars seemed little in more ways than the physical: hard and easily hurt, they were just experienced enough to know how to turn their innocence to advantage. Their sauciness was shy, their bashfulness was brazen. One minute, they were repeating endearments imperfectly picked up from some American movie; the next, forgetting themselves, they would admit to daydreaming about the right man or a fairy-tale future. They loved the *Star Wars* movies, many of them confessed, but their all-time favorites were *Rocky* and *Flashdance*. Because they showed that dreams come true.

Inevitably, this elfin wish for happy endings rubbed constantly against the details of the lives they led. Nearly every girl had a tale to tell, and nearly always it was the same one. She grew up in a village in a family of twelve. A local man came along when she was in her early teens and promised to make her rich. He said she would make her fortune, but she ended up making his. He said she would be "a maid," then forced her to become a slave. She bore him a child, she returned alone to her village, she worked without joy or profit in the fields. Now she could support her offspring only by coming to Bangkok. Who looked after the child? "Mamá." Did her still-devoted parents know what she was doing in Bangkok? "No. I tell them I work in a boutique. They know I work in bar, they kill me." Sometimes there were hazards in her job: a boss would force her to sleep with him, or lock up the bar and screen blue movies. But she could always find another opening, another show. In the countryside, she could earn only $15 a month; here she took home thirty times as much, leaving her more than enough to send $100 each month to her little brother or widowed mother.

One day, she hoped, she could make enough money to return to her village and raise her child (though, schoolgirl to the end, she squandered her cash as soon as she got it on discos and flashy clothes). And one day, she hoped, she would fly off to live with her husband. After the wedding, he had been forced to return to Australia, or California, or Holland. But he promised, he really promised, to send her a visa. The plane ticket, he wrote, was in the mail.

Sometimes, there were variations on the standard theme: Somchai had been bustled out of Phnom Penh by her uncle as soon as the town was stormed by the Khmer Rouge and had landed up in Bangkok, penniless, uneducated, and unqualified; Vaitnee had been studying at a local university when Papá died, forcing her to drop out to support Mamá. And some of the tales might have been fact, and some of them fiction—in the half-light of the bar, who could tell?—but it was hard not to shiver, just a little, when Somchai said that she was frightened of sleeping alone because ghosts from Cambodia came back to her in the night; or when Vaitnee admitted that her favorite night of the month was the night she returned to Mamá and was lullabied to sleep as if she were once more a little girl.

Together with their anthology of sad stories, all the girls cherished, as souvenirs, their albums of photographs. These were invariably small and tatty things, their plastic covers adorned with pictures of a smiling kitten, or a cartoon bee. Inside was a heart-breaking gallery of treasured moments: Pen, for example, in a hundred places with a thousand men, her face always smiling, her eyes sometimes red in the flashlight glare. Usually, she was dressed in a bikini, or simply a pajama shirt, and her companion was fully clothed; sometimes she was nestled in the lap of a shirtless Westerner, sometimes her hand was draped around him. In most cases, they were sitting in a bedroom or a bar. "This man from Switzerland," she explained. "This me in Phuket. This outside bar. This very good man. He give me kangaroo bag. This," she said proudly, pointing to a portly, disheveled character in his late forties, "my boyfriend."

Their other most precious mementos were the letters or postcards they received (translated for $2 a shot, and sometimes answered too, in the great tradition of Samuel Richardson, by a man who hung around the entrance to the Grace Hotel). These too recited the formulae of uncertain affection as ritually as thank-you notes. "I still think of the time we spent together," they always said. "I hope I will see you again soon," they usually continued. "I love you," they invariably concluded. A Pakistani sent a greeting card showing two blond lovers in a California sunset. Bart from Holland wrote, "I love your mind, your body. You are all I want in a woman." A firm in New Jersey replied, in Xeroxed typescript, "We are sorry to inform you that Mr. David Jackson, to whom you wrote, is no longer employed by this company. We sincerely apologize for any inconvenience this may cause you."

One afternoon Janjira invited me to see her room. Down a dingy alleyway we went, and up some narrow stairs. She turned a key and let me into a tiny, ill-lit cell, bare except for a mattress and some bedding on the floor (the mattress for her, she explained, the sheets for her roommate—a loquacious, lipsticked transvestite from Laos). A stale loaf of bread sat on a small table; underneath was a bowl of old water. Mickey Mouse grinned down from the bathroom. On a shelf above the mattress, Janjira kept her most valuable possessions: a savings account book and a crumpled manila envelope stuffed with letters. She didn't sleep here very often, she said by way of apology.

Two pieces of decoration dominated the place. Above the mattress was a two-by-one-foot framed glossy photo of Janjira completely naked, with the hands of a clock attached to the glass. Her face was her fortune, I knew, and her picture, she implied, was her résumé. The only other furnishings were two three-foot-tall stuffed animals, with cartoony faces and silly smiles, suspended from the ceiling. Why keep these? I asked. She turned a little bashful. Sometimes, she said, she took them down and slept with them in her arms, one on either side of her. "I dream I have one little girl," she said. "And also one little boy."

Yet the system had little room for such indulgences. What it promised was something more than sex, but a good deal less than security. The girls were to offer love for a price; the men to return it for a while. Both parties were to swear eternal love for a week, or maybe a month. Constancy, like everything else, could be imagined into existence. But let affection or desperation or yearning intrude, even for a moment, and you were lost. Bangkok was home to what was truly the oldest profession in the world: of love, where there was only uncertainty.

I first met Ead in the corner of a bar, dressed in a housewife's buttoned-down frock and white sneakers that looked like a pixie's playthings, gravely keeping to herself. I was surprised to find a shrinking violet in this place of wildly blooming orchids. And doubly surprised when Ead, as we began to talk, swallowed a couple of pills. For what? "The doctor say I think too much." Of what? Sometimes of her seven-year-old daughter, sometimes of her present calling.

As Ead went on speaking, it became clear that her sorrow lay in an intelligence that could not easily accept the paradoxes of her life: unless she gave herself, she knew, she could not enjoy herself; but unless she kept something of herself to herself, she could not survive. Worse than that, she was still old-fashioned enough to chafe against the moral complexities of her position: unable to respect herself, she found it hard to trust herself. So, like many of her colleagues, she kept on reminding me of all her acts of charity, as if to remind herself. Once she gave her boss $1,000, she said. Again and again she reiterated that she had slept with only seven men in thirteen months. Two men had proposed to her. Another had promised to open a bar just for her. "But," she said, eyes shining, "I no have good luck."

To me, it sounded as if she had all the luck in the world. But as she continued, I began to see that she—like any girl who could not happily give herself over to pleasure or profit—was entangled as fatally in the cat-and-mouse game as the men she attracted. These girls were looking for love in all the wrong places, receiving every proposal except the one they might be tempted to accept. For the men they encountered in bars were generally sweet-talkers, lonely transients, "butterflies" who flitted every night from one flower to the next. So Ead had to remember not to forget herself, had to force herself not to believe the compliments she had heard. If her self-respect depended on accepting praise, her sense of self-protection bet he said that to all the girls.

For the sensitive bar girl, then, there was only one thing worse than attaching herself to a man she despised, and that was finding a man she really did care for. Ead's Swiss boyfriend had told her she meant everything to him and they had spent three weeks together. She never heard from him again. For six weeks she had gone everywhere with her Australian boyfriend, who had said they should get married. But now he was back in Sydney, and she did not know when or whether he would return, whether he would ever send for her, whether he was back with a girlfriend or a wife. She had thought about spending $500 to fly to Australia, just so she could be sure. In the meantime, in a mood of self-mutilation, Ead had cut off her long hair. "I think," she said simply, "I have a broken heart."

Bangkok's intricate blend of dynamism and languor had long intrigued me. But as I spent more time in the country, Thailand began to betray other combinations I found more difficult to square. For savagery and grace were so cunningly interwoven here that beauty often seemed brutal and brutality itself quite beautiful. At official performances of Thai classical dance, sketches that featured lissome girls making supple turns were juxtaposed with others that showed off bruising, but no less sinuous, displays of sword fighting. Meanwhile, bouts of Thai boxing resembled nothing so much as ritualized ballets, in which two agile boys bowed their heads before the spirit of the ring, then pounded each other to the accompaniment of weird pipes, ominous drums, and a steady chanting.

Late one evening, as I wandered through the streets of Chiangmai, I came upon groups of men flinging themselves through a game of volleyball played entirely with head and feet. Their suppleness was a marvel. They somersaulted and pirouetted, making corkscrew pivots in the air; they lunged and twisted high above the ground; they dazzled with their slinky acrobatics. Yet all the while, feet kicked faces, heads banged nastily together. And all around the dusty floodlit square hung a cockfight air of menace.

The Thais, wrote le Carré, are the world's swiftest and most efficient killers. Yet executioners would shoot their victims through gauze so as not to offend the Buddha, and monks would strain their water through their teeth so as not, by chance, to harm a single insect.

But at least, I thought, there was one clear-cut division here, in the Manichean setup of Bangkok. The city's two most common and appealing sights,

You get pretty dirty in Bangkok—clothing rimmed with dirt, diesel fumes in your lungs, fingernails gritty. Businessmen need two shirts to see the day through. But there are body overhaul places in Bangkok that will make you feel on top of the world again. Service is excellent and cheap. Expert haircutting or shaping? Facial massage? Manicure? Afro-style braiding? Full beauty treatment and Jacuzzi with fresh milk? All of this, and more, can be arranged in Bangkok. The Yellow Pages, under Beauty Salons, is a good place to start— many of the places listed are unisex.

— Michael Buckley,
Bangkok Handbook

after all, were its holy men, in spotless saffron robes, and its scarlet ladies. By day, the monks evoked a vision of purity, of hallowed groves filled with golden novitiates; by night, the whole grimy city felt polished, renewed, and transformed as sequined girls sang the body electric. At least, so I thought, this day-and-night division would ensure that good was good, and evil evil, and never the twain would meet.

But no. For after a while, I began to notice that, as the whores were engagingly girlish, the monks seemed endearingly boyish. I saw them poring over Walkmans in electronic stores with shopping bags slung over their shoulders, puffing ruminatively on cigarettes, playing tag with their friends in temple courtyards. Once, on venturing inside a monastery on a drowsy afternoon, I chanced upon a group of monks, with beautiful faces, huddled, in the cool shadows, before a TV set that was blasting out cartoons. Then I registered a deeper confusion: some monks, I gathered, were criminals on the lam, while others scattered blessings each night upon the go-go bars; many bar girls, for their part, paid regular visits to Buddhist temples, joined palms together whenever they passed a shrine and knelt in prayer before undertaking their bump and daily grind. Finally, quite flummoxed, I was coming to see the girls as something close to martyrs ("72 prostitutes rescued," proclaimed *The Nation*), and the holy men as something close to con men (the Bangkok *Post* told how five monks had killed one of their fellows with axes and knives, because he dared to criticize them for shooting another monk during a party).

Thus the real sorcery of this dizzying place was that, before one knew it, it could work on one not just a physical but a moral seduction. For here was decadence so decorous that it disarmed the criticism it invited; amorality expressed with the delicacy of a ballerina's nod. And amid such a guiltless marketing of love, righteous indignation could only bounce off the mirrors and the shadows. Slowly, I saw, the city would unbutton your beliefs; gently, it would unbuckle your scruples; cooly, it would let your defenses slither to the floor. Buddhism did not forbid pleasure, the Thais kept saying—just the infliction of pain. So why find shame in enjoyment, and why take enjoyment in shame? What is so harmful or unnatural about love? Must sweetness be seen as a kind of laxness? Why not see sex as an act of communion? "*Mai pen rai*" ran their constant refrain. No matter. No sweat. Never mind. "Everyone make love," cooed sweet-smiling Nitya. "What is so wrong? No problem, dahling, no problem."

And for all my unease in Bangkok, I could not deny that it was quite the most invigorating, and accommodating, city I had ever seen—more lazily seductive than even Rio or Havana. For elegance here was seasoned with funkiness, and efficiency was set off by mystery. Sugar was blended with spice. On Sunday mornings, I often went early to the Temple of the Dawn, and spent several noiseless hours there, surrounded by Buddhas and gazing at the gilded temples that lay across the river like slumberous lions; the minute I grew hungry, however, I could jump into a ten-cent local bus and savor a delectable lunch of watermelon juice and spicy chicken while watching Eurythmics videos in a spotless air-conditioned café. In the evenings, I would sip Twining's tea from porcelain cups in an exquisite teak-tabled restaurant, soothed by the sound of George Winston, then saunter outside to find the wind blowing around the sleeping canals and three-wheeled *tuk-tuks* puttering through the tropical night.

Bangkok was the heart of the Orient, of course. But it was also every Westerner's synthetic, five-star version of what the Orient should be; all the exoticism of the East served up amidst all the conveniences of the West ("It seems to combine," a fascinated S. J. Perelman once wrote, "the Hannibal, Missouri, of Mark Twain's boyhood with Beverly Hills, the Low Countries and Chinatown"). And all the country's variegated Western influences seemed, finally, nothing more than decorative strands that could be woven at will into the beautiful and ornamental tapestry of the country's own inalienable texture ("We provide attractive Thai, Australian, Japanese, Chinese, Swedish, Dutch, Danish, Belgian, Austrian, and French girls," offered one escort agency. "Also handsome and nice boys [gay] entirely at your service.") The Thais, moreover, seemed to know exactly what their assets were—melting smiles, whispering faces, a beseeching frailty, a luxurious grace—and exactly how to turn those virtues into commodities that the West would covet. The carnal marketplace known as the Grace Hotel was, to that extent, aptly named. "Experience unique courtesy only Thai girls can offer."

In the end, then, the lovely doubleness with which the bar scene enthralled its foreign votaries seemed scarcely different from the way in which the stealthy East had often disarmed its visitors from abroad. For had not the Buddha himself said that all that we see is illusion? And had not the war in Vietnam turned on much the same conflict between straight-ahead assault and tricky depth? Perhaps its truest representation, Tim O'Brien's *Going After Cacciato*, had, after all, suggested that the struggle on the battlefield, as in the mind, opposed the usual hard slog of war with the phantom forms of imagination. And the war too, the result had been the same. Bombs could not annihilate shadows; guns could not demolish mirror images. Strength could not deal with what it could not understand. Throughout the fighting, the Americans had held their own by day. But the Vietnamese had ruled the night. So too, it seemed, in Bangkok.

Ultimately, then, it began to seem no coincidence that Thailand, the most open and most complaisant of all Asian nations, was also the only one that had never been conquered or colonized. The one woman who *never* gives herself away, D. H. Lawrence once wrote, is the free woman who always gives herself up. Just so with Thailand, a place, quite literally, more ravishing that ravished. For though it was known as the "Land of Smiles," the smiles here really gave nothing away; Thai eyes often seemed to laugh, and Thai smiles shone with the light of all that was left unsaid. Many years ago, some Americans had tried to unravel the mystery by calling the Thais "the nicest people money can buy." But even now, the Thais, with a gentle smile, continued to confound their visitors from abroad. A Westerner was not exactly in the dark here; just always in the shadows.

The effects of this silken sorcery were clearest, perhaps, in the alien residents who studded the country. For the expats I ran into in Thailand were very different, by and large, from the industrious yuppies who crowd Hong Kong, the vagabond artists who drift through Bali or the beaded seekers who traipse around India. A surprising number of them were underground or marginal men— professional renegades, mercenaries, freelance writers, drug dealers, proprietors of girlie bars, men (and only men) whose wanderlust was spent. And all of them, in their way, seemed to have slipped into the city's restless lifestyle as into the tempting embrace of a goddess. By now, therefore, they seemed almost stranded here, im- mobilized by their addiction to cheap drugs, to memories of the war or to the same "soft beds of the East" that had once seduced Mark Antony away from his official duties. "This," said Emmanuelle, "is a place where doing nothing is an art."

Yet the hardened expats were at least victims of their own worst selves; visitors to Bangkok with even a touch of naïveté were more likely to fall prey to their better impulses. For the bars provided a perfect setting in which susceptible visitors could lose themselves in thinking they had found themselves, shadow-loving their mirror girls, playing hide-and-seek with their consciences. They tempted their subjects to exchange ideals for fantasies. They teased them into circles of self-doubt. And they invited them to ignore the prudent spinster's voice of reason, in favor of the coquettish flirtations of pride—I am the one who can save her, I only think of her as a daughter, she really does care for me. Girls with dreams trigger daydreams in men, and make them feel like boys again.

One man, Ead told me, had stayed with her for five weeks, and had never laid a hand on her; when he left, he had given her a video-machine. Others I knew invariably kept up two girls at once, in the hope that they would fall in love with neither. But even that seemed something of an illusion, and on my third day in Thailand, the Bangkok *Post*, ever sagacious about the salacious, ran on its front page a pointed warning from Auden, "Men will pay large sums to whores for telling them they are not bores."

Yet still each day, the would-be conquerors kept flying into town in droves, old men and young, Arabs and Australians and Americans, on pleasure or a kind of business. Some of them had come many times before, some still had a first-time innocence. And as the airport bus left John behind and drove past the Garden of Eden, Ltd., they could still be seen in the half-light, poring over crumpled pieces of paper (this is Soi Nana, the sex show is here), asking whether the girls were pretty and clean and safe, and concluding, with somewhat shaky assurance, "I think I'll relax this evening with a good Thai massage."

And all night long, in darkened hotel rooms across the length and breadth of the city, from the Sukumvhit Road to Suriwongse, uncertain foreigner and shy-smiling girl kept whispering a ritual litany amidst the mirrors and the shadows.

Do you really like me?
Do I really like you?
Why did you choose me?
How much? How much? How often?
When again? How much? Why not?
You have a good heart? You will write to me soon?
Can you? Will I? Should we?
No problem, dah-ling. No problem.

Pico Iyer is the author of Falling off the Map, The Lady and the Monk, *and* Video Night in Kathmandu, *from which this story was excerpted. He was born in Oxford, England, and lives in Santa Barbara, California, when he's not on the road.*

★

A visitor quickly learns that to ensure he receives accurate, relevant information, never ask a question which can be answered with a "yes" or "no." "Yes" can mean "Yes, I heard you" without a modicum of understanding of its content.

—Steve Van Beek, "Thailand Notes"

MICHAEL BUCKLEY

✦ ✦ ✦

The Secrets of Tham Krabok

Travel can be a form of escapism as addictive as drugs.
The monks at Wat Tham Krabok seem to
have an answer for both.

WAT THAM KRABOK, 7 A.M.: THIRTY YOUNG MEN ARE KNEELING in two long lines, heaving their guts into buckets—the sound of violent retching shatters the air. A motley crowd of monks and onlookers is banging drums and cheering them on. And why, you ask, cheering them on? Well, this all has a perfectly rational explanation: we're spectators at the world's most unorthodox—and successful—cold turkey program. It's an awful way to start the day, but in this fifteen-minute session, Thai heroin addicts are given a vile brown liquid that induces vomiting, and then consume a pail of water. The session is supposed to rid the body of toxins.

The secret potion is brewed from scores of wild plants that grow in the valley around the monastery; it also appears to contain nicotine, which acts as a harsh emetic. It is rumored among addicts that traces of the brown elixir stay in the body forever, and will kill the recipient if he or she ever touches hard drugs again.

The abbot of the monastery, Pra Chamroon Parnchand, claims he can wean any addict off a habit in an intense ten-day period; addicts often stay up to a month to consolidate their cure. Upon entering the monastery, addicts make a commitment never to touch drugs again—the oath is written on rice paper and swallowed. This amounts to a religious vow: drug addiction, it has been suggested, is a spiritual thing, and requires a spiritual cure. For the first five days, patients take herbal medicines; for the next five days they have steam baths, which ease aches and pains and lead to a feeling of cleanliness and well-being. They are given spiritual counseling to strengthen their resolve and abandon drug use. After this period, patients can opt to stay on—joining work crews to cultivate the monastery's maize fields, or helping with other projects.

Pra Chamroon claims a phenomenal 70 percent success rate, based on follow-up research with clients interviewed two years after taking the treatment. If this is so, the rate is exponentially higher than any rehabilitation program in the West. To date, over 80,000 addicts have passed through the gates of the monastery.

Pra Chamroon is a living legend. In his twenties, he was a police officer with a family. His work involved highly dangerous detection and arrest cases—some of them undercover narcotics operations. Like the historical Buddha, he had a powerful vision of saving people from suffering: he turned his back on police work, left behind his wife and children, and disappeared into the jungle for a lengthy period. He decided to become a monk, but wasn't interested in following an established Buddhist school. His aunt, Luang Poh Yai, was his spiritual mentor.

Wat Tham Krabok lies in a valley midway between Lopburi and Saraburi, and 130 km from Bangkok. It can be reached on a daytrip from Lopburi. Tham Krabok means "Bamboo Cave"—in 1957, Luang Poh Yai, Pram Chamroon, and a few monks withdrew to a cave among the limestone crags behind the present monastery to meditate. In 1959, bowing to international pressure, the Thai government outlawed the use of opium. When two addicts approached the caves asking for treatment, Luang Poh Yai—an expert herbalist—recommended some medicines. The word spread that addicts were being cured at Tham Krabok, and buildings were put up to house patients and their relatives, with projects paid for entirely by donations. In 1975, Pra Chamroon won the prestigious Ramon Magsaysay Award for Community Services for his work with addicts. Such is the reputation of the monastery nowadays that entire Hmong tribal villages from the north have arrived for the detox program, prompting opium barons to issue threats on Pra Chamroon's life because of loss of "customers." Other steady clients at the monastery are the "walking dead"—heroin addicts from the slums of Bangkok.

I got to try out the detox process—well, the more pleasant part of it: the herbal steam bath. The sauna is wood-fired, and heavily scented with lemongrass and morning glory. The fire was being stoked by Gordon, a black American who didn't care to talk about his experiences, although he did let slip that he was a Vietnam War vet, and that he'd taken a lifetime vow to stay at the monastery. There are two sets of saunas at Tham Krabok—one for addicts, one for monks. Wrapped in a sarong, I spent a volcanic twenty minutes in the monks' sauna—sweating like I'd never sweated before. But afterwards I felt terrific—renewed, invigorated, ready to take on the world.

In the afternoon I was adopted by the resident photo-monk, nicknamed "Aye" (pronounced "eh?" with a rising tone). Speaking in broken English, Aye did an admirable job of showing me around. He was in charge of a work-squad of rehabilitated addicts—so he conscripted me to help lug equipment up to a building site. When this task was completed, he decided to take me off to a vantage point in the hills to photograph the monastery. Or rather, he bounded over rubble and rocks like a mountain goat, leaving me behind—huffing and puffing and cursing, and scrambling for footholds on the steep rocks. At the top of this climb, I got a rude shock: we were standing on a pile of rocks that formed a precarious overhang—right over a huge cliff. He flourished his Nikon and started taking photos of the monastery far below, and indicated I should stand right on the edge of this rock-pile overhang so he could include me in the picture. *What kind of crazy monk is this?* I thought, as he perched on the very edge to demonstrate.

I found out why Aye was so nimble-footed. The monks at Tham Krabok belong to a separate order: by Thai Buddhist standards, they are a radical group. One of the vows the monks here take is never,

ever, to use any kind of transport—no bicycles, no roller-skates, no elephants, nothing—just a pair of feet. This promotes a tighter-knit community as monks have to think twice about walking off to Bangkok—130 kilometers away—a trip of five days on foot, as opposed to three hours by bus. Wat Tham Krabok does have its own vehicles—but these are operated only by lay-people attached to the monastery.

An understanding of "Jai Yen" ("cool heart") is vital to smooth navigation. Losing one's temper is a sign of bad breeding and a sure way to shut the door on a social or commercial transaction. Under the old royal legal codes, the punishment for a prince striking a commoner in anger was harsher than that for a commoner hitting his patron. The law reasoned that while it was expected that an ordinary man might lose his temper, a royal was an exalted, more fully-evolved person and should be above petty annoyances.

—Steve Van Beek, "Thailand Notes"

Cameras, on the other hand, are permitted. Aye proudly showed me his high-tech photo and video equipment. Decorating walls of his humble room were large black-and-white prints of activities around the monastery— Aye had taken all the photos. This surprised me because Thai monks don't paint, take photos, compose music or make videos—indulging in such creative self-expression is something that no Theravada monk is permitted in Thailand, because these pursuits are thought to be forms of craving. Nor do Thai Buddhist monks make statues or temple decorations—at Tham Krabok, however, it is the monks who cast huge Buddhas for shrines at the monastery. And the brown-robed monks at Tham Krabok are actively involved in all the building and farming projects around the monastery—producing their own rice, maize, peas, honey, and other foodstuffs. These practices run contrary to the Vinaya, the 2000-year-old code of conduct for Buddhists, which forbids heavy labor, such as tilling the soil.

Five percent of the addicts treated are female—the fact that monks at Tham Krabok deal directly with female addicts (often prostitutes) is another unorthodox procedure for Buddhism. In addition to the 200 monks, there are 20 nuns attached to the monastery, and about 150 supporting lay people. At any time there can be up to 150 patients and relatives in residence (an average of 50 addicts a week pass through the program.)

Once a year, the monks of Tham Krabok go on "vacation" for a week, or maybe a month. Their idea of a holiday is very different from yours or mine. They go on foot, with a retinue of lay followers. Aye showed me photographs from one of these trips. Each monk shoulders a ten-kilogram (22-pound) white umbrella, which is used as a tent at night—the weight comes from a wooden staking pole, and from attached mosquito netting. The entire band of 200 monks and retinue carry their own supplies; at night the monks form a circle of umbrella-tents, light their lamps and create their own village. This may sound like a camping trip but it's not—the monks look at travel from a purely spiritual angle. Aye informed me that this walkabout is a kind of pilgrimage—to gain merit, and accumulate wisdom. Travel is limiting the comfort of the body to gain freedom of the mind.

I mention all this because it is my firm belief that travel involves experiences, not sights. Real travel is coming across people whose viewpoints are completely different from your own, finding out that you still have much in common, that you can communicate regardless—and that you can learn a lot. Travel is transformation—if the trip shook your ideas up, if the experience changed you, then the journey was a success.

From the addict's point of view, it's a very different kind of learning experience at Tham Krabok: how to regain confidence in body, mind, and soul. Peter, from West Germany, was addicted to heroin for 25 years before visiting Tham Krabok. He underwent a month-long session, was completely cured, became a monk, and has been at the monastery since.

How is it that the staff of Tham Krabok have succeeded in rehabilitating addicts where most Western programs have failed? I asked Peter if Tham Krabok's methods could be applied elsewhere. No, he said—the secret herbal medicines cannot be exported because the abbot is afraid they will be misused. But that's beside the point: most of the cure is counseling—it depends on the Thai reverence for monks. A monk plays the role of guard, nurse, and confidant—half the monks are ex-addicts. The monks use every trick in the book—peer pressure, pressure from relatives-in-residence, marriage counseling, spiritual counseling. Without the monks there is no cure, but the monks cannot travel to other countries because they cannot walk there—so the program remains at Tham Krabok. Westerners, if interested, simply have to go there: the week after my visit, 30 Australian addicts were on their way to the monastery.

Michael Buckley is a writer and photographer who lives in Vancouver, Canada. He is the author of Moon Publications' Bangkok Handbook, *and is co-author of Lonely Planet's* China - a travel survival kit. *He is working on another guidebook for Moon on Vietnam, Laos, and Cambodia.*

⋆

Pointing at anyone with your foot is extremetly rude. In fact, using one's foot for any purpose for which hands are normally used, such as kicking a door shut, is also very bad manners in Thailand. We Westerners are apt to use our feet for un-footlike actions much more than Thais do, and this has given rise to a very telling Thai expression for the feet—*meu farang* or *"farang* hands!"

—Denis Segaller, *Thai Ways*

CHARLES NICHOLL

* * *

Moonsong and Martin Luther

In northern Thailand, a former tuk-tuk *driver tells the story
of Buddha and Mara to the author and his Thai friend,
and wonders about that turbulent priest.*

KATAI AND I MET THE OLD MONK THE NEXT DAY, IN THE BIG OPEN-
sided *sala* of Wat Pa Sak. We sat beneath a large gilded Buddha in
the sleek etiolated, Burmese-influenced style of Lan Na. His name
was Moonsong. He was a thin, knotty, myopic man. He said he was
seventy but he looked younger. He was unshaven, his orange
robe creased and tattered, his heavy spectacles sellotaped at the
hinges. He had once been a *tuk-tuk* driver in Bangkok. He showed
us an old photo: a tough bare-chested man leaning against the door
of a repair shop. It's odd how the monk's robe seems to partition
the wearer off from "normal" life, so one is surprised at this secular past. He had gone into the monkhood twelve years ago, seven
of those spent as a novice.

Did he prefer being a monk?

"Of course." Then, with a little laugh, "Most of the time."

He was keen to practice his English. He taught English to the
temple boys of the locality. There were certain rather specialist
points he wanted me to explain to him. On the blackboard in the
sala I defined as best I could the distinction between angels and
fairies. I corrected his impression that Martin Luther was a "famous
English monk", and that Henry VIII had murdered him. I said

41

he was thinking of Thomas à Becket and Henry II. Luther is a well-known figure in Thai religious circles, because he opposed a corrupt and mercenary clergy, and because, as Moonsong now put it, "he taught that God was inside us, not"—he gestured to the raftered roof of the *sala*—"up there. So it is with Buddhism. It is just following the good inside you, and putting aside"—an effortful pushing-away gesture—"the bad."

I said, "It is difficult to put aside the bad."

"Of course," he said quickly, a touch of irritation in the reedy voice. "Of course. The spirit of Mara is always ready to make trouble. But look." He gestured up at the bronzed Buddha above us. "You see our Buddha here. He is seated on Mara. Mara is all that you wish for, all you desire. The Buddha has risen above this, and now he may sit in meditation on top of Mara."

Mara was in the form of a serpent coiled up like a cushion beneath Buddha. I remembered Katai talking of the *naga* performing this office for the Buddha, and asked if they were the same.

"Mara is much greater," said Moonsong. "The evils of water brought by the *naga* are perhaps a part of Mara's work, but the *naga* brings the good things of water too. No, Mara is *phanyaa mahn*, the Prince of Demons. If you do not know it, I will tell you the story of Buddha and Mara."

We settled at his feet, which were dusty and crooked.

"When our Buddha attained to truth beneath the *bodhi* tree, Mara gathered an army of demons to bring fear to him. Mara rode at the head of the army on his war elephant, Giri Mekhala. But the goddess of the earth, who we call Nang Thoranee, saw that the Buddha was about to be engulfed by demons. She squeezed all the waters from her hair and sent down a flood to drown the demons.

"So next, Mara sent a plague of rats to devour the holy scriptures. The Buddha created at that moment the first cat in the world. She is called Phaka Waum. She chased away the rats, and preserved the truth of the Buddha's teaching, and to this day we consider it a great wrong to kill a cat.

"Now Mara hurled his most terrible weapon, a great thunderbolt, but the Buddha caught it in his hand, and there and then he turned it into a garland of flowers, like the *puang malai* you see hanging on his neck now.

"Last, Mara sent his three daughters to tempt the Buddha. His three daughters are Aradi, discontent; Tanha, desire; and Raka, love. Well, this was the hardest fight for Buddha, because now he was fighting the dangers inside himself. But the Buddha resisted their charms, and so today we say: the power of *dharma*—the truth of the Buddha—can save us from all the dangers inside us and around us.

"So, yes, of course it is difficult to put aside the spirit of Mara. We must learn to turn our desires into beautiful flowers. We must learn to place ourselves above Mara, like the Buddha does. Not only so that we can be above Mara, but so that we can *see* the dangers. They are outside us: desires and discontents. They are no longer part of us."

"They are part of life."

"Yes, in one sense. But we Buddhists say, rather they are part of death. They are part of the world that dies. Mara is a principle of death. That is why he is not the same as *naga*. The *naga* is dangerous, but he is a principle of life. In the Festival of Lights in Thailand, the Loi Kratong, it is said that it was a king of the *naga*, Phra Upagota, who finally helped to capture and conquer Mara. This was in the time

In almost every Buddhist temple in Thailand you'll find representations of naga-serpents, mythical creatures from pre-Hindu days. Usually these naga appear as balustrades on the side of bridges or stairway entrances. According to one ancient myth, the gods on Mount Meru sent naga across the water to the shores where man lives. From here they were to carry all men wishing and worthy to be in the realm of the gods. Passengers were to walk the serpent's back while meditating on love and kindness. Thus, these statues symbolically take anyone entering the wat into the realm of the spirits.
—Wayne Stier and Mars Cavers, *Wide Eyes in Burma and Thailand*

Naga serpent

of King Asoka, who brought the Theravada teachings of Buddhism into Thailand."

"But aren't desire and discontent a principle of life too?" I persisted.

His lined face looked down at me, a little rabbit-toothed pout. He said cryptically, "After noon a monk may not eat, but he may take water any time."

Thais very rarely shake hands, using the wai *to greet and say goodbye and to acknowledge respect, gratitude, or apology. A prayer-like gesture made with raised hands, the* wai *changes according to the relative status of the two people involved: Thais can instantaneously assess which* wai *to use when, but as a* farang *your safest bet is to go for the stranger's* wai, *which requires that your hands be raised close to your chest and your fingertips placed just below your chin. If someone makes a* wai *at you, you should definitely* wai *back, but it's generally wise not to initiate.*

—Paul Gray
and Lucy
Ridout,
*The Rough
Guide Thailand*

"I don't understand."

"Food is what you want, water is what you need."

He went still for a moment, eyes focused on something beyond us, mouth still showing two yellow teeth. I started to say something, but Katai laid a hand on my arm, and put a finger to her lips.

I heard the leisurely rattle of a dried-up teak leaf tumbling from the tall canopy. The temple was called Wat Pa Sak because two hundred teak trees had gone into making its enclosure.

After a bit he looked at me and smiled. "Your Luther says: *Pecca fortiter, sed fortius fide.* Sin strongly, but believe more strongly. I think that is a good beginning for us all."

He climbed wearily to his feet, and began to rummage in a wooden chest near by. He brought out a little medallion: a tiny tin Buddha inside a triangular blob of perspex [transparent plastic]. Katai said, "It is a *phra kliang* to hang around your neck."

I made a *wai* and took it from him. Katai too made a *wai*, and I got the feeling she was thanking him for what he had done to "enlighten" me, a poor *farang* who knew nothing. Phra Moonsong received our thanks with a slight bow, but no *wai*.

Katai said quietly, "He would like you to give money for the temple." I handed some notes to him. She too gave him money, but she placed the notes on top of the wooden chest. A monk may not take anything directly from a woman's hand.

"Thank you," Moonsong said, "for teaching me about Martin Luther, and about Thomas the Becket. I shall tell my pupils." He thought for a moment. "So. Is it right: 'Who will rid me of this turbulent priest'?"

"Perfect," I said.

He grinned, impish, pedantic. "Never perfect," he said. He ambled off. At the edge of the *sala*, where its shade met the shimmer of the midday light, he met another monk. They conversed for a moment, a faint breeze catching their robes, a few more teak leaves slowly falling, and then they went their separate ways.

Charles Nicholl is the author of The Reckoning, The Fruit Palace, *and* Borderlines: A Journey in Thailand and Burma, *from which this story was excerpted. He lives with his wife and four children in Hereford, England.*

*

If you dine in a Thai home, don't wait for your hostess to sit down before beginning to eat. She may not eat or drink with the guests. Begin when your host does.

Never finish the last bit of food in the serving dish. It's considered an honor to have it. Wait until it's offered to you. Refuse it politely, and, when asked again, accept.

—Elizabeth Devine and Nancy L. Braganti, *The Traveler's Guide to Asian Customs and Manners*

ALAN RABINOWITZ

* * *

"To Eat" Means
To Eat Rice

In Thailand, rice is not just food.

I THOUGHT OF THE DAY I TOOK ONE OF THE WORKERS TO HIS family's home outside of Lan Sak [in the central plains region]. Sitting in one of those little island pockets on a bamboo mat outside the house, I gazed out at eye level with the fields. Before eating our meal of rice, dried fish, and fruit, his father put some rice to the side for the insects and birds, so that they could share in a bounty that was not seen by these farmers as being entirely their own. As each family member finished his meal, he gave a quick *wai* over his plate, to show respect to the Rice Mother. Later, we walked to the temple compound, where I was shown the new roof that the village was putting on one of the temple's buildings.

This little Thai community was like thousands of others around the countryside, the end product of millennia of tradition. The farmers' homes were simple wood or bamboo structures and the villages were self-governing units. The temple was the focal point of the community and often served as the school, the hospital, the community center, and a refuge for the poor, the aged, and the mentally disturbed all at the same time. Until 1921, these temples were the only places for children to get a basic education in Thailand. These small villages represented Thai life at its purest, nearly undiluted by outside cultural influences. In a place like this, I could believe in magic and spirits.

At different times of the year, the scenes and colors of the central plains change. Around May, toward the end of the dry season, the farmers and water buffalo labor at trying to till the brown parched ground for the next crop. Up before dawn and working in the fields by first light, they don't return home until dusk. This is also the month of Visakha Puja, Thailand's greatest religious holiday, commemorating the Buddha's birth, enlightenment, and death. Even those who have been out all day in the fields go to the temple at dusk and join the procession, circling the chapel three times with flowers, a candle, and three incense sticks representing the Buddha, the *dharma* (his teachings), and the *sangha* (the monastic order).

When the monsoons arrive a month or so later, water inundates the paddy and the young, green rice plants start to emerge. As the plants seed, and the fields become "pregnant," a spirit ceremony is held to strengthen the plants through this period of weakness and vulnerability. By early November, when the rains cease, the grain turns golden. In late November or early December, harvest time arrives. The work continues now well into the night. The fields are lit by lamplight, and some villagers sleep among their crops in make-shift

> *If you visit a family outside Bangkok, expect to find a mat on the floor and a small table with food on it. When you sit, do not cross your legs. Bend your knees and keep your feet behind you or to the side.*
>
> —Elizabeth Devine and Nancy L. Braganti, *The Travelers' Guide to Asian Customs and Manners*

shelters. During the harvest, the paddies are filled with women and children, their wide-brimmed straw hats hiding their faces, their voices occasionally drifting through the hot, still air.

This system of paddy growing, called *sawah* agriculture, is practiced throughout Asia's most populated areas. Because these irrigated paddies often produce similar or increased yields from the same land for centuries, this type of agriculture is capable of absorbing and feeding expanding populations in a way other forms such as "swidden" or slash-and-burn agriculture cannot.

But rice is more than just a commodity to the Thai people. Symbolically, it represents a gift to be respected and shared. Rice grains are not to be intentionally thrown on the floor and, if seen on the ground, should not be stepped over. The Thai words "to eat," *geen cow*, literally mean "to eat rice." Eight out of every ten Thais are rice farmers. As of 1986, more than twenty million tons of rice were produced a year. Over a quarter of this yield was for export; Thailand is the only developing country in the world that is a net food exporter.

Yet the irony is that as Thailand's wealth increases and the number of Mercedeses and skyscrapers in Bangkok mushrooms, the Thai rice farmer finds himself plummeting to the bottom of the Thai economic pyramid. The farmer, who is often merely a tenant on the land, is a frequent victim of usury. Sometimes the farmer is forced to sell even his most cherished belonging, his water buffalo, just to survive. A 1987 survey estimated that 80 percent of Thailand's villages were in debt. The enormous sums owed averaged over $80,000 per village. This economic instability causes chronic hardship that often results in landlessness, poverty, and collapse of family units.

Alan Rabinowitz is a research zoologist with Wildlife Conservation International, a division of the New York Zoological Society, and the author of Jaguar *and* Chasing the Dragon's Tail: The Struggle to Save Thailand's Wild Cats, *from which this story was excerpted.*

★

When a baby is put in the cradle for the first time, a cat is placed there first and rocked to and fro for a minute before the baby is put in it. Undoubtedly, a domestic cat was in the past a necessity in a house infested by rats, especially in the vicinity of rice fields.

—Phya Anuman Rajadhon, *Some Traditions of the Thai*

KUKRIT PRAMOJ

⋆ ⋆ ⋆

The Reverend Goes To Dinner (at 8 a.m.)

A Thai statesman tells how King Mongkut (1851–1868)
made use of an American missionary and
learned to use a spoon and a fork.

AND SO WE ADOPTED WESTERN TABLEWARE. WE DIDN'T REALLY adopt it, we only picked out a few to adopt. Two. The *farangs* turned up with tableware—20 knives, 20 forks, 100 spoons and so on—and put them all over the table. When that happened the Second King, Phra Pinklao, the younger brother of King Mongkut, invited Dr. Bradley, an American missionary, to go and have dinner with him at 8 o'-clock in the morning. The invitation was in English and specifically said "dinner." But at 8 a.m. The Dr. and his wife, Mrs. Bradley, were rather mystified about dinner at 8 o'clock in the morning but they couldn't refuse it; the invitation had come from the Second King himself. So they went in full dinner at-

This is the same Dr. Bradley who took Anna Leonowens, of Anna and the King of Siam *fame, under his wing. For an account of Anna's imaginative life in Siam, see William Warren's "Who Was Anna Leonowens?" later in this section.*

—JO'R and LH

tire, to dinner in the palace. They found a table set with all the *farang* tableware—knives, forks, and spoons, soup plates, and so on. They were requested to sit down. Just the two of them, and

49

Western food was served accordingly. Like a grand dinner. Six courses.

And the King was there sitting on a chair with all his family and his Royal court behind him, looking at how the *farangs* made best use of these implements. Dr. Bradley and his wife went through the dinner using each instrument correctly, and each plate, each cup, everything, wine glasses, and so on. After that, they took leave and went back home. And the King knew how to make use of each implement.

But the Thais themselves didn't keep up in grand style after that. They only adopted the spoon and the fork because Thai food is cooked in the kitchen and the cooking operation is not carried to the table. You don't need the knife to cut anything when it has already been chopped up or is served in small pieces. So they adopted only two. The rest they discarded. And they adopted the soup plate to eat rice with. That's how the Thai people deal with a foreign culture when it arrives. Dr. Bradley made a note of this to himself.

He was surprised. He just thought it was so strange. He probably thought, oh well, we must humor him, so he took his wife along in all her fineries to a dinner party at 8 o'clock in the morning and they made an exhibit of themselves.

The late Kukrit Pramoj was Prime Minister of Thailand, scholar, and author of the epic Thai novel The Four Reigns.

✳

Among the voices of democratic opposition, Kukrit was prominent as a courageous journalist and parliamentarian. In the early 1960s, when Hollywood made *The Ugly American,* on the struggle to save democracy in Southeast Asia, Kukrit was asked to play the "Sarkhan" prime minister, opposite Marlon Brando as the United States ambassador. Kukrit later recollected:

I was important cast.... Marlon Brando had his own dressing room which was a trailer with everything inside, air conditioning, gin flowing from the tap. I had the same thing, identical and Marlon insisted on that...I'm born a one-movie actor. You see, Hollywood calls a person like me a type actor. You are only called when they need another Oriental prime minister....

Oddly enough, Kukrit went on to become the real-life prime minister, not of "Sarkhan," but of Thailand itself. He took on the task early in 1975, when South Vietnam was about to fall to the Communists, and many people in Southeast Asia feared that Thailand as well might fulfill the prophecies of the domino theory. To the great dismay of the timid, Kukrit decided to close American air bases in Thailand, then went to Beijing to establish friendly relations with Communist China. He was the architect of the Thai-Chinese alliance against Vietnam.

—Richard West, "Royal Family Thais,"
New York Review of Books

* * *

Ghosts of Siam

How the Wild West came to Hat Yai,
the ancient shadow play disappeared,
and what became of Uncle.

THAILAND, UNTIL 1953 GENERALLY CALLED SIAM, WENT MODERN just before my first visit there, later in that year. Marshal Pibul Songkhram, the ruling autocrat, ordered the nation to cease to look to the past, and to take the future in a firm embrace. A commission sent to the U.S. to investigate western culture returned with its findings. Its members believed that it was rooted in whisky drinking, dancing in public, and the strip-tease, and urged the introduction of these customs into Siam. It was at first stipulated that the strip-tease should be performed under religious auspices in the precincts of a temple—although this provision soon went by the board.

Hat Yai, a provincial town in the south within a few miles of the Malaysian frontier, was chosen for an experiment in instant modernization, and I went there to see what was happening. There was a tendency in Siam for the words "modern" and "American" to be used interchangeably, so when the order went out for Hat Yai to be brought up to date, most Thais accepted that it was to be Americanized. Little surprise was aroused when the model chosen for the new Hat Yai was Dodge City of the 1860s revealed by the movies.

In due course the experts arrived with photographs of the capital of the wild frontier in its heyday, and within weeks the comfortable muddle of Hat Yai was no more. Its shacks reeling on their stilts were pulled down, the ducks and buffaloes chased out of the ditches, and the spirit houses (after proper apologies to the spirits) shoved out of sight. It became illegal to fly kites within the limits of the town, or to stage contests between fighting fish.

Where the bustling chaos of the East had once been, arose a replica of the main street made famous by so many westerns, complete with swing-door saloons, wall-eyed hotels, and the rickety verandas on which law-abiding citizens had been marshaled by the sheriff to go on a posse, and men of evil intention planned their attack on the mail train or the bank. Hat Yai possessed no horses and the hard men of those days rode into town in Jeeps—nevertheless hitching-posts were provided. For all the masquerade, Hat Yai in the 1950s did bear some slight resemblance to the Dodge City of a century before, and there were gun-fighters in plenty in the vicinity. It was at that time an unofficial rest area for Malaysian communist guerrillas from across the frontier, tolerated simply because the Thais lacked the strength to keep them out. The communist intruders were armed to the teeth, and Thai law enforcement agents—part of whose uniform included Davy Crockett fur caps from which raccoons' tails dangled—were few in number. Reaching for one's gun was a matter of frequent occurrence in the main-street saloons. Although it was largely a histrionic gesture and few people were shot, newcomers like myself were proudly taken to be shown the holes in the ceilings.

The arrival of the movies played their part in Pibul Songkhram's vision of the new Thailand. In a single year, 1950, hundreds, perhaps thousands of movie-theaters opened up all over south-east Asia, the first film on general release being *Arsenic and Old Lace*. With this the shadow play that had entertained so many generations of Thais was wiped out overnight. A multitude of mothers throughout the land had worked tirelessly at pressing back their daughters' fingers from the age of five to enable them to dance with style in dramas such as the *Ramayana*. From this point on it

was all to no purpose, and the customers who befuddled themselves in the saloons with Mekong whisky, drunk hot by the half-
pint, were waited upon with sublime grace by girls whose days as
performers were at an end. Real-life theater demanded the imaginative effort of suspending belief; cowboy movies did not.

Investigating the threatened disappearance of the puppet show, a
Bangkok newspaper reported that it had only been able to discover
a single company surviving somewhere in the north of the country,
working in Thai style with life-size puppets manipulated not by
strings, but by sticks from below stage. It took 40 years to train a
puppeteer to the required pitch of perfection in this art, and it
seemed worthwhile to the newspaper to bring this company down
to Bangkok to film what was likely to be one of its last performances.

This was given in the garden of the paper's editor, Kukrit
Pramoj, and attracted a fashionable crowd of upper-crust Thais,
plus a few foreign diplomats, many of whom would see a puppet
show for the first and last time. So unearthly was the skill of the
puppeteers, so naturalistic and convincing the movements of the
puppets, that, but for the fact that their vivacity surpassed that of
flesh and blood, it would have been tempting to suspect we were
watching actors in puppet disguise.

After the show most of the guests went off to a smart restaurant, filling it with the bright clatter of enthusiasm that would
soon fade. Such places provided "continental" food—the mode
of the day. In this land offering so many often extraordinary regional delicacies, successful efforts were made to suppress flavor
to a point that only a soporific vacuum remained. Kukrit, always
a champion of Thai culture, made the astonishing admission that
he knew nothing of the cuisine, now only to be savored at night
markets and roadside stalls. In a flare-up of nationalist enthusiasm,
he announced his determination to put this right. He made inquiries among his friends and a few days later I received an invitation to lunch with him at the house of a relation, a prince who
was a grandson of King Chulalongkorn. The prince, said Kukrit,
employed a chef trained to cook nothing but European food, and
he could not remember whether—if ever—he had tasted a local

dish. Entering into the spirit of adventure, he had been able to track down a Thai cook with an enthusiastic following in the half-world of the markets, who would be hired for this occasion. The meal thus, for him too, offered the promise of novelty and adventure.

The prince lived on the outskirts of Bangkok in a large villa dating from about 1900. It was strikingly English in appearance, with a garden full of sweet peas, grown by the prince himself, which in this climate produced lax, greyish blooms, singularly devoid of scent. He awaited us at the garden gate. Kukrit leaped down from the car, scrambled towards him and despite Songkhram's injunction to refrain from salutations of a servile kind, made a token grab at his right ankle This the prince good-naturedly avoided. "Do get up, Kukrit, dear boy," he said. Both men had been to school in England, and, as well as their easy, accent free mastery of the language, there was something that proclaimed this in their faces and manner.

My previous experience of Thai houses had been limited to the claustrophobic homes in which the moneyed classes had taken refuge, shuttered away from the menacing light of day in a gloom deepened by a clutter of dark furniture. The villa came as a surprise, for in the past year an avant-garde French interior designer had flown in to bring about a revolution. He had brought the sun back, filtering it through lattices and the dappled shade of house-plants with great, lustrous leaves, opening the house to light and diffusing an ambiance of spring. This was from the womb of the future. We lunched under a photo-mural of Paris—*quand fleurit le printemps*—and a device invented by the designer breathed a faint fragrance of narcissi through the conditioned air. The meal was both delicious and enigmatic, based, we were assured, on the choice of the correct basic materials (none of them identified), and colours that were auspicious given the phase of the moon. Kukrit took many notes.

The entertainment that followed was in some ways more singular, for the prince told us that he had inherited most of his grandfather's photographic equipment, including his stereoscopic slides, and he proposed that we should view them together—"to give you some idea of how royalty lived in those days."

King Chulalongkorn, who reigned from 1868 to 1910, was a man of protean achievement. On the world stage he showed himself more than a match for the French colonial power that entertained barely concealed hopes of gobbling up his kingdom. At home he pursued many hobbies with unquenchable zest; organizing fancy-dress parties, cooking for his friends, but above all immersing himself in his photography. He collected cameras by the hundred, did his own developing, and drew upon an immense family pool of consorts and their children for his portraiture. We inspected photographs, taken at frequent intervals, of his sons lined up, ten at a time in order of height, for the king's loving record of their advance from childhood to adolescence, all of them, including the six-year-old at the bottom of the line, in a top hat. Toppers had only been put aside in one case when four senior sons had been crammed into the basket of a balloon.

King Mongkut was a gifted, enlightened ruler who successfully ushered Thailand into the modern world. That he is chiefly remembered as the light-hearted libertine of the film The King and I—*based on the fanciful recollections of Anna Leonowens, the English governess hired as tutor to his children—is indeed unfortunate. The sybaritic demagogue portrayed in the film bore little resemblance to the austere, venerated monarch who had spent 27 years in a Bangkok monastery. Significantly, the king's voluminous state papers contain just one brief reference to Anna— as an appendix to a shopping list!*

—Frank Kusy,
Cadogan Guides: Thailand

The queens and consorts were of even more interest, and here they were seen posed in the standard environment of Victorian studio photography; lounging against plaster Greek columns, taking a pretended swipe with a tennis racquet, or clutching the handlebars of a weird old bicycle. Fancy-dress shots, of which there were many, bore labels in French, the language of culture of the day: *L'Amazone* (Queen Somdej with a feather in her hair grasping a bow); *Une Dame turque de qualité* (the Princess of Chiang Mai, with a hookah); *La Cavalerie Legère* (an unidentified consort in a hussar's shako); *La Jolie Chochère* (another consort, in white breeches and a straw hat, carrying a whip). The impression given by this collection was that the Victorian epoch produced a face of its own, and that this could even triumph over barriers of race. Thus Phra Rataya, Princess of Chiang Mai, bore a resemblance to George Sand; Queen Somdej had something about her of La Duse, while a lesser consort, well into middle age, reminded me of one of my old Welsh aunts.

The prince put away the slides. Like his grandfather, King Chulalongkorn, and his great-grandfather, King Mongkut—an astronomer and inventor who designed a quick-firing cannon based on the Colt revolver—he had a taste for intellectual pleasures. He showed us his Leica camera with its battery of lenses. Candid photography was in vogue at the time. By use of gadgets, such as angle-view finders, it was possible to catch subjects for portraiture off-guard, sometimes in ludicrous postures. There was no camera to equal it for this purpose, said the prince. As for his grandfather's gear, it took up a lot of space, and he said he would be quite happy to donate it to any museum that felt like giving it house-room.

As we strolled together across the polished entrance hall towards the door, my attention was suddenly taken by what appeared to be a large, old-fashioned, and over-ornate birdcage suspended in an environment in which nothing was more than a year old. I stopped to examine it, and the prince said, "Uncle lives there."

Although slightly surprised, I thought I understood. "You mean the house spirit?"

"Exactly. In this life he was our head servant. He played an important part in bringing up us children, and was much loved by us all. Uncle was quite ready to sacrifice himself for the good of the family."

The prince had no hesitation in explaining how this had come about. When the building of a new royal house was finished, a bargain might be struck with a man of low caste. The deal was that he would agree to surrendering the remaining few years of the present existence in return for acceptance into the royal family in the next. He would be entitled to receive ritual offerings on a par with the ancestors. Almost without exception, such an arrangement was readily agreed to.

"How did Uncle die?"

The prince answered enigmatically: "He was interred under the threshold. Being still a child I was excluded from the ceremony, which was largely a religious one. Everyone was happy. Certainly Uncle was."

I took the risk. "Would a Western education have any effect at all on such beliefs?" I asked.

"That is a hard question," the prince said, "but I am inclined to the opinion that it would be slight. This appears to be more a matter of feeling than conscious belief. Education is an imperfect shield against custom and tradition." We stood together in the doorway and the cage swayed a little in a gust of warm breeze. "In some ways," the prince said, "you may judge us still to be a little backward." His laugh seemed apologetic. "In others I hope you will agree that we move with the times."

Norman Lewis has written thirteen novels and nine non-fiction works. His A Dragon Apparent *and* Golden Earth *are considered travel classics, and* Naples '44 *is considered by some to be one of the best books written about World War II. He lives with his family in Essex, England.*

★

Most Thais are fanatic royalists, and you risk offense if you speak of the king without due deference. Centuries of absolute monarchy ended with the revolution of 1932, but the ethos remains strong. Unlike some of his predecessors, who blithely murdered their way to the throne—the traditional mode of execution for those of royal blood was to be placed inside a velvet sack and bludgeoned to death with sandalwood clubs—King Bhumibol seems to deserve the adulation. He is an attractive, high-profile figure, who spends a lot of time helicoptering around the remoter regions of the kingdom, setting up the Royal Projects one encounters everywhere: irrigation projects, hydro-electric schemes, schoolhouses, medical centers, immunization programs, temple restoration, road construction, etc. The hill tribes are devoted to him for championing their cause.

Historians say he has revived the "open monarchy" ideal of Sukhothai, when the famous King Ram Khamkaeng was said to be accessible to the meanest of his subjects. He is a cosmopolitan man: he was born in America, grew up in Switzerland, and speaks fluent English and French. He is a typical Thai blend of tradition and modernity, and the people love him.

—Charles Nicholl, *Borderlines: A Journey in Thailand and Burma*

ALAN RABINOWITZ

✳ ✳ ✳

Elephant Scream

*Acceptance sometimes comes
in an odd guise.*

IN ADDITION TO THE MONKS, THE BEGINNING OF THE RAINY season brought other visitors as well: ants, a group of animals that must have evolved solely to torture man. At first there were just the tiny, innocuous varieties. I'd find them stuck between the bristles of my toothbrush, running across the pages of my book as I read, emerging from the switches on my tape player, or floating in their final resting place in my morning coffee or rice. After a while I stopped picking them out of my food and just ate them along with the vegetables. When I finally adjusted to their constant presence, another, more insidious species entered my life.

Lying half awake in the darkness slapping at myself, I wondered how mosquitoes had gotten inside the net. Then I felt painful little stings and I switched on the flashlight that I kept under my pillow. Large red ants, which until now I'd only seen in little groups around camp, were all over the lower part of my body. They were moving *en masse* through the window beside my bed. I slapped at them frantically and jumped out from under the net, only to have them retaliate by biting me more ferociously. When I felt them marching across my feet, I swung the flashlight around to see that they were all over the floor and spreading quickly into the other two rooms of the house.

I ran into the bathroom, dumped water over my body, and then ran outside feeling like I had just emerged from a late-night horror movie. Around me the forest was dark, quiet, and peaceful. It was peaceful, I thought— except for the ants, scorpions, snakes, gaur, elephants, tigers, and leopards. I crawled into the front of my truck and tried to sleep, but my heart was still racing. Every now and then I'd feel the movement of an ant that had been stranded somewhere on my body. It was two days before I could move back into my house. It was much longer before I could sleep easily again.

When Lung Soowan appeared at my door the day after the ant invasion, I found myself staring into the face of a scarred, tough-looking 42-year-old man. He was dressed only in a short, saronglike wraparound called a *pacomah* and his chest and back were covered with tattoos, a practice common among men from the northeastern part of Thailand. He'd never worked with a *farang* before and spoke mostly Isarn, a northeastern dialect, different from both the northern dialect Amporn was teaching me and the more common central or Bangkok Thai which I had been learning on my own. I was just beginning to make myself understood, I thought. Now this.

Soowan arrived alone. His family remained in his village about an hour from the sanctuary. After agreeing on a salary of fifty

The idea of working in the Huai Kha Khaeng Wildlife Sanctuary was, in many ways, intriguing. This thousand-square-mile sanctuary forms the core of a forest area more than four times that size, one of the largest protected forests in Southeast Asia. Still relatively pristine and remote, this preserve supports wild populations of tigers, leopards, tapirs, wild cattle, and elephants; it is the last refuge in the country for the wild water buffalo and green peafowl. Much of the sanctuary is comprised of dry deciduous forest, containing trees that shed their leaves seasonally. These forests contain good soil for agricultural development and thus have been quickly destroyed in most areas where they once existed.

—Alan Rabinowitz, *Chasing the Dragon's Tail: The Struggle to Save Thailand's Wild Cats* baht (two dollars) a day, he moved into part of Beng's house and started coming over every morning at sunrise to go into the forest with me. Though he understood my Thai, at first he rarely acknowledged anything I tried to say. I made the situation worse when, several days after we had started to work together, I gave Soowan a hunting knife as a present. When he refused it, I thought he was being polite, so I stuck the knife in his belt. He turned and left abruptly. When I told the story to Noparat, I learned that in Thailand a knife is only given to someone you wish to hurt. It can be given as a friendly gesture only if you accept something in return. Noparat talked with Soowan, and the next day I accepted one baht (four cents) for the knife.

Despite the initial lack of rapport between us, I could tell from our first day together that Lung Soowan was at home in the forest. He would glide through the underbrush, clearing vegetation with no more than a flick of his razor-sharp knife, all the while pointing out sights and sounds that I had difficulty discerning even after being shown them. Sometimes he'd pull up and freeze suddenly, eyes flashing, as he watched a sambar deer grazing by the water or a group of macaques moving through the trees overhead. But when it came to communication, he was Lung Galong's exact opposite. Words were spoken only when necessary.

The initial breakthrough came during the third week we worked together. As we chopped our way through a rough, scrubby area, I grabbed a thorny, poisonous plant that caused me extreme pain and made my hand start to swell immediately. This sent Lung Soowan into fits of laughter, producing the first smile I'd seen from him.

"What was that?" I demanded in Thai, not at all pleased.

"Elephant scream plant," he answered, a big grin still on his face. "Even elephants cry when they touch it. It'll hurt for many days."

"Why didn't you tell me about it?" I asked unreasonably.

"I forgot you're a *farang*," he said, laughing.

I suddenly realized that not only did Soowan have a nice smile but we had just held our first conversation. I laughed too in spite of the pain. Later, I learned how Thais often laugh at the misfortunes of those closest to them. If Lung Soowan had disliked me, he would have shown no emotion.

Alan Rabinowitz contributed other stories to this book which are also excerpts from Chasing the Dragon's Tail: The Struggle to Save Thailand's Wild Cats.

★

The word *farang* is actually a Thai derivation from *"français,"* but it is used to describe any fair-skinned, round-eyed foreigner from Europe or the USA. According to Thai tradition, the *farang* inhabit a far-flung region called the *muang nauk,* the "outside kingdom." One chronicle, the *Thai Nya Phuum,* sums them up as follows: "They are exceedingly tall, hairy, and evil-smelling. They school their children long, and devote their lives to the amassing of riches. Their women, though large and round, are very beautiful. They do not grow rice." When the Thai call you *farang* it is not pejorative. They disarm the word with a grin or a giggle. But they remain cautious. The *farang* does not have the great Thai virtue of *jai yen,* a "cool heart." His heart is liable to overheat.

—Charles Nicholl, *Borderlines: A Journey in Thailand and Burma*

JOHN CALDERAZZO

✦ ✦ ✦

Meditation in a Thai Forest

An extraordinary monk and two determined women are
working to restore Siladhamma, *the balance of*
nature, in Thailand's imperiled forests.

IT'S DAWN IN THE SHRINKING, DROUGHT-PLAGUED FOREST OF
northern Thailand. Sitting cross-legged on the open platform of a
hillside cabin, SueEllen and I listen to a faint clanking of bells
ringing from the floor of the Mae Soi valley—the sound of water
buffalo trudging to their fields. I take a sip of tea and smile drowsily
at Nuni, our host and interpreter. Later today she'll show us a
meditation cave a short walk from here where her friend and
colleague Ajarn Pongsak, a remarkable Buddhist monk, has con-
ceived a plan to change the weather.

But right now Nuni is eyeing us strangely. Then, in her crisp
Queen's English, she says, "I don't mean to alarm you, but when
I woke up this morning I found a snake on my kitchen counter.
Big, smooth, olive-brown fellow. Cobra, I'm afraid."

I keep on smiling, but suddenly I find myself peeking nervously at the teak branches over my head. Snakes give me the
creeps. My uneasiness will eventually pass, but I try to rush matters by telling myself that a snake *belongs* out here in the forest, by
reminding myself that a huge snake, possibly a king cobra, once
slithered peacefully across Ajarn Pongsak's lap while he was deep
in meditation.

It's no use. My equilibrium's gone; gone yet again, for during the month that SueEllen and I have been traveling through Thailand, exploring national parks and wildlife preserves—or what we could find left of them—almost nothing has turned out as I expected.

On our first day in the country, SueEllen and I sat in the atrium of our modern Bangkok hotel and watched a mandarin duck waddle hopefully under our breakfast table. After a while it plopped into a goldfish pond surrounded by enormous ferns. Above us, seven floors of hanging bougainvillea framed a square of blue sky, and when a breeze riffled the blossoms, a pink shower came fluttering down. Christmas was about a week away.

The architects had done a spectacular job. And, as our first stroll outside the hotel walls made clear, it was also a necessary job. As we walked in shimmering 95-degree heat along Rama IV Road, one of the many cemented-over canals, unmuffled motorbikes whizzed past us like furious bees, and *tuk-tuks*—three-wheeled taxis which resemble souped-up golf carts—zigzagged through the crush. We came to a major intersection and just before the light turned green, the ratchety two-stroke engines began revving up with a noise like that of a thousand chainsaws. We looked up at each other with disbelief. SueEllen, shouting millimeters from my ear, sounded far, far away.

Within minutes she had pulled out a handkerchief and clamped it to her mouth, a habit she'd picked up in the murky, coal-fouled cities of China. Over the years, we'd both breathed a lot of awful air, but I couldn't recall ever inhaling so much smoky oil and pure leaded gasoline.

Traveling on the Chao Phraya River a few days later, it was much cooler. As we moved upriver past floating vegetable markets, golden-spired *wats,* and the delicate rooftops of the Grand Palace, it was possible to see the charm and beauty of Bangkok. I momentarily forgot about the frantic traffic, the blocks and blocks of all-night sex bars, the hundreds of thousands of prostitutes, many of them refugees from the severe deforestation and drought of the northeast. As I listened to the soothing slap of water against the pier pilings, I could see why the city had once been called "The Venice of the East." But every thirty seconds or so everything was drowned out by the airplane-engine yowl of "long-tailed" boats, river taxis that slashed through the water like food mixers gone mad.

Now and then I caught some spray, but I knew enough to keep my lips pressed tight: Bangkok's seven million residents (and another four million are projected within ten years) dump thousands of tons of raw sewage into the river every day. As we passed a series of barges plowing downriver with gigantic logs, I watched some dead fish bob gently towards the Gulf of Thailand.

The architects of our hotel were looking more sensible by the minute.

So were the builders of Bangkok's nearly four hundred *wats,* those walled-in way stations of peace and quiet (and widely varying degrees of commercialism). Their leafy courtyards and blissful Buddha images were probably keeping a lot of Thais from going crazy. At least, during the four days before SueEllen and I made our escape to the south, that's how they worked for *me,* and I'm not even a Buddhist.

There were probably a hundred and fifty of us crammed into a peeling wooden boat designed for sixty. As we burbled along through the Andaman Sea south of Phuket, Phi Phi Islands National Park rose from a calm jade sea with the laconic speed of myth. First I could make out only two green specks floating on the horizon, then their fuzzy toppings of jungle, then their sheer cliffs steadily growing. Finally the two islands stood above us like moss-

Longtail boat

draped Chinese rock sculptures, unreal and unbelievably steep. They were spectacularly beautiful.

We chugged around the schist walls of the larger island into a bowl-shaped harbor fringed with white beaches and swaying co-conut palms and joined half a dozen boats at least our size sitting at anchor. When we got close to the beach I could see, behind the thick vegetation that started perhaps ten yards from the water, long lines of brand-new thatched-roof bungalows. Nearby were a couple of open-air cafeterias where several hundred other day tourists—Americans, Australians, Germans, Italians—were washing down curried chicken with Singha beer.

Officially, Thai national parks allow five percent of the land to be used for development. Here, that five percent—if that's all it was—took up just about all of the inhabitable land.

After lunch, I tried to take a tourist-in-paradise picture of SueEllen on the beach, but

The Western liberalism embraced by the Thai sex industry is very unrepresentative of the majority Thai attitude to the body. Clothing—or the lack of it—is what bothers Thais most about tourist behavior.... You need to dress moderately when entering temples, but the same also applies to other important buildings and all public places. Stuffy and sweaty as it sounds, you should keep shorts and vests for the real tourist resorts, and be especially diligent about covering up in rural areas. Baring your flesh on beaches is very much a Western practice: when Thais go swimming they often do so fully clothed, and they find topless and nude bathing extremely unpalatable. It's not illegal, but it won't win you many friends.

—Paul Gray and Lucy Ridout, *The Rough Guide Thailand*

things kept getting in the way: floating oil and toilet paper (ominous hints of the septic system) and nude bathers who seemed to think they were on the Italian Riviera. The sea gypsies who once lived here were long gone.

A few years ago there was nothing here but island. In a few more years this "national park" will look like Ko Samui, where we spent Christmas Day strolling past hundreds of bungalows on once-empty beaches. And Ko Samui will soon catch up with Phuket, where a lush rainforest has fallen to plantations—rubber, pineapple, and papaya—and the shabby sprawl of uncontrolled tourism. Almost everywhere we went, incredible natural beauty was fading fast, one ecosystem after another on the brink of disaster.

SueEllen and I walk with Nuni through the forest. As I watch the stars come out, I feel as though a calm has dropped over everything—the well-worn path, the trees, my uneasiness about cobras. We come to a campfire, and sitting before it in a wicker chair is Ajarn Pongsak, his skin glowing as deeply orange as his robes. He's fiftyish, short and sturdy, a farmer's son, slightly jug-eared. He shakes my hand warmly, bows slightly to SueEllen. We take places around the fire and sip tea. After a while Nuni begins to translate my questions.

"When you are in the forest, you feel its coolness in body and in spirit," Ajarn says. "This is harmony, the correct balance of nature, or what we call *Siladhamma*." He leans forward and pokes a stick into the flames. The fire crackles, and a few sparks sail up into the dark. "The balance of nature. It's achieved and regulated by the functions of the forest. Hence the survival of the forest is essential to the survival of *Siladhamma* and our environment. It's all interdependent." For a moment Ajarn looks sadly bemused, as though what he's saying should be, but isn't, obvious to everyone. "When we protect the forest, we protect the world. When we destroy the forest, we destroy that balance, causing drastic changes in global weather and soil conditions, causing severe hardships to the people."

Until a few years ago, like many meditation monks (and unlike the more worldly "study monks" of the cities), Ajarn spent his life wandering the cool forests of the countryside. Occasionally he came here, to the Mae Soi valley, and from the highway he would follow a path to an ancient meditation cave. The path wound five miles through a forest laced with streams and shaded by enormous teak, ironwood, and mango trees, some of them seven hundred years old and wider than his arms could stretch. The forest was alive with great hornbills, civets, sambar, and barking deer. Sometimes at night he heard the cry of a leopard. The mist-shrouded ridgetops above the cave were chilly even in the hot season.

Then one day, after an absence of several years, he returned to find that the forest had disappeared. Now there were almost no trees at all—only miles of knee-high stumps and bushes, cracked gullies, and scorched hills. Standing in the blazing sun alongside the road, he stared at a landscape that belonged more in the American Southwest than in what was once the lushest country in Asia. The valley was suffering unprecedented drought, and farmers in the lowlands told him they were getting only one poor crop a year instead of three good ones.

How could this have happened?

First, Nuni explained to me, a company which wanted wood to cure tobacco logged almost all of the forest from the roadside halfway to the ridgetops. They had a concession to cut only smaller trees, but they ignored it.

Second, Hmong hill tribes moved onto the ridgetops with their traditional slash-and-burn farming practices, which shave bare the tops of the mounts. (Several years ago I saw evidence

The forest was always quick to remind me that becoming too comfortable was dangerous. One day, while crossing a stream, I was busily concentrating on the pronunciation of some Thai words when I stepped up onto the opposite bank; a break in the normal pattern of grass made me freeze instinctively. Just inches below my boot was the mottled, diamondlike pattern of a coiled Russell's viper, one of the most poisonous snakes in the region.

As I pulled my foot back slowly, the snake became rigid, head up, ready to go into action. I froze, holding my breath with my foot still in the air, not wanting even the backward movement to appear threatening. Finally the snake uncoiled and moved off into the underbrush.

I sat down on a rock by the stream, letting my heartbeat return to normal, and pictured the consequences of this snake's bite. Descriptions of vomiting blood, bleeding out of the eyes and nose, organ failure, and cerebral hemorrhaging came easily to mind. That was enough. The snake reminded me to tread much more carefully.

—Alan Rabinowitz, *Chasing the Dragon's Tail: The Struggle to Save Thailand's Wild Cats* of this in southern China, the original home of many of Asia's hill tribes.) According to Nuni, when the Hmong and other nomadic farmers first came to Thailand, their impact was small, but during the last few decades political instability in Vietnam, Myanmar (Burma), Laos, and Cambodia have sent them pouring in by the thousands.

Now, whatever rain falls on the denuded ridgetops races instantly away, carving deep grooves in the sandy, treeless soil below.

B uddhists cannot slaughter or witness the slaughter of animals; but they can eat animal flesh as long as they are not responsible for the termination of the animal's life… As Buddhists grow older they worry a great deal about complying with the ban on killing animals, but they can always get someone else to do the dirty work. In Thailand and Burma, to be truly virtuous, one should never crack an egg. Shopkeepers routinely evade this restraint by keeping a supply of eggs that have been "accidentally" cracked. Wealthy Buddhists ask their servants to break their eggs; the master escapes blame because he didn't do the killing, and the servant escapes blame because he was ordered to do it.

—Marvin Harris,
The Sacred Cow and the
Abominable Pig

Third, the Mae Soi villagers, whose previously wasteful wood-gathering practices depended on having an enormous forest all around them, ran out and chopped down everything that was left.

After meditating on what the villagers told him, Ajarn decided to stop his wandering and start a monastery in one of the small remnants of forest that had survived the devastation. "As a monk," he tells me now, his gold tooth glinting in the firelight, "it is my duty to strive for balance in society. As the villagers lacked this aspect of *Siladhamma*, it was for me to bring it back to them."

Nancy Nash knew nothing about Ajarn Pongsak, but during the same year that the Mae Soi watershed was being destroyed, she happened to find herself one afternoon on the grounds of a large Buddhist temple near Bangkok. She was staring at a tree.

Nash had come to Thailand for a break from her work with the World Wildlife Fund for Nature in Hong Kong. A self-taught journalist and environmentalist (more than twenty years ago, she'd left high school in Kansas City to see the world and never went back), she's often called "The Panda Lady." Somehow, after hundreds of phone calls and letters and dozens of trips to China, she had pulled off a bureaucratic miracle and persuaded the Chinese government to start its now famous "Save the Panda" program.

But now she was too excited to rest. The tree she was staring at was crowded with rare open-billed storks placidly whitewashing the lower limbs with their droppings. Without the protection of the monks' belief in the sacredness of all life, Nash realized, the storks would probably already have become extinct. Like most of the hundreds of *wats* in rural Thailand, this temple was an unofficial wildlife preserve.

She remembered something the Dalai Lama, Tibet's leader-in-exile, had once told her during an interview: the destruction of nature results from ignorance, greed, and a lack of respect for the Earth's living things; the Buddha, who was born under the branches of a *sal* tree and attained enlightenment while seated beneath a *bodhi* tree, took great care not to harm his natural surroundings.

Thai scholars said much the same. Ancient Buddhist texts and folklore are filled with sound advice about the interdependence of humans and nature, the dire consequences of cutting trees, the follies of poaching. Centuries before contamination of the Earth's water would be the widespread threat to human health that it is today, the Buddha set down rules forbidding the pollution of water resources.

Nash was all too aware that conventional approaches to conservation weren't working. But the rare storks gave her an idea. Since 89 percent of Thais are literate and 95 percent are Buddhists— many of them educated in rural *wats*—why not use the wisdom of their religion, the major cultural force in the country, to teach environmental ethics? "A Buddhist Perception of Nature" was born. With Nash as the galvanizing force, Thai and Tibetan scholars, educators, and conservationists began putting together books—

environmental catechisms, really—that monks could use to teach conservation at grassroots levels, where in fact many problems began. Perhaps the program's influence would trickle up through the power structure, which recognized Buddhism as the official state religion. Perhaps, eventually, the program might be used as a blueprint for other cultures, other religions.

In November, 1988, five days of rain fell on the mountainous jungles of the Malay Peninsula, the slender arm of Thailand that reaches south to Malaysia. Soon, flash-floods began to race through hillside communities in the provinces of Surat Thani and Nakhon Si Thammarat. Then the mountains themselves started to go. Entire hillsides pulled loose in great swatches the size of ski runs, and tidal waves of mud and thousands and thousands of flood-washed logs crashed down the slopes. In seconds, buildings that had stood for generations were turned to rubble, villages were entombed in mud a hundred feet deep, and more than 350 people were killed. Tens of thousands were left homeless. It was the worst natural disaster in Thailand's history.

It was also undeniable proof of what many environmentalists, forest monks, and villagers had been saying futilely for years. Illegal and unwise logging had been occurring on a massive scale, local corruption in the granting of concessions was endemic, and the legacy of logging-company and old U.S. military roads running deep into forest reserves let squatters and others get in to strip the forests. All of this helped make the floods more deadly. In addition, the huge hardwood forests of the northeast were all but gone. ("Just sand," was the way one environmentalist put it.) Overall, Thailand had lost more than *three-quarters* of its original forest in only 50 years—from 80 percent of the land surface in 1939 to just 19 percent in 1991.

These figures shocked even the *laissez-faire* Thai government, which within weeks of the floods declared an unheard-of nationwide ban on commercial logging. The decision launched a bitter debate which ran for months on the front pages of the major newspapers.

One story quoted a timber industry representative's claim that the ban would put logging elephants and their *mahouts,* or keepers, out of work. The result, he argued, would be a national crisis in "redundant elephants."

Nuni bends down and touches a spindly plant. "This one's called 'the little doctor' because it's used for so many cures. It once grew everywhere here. And this"—she drops a seed the size and color of a red-hot into SueEllen's cupped hand—"will grow into *that.*" We all look up at a tree that must have been one hundred feet tall. She pockets the seed—saving it for the nursery where she'll coax it along until it's ready to transplant.

She and Ajarn Pongsak and the Mae Soi villagers are trying to grow back an entire forest from seed.

Nuni points out the tiny hut where Ajarn lives and the buildings for visiting students. She knows the name of every plant—in Latin, English, and often Thai. As a child in England, she spent hours exploring the woods and fields near her home. "I'd bring home lots of mushrooms," she tells us, "and we'd eat them for supper. My parents always trusted me not to poison the family." Now, after a successful career as a batik artist in Bangkok, she's using her knowledge, the proceeds from her business, and her family inheritance to help finance this project. It's still not enough, and so she and Ajarn, who's an old family friend, have established the Dhammanat Foundation, which recently received a $44,000 grant from the Ford Foundation.

We stroll through a field where Ajarn led the villagers in planting 20,000 seedlings one afternoon. Though he has no background as an engineer, he's supervising construction of bridges and huge holding tanks of water for irrigation. "He seems to have remembered everything he's ever seen during his travels," says Nuni. "I don't know how he does it."

She shades her eyes from the sun. "Of course we'll never get our original forest back, but we're lucky about one thing: what soil is left is rich in lime. If we can keep the water coming, things will grow quickly." She shows us their teak grove—rows of thin trees some twelve feet high, all of them only two years old.

Ajarn and the villagers have also been trying to work with the hill tribes, talking to them about the problems caused by slash-and-burn farming and offering to sell them valley land very cheaply if they'll relocate. But hill-tribe issues are often politically delicate in Thailand, and so their success here has so far been limited. Besides, the plan would radically change the life-style of the Hmong. Meanwhile, to prevent further damage to their watershed, Ajarn and the villagers have fenced the ridgetops and set up 24-hour patrols.

For Ajarn, the heart of the matter is education, and so he sits under an enormous mango tree and talks with the villagers. "The forest is our first home. Your own house that you cherish so dearly is in fact your second home. Without your first home, you cannot have your second home. So how can we live off the forest so thanklessly?"

Thailand can always put its redundant elephants here, in Khao Yai National Park, northeast of Bangkok. That's what I thought as SueEllen and I stood in an elephant path and craned our necks to see what the ruckus was up in the treetops. There was a whooshing of wings, a furious scraping of branches, and then SueEllen spotted a great hornbill, bright yellow and black, hooked to a tree trunk a hundred feet above us. Then: *whoopwhoop-WhoopWHOOPWHOOP!* Through a profusion of air plants, giant ferns, and waist-thick, dangling vines, I caught a glimpse of a gibbon swinging through the branches of the same tree.

We watched until our necks hurt. Then we moved a few more miles along the trail, a ragged, elephant-sized tunnel through undergrowth. Several hundred wild elephants live here. Although we didn't see any of them, we found their signs everywhere— freshly broken branches, recent droppings. Once, from somewhere in the impossibly thick undergrowth, there came a slow and heavy crunching that couldn't have been anything else. (Or at least that's what I told myself. Some of Thailand's last tigers roam this park, too.) Occasionally a hand-sized butterfly fumbled along through the late-afternoon sunlight, and we passed trees with buttresses so large that SueEllen, standing between two of them, disappeared. I was ecstatic: at last we seemed to have found a park free of frantic development and destruction.

And so when we emerged from the trance of the jungle and walked into the clearing around the park headquarters, we were shocked to find ourselves surrounded by hundreds of Boy Scout leaders—singing, laughing, smoking like mad, drinking from bottles of Scotch that must have cost several days wages. As I watched, blinking, a few men strolled off down the asphalt road that ribbons through the park. One stopped for a moment to gaze into the green curtain of jungle, then walked on. The rest of them might as well have been in Bangkok.

That evening, after SueEllen and I checked our feet for land leeches and pulled ticks off each other's legs and arms, we met Randle Robertson, an education specialist at Canada's Yoho National Park who had volunteered to work the winter season at Khao Yai. "This is one of the world's greatest parks," he said. "But in two months here, I've seen only one Thai couple walking the trails. Everybody else was a foreigner."

Raucous laughter rose from a nearby cabin of scout leaders. "Weekends," said Randle, rolling his eyes. "But maybe you can't blame them. Snakes, ticks, leeches, man-eating tigers, the chance of getting lost—no wonder they don't like the jungle."

Then he told us about The Car. On a recent night a carful of weekend revelers came upon an elephant standing in the road, its trunk resting on the still-warm asphalt. Apparently the driver thought he'd have a little fun, so he honked the horn and flashed his headlights while his friends called out good-natured insults. For a moment, the elephant stood perfectly still in front of the car. Then it placed a foot on the hood, took one lumbering step, and crushed the engine. It kept on walking, shattering the windshield and caving in the roof. The terrified passengers scrambled out just in time.

It's too bad nobody captured that little morality tale on film. The park could use it. Like every place else in Thailand, Khao Yai, it turns out, is under siege. Poaching—of animals and trees both—is so frequent that armed guards keep watch every night. A villager on a dirt bike with a chainsaw slung over his shoulder can slip into the woods, cut a two-hundred-year-old tree in a few hours, drag out the pieces with elephants during the next week and build himself a new house.

Park officials, helped by Wildlife Fund Thailand fieldworkers, are trying to convince the local villagers that they're cutting down their own future.

From where Ajarn Pongsak often sits, you can look up through a jagged hole in the cave roof—through a network of roots, clumps of earth, pebbles, and a silky, backlit spiderweb—and you can see blue sky. It's like looking at the world from the inside out, like sitting in the middle of a seed.

Over the fire the last night, Ajarn warned, "Times are dark and *Siladhamma* is asleep. We must wake it up." In Bangkok the engines roar on. The fish die. The beaches fill up, and forests full of animals turn to dust. "Thailand is the whole world's ecological history in microcosm," says Nancy Nash. "We keep treating the Earth as if everything is still endless."

Several times during my travels I stood just 50 feet inside a once-vast jungle that had shrunk to a few protected acres. Even with my outsider's perspective, it was easy to imagine that the huge trees and chaotic undergrowth ran on forever.

Against all this, what can be accomplished by ecological catechisms or monks padding around in robes and sandals?

It's hard to be an idealist. But some Thai villagers have already changed their ways. The logging ban has caught the people's attention—and the government's. Activists from all over the country killed a gigantic hydro-electric project that would have flooded the largest wildlife reserves in Southeast Asia, home to more that 350 species of birds. Scientists have endorsed Nancy Nash's project.

And one night not long ago, Ajarn Pongsak, sitting in the forest, heard the far-off cry of a leopard.

John Calderazzo is an Associate Professor of English at Colorado State University, Fort Collins. He has traveled widely in China and Africa, and he is finishing a book of personal essays.

✳

In the West, a philosopher's theories and beliefs can be accepted as valid even though they remain entirely unrelated to his personal way of life. In Buddhist opinion, mere theoretical notions are considered useless, representing only sterile mental exercises. A man must act and live by what he has discovered to be true. Said the Buddha: "The man who talks much of his teaching but does not practice it himself is like a cowman counting another's cattle." And: "Like beautiful flowers full of color but without scent are the well-chosen words of the man who does not act accordingly."

—Nancy Wilson Ross, *Three Ways of Asian Wisdom*

✦ ✦ ✦

Island Entrepreneur

Exploitation can be a two-way street.

"WE DO NOT CALL OURSELVES THAI. WE ARE *CHAO SAMUI*." BUT Naret looks Thai to me. True, he somehow seems even more relaxed than his mainland counterparts. His round, shining face absorbs rather than reflects my attention. He is certainly well-fed, and he wears his extra weight proudly. Like rural Thais in only the most remote areas of Thailand, he wears a *phakhamaa*, the all-purpose cotton wrap-around, knotted at his thick waist. Dressed for comfort.

"Our food is different. Our language is different. Living here on Ko Samui is different from living in Surat Thani." Surat Thani is a port on the east coast of the southern Thai peninsula, between the Isthmus of Kra and Malaysia. It is the closest mainland point to Samui, which is three hours away by boat. Traditionally-minded *chao Samui* ("Samui folk") spend as little time as possible on the mainland, if they go there at all, marketing coconuts, the mainstay of Ko Samui's economy. Thirty-six-year-old Naret has only been to the mainland twice in his life, and he is no longer in the coconut business.

"Samui has everything I need. Why go to the mainland? Now the world comes to me."

The world comes to Naret to rent his beach bungalows—thatched palm-leaf and bamboo huts spread around a small Samui bay called *Ha Phra Phuttha Yai* or "Big Buddha Beach." A colossal Buddha image seated on a minuscule island in the bay gives the beach and Naret's bungalow village its name.

Asia backpackers making the perennial trek between Goa in India and Kuta Beach in Bali often stop over for several weeks on this 247-square-kilometer tropical island of just over 80,000 people. Although international-style resorts have arrived at the island's more well-known Chaweng Beach, Naret's one-room huts still offer a cheap sleep for travelers who must weigh every baht. His wife cooks their meals, mostly fresh seafood and curry.

Naret once had a family share in one of Samui's several coconut growing enterprises—Samui ships well over a million coconuts to Bangkok each month, as well as a modest amount of durian, rambutan, and langsat fruits in season. At the end of a particularly good year, Naret took his profits and, instead of putting them back into the coconut business, built a handful of huts on Big Buddha Beach.

"Now I make more money in six months than I did in a year of coconuts. I meet interesting people, too." He smiles broadly and glances over at the young Frenchman who is drinking tea and smoking a cigarette. The previous evening the French traveler had sighted a very large flying beetle which frightened him out of his rattan chair as he was eating some of Naret's famous grilled *kapong* fish. Naret promptly captured the insect, managed to kill it without disfiguring the body, and now kept it in a Chinese matchbox wedged in his *phakhamaa*. Today he was having great fun chasing the Frenchman around the village with the dead beetle. The harassed young man somehow enjoyed it, too.

In the water there are fish, in the fields there is rice. Whoever wants to trade in elephants, so trades....Whoever wants to trade in silver and gold, so trades. The faces of the citizens are happy.

—Words inscribed on a stone in the ruins of the former Thai capital of Sukhothai

"Every nationality is different. The French keep to themselves. They eat together and swim together, and they aren't interested in meeting the others. The Americans and the Australians are the opposite. They like our food and like to meet other nationalities. The Germans and the Swiss are lazy. They smoke too much *ganja*."

Earlier when I had arrived Naret had brought out a large tin box from his bungalow, which also served as the village kitchen and laundry. He had opened the box and proudly displayed his plentiful supply of "Thai sticks," potent marijuana tied to six-inch bamboo slivers. When I declined his offer, he said he didn't smoke it either and never had, but that it was all part of the "bungalow business."

"I ask these tourists where else they have been in this part of the world. India, Sri Lanka, Malaysia, Bali, but always on the beaches. *Chao Samui* never go to the beach except to catch fish."

Naret smiles as he talks. He seems to find it all very humorous. Was there anything that really bothered him about the foreigners who brought him a life of ease?

"Not really. But some of us *Samui* don't like it when they swim without their clothes. For them it means freedom, but it is offensive to us and to Thai people. My brother says it means they have no respect for us."

Naret's brother is in the bungalow business, too, on another beach on the large island. In fact, different members of Naret's extended family own nine different bungalow villages among the twenty or so on this end of the island. The tourists don't know this so they go from one to the other, thinking one village may be cheaper than the next.

"We change rates depending on how many travelers are on the island. Sure we bargain—but they aren't very good at it." He grins.

When I first walked into this village on Big Buddha Beach, Naret had appeared before me with a smile and "*Sawatdi khrap,*" the traditional Thai greeting. He then grasped my arm and we went for a stroll down the beach, as if we had been old and dear friends. He took me to his bungalow where his wife, or his "girl friend" as he called her, was cooking an orange-colored fish curry over a charcoal fire pot. He poured me a glass of rice whiskey and asked me where I was from. His hut was identical to the others, except it had a more lived-in look. On the raised wooden floor were straw mats. Brightly colored *phakhamaas* hung from lines strung across the room. There was a calendar printed in Chinese and Thai on one wall. A low table beneath the calendar held a ledger in which I assumed he kept business records. He lived simply yet he was probably a wealthy man on Ko Samui.

"I was born on Samui and I will die here. The people of Samui work together." Gesturing to the west toward the mainland, he says, "I don't see why others can't do the same."

Joe Cummings is the author of Lonely Planet's Thailand – a travel survival kit, *Moon's* Baja Handbook, *and co-author of Lonely Planet's* Vietnam, Laos and Cambodia – a travel survival kit. *He has spent much of the last fifteen years in Thailand and was an extra in the movie,* The Deer Hunter. *He is profiled in Part Three in "Farang Correspondent," by Michael McRae.*

★

Remember that if a shopkeeper accepts your price, you are obliged to buy the item. Try to make the seller mention prices, so that you are in a position to accept or reject offers.

—Elizabeth Devine and Nancy L. Braganti, *The Travelers'
Guide to Asian Customs and Manners*

ALAN RABINOWITZ

✦ ✦ ✦

Echo of the Forest

City sounds jog memories of
unexpected encounters.

IT WAS NOW MIDNIGHT, AND THE STREET NOISES OF BANGKOK outside my hotel room were just reaching a crescendo. As my mind drifted back to the Huai Kha Khaeng [Wildlife Sanctuary], I thought how different these sights and sounds were from those of the forest. There I had been lulled to sleep by the monotonous rhythm of geckos called *too-kay* in Thai because of the strange throaty sound they make to each other, and I had awakened to the howling of male gibbons. Fresh tiger and leopard tracks lined the riverbanks and trails, the various shapes and sizes telling a different story about each animal. I remembered the huge clumps of fresh elephant droppings and the afternoons when I'd been shaken from my reverie by the high-pitched, almost mournful trumpeting of an elephant herd nearby.

My most vivid memories didn't stem from anything I had seen or heard in the forest, but from what I had felt. This forest possessed what I can only describe as an "oldness." Inside this sanctuary the modern world had yet to fully intrude. The pure essence of this place was still somehow undisturbed.

Two scenes in particular played back in my mind. I remembered sitting on the steps of a thatched hut in the forest watching a golden-backed woodpecker search for its morning meal. Peering around a corner of the hut to follow the bird's flight, I found myself instead facing the calm countenance of a thin, medium-sized man. I'd had no idea he'd been standing there. His head was completely bald and he was wearing nothing but an orange cloth around his body. I had just met my first forest monk.

We stared at each other for several seconds, then he pointed to the bird, which had landed nearby, and said something in Thai. Seeing I couldn't understand him, he smiled and beckoned me to follow him down the path from which he'd come. I wanted to go with him but to my surprise I turned away instead, and walked quickly back toward camp.

Two days later, I was following leopard tracks along an old elephant trail when I smelled a strange, sweet odor. Glancing around until my eyes adjusted to the shadows, I suddenly noticed there were people standing quietly among the trees watching me. They were Hmong tribesmen whose villages were near the Burma border, at least a two-day hike from where we were standing. There were five of them—three boys and two old men—and a water buffalo, making their way to purchase or trade supplies in the nearest village outside the sanctuary. As I moved among them, the boys looked at me curiously, while the glassy-eyed old men looked toward the ground. The strong, sweet smell that had first caught my attention permeated their clothes. It was the smell of opium.

Alan Rabinowitz is a research zoologist who contributed five other stories to this book from Chasing the Dragon's Tail: The Struggle to Save Thailand's Wild Cats.

*

The Hmong, called Meo by the Thais, are a fiercely independent people who fled Chinese persecution over the last century for the relative peace of northern Thailand. Today the second-largest tribal group in Thailand, Hmong have become the country's leading opium producers by establishing their villages on mountaintops since higher elevations are considered best for opium cultivation. Thai Hmong are subdivided into White and Blue, color distinctions which refer to costume rather than linguistic or cultural differences.

Despite their isolation, Hmongs are not shy or rare; you will see them in Chiang Mai's night market selling exquisite needlework and chunky silver jewelry.

—Carl Parkes, *Thailand Handbook*

WILLIAM WARREN

✦ ✶ ✦

Who Was Anna Leonowens?

Western theatre and movie-goers have believed the story of
Anna and the King of Siam to be based on fact, but the
English governess was more than creative with reality.

THE APPEARANCE OF *THE KING AND I*—FIRST AS A BROADWAY
musical comedy in 1950, then as a movie seen by millions all over
the world—stirred considerable emotion in the kingdom where
the story allegedly took place. Angry editorials appeared in
Thailand's newspapers, the movie was banned, and prominent
novelist and political leader, M. R. Kukrit Pramoj, on hearing that
other figures from the Thai past might be subjected to similar
treatment, advised his readers that "the best we can do now is to
shut our eyes tightly and pray 'God save our ancient Kings.'"

The outrage is not difficult to understand. The ruler portrayed
was supposed to be King Mongkut, one of the most revered monarchs in modern Thai history, and even a cursory knowledge of
the real man was more than enough to shatter the image of a comic
character dancing a spirited polka through the hallowed halls of the
Grand Palace. Just as painful to Thai minds was the fact that countless innocent Westerners apparently believed they were viewing a
true story, not only regarding the King but also the importance
of Anna Leonowens, whom he hired to teach some of his wives
and children. Even so shrewd an observer as the noted Middle
Eastern traveler Dame Freya Stark praised Anna's alleged achieve-

ments, writing that "few people can have wielded a stronger influence in that corner of Asia."

Trained historians quickly began the task of setting the record straight, going back to Anna's original works, *The English Governess at the Court of Siam* (1870) and *Romance of the Harem* (1873). Both had formed the basis for Margaret Landon's 1943 best seller *Anna and the King of Siam,* which in turn became a seldom-seen, non-musical movie (with Irene Dunne as Anna and Rex Harrison as the King) and, eventually, *The King and I.*

It proved easy enough to demolish Anna as a trustworthy historian because both her books are filled with glaring errors. Even the title of the most famous is inaccurate for, as King Mongkut's correspondence makes clear, she was hired not as a governess, which implies a broad range of duties, but merely as a teacher of English. In the text, she makes elementary blunders regarding Thailand's past, offers an explanation of Buddhism that is either hopelessly confused (she never understood the use of Brahmanic rituals at the Thai court) or shamelessly lifted from other writers, and identifies a picture of Prince Chulalongkorn (her most prominent student) as being that of a princess. Though she claims to have spoken fluent Thai, most of the examples she offers are incomprehensible even with all possible allowances made for clumsy transliterations.

Her worst errors occur in *The Romance of the Harem,* when, one historian suggests, "her store of pertinent facts was running low." In this she claims that the King threw wives who displeased him into underground dungeons below the Grand Palace and, most horrific, that he ordered the public torture and burning of the consort and a monk with whom

> *Before King Chulalongkorn succeeded to the throne, he traveled extensively throughout Southeast Asia and Europe. As a result of his travels, when he became king, he began to modernize Bangkok. One project was to carve a wide avenue from the Grand Palace to the new Dusit Palace, patterned after the Champs Elysées in Paris. The avenue as we see it today is called* Rajdamnern, *or Royal Progress Avenue.*
>
> —Harold Stephens, "Searching for Joseph Conrad's Asia," *Sawasdee*

she had fallen in love, a spectacle Anna claims to have witnessed with her own eyes.

But there were no underground dungeons at the Grand Palace or anywhere else in Bangkok, and there could not have been in that watery soil. Nor was there any public burning, or, if there was, it escaped the attention of every other foreign resident, many of whom also wrote accounts of the same period. Anna simply invented such tales, perhaps to add some spice to what would otherwise have been a rather tepid work, just as she also exaggerated her own influence. As one of Mongkut's biographers, Alexander Griswold, observes, "Virtue was not unknown in Siam before her arrival, and a cool assessment suggests that she did not loom very large in the life of King Mongkut or his children."

Anna, then, stood exposed as hopelessly unreliable, and *The King and I* as a pleasant fantasy with little historical content beyond the simple fact that King Mongkut did hire an Englishwoman and she did hold classes in the palace. The case seemed closed; there was nothing else to reveal. But there was, and it proved as surprising as Anna's fictions had been deplorable.

Who exactly *was* Anna Leonowens? Even her most determined detractors never really applied much effort to that question, all apparently accepting what she claimed about her pre-Thai life. This, as we shall see, was a mistake; for in the answer lay the key not only to much of what she wrote, but *why*.

Anna was born, she said, in Wales, on November 5, 1834, which would have made her 28 when she arrived in Bangkok in 1862. Though not wealthy, her family was distinguished, her father being an army captain named Thomas Maxwell Crawford. When Anna was six, she and a sister were left behind while her parents were posted to India where, shortly afterwards, Captain Crawford died in battle during a Sikh uprising.

After completing school at the age of fourteen or fifteen, Anna and her sister sailed for India and an unpleasant surprise in the form of a new stepfather to whom Anna took an intense dislike. One reason for this was that he wanted to marry her off to a wealthy merchant twice her age, while she in turn had fallen in love with a dashing young army officer named Thomas Leonowens. To escape the situation, she went on a long tour of the Middle East with a well-known scholar, the Reverend Percy Badger, and his wife, presumably friends of the family.

It was on this trip, writes Dame Freya Stark (following Anna's account) that "her vision of Asia was widened in a manner impossible in an India verging on the Mutiny; and she returned to her family after nearly a year's absence with a character already strongly formed, both for tolerance and independence."

She was independent enough to defy her stepfather and elope at the age of seventeen with her young officer. They were blissfully happy, despite the death of their first two children in infancy; two more, however, a girl and a boy, were born and survived, both in London where the couple resided in the fashionable St. James district for three years. In 1857, Leonowens, by then promoted to major, rejoined his regiment in Singapore, and it was there that Anna received the news that a small fortune left to her by her father had been lost with the collapse of a bank during the Indian Mutiny. A year later, Major Leonowens suffered sunstroke on a tiger hunt and died, leaving her with two small children and no money.

Friends rallied round to help and she began a small school for officers' children, bringing in enough money to send her daughter Avis back to England but not much more. A new challenge came with the offer to go to Siam and, with characteristic pluck, off she went, accompanied by her young son Louis.

A refined gentlewoman, marked by personal loss but brave and determined to bring light to other less fortunate lives: that is the image of Anna drawn by herself, by all the actresses who have portrayed her on stage and screen and even by historians who also accused her of willfully maligning a great man.

The first person to question the image, almost accidentally, was Dr. W. S. Bristowe, an English scholar whose specialty was spiders but who also wrote on other subjects. A lover of Thailand, he had been visiting the country since 1930, and in the early 1970s decided to write a biography of Louis Leonowens, who founded a company in Bangkok that still bears his name. Not many people read the work that eventually appeared, entitled—perhaps inevitably—*Louis and the King of Siam*, which is a pity, because Dr. Bristowe's deft detective work on Anna's past revealed an extraordinary tale.

It began when he made a routine check of London records to ascertain the exact date of Louis' birth. He found nothing, either for Louis or for Anna's daughter. Nor, when he looked further, could he find a record of anyone named Thomas Leonowens who had served in the army in either India or England. Nor did the army know anything about the man Anna claimed to be her distinguished father. Strangest of all, archives in Wales failed to provide any mention of Anna herself.

By now, Dr. Bristowe's curiosity was thoroughly aroused, and he set about tracking down the elusive Anna with all the enthusiasm he normally gave a rare species of spider. Here is what diligent research in the India Office records eventually uncovered:

Anna was born not in Wales but in India and not in 1834 but in 1831. Her father was Thomas Edwards, a cabinetmaker from Middlessex who enlisted in the Bombay infantry and went to the subcontinent in 1825. There he married Mary Anne Glasscock, the daughter of a gunner in the Bengal Artillery and a local mother who, in all likelihood, was Eurasian.

Thomas and Mary Anne Edwards had two daughters, Eliza and Anna, and he died three months before the birth of the latter, leaving his widow penniless after his debts were paid. When Anna was two months old, her mother remarried, this time to a corporal in the Engineers who, not long afterwards, was demoted to private for some unknown misdemeanor.

Here the record blurs for a time, but somehow—probably through the assistance of a charity—Anna and Eliza were sent to her father's relations in England, where they presumably received an education. They returned to India in their early teens and entered a home which Dr. Bristowe says "must have appalled them," for the life of a private soldier at the time was a squalid one of "drunkenness and fornication."

Eliza was married off at 15 to a 38-year-old sergeant and something similar was clearly planned for Anna—this is one of the few points where her own version and the truth coincide. Instead, at 14 she went off to the Middle East with the Reverend Badger, who was serving as an assistant chaplain. How she met the clergyman (later to gain distinction as an Oriental scholar) is uncertain. He was not married, however, obviously liked young girls (Dr. Bristowe discovered he eventually married one of 12), and their tour may not have been character-building in quite the way Dame Freya Stark believed.

Anna's marriage came when she was 18, not to a dashing young officer but to a lowly 22-year-old clerk whose name was not Leonowens but Thomas Leon Owens. He did not seem to hold any job for long and the couple was constantly on the move; Dr. Bristowe never did pinpoint the precise birthdates of Louis and Avis and finally concluded that they must have taken place on board a ship or perhaps in Australia, where the couple lived for a time. At some other unknown point, Leon Owens changed his name to Leonowens, and the doctor did find a record of his death in Malaya: of apoplexy, in Penang, on May 8, 1859, where he was listed as a "hotel master."

Anna was already busily burying this past when she arrived in Singapore and was eventually so successful that not even her own children ever penetrated her disguise. Among other things, this required a complete break with her sister Eliza back in India, a step she may have been doubly glad she took—given the social prejudices of the time—if word ever reached her that Eliza's eldest daughter married a Eurasian. As thorough as ever, Dr. Bristowe traced that family, too, and made the engaging discovery that the youngest child of the union—that is, Anna's grand-nephew— ultimately became the actor Boris Karloff, of *Frankenstein* fame.

Adept as it was, Anna's performance may not have been flawless, at least during her time in Bangkok. This would explain her notable failure to become a part of the small British colony of merchants and consular officials. "The consul and his two assistants," writes Dr. Bristowe, "came from good families and she must have been quite unable to sustain her pretenses of breeding either in her manner of speech or in her manners for them to have taken no notice of her."

The only respectable foreigners willing to take her at her word were American Protestant missionaries, particularly Dr. Dan Beach Bradley, their senior member. They gave her the friendship and support she needed so badly and in return she adopted their prejudices, especially concerning royal polygamy, about which Dr. Bradley had strong feelings. The inventions and distortions of her books may have been partly designed to boost sales, but they were also aimed at convincing her missionary friends that Anna Leonowens was truly a virtuous Christian, worthy of their trusting kindness.

Dr. Bradley also appears in "The Reverend Goes to Dinner" earlier in this section.
—JO'R and LH

After leaving Thailand, Anna spent some years in America, where her books were written, and eventually settled in Canada with her daughter. There she died in 1916 at the ripe age of 85 (not 82 as her family and friends thought), still playing, by now with accomplished skill, a role that might have challenged the best of her later impersonators.

William Warren, a native of Georgia, has lived in Bangkok since 1960. He is the author of Thailand, Seven Days in the Kingdom, *and* The House on the Klong, *and he has been called "the dean of English-language authors in Thailand."*

*

Thais consider the head the most important and honored part of the body; and, conversely, the foot is the most degraded. Touching anyone on the head is a great insult. Even a friendly pat on the head, or tousling someone's hair, is only done between brothers, sisters, or the closest friends—and, even then, only if there isn't too big a difference in age.

The late Phya Anuman Rajadhon, in his monograph "Thai Traditional Salutation," throws some interesting light on this question of the head.

He says the Thai deems his head sacred, probably because it is the seat of an individual's *kwan* or vital spirit which confers strength and health. The *kwan* is very sensitive, and if subjected to indecorous behavior it will feel injured and leave its abode in the body to stray somewhere in a forest. While the *kwan* is absent, its owner will suffer a weakening of his "dignified splendor" followed by bad luck and ill-health.

With such an idea handed down from generation to generation over a very long period of time, the sacredness of the head is deeply embedded in everyone's mind. If the hand that touches another's head is that of a woman, the man will instantly lose his "dignified splendor," for a woman's hand is acutely adverse to the *kwan*.

This explains why Thai people, especially men, refuse to walk beneath a clothesline on which female clothing is hanging, especially lower garments such as sarongs or skirts, for fear their head will be touched by them. So when women's clothes are hung out to dry a very low clothesline is used, and everyone walks round it instead of under it.

And while we're on the subject of walking round something or somebody, if anyone—even a young child—is lying on the floor resting or asleep, no Thai will ever step over such a prostrate person, no matter how much of a hurry he's in. Again, it simply "isn't done." One must always walk round—never step across.

—Denis Segaller, *Thai Ways*

CAROL HOLLINGER

✱ ✱ ✱

Where the Footnotes Went

In which a young Foreign Service wife discovers the
secret of a culture—and her elusive master's
thesis—in a single phrase: mai pen rai.

IF YOU ASKED A CHILD TO CONFRONT HIS WRINKLED, ELDERLY future self without the intervening decades of gradual aging, that child would feel as I felt. Departure was close upon us. It was time to return home and face up to the suburban matron I had abandoned so long before in the irrational chronology clocked by the human experience.

When I had set out for Thailand I think I was unbalanced mentally. I had had giddy intentions of living in an underdeveloped country and sharing with the natives, whom I regarded with great affection from afar, our civilization. I even studied in graduate school the technique of accomplishing this. I attended meetings of American Buddhist groups and listened to pale, otherworldly ladies discuss "non-being" and "Om." Foreign Service officers lectured to me on methods of adjusting to strange cultures and I listened as though their word was gospel.

Although published in 1965, the era of The Ugly American, *the author's impressions of Thailand are for the most part still valid.*

—JO'R and LH

Thus I was somewhat prepared not to be an "ugly American," but I was not at all prepared for the fierce reality of the East. Once there, all my absurd pretensions collapsed and I found myself deflated, purposeless, and frightened. It amazed me to find the Thai so capable, so charming, and, worst of all, so skillfully in charge of their own country. After two years of studying Southeast Asia it was a shock to discover that almost everything I had so earnestly studied was nonsense. Neither books nor professors had informed me that the Thai had a secret weapon called *mai pen rai*. I had not been warned that Americans crumpled by the score when they encountered the intangible atmosphere of "never, never mind."

Near the turn of the century a Bangkok editor remarked that Siam was obviously being added to the "globe trotter's route" for visitors were "dropping in at the rate of sometimes as many as two or three a day!"

—Bonnie Davis, "Early Siam Through Foreign Eyes," *Sawasdee*

Who can chart with accuracy the whirlwind effect on a dubious scholar of *mai pen rai*? The slender erudition I did possess was almost immediately ambushed. For example, I read an authentic history of the T'ai people written by a respected Siamese scholar. I had often seen it used in bibliographies and footnotes by academic and specialized Western historians. The Thai edition was charmingly packed with proof from Thai mythology and acknowledged aid from the Lord Buddha. The Thai historian, Phra Sarasas, had more integrity than some of those who impressively weighted their footnotes with quotations from his book. In his introduction he says simply:

> Conscious of the mentality of the Thai historians I have to handle with gloves the Thai history in the Thai language. After adding the necessary salt of incredulity, I accept the records by the Thai with the most scrupulous precaution. The word history in the Thai language is *Bongsavatar,* which means the biography of the kings, that is to say, Thai's own history is intended for the glorification of the Thai monarchs.

...Since a true Thai historian's possession is almost entirely locked up in his head, are we to believe what we are told by Thai annals? Ordinary prudence would suggest a careful handling. The very obviousness of the aim and purpose of Thai's own history somewhat discounts our idea of taking it as the whole truth.

The complacence with which so-called serious scholars take all the hocus-pocus that comes out of Southeast Asia appalls me. A few of the universities, among them Cornell, do a good job in publishing objective writing, but most of the writing on Southeast Asia should be labeled fiction so as not to mislead the public. From whence come the imposing battalions of statistics and historical documentation? No statistic in Southeast Asia is trustworthy (indeed, are statistics anywhere? *Mai pen rai*). In addition, Thai written history dates back to the destruction of Ayudhaya by the armies of Burma only a few centuries ago. Before this the only history is the sparse account of visiting Chinese writers.

Instead of the orderly master's thesis I had once dreamed of writing (I used to dream of pages half filled with gloomy, impressive footnotes) I now switched to composing imaginary footnotes for an imaginary thesis. They went something like this.

1. ไม่เป็นไร (*mai pen rai*), from conversations with the natives.

2. Lord Buddha.

3. *Conversations of Narasuan the Great with his Sacred Cobra.* Scroll Four, Royal Bangkok Museum (underneath King Mongkhut's favorite teapot).

4. *Ibid.*

Current reports are equally suspicious. After meeting the correspondents and the men responsible for the stories in our most respected newspapers I regard everything in print as suspect. It isn't because I think I know more; I am simply aware of how little anybody knows. Behind the staid, factual reports on Southeast Asia in *The New York Times* and the London *Times* I now see only the

faces of the stringer correspondents who were my friends and I
know where the news came from. They do a good job...the best
possible...and I am not criticizing, I am merely pointing out a
complexity largely unrealized by the American public. You have to
be God to distinguish truth from fiction in Thailand. And on second thought I think God might have difficulty unless he were Thai.

American matrons, who played bridge all day long with other
American matrons, discussed the Thai with the utmost authority.
After all, they were there weren't they? I found myself, up to my
ears in Siamese around the clock, growing ever more confused.
In no way but the most superficial did I ever understand the Thai.
No Westerner comprehends an Oriental country because he has
lived there a few years. Even those who spend a decade or so in the
East and who go ostentatiously native are deluding themselves if
they claim to understand the country. The delusion is complete if
they think they are accepted by the Asians. Orientals are the worst
snobs on earth. You are called a *farang* by the Thai the first day
you set foot on Thai soil and the term will still apply, if your face
is white, although you remain there a score of years. In the most
familiar situations the unfathomable will suddenly arise, a specter
to confront the smug who believe themselves assimilated. Even
those who learn to speak fluent Thai find that their real friends
are either Western educated or from the upper class. There are a
few exceptions, but very few. There is a line beyond which the
millions who are Asia sleep and eat and breed in un-American
poverty and of whom the Westerner knows nothing.

Propaganda was another shock. When I left America I understood the formation of public opinion in Southeast Asia. I had had
the best course possible, taught by a famous Asian expert. Two
minutes at Chulalongkorn University taught me that I might just
as profitably have studied the zither. Readers know enough to
suspect the writer who dashes off an authoritative article on a
country in which he has spent three weeks or less, but the scientific studies arouse less suspicion. Americans have a thing about
statistics and are thoroughly intimidated by them. More of us
should have a little Harry Truman in our makeup. The polltakers

have hoodwinked the American public into thinking that their intuition is an exact science.

Let us follow the polltaker as he stalks the jungle and talks to hill tribes. Accompanying him is a bright interpreter, who is probably a graduate of Chulalongkorn and is provided by the Thai government. You would trust this boy with your sister's honor or your last dollar, so honest of face is he. However, he is Siamese; he has a tremendous pride in his country and he has the most beautiful manners on earth. He is embarrassed for his country when villagers look blank at the mention of such key words as Communism or Democracy. These villagers are usually dimly aware that they have a king and this is about all they understand on a national level, although their community government is thoroughly understood. The interpreter dislikes disappointing the nice expert from America so he fills the massive vacuum with glowing phrases of his own invention.

A public opinion expert I know visited Thailand on his way to Laos to conduct a survey for the United States government. He spoke only English and used an interpreter. It was the first time he had been in Southeast Asia. It was the first time he had been out of the United States. I had known him in Washington and had admired him for his massive intellect and his Ph.D. in statistics.

We both attended the same dinner party upon his return from Laos. He had been in Laos for one week. It was a large garden party and individual tables for four had been scattered over the lawn. At our table were two Englishmen who had lived for years in Thailand and who had been interned in prison camps during the war. One of them politely asked my friend what he was doing in the area.

"I have been ascertaining political awareness among the Lao," announced the learned statistician.

There was a moment of consternation. I could see by the expressions that washed over the faces of the Englishmen that, for a fleeting moment, they thought the newcomer a superb humorist. The pompousness of the public opinion expert evidently cautioned them to the contrary. An extremely fragile conversation prevailed during the rest of dinner. The story was all over Bangkok the next day.

If no one knows anything, why write a book? It is a good question. The answer is that this is not a book, it is a master's thesis that boomeranged. It is not what I intended to write. The whole impossible thing is a sepulcher for my scholarly remains. "Very dry," as Khun Chit said of his deceased mother-in-law, "nothing but bare bones."

The bare bones of this renegade master's thesis became the script of an overdeveloped American crashing head-on with an underdeveloped people. They, of course, won. I learned how incredibly provincial an American can be by starring as a horrible example. I learned, although I thought I knew it, that civilization means more than the number of television sets per capita. I learned this the hard way and I have tried in my disorderly manner to share the experience.

Because a nation is underdeveloped does not mean that it is populated by underdeveloped citizens. An underdeveloped nation is one in which the gross income per capita is too low. The term tells us nothing about the individual living in the country except that he is probably too poor. He is as developed as we are. The Thai civilization is different, not lower. I once asked a Chula science student if he would like to be the first man on the moon. He took the question seriously and after deliberation replied, "Let the Americans do it." Was one of us brighter than the other? The answer to that question leaves me uneasy.

There is no such person as a simple man. The pathos and absurdity of human life is as complex in a tribal village as it is on Fifth Avenue. The man who lives in a thatched house on stilts has wisdom and ignorance, love and death, mirth and tears, anger and peace, youth and age in his life as we do. There is no East, no West…there are people and no one of these people is a statistic to himself.

Many otherwise educated Westerners are victims of a strange belief that the white man and not Homo sapiens is the present pinnacle of evolution. To them aborigines, pygmies, hill tribes, and dark foreigners are illustrations of an evolutionary step like Neanderthal man. At Chulalongkorn I saw boys who came from tribes which, a few decades before, were scarcely cognizant of the wheel settle down with brilliance to the study of twentieth century science. Without statistical proof I now take the stubborn position that genius, talent, and brains are a magic that may evolve any-where...perhaps in your home, perhaps in your neighbor's, or, perhaps, in a lonely, backward village where a solitary youth broods in a primitive culture and dreams of events beyond his own hori-zon. Education not evolution finds such a boy.

One evening I attended a dinner party. There were no Thai present and the British and Americans there relaxed, as people do in a foreign country when they are surrounded by their own kind. Everybody bristled with Anglo Saxon virtue and complained. They raved about the absolute lack of honesty, goodwill, duty toward country, and the all around amorality of the Thai. When I protested, my friends countered with accusations of sentimentality and gullibility. I subsided, victim to majority squashing, but I wished that I could introduce them to a student with whom I had had an hour's conversation that morning. In talking to him I had again been comforted by a realization that, although the evil in man lends itself to bigger headlines, the good in him, though scarcer, is tougher. Formerly I had believed in an environmental explanation of character, but this conviction faded in Thailand. A sober fate kept pushing Siamese into my path whose uncompromising virtue could never be explained by their ethical environment.

My friends were wrong when they said I did not understand the extent of the corruption and deviousness of the Thai officials. It oppressed me everywhere, even at the university. I learned to look with jaded eyes at most of the Thai politicians and many of the high-ranking civil servants...but they were not all of Thailand. The corruption was, after all, a way of life. In Siam a bribe is considered part of an official salary, for even an important official receives only a small legal wage. It is assumed that he will live by manipulation of his public power. I remember a headline in a Thai paper that illustrated this concept perfectly. The Thai government, bedeviled by American exhortations to abolish corruption, made a proclamation that henceforth all bribes over 200,000 baht ($40,000) were declared illegal. The official morality was a matter of degree.

The Thai were as honest in their way and in terms of their own culture as we are. One of the most honorable men I ever knew was a Thai. He was our closest Thai friend in Bangkok, but it took me a long while to appreciate his character. His name was Khun Amorn. Like many men rich in spiritual values he did not take himself or the rest of mankind very seriously and his witty nature, flashing white teeth, mischievous eyes, and an uncanny resemblance to Yul Brynner in *The King and I* deceived me for a long time. There was a solidity about Amorn that impressed me and I became aware that he watched and observed and knew more than he spoke.

He was poor. Khun Chern, the wealthy hostess of the Friday Night Group, was his cousin. She allowed him to live rent free in a tiny Thai house set toward the back of her enormous compound. In return his wife managed her household and servants, for Khun Chern despised this job.

We could see his house from the veranda and when I listened to the versatile, witty, and sophisticated conversation of the well-traveled Amorn I found it difficult to reconcile him with the small lower-middle-class teak house on stilts. The Friday Night Group were gossipy about themselves and the whole of Thailand. No one was spared their caustic barbs save Khun Amorn. At parties and dinners and celebrations someone from the group was always at my side gleefully pointing out mistresses, second wives, and people afflicted with venereal diseases, but if one questioned about Khun Amorn their faces would soften and they all answered with exactly the same sentence, "Khun Amorn is a good man."

He had a high position in the Thai Civil Service and one night, when we were discussing corruption in high places, I stopped in the middle of a sentence.

"Khun Amorn," I asked, the words slipping out before I realized what I was saying, "why are you so poor when your position is so high?"

It was not a polite question but Amorn did not take offense. He answered simply, "It is because I must maintain a cool heart."

In America we favor a warmhearted person, but a cool heart is the ideal of a Buddhist. It does not mean lack of compassion. It stresses the need to keep your heart free of entangling and destructive emotions of both joy and sorrow that assault you from the material world and make you act from greed instead of pure intent. If you seek more than your share of worldly goods you are not maintaining a cool heart.

"I cannot take bribes," continued Amorn, "because I have the knowledge that this is wrong and I am sickened. If you do not recognize the evil it is easier to do. One night I returned from work to find that a rich man had left an expensive gift with my wife because I had made a judgment in his favor. I had done this because it was the law and he was right. I took the gift and bicycled fifteen miles to his house to return it to him. He was very angry and shouted at me that I was a crazy man."

I stared out at the tiny thatched house on stilts in which he lived. There was nothing for me to say, but at that moment the dignity of man walked out of books and became as real to me as the bread I eat.

Carol Hollinger went to Thailand in the 1950s as a diplomatic wife and university teacher and wrote an engaging book about her experiences, Mai Pen Rai Means Never Mind, *from which this story was excerpted.*

＊

"We were led to expect that we should find rapacity intrusive, insatiable, and extortionate—every art employed to obtain much, and to give little in return. Far different was my experience. It seemed as if nothing was expected from me, while upon me and around me every kindness was profusely and prodigally showered…. In great things as in small, I found a hospitality that was almost oppressive, and of which I retain the most grateful memory."

—Sir John Bowring, writing about his 1855 visit to Siam in
The Kingdom and People of Siam, quoted in *Thailand,*
Seven Days in the Kingdom, by William Warren

PART TWO

SOME THINGS TO DO

THURSTON CLARKE

✦ ✦ ✦

Lure of the Chao Phraya

*Unable to reach a friend a few miles away because
of Bangkok's choking traffic, the author discovers
a better route to the city's treasures.*

TRY TO IMAGINE VENICE, IF YOU CAN BEAR TO, WITH ALL ITS
canals (except the Grand Canal) converted to roads for cars. Add
to this an economic boom, vast traffic jams, and pollution. Imagine
all this, and you are imagining Bangkok, home to 90 percent of all
motor vehicles in Thailand. Question: If you were visiting such a
Venice, would you not prefer a hotel facing the Grand Canal?

Well, Bangkok's "Grand Canal," its last great "unfilled" waterway, is the Chao Phraya, a glorious working river, filled with
sampans, barges, and ferries, beautiful in its wide curves, lined by
many of Thailand's best hotels, liveliest markets, and historic
temples, and again becoming what it was a century ago, the city's
widest and most convenient highway.

It was only after staying in Bangkok for several days that I discovered the Chao Phraya and its riverine pleasures. This tardiness
was my own fault. My pre-departure Bangkok inquiries yielded
mostly descriptions of traffic and pollution. My friend Martin, a
fifteen-year resident, wrote back warning that, if I stayed in my
proposed hotel, less than five miles from his home, he was afraid
they wouldn't be seeing very much of me. The journey, he explained, could easily take an hour and a half. My wife reported

being told Bangkok's air was so polluted that walking is "like a stroll through an underground car park."

Meanwhile, I read news clips lamenting, "Heavenly Bangkok is a traffic hell." "So severe are Bangkok's dawn-till-late-night traffic jams," claimed the Sydney *Morning Herald*, "…[that] a lunchtime meeting across town can take most of the day, and an evening concert often may be reached only by abandoning the car and setting off for a long, hot, and choking walk."

The more I heard how impossible Bangkok was, the more determined I became to enjoy it. I would simply travel early or walk. I would be the kind of sensitive visitor who, according to one guidebook, is wise enough to look beneath Bangkok's surface and "begin turning up shovelfuls of pure gold."

My first afternoon in Bangkok I set out at 3 p.m. in a taxi to surprise that friend who had warned I would not be seeing much of him. The first hundred yards took fifteen minutes. A half hour later, I had traveled a mile. There was no accident or breakdown; just too many vehicles trying to cross two busy intersections. The air conditioner seized up, and we rolled down the window. The pollution set my eyes itching. Other

Established in 1782 by King Rama I, Bangkok was originally a walled city. It began as an artificial island, formed by a canal that was dug at a point where the Chao Phraya river curved. The earliest palace buildings and Buddhist temples, many of which can still be seen today in the Grand Palace area, were conscious evocations of structures in the former capital of Ayutthaya. As in the old city, an intricate network of canals, lined with floating teak houses and shops, formed the main avenues.

This riverine, essentially medieval Bangkok, lasted barely a century. The city prospered from trade, and soon the Chao Phraya was crowded with ships from all over the world. Thousand of Thais came from the provinces to seek their fortunes in the capital, while other Asians, mostly Chinese, immigrated in growing numbers. The first proper street, Charoen Krung (New Road) was built in the mid-19th century. Others followed quickly, spreading out and replacing rice fields to the east and extending in time all the way to the Gulf of Thailand.

—Gault Millau:
The Best of Thailand

drivers read, dozed, or stared glassy-eyed. My driver muttered to himself, manicured his fingernails, and handed me tissues for wiping my face. At five-minute intervals he slapped his forehead and then turned to flash a beatific, apologetic smile.

After an hour I abandoned the taxi and walked. The sidewalks were narrow and lined with monotonous concrete "shophouses"— with a store on the ground floor and apartments above. A yellow fog hung over the road. The air was thick with diesel fumes and tasted like the inside of New York's Lincoln Tunnel. It was 95 degrees and humid, and in ten minutes I had sweated through my clothes. Some pedestrians and motorbike passengers wore gauze masks. A terrified family of tourists gripped one another like a string of paper dolls as they inched across a murderous intersection. Later, a Thai asked me, "Do you know what we call someone who crosses a Bangkok street safely? We call him 'the winner'!"

I hailed a second taxi but soon abandoned it in front of a hotel on Sukhumvit Road. It was now 4:30, the rush hour, and I was still two miles short of my destination. Through the tinted windows of the second-floor bar I saw stalled traffic to the horizon, a "traffic hell." I spread out a map of Bangkok and circled the places I wanted to see. Almost everything was near the Chao Phraya river. A dotted line down its center showed the route of an express ferryboat. The next morning I checked out of my hotel and moved to the river.

The Chao Phraya turned out to be everything the rest of Bangkok was not. The climate was cooler, and there was often a breeze. A trip that took an hour inland could be accomplished by ferry in ten minutes. Instead of the low growl of traffic, I heard the chugging ferries and tugboats. Instead of red brake lights, I saw fast-moving running lights and the colored bulbs of riverside restaurants. Instead of eating indoors in air-conditioned caverns, I ate on outdoor terraces.

Inland, the view was of concrete skyscrapers, hermetically sealed atriums, and bowling-alley avenues decorated with signs advertising all the familiar cars, fast foods, and electronics. Along the river, you saw domed Portuguese churches sandwiched between pagodas and the colonial-era "palaces" of the European trading companies alternating with the river villas of Thai royalty.

It is no mystery why riverine Bangkok is more interesting and pleasant than the rest of the city. The city was not settled until the late 18th century, after Burmese invaders destroyed the royal capital, at Ayutthaya. Bangkok's first temples and government buildings, trading houses, and consulates were all built on the river. Wheeled transportation consisted of ceremonial carriages; for a century roads were thought unnecessary. Canals were Bangkok's principal arteries until well after World War II. Once you realize the city was built for *sampans* rather than trucks, its chaos becomes understandable.

The contrast between the river and the interior became most apparent during a combination bus-and-boat excursion to the ruins of Ayutthaya. First we drove north along Thailand's ugly version of the New Jersey Turnpike. Billboards and plumes of black smoke marred the views, such as they were. The roadside towns were slapdash affairs, concrete egg boxes facing ditches black with waste water. There were prosperity and energy here but no beauty, and enough garbage to justify Claude Levi-Strauss's observation, "The first thing we see as we travel round the world is our own filth, thrown into the face of mankind."

Hopefully you won't have an [auto] accident, but if you do, it's very important to choose with whom you have an accident. It's much better to have an accident with a cheaper second-hand car than it is to crash into a Mercedes driven by a police general. Avoid accidents with army personnel above the rank of colonel. Most Thai drivers do not carry insurance: minor traffic accidents are settled on the spot between drivers; other accidents are settled at the nearest police station. Taxi and tuk-tuk drivers are prone to taking off from the scene of an accident, and hit-and-run accidents are on the rise. I once saw a truck-driver come out of a sidestreet onto Sukhumvit and smash into a motorcyclist, flipping him through the air. The truck screeched to a halt, then turned around to take off. Dragging a limp leg, the motorcyclist leapt onto the back of the truck as it disappeared down a soi.

—Michael Buckley,
Bangkok Handbook

But in Ayutthaya everything changed. The ancient ruins covered acres of moldering palaces and shattered temples, lines of decapitated pillars, and bell pagodas stripped of ornamentation and losing their brickwork but still showing graceful lines. The grounds of the Victory temple were a functioning monastery where monks lived in airy wood houses raised on stilts. The porches were decorated with flowering plants chosen for their lucky qualities. Signs tacked on trees carried Buddhist teachings, such as "The wise tame themselves" and "Contentment is the greatest wealth."

In this, as in other Thai temples, it was easy to find contentment. The compound was shady and silent except for tinkling prayer bells and songbirds the monks kept in cages. But just outside, our bus idled away in a parking lot made hot and noisy by tour drivers running their air conditioners so that they could stay cool while their passengers were off marveling at this oasis of beauty and calm.

The trip back by boat was the opposite of the drive. Instead of concrete and cars, we saw water and wood. On the bus, passengers quickly tired of the scenery, and some dozed or read. On the river, no one slept or became bored. At first, the river widened; then it narrowed, in places becoming a jungle-hugged waterway, bordered by coconut plantations, fishing shanties, and fine villas perched on teak platforms over the water. Some had elegant peaked roofs; all had ladders leading to the river and a *sampan*. Flowers decorated their balconies, reminding me of alpine chalets with geranium-filled window boxes.

As we neared Bangkok there was more industry. First a ramshackle café with three tables and a weathered Pepsi sign; then a huge Pepsi-Cola terminal plastered with the familiar logo, its crates stacked several stories high. Lines of black-hulled barges, loaded to their waterlines with sand or fuel, glided past buzzing sawmills and humpbacked rice barges. As we entered the city, golden spires and temple roofs glittered in a late-afternoon sun. The rush hour was on. Above us, every bridge was filled with double lanes of stalled traffic. On the water, express ferries and longboats sped between landings.

Once I began relying on river transportation, it was easier to appreciate things that make Bangkok so alluring to foreign residents: its temples, markets, and food; its surviving canals; its splendid people. Unlike Hong Kong and Singapore, which have obliterated most of their traditional neighborhoods, this city of six million retains much of its Asian atmosphere, preserving its unique mixture of the traditional and the modern, the chaotic and the peaceful, the beautiful and the garish.

The temples of Bangkok reflect this dichotomy. Serious places for worship and contemplation, they are also friendly and accessible to foreign visitors. As one sign in a Chinatown temple put it, "Tourists are welcome to visit and take photographs. Taking off of shoes not necessary!"

A few important doors in Bangkok now have notices in English to request you to "Please step over the threshold." This is not simply an invitation to enter. Apart from a desire to save wear and tear on historic buildings, there is a deeper, spiritual reason for such signs.

Bangkok's scandal-loving newspapers and famous sex-trade areas might lead one to conclude that irreverence is a major Thai trait. Yet the Thais do not take their religion or monarchy lightly. Foreigners are forbidden to export certain replicas of Buddha, *The King and I* is still banned as disrespectful to the monarchy, and temple signs remind visitors not to eat or smoke or sit with their feet pointing at the Buddha image. Even so, commerce seems to be the handmaid of religion. No temple compound is complete without souvenir stands, cafés, palm readers, astrologers, and masseurs.

At Wat Arun you can have your picture taken as you stand behind a cardboard cutout of a Thai prince and princess. In the

In ancient times, only Buddhist temples were built of stone. Gods were eternal, humans ephemeral. In the museum at Bangkok's Wat Bovornivet a series of slide viewers is arrayed along a table. A novice monk peers into the first and observes a cadaver. In the second, it has been skinned. He views each successive state of decomposition until, at the final viewer, he is looking at a skeleton. From it, he learns that even too solid flesh melts with time and he must order his life accordingly.

*—Steve Van Beek,
"Thailand Notes"*

Grand Palace compound, near the temple of the much venerated Emerald Buddha (carved from a single piece of jade), is a snack bar with a jukebox. At Wat Po monks sit around reading newspapers, men play checkers underneath shade trees, children suck mango juice from plastic bottles, an astrologer's sign says, "Please check your fate.... Your past, present, and future now available here," and not far from the Reclining Buddha the temple massage school offers visitors an hour-long introductory rub.

In all these temples you see visual clues that suggest why the sensitive Thais, possessed of such a fine eye for grace and beauty, could have built a modern city that is, as Alistair Shearer warned in his book *Thailand: The Lotus Kingdom,* "a smack in the mouth." The temples' curving roofs and pagodas barely escape being gaudy. They glitter with gold, verging on excess. Their colored tiles and gilt are not quite vulgar but are surely flashy and a bit too cute. When Bangkok began sprouting tacky modern architecture, the Thais perhaps crossed the taste line they had nudged for centuries.

Some of the Bangkok canals in Thonburi, on the western side of the Chao Phraya, were never filled, and the trip I took there made it possible to imagine 19th century Bangkok. Here, in the heart of a great city, were small river villages with stores, bars, and barbershops, all accessible by water and sometimes connected by wooded walkways. There was a musty, tunnel-of-love odor of wet wood and recycled water. Sunlight filtered through thick foliage, giving everything an aquamarine tint. The best time to visit these canals is early morning, before tourist longboats descend, churning the water and shattering the peace.

I had heard Thais endlessly praised for their gentle dispositions and smiles. The famous Thai tendency to compromise and avoid conflict may explain why they seem able to tolerate their ghastly traffic with such equanimity.

The legendary Thai smiles are marketed by the Thai tourist industry with a cunning reminiscent of Hawaii's effort to retail "aloha." But the quality and quantity of the smiles in Bangkok were indeed remarkable. There was apparently a smile for every eventuality, even a tight little grimace I took to signal anger. But the smiles were not a façade; behind them was genuine concern. I won't forget the woman measuring me for a suit who talked me into choosing a less expensive fabric. Or the two students at Wat Saket who guided me around the observation terrace naming every temple and insisting we be photographed together. Or the man who, thinking I was lost, walked with me to the nearest ferry landing.

Sometimes the Thais seemed too polite. So many smiles and *wais*. So many eyes studying my face and body language for signs of discomfort or disapproval. Did I really need my water and beer glasses refilled every time I took a sip? Would my beer not stay colder left in its bottle? After a while, I began feeling clumsy and graceless, like someone who dreams of himself arriving at a fancy-dress ball in underwear. If you think I exaggerate Thai sensitivity, just consider what one Thai guide told me about U Nu, the first leader of independent Burma. When U Nu made a state visit to Thailand shortly after the war, he said, the government hurriedly reconstructed parts of Ayutthaya so that "he would not feel bad" about his people's having sacked the city two centuries earlier.

But there was so much to like about the Thais that I came to agree with the Australian expatriate who had answered my questions about the city's appeal, "The people, mate, they're the attraction of this place." I liked it that nobody, even the woman selling fake Gucci shirts on the street, tried to hustle or pressure me. The bargaining was always good-natured; it had none of the desperate undercurrent found in India and the Middle East. I liked it when even the seediest touts stepped back and smiled when I refused their approach. I liked the way waitresses, following the Thai sensitivity to relative tallness, kneeled down to take my drink order instead of towering over me.

I liked the pleasure the Thais took in their food and the way they had liberated it from the straitjacket of breakfast, lunch, and dinner. Instead, they snacked constantly at gimcrack outdoor restaurants so cheap that even the poor had enough baht for a bowl of spicy noodles. These were companionable places, arranged like sushi bars, with low tables set up along a sidewalk so that diners faced cooks who created miracles with a handful of utensils, boiling water, and a charcoal fire.

I liked the way the Thais had woven the spiritual and the temporal together: the dollhouses on poles, known as spirit houses, that sat in front of homes, stores, and even gas stations and, with their daily offerings of flowers and incense, appeased the spirits believed to inhabit these places; and the sunrise spectacle of saffron-robed monks, walking barefoot across highways soon to be clogged with traffic as they collected donations of food in plastic buckets. On my first morning, I woke to see the staff of my hotel, turned out in suits, morning coats, and elegant uniforms, standing behind trestle tables covered with starched white tablecloths and handing out food plates wrapped in yellow cellophane and ribbons to monks who moved down the line like diners in a cafeteria.

After I learned how the express ferries worked, I began making short excursions on foot back into the interior of the city. I found I could take a boat to the Pak Klong Talad vegetable market and then walk half an hour on roads paralleling the river to the Grand Palace, where there was another ferry dock. Farther up the river, I walked to the National Museum, and on my last day I discovered walking to be the best way to see Chinatown. By car, it was a horror, and several times I was told it was the city's most polluted and congested neighborhood. But on foot I could follow a maze of pedestrian alleys detouring around the traffic-clogged arteries and leading to fabulous temples and markets. My favorite alley was Soi Issaranuphah, where bins of food and clothing spilled out of stores, almost meeting in the middle, and where overhead awnings created a perpetual twilight and neon signs burned brightly at midday.

After a half mile of spices, silks, sea slugs, and flowers, I came upon lines of stores selling what I took to be children's toys. There were elaborate dollhouses and telephones, computers and luxury cars, all constructed of paper. It was only when I arrived at the Dtai Hong Kong shrine, at the end of the lane, that I understood these were not toys but *kong tek* items, purchased to be burned and sent into the afterlife for the enjoyment of deceased relatives. A casual ceremony was in progress, and believers were slipping items into an urn. Most offerings were folded pieces of orange paper representing money. But it occurred to me that, if I waited long enough, I might see, if only in my own imagination, undisguised joy on the faces of these Bangkok worshipers as they turned their automobiles to ashes.

Thurston Clarke is the author of Equator, *a chronicle of a journey around the world, and* California Fault, *an account of travels along California's San Andreas Fault.*

★

For many Westerners, death is horror. Yet it is the Western religious creeds which dwell on death and instruct the followers on how to avoid the fear of death. Religious people and death-bed rites are available to aid the dying to accept death, yet death remains, for many, a trauma of the gravest dimensions.

Buddhist teachings focus on life—since life and death are one. Death (or changing) is only a part of life. Of course, there are rites and rituals attached to the cremation or burial of a Buddhist and the families reflect sadness. But because many Theravada Buddhists believe that they have many lives to lead—hundreds, perhaps hundreds of thousands, yet to come—there is an absence of finality in the cessation of one. For the Buddhist, death is not a trauma, but more the continuation of a constant process of changing, decaying and arising, that somehow lies outside the notion of death as a finality.

The essence of this understanding of death is softly chanted by monks at funerals—"All things in '*samsara*' (the world of birth and death) are impermanent. To be happy there can be no clinging."

—Jane Hamilton-Merritt, *A Meditator's Diary*

GENA REISNER

✦ ✦ ✦

Siriraj Hospital Museum

Looking for Thailand's most famous killer?
You'll find his pickled remains at
Bangkok's offbeat museum.

IT'S EASY TO GET TO BANGKOK'S SIRIRAJ HOSPITAL. THERE'S AN express boat stop right there, and the name is written in large letters across the white building, clearly visible from the river.

The difficult part is finding the hospital's museums, even though there are several of them. But once you do, be sure to visit the Prehistoric Museum and Library. This collection represents a life's work. Dr. Sood Sangvichien, 86, who is emeritus chief of anatomy at the hospital, gave us a personal tour.

"I built this museum because I wanted to know where the Thai people came from," the doctor explained in English as he ushered us into a large, hot room. His quest began during World War II when a Dutch archaeologist—held by the Japanese as a prisoner of war in the Thai countryside—found six pebble tools. "After the war he had the pebbles analyzed at Harvard," recounted the doctor. "They had been made by people 500,000 years ago. When I heard this, I became convinced—contrary to most theories— that the Thai people originated here in Thailand." The pivotal pebbles are on display in the museum.

Fifteen years later, Sood joined an archaeological expedition and traveled by boat and elephant to Three Pagodas Pass. Digging its first pit, the team hit the jackpot—two four-thousand-year-old skeletons. These were the first Neolithic skeletons found in Thailand. A display compares a model of one of these skeletons to a modern Thai skeleton, pointing out numerous similarities.

We concluded there was no difference in the characteristics of the two skeletons," the doctor said. "Thais lived here four thousand years ago."

The museum also contains a display of Stone Age tools, complete with drawings of how the tools were used. One set of these ancient tools was found by chance. "We bought one in a market across the river, and the lady refused to tell us where she had gotten it," Dr. Sangvichien explained. "But luckily, a student recognized the tools as coming from his part of Thailand, and we were able to go and get more."

Two long wooden objects that look like dugout canoes remain a mystery. "They might be boats, but they might also be coffins with room for traditional objects to be buried with the dead," the doctor said. As evidence, he showed us a rock painting of a funeral procession, where the "dugout canoes" were carried aloft.

After we finished seeing Dr. Sangvichien's prehistoric museum, his son, Dr. Sanjai Sangvichien, the current chief of anatomy at the hospital, took over the tour and showed us several more of the hospital's museums. We started at the anatomy museum, which included a dissection of an entire human nervous system.

Also in the collections are skeletons of several important people, including members of the faculty. One particularly important person's skeleton is varnished, polished, and kept in a case topped with his photograph.

The most macabre of the hospital's museums is the Museum of Forensic Medicine. Here we saw the most famous killer in Thai history, his body preserved and on display in a wooden case. Other preserved bodies on display included murder victims and more notorious killers. On one case containing the body of a particularly nasty criminal, someone had draped a flower garland—a typical Thai offering. "Some kids were joking about the body, then got scared, and wanted to propitiate its spirit," the doctor explained.

The Museum of Thai Medicine showcases traditional methods of Thai healing. A set of dioramas shows treatments being administered in a village. In one diorama, a pregnant woman inhales vapors while her shoulders are pounded with heavy sacks. In another, a healer cuts the umbilical cord with a shell. In a third, the mother is massaged after childbirth.

Another exhibit shows Thai herbal medicines. For those interested in native remedies, hundreds of these medicines, collected throughout the country, are catalogued here. Signs give the Latin terms for the various herbs. Some of the same medicines can be seen on display in Thai country markets.

In another Siriraj Hospital museum [there is] a pair of conjoined twins, usually known in the West as Siamese twins. The famous originals were first spotted in 1824 by an English resident of Bangkok. The twins were swimming in the Chao Phya river not far from where the hospital is presently located.

—William Warren, Thailand, Seven Days in the Kingdom

According to Dr. Sanjai Sangvichien, Siriraj is the Thai's favorite hospital. "It's Thailand's oldest hospital, so everyone knows it," he said. "And with 2,400 beds and 1.1 million outpatients, it's the third-largest hospital in the world."

Gena Reisner is a free-lance travel and technical writer who lives in New York. She was a Peace Corps volunteer in Togo, West Africa, from 1964 to 1966.

*

To get an idea of what shopping in Bangkok used to be like before all the canals were tarmacked over, make an early-morning trip to the floating markets (*talat khlong*) of Damnoen Saduak, 60 km south of Nakhon Pathom. Vineyards and orchards here back onto a labyrinth of narrow canals thick with paddle boats overflowing with fresh fruit and vegetables: local women ply these waterways every morning between 6 a.m. and 11 a.m., selling their produce to each other and to the residents of weatherworn homes built on stilts along the banks. Many wear the deep blue jacket and high-toppped straw hat traditionally favoured by Thai farmers. It's all richly atmospheric, which naturally makes it a big draw for tour groups—but you can avoid the crowds if you leave before they arrive, at about 9 a.m.

—Paul Gray and Lucy Ridout, *The Rough Guide Thailand*

JEFF GREENWALD

* * *

Bite-sized Buddhas

*Amulets are serious business
at the Buddha bazaar.*

WHEN I HEARD THAT ONE COULD BUY MAGIC BUDDHAS IN Bangkok—small, sculptured images which, worn around the neck, protect the wearer from harm—my only question was, where? The answer was, Wat.

Wat Mahathat is the site of the Saturday bazaar, the best place to find these magic buddhas. I took a *tuk-tuk* to the Oriental Hotel, where the Chao Phraya River Express taxied me over the waterways to Mahathat. Then, after navigating a labyrinth of back alleys (clouds of oily

According to Joe Cummings, author of Thailand – a travel survival kit, *the money exchanged for Buddha images is actually "rent" paid to the* wats *or monks associated with them, and thus is neither a purchase nor a donation.*

—JO'R and LH

wok-smoke, the ground littered with banana leaves, pressed dried squid stacked in straw baskets), I emerged into the light.

All along the sidewalk, tables stood covered with tiny, exquisite Buddhas. Shoppers leaned over the displays, examining the wares through loupes. Each amulet, I knew, was meant for a specific purpose. Some were ancient, worth many thousands of baht; others, mass produced, might be had for the equivalent of a dollar

119

or two. Traditionally, of course, nobody may buy or sell a magic Buddha; any money that changes hands is merely a donation.

I spent hours at the Buddha bazaar, fairly oozing from stall to stall in the hot-tub humidity. Finally I returned home, four bite-sized Buddhas in hand. Speaking no Thai, I hadn't a clue what their various powers might be. I showed them to the cashier at my hotel, who perused the lot and eyed me quizzically.

"This one will protect your jackfruit crop from hail," he said, "and this one will ensure success on your high school equivalency exam. This third one you must wear around your waist when kick-boxing; it will safeguard your testicles. And this fourth one will make you invulnerable to bullets."

"Hmmm. That last one might come in handy in my country," I admitted. "But how do I know that it works?"

"You may be very sure," the cashier replied, dead serious, "that all these amulets have been carefully tested."

Jeff Greenwald is a contributing editor for Wired *magazine and the author of* Mr. Raja's Neighborhood, The Size of the World: Once Around without Leaving the Ground, *and* Shopping for Buddhas.

★

Few Thais would leave home without an amulet (or two, or three) dangling on a chain around the neck. This may seem peculiar to Western minds, but not so peculiar when you consider that the average Thai has very little insurance—car insurance, life insurance, medical insurance, or otherwise. Insurance provides coverage after an accident happens; amulets give the wearer reassurance that no accident will happen in the first place. Like different kinds of insurance, there are different kinds of amulets— some are good against air crashes, others against theft or bullets or snakebite. All-round invulnerability is possible—but such an amulet is highly prized and therefore expensive.

—Michael Buckley, "The Arcane Power of Amulets"

KEMP M. MINIFIE

⋆ ⋆ ⋆

A Cooking School
in Bangkok

*Thai food is aromatic, pungent, spicy, and sweet. Learning
to prepare it offers unique insights into Thai culture,
and gives a fresh view of local markets.*

TALK TO ANYONE WHO HAS BEEN IN THAILAND AND INVARIABLY
you will hear excited descriptions of the food, with virtual rhap-
sodies on the exotic flavors. But even though one of the most
vivid pleasures of travel in Thailand is the cuisine, it is one of the
most elusive memories.

Thanks to the foresight of the Oriental Hotel in Bangkok,
travelers interested in returning home with some of the secrets of
preparing Thai food can enroll in the Thai Cooking School run
by the hotel. During a week-long course that combines lectures
with demonstrations and some participation, I learned why Thai
food tastes the way it does and how to achieve the balance of key
flavors with what for many of us are new, exotic ingredients.

To be honest, a hotel-sponsored cooking program sounded at
first like the ultimate tourist trap. Despite glowing reviews I'd
heard about the school I had my doubts, but I should have known
that the Oriental, with its reputation as one of the finest hotels
in the world, would not get involved in anything that was not
first rate. I left the school most impressed; I had gained more
knowledge in one week at the Oriental than I had in much

longer courses at other cooking schools, in both the United States and Europe.

The direction of the school and the man largely responsible for its excellence is Chalie Amatyakul. A native Thai, Chalie is a cosmopolitan fellow who studied literature in France and interior design in Vienna for several years after graduating with a degree in political science from Bangkok's prestigious Chulalongkorn University. He has traveled extensively around the world pursuing a career that has included stints as sales manager and food and beverage director for the Oriental. Successful as he's been in the hotel business, he seems to have found his real métier with the Thai Cooking School. A born teacher, Chalie is passionate about Thai food, and he shares that enthusiasm with an almost missionary zeal. He is both knowledgeable and articulate on the subject, and not just in his native tongue. His fluency in English, French, and German has served him well in tutoring the large number of American and European students who have attended the school since it opened in June, 1986.

Chalie has since moved on from the Oriental's cooking school, but the school is now in the capable hands of Sarnsern Gajaseni.

—JO'R and LH

Chalie's interest in food goes back to his childhood when, as the youngest of five children in an old aristocratic family, he learned to cook by hanging around the kitchen and helping out when needed. "To know how a dish was supposed to taste I had to learn how it was made," explained Chalie. "My mother supervised the household and trained her children to supervise, which included being able to tell servants how to do something."

As food and beverage director of the Oriental in the early 1980s, he was instrumental in setting up the hotel's Thai restaurant, the Sala Rim Naam, and many of the recipes prepared there today are taught at the school. He also helped develop the catering and banquet business for the Oriental, getting involved in all aspects of party planning from costumes and decorations to flower arrangements. So creative were his events that he caught the attention of Thailand's Queen Sirikit, who continues to hire him to cater state functions. He even accompanied the queen on her 1985 tour of the United States and single-handedly organized receptions she hosted in New York and Los Angeles.

Thai cuisine conveniently falls into five general categories of dishes, giving Chalie a natural structure for the week's classes, beginning with snacks and salads and moving through soups and curries to stir-fried, steamed, and grilled dishes before ending with desserts.

Despite its hotel connections, the Thai Cooking School is open to anyone, but the extras such as meals and tours are available only to guests at the Oriental. The complete course runs from Sunday night, with an introductory dinner at the Sala Rim Naam, through Friday noon and features such added amenities as breakfast every morning at the Oriental's Verandah restaurant and a lunchtime sampling of the hotel's other restaurants, including Lord Jim's. Also included in the tuition are a private tour guide for two afternoons of sightseeing and three dinners: a barbeque buffet at the Oriental's Riverside Terrace; an elegant French respite from Thai food at the Normandie, and an interesting interpretation of what's been called "nouvelle Thai" at the Lemongrass, a local Bangkok favorite lodged in an antique-filled converted townhouse. There are clearly more than enough opportunities to eat during the week's course, and tastings of the dishes prepared in class each morning were so ample that I often skipped the hotel lunch.

The school can handle up to twenty people, but I was fortunate to have chosen a week when only one other student, a horticulturist from Greenwich, Connecticut, had signed up for the full course. Except for the two days when we were joined by an Australian homemaker and a New York-based book editor, my classmate and I had virtually private lessons. For someone visiting Bangkok for less than a week, it is possible to spend as little as one day at the school.

What I particularly liked about the classes is that they gave me a structure for my time in Bangkok. By steeping myself in Thai cooking each morning, my forays into the city streets each after-

noon became more meaningful. Whether I was headed for a shopping spree or sight-seeing, I was bombarded with the sights and
smells of food, which were always exotic and often quite pungent.

Bangkok, among its other reputations, is clearly a city of gustatory pleasures. Never before had I seen so many stalls selling all
manner of snacks and freshly sliced fruit, or wandered in so many
street markets, or passed so many individual farmers who had
staked out a square of sidewalk from which to sell their produce—
all of them offering countless opportunities, if not to indulge then
at least to view the incredible variety of raw ingredients and in
many cases to watch them being cooked. Whatever questions I
had about what I'd seen would be answered in class the next
morning.

The school is housed—rather appropriately it seemed—in a
19th-century colonial teak structure that was formerly a riverside
mansion. It stands next to the Sala Rim Naam restaurant, which is
across the busy Chao Phraya river, directly opposite the modern
River Wing tower of the Oriental. Each morning, after a breakfast
of fresh papaya and toast, the latter serving purely as a vehicle for
the dark and bittersweet pummelo marmalade made by the
Oriental, I headed for the hotel dock to catch the private ferry. I
looked forward to this ride, during which the ferry crossed the
commercial lanes of traffic like a fearless jaywalker to the Thon
Buri bank of the river. When the Oriental's boat wasn't immediately available, I'd spend the equivalent of a nickel to take the local
ferry filled with Thais on their way to work. From the Thon
Buri dock it was a short walk past lush greenery and through the
veranda-like private dining rooms at the front of the building to
the two classroms in the rear.

Despite the fact that both rooms were air-conditioned, Chalie,
who helped design the school facility, left intact the natural venti-
lation that was ingeniously incorporated into the original building.
The system takes the form of an open-air clerestory: decoratively
shaped holes are cut out repeatedly along the top of all four walls,
like a string of paper dolls. Hot air rises up and out of the rooms
through the clerestory, and fresh breezes find their way in.

We reported each morning to a room filled with rows of mahogany desks facing a blackboard. Each desk was topped neatly with a stack of recipes, a small vase of orchids, and a cup and saucer for coffee—a far cry from the classrooms of my youth. On our first morning we opened our desk drawers to find an apron and sacks of Thai spices to take home, as well as such staples as *naam pla,* the fermented fish sauce that is to the Thais what soy sauce is to the Chinese, and a bottle of Chalie's favorite brand of Sriracha chili sauce.

Each class began with a brief but by no means lightweight lecture on the background of the dishes to be demonstrated that day. Chalie made active use of the blackboard, which simplified our personal note taking. After about a half hour we would move to the demonstration room, which resembled a chemistry laboratory, with three long marble-topped teak units and an overhead mirror.

The ingredients for each dish, already pounded, chopped, or shredded, would be waiting in small bowls arranged on large platters, a welcome sight consid-

*D*ining choices in Thailand range from five-star hotel restaurants to simple foodstalls on the side of the road. First-time visitors sometimes dismiss hawker food as unclean and assume that any meal served on a rickety aluminum table must be inferior to a first-class restaurant. Nothing could be further from the truth. If a steady queue of Mercedeses waiting for noodle soup is any indication, hawker food provides stiff competition for many of Thailand's finer restaurants.

In fact, street food should be your first choice for several reasons. Large congregations of foodstalls in a single location ensure a greater array of food than in any single restaurant. Secondly, since there is virtually no overhead, prices are kept low—a filling and delicious meal can be served for less than $2. But perhaps most importantly, foodstall dining is a great way to meet people, make friends, and gain some insight into Thai lifestyles.

—Carl Parkes,
Thailand Handbook

ering this labor-intensive cuisine. Chalie, with the help of his assistant, Sarnsern, performed a show-and-tell with the components of the recipes, encouraging us to smell and taste the raw ingredients to get a better understanding of their unique role in the complexity of flavor in Thai food.

For me it was my first encounter with certain exotic fruits, vegetables, herbs, and other seasonings that until then I'd only heard about or seen in their barely recognizable dried state. Here, at last, in the raw, was *kha,* or greater galanga, the ginger-like rhizome native to Indonesia. A sniff of greater galanga revealed its kinship to turmeric, itself another rhizome used fresh in Thai cooking; I was reminded instantly of ball-park mustard, which derives its characteristically bright yellow color from powdered turmeric.

Also new to me were *kaffir* limes and their leaves. Years before I'd seen dried *kaffir* lime leaves stuffed in little plastic bags in New York's Chinatown and never knew that they grow in pairs, almost piggyback style on the stem, the tip of one leaf barely overlapping the end of the one ahead of it. Infused with a citrus perfume, the bright green leaves were shredded fine and added at the last minute to soups and curries. The *kaffir* limes resembled the limes we are accustomed to in color only. In stark contrast to the smooth-skinned fruit we're familiar with, the *kaffir* limes were a mass of knobby little bumps, a curious trait that didn't prevent the rind from being grated and added as still another lemon-lime accent to Thai food.

As we were led through each step in the preparation of a dish, Chalie proved to be an overflowing font of information, suggesting all kinds of variations and substitutions. We often found ourselves scribbling down extra recipes and procedures Chalie rattled off from memory.

For the actual cooking we gathered around large, free-standing gas burners in the kitchen, which was separated from the demonstration room by glass doors. Although the classes were predominantly demonstration here, we had the chance to try our own hand at certain techniques, sometimes quite literally as when we learned to drizzle beaten egg from our hands in a crosshatch pattern onto a skillet to make a woven-looking egg sheet.

The cooking equipment was unlike any I'd seen before, especially the striking brass woks, with their gleaming golden color and distinctive, unusual shape. Unlike Chinese-style woks, which feature narrow bottoms and sharply sloping sides, the Thai brass woks had wide, softly rounded bottoms and barely flaring sides. Originally designed for the preparation of desserts, the woks eventually proved their versatility as efficient vessels for stir-frying, deep-frying, and the reduction of liquids. Although Chinese woks are used widely in Thailand, Chalie prefers the elegance of the brass version. The brass woks retain their shiny look even after long contact with flames on the stove, and so, frequent usage notwithstanding, the woks stay as beautiful to cook in as they are to serve from—the ideal kitchen-to-table-ware.

The mottled brown ladles and spatulas at the school were fashioned from coconut shells, a testament to both the ingenuity of the Thais and the profusion of coconuts. Made by the hill tribes near Chiang Mai in the northern part of Thailand, the coconut utensils are not readily found in Bangkok, but by sheer luck I happened upon a woman selling them at the sprawling weekend market just outside central Bangkok in Chatuchak Park. Whether one is interested in coconut utensils or not, the Chatuchak market is well worth the taxi ride to see the assortment of items—produce, jeans, dried fish, pets, plants, fabric, ceramics, counterfeit tapes, and the like—all being sold in one vast, tented area.

In designing the curriculum for the cooking school, Chalie researched recipes in many cookbooks, some of which were over a hundred years old. He tried several versions of a classic dish before determining the best one for the classes, keeping in mind not only what would be most representative of Thai cooking but what would translate easily to a typical Western kitchen. From his travels Chalie was aware of the limited availability of Thai ingredients in the West and kindly considered that fact when choosing recipes to demonstrate.

If I had to describe the classes in one word, it would be intensive. For a Westerner there is a great deal to learn about the raw materials even before commencing on the procedures for combining them in a recipe. Take coconut milk, for example, one of the most distinctive flavors in Thai food. Although a vessel of coconut milk is always on hand at the school, and freshly grated coconut is sold in all the markets, we had to learn to make it from scratch. That process alone involved cracking open a mature coconut, prying out the flesh, finely grating the meat, mixing it with water, and squeezing out the milky white liquid. The result was coconut milk in its simplest form.

But it didn't stop there. In some recipes the Thais make a distinction between coconut cream and coconut milk. The cream is a more concentrated extraction using half the amount of water used for coconut milk. This procedure can be followed by a second extraction, using more water and the same grated coconut to make a thin milk. In these coconut extractions the Thais have both a fat and a dairylike liquid. The cream, when boiled and reduced to release its oil, becomes the fat for cooking seasonings, and the milk becomes the liquid base for curries and soups.

Needless to say, making coconut milk is a time-consuming process, and the results depend on flavorful coconuts, which are often difficult to find in Western markets. Fortunately, good, unsweetened coconut milk is available either frozen or canned in Asian markets in major cities in the United States.

Thai food uses three varieties of fresh basil. The Thais are quite particular about their herbs. Each type of basil has its specific role.

Bai horapha is similar to the Italian basil that Americans and Europeans sprinkle over sliced tomatoes or blend into pesto as a sauce for pasta. In Thailand *bai horapha,* or basil-basil as it is also called, tends to be confined to the more refined, city-style of cooking, making frequent appearances in coconut milk-based dishes. When we prepared *panaeng nuea* (beef curry) in class, *bai horapha* leaves were stirred into the mixture at the last moment to wilt them and infuse the curry with their mild anise flavor.

Bai manglug, known elsewhere as sweet balsam or lime basil, has small, paler leaves reminiscent of our dwarf basil. In Thailand sweet balsam is usually added to soups, although it is sometimes sprinkled raw over salads and fish curries.

Most intriguing of all was *bai gaprow,* or holy basil, which derives its mysterious appellation from its Latin name, *ocimum sanctum*. Thai restaurant aficionados in the United States are probably familiar with this herb as the predominant flavor in what is fast becoming a ubiquitous classic, chicken with holy basil. Similar in appearance to Italian basil, holy basil is recognizable by its purple stems and green or reddish-purple leaves, which are slightly smaller and thicker than Italian basil leaves. Holy basil is treated by the Thais as a lusty herb, suitable for the robust chili dishes that have not been soothed with coconut milk. In the version of chicken with holy basil that we learned in the school, the fresh leaves were fried first, forming bright green crisps that tasted faintly of artichoke, before being added to the stir-fried chicken mixture.

Despite the subtle differences among the three basil varieties, fresh Italian basil can be substituted for the other two, and, in fact, it is preferable to the dried holy basil that is sold by some Asian markets and mail-order companies. Fresh holy basil is available sporadically in Thai markets in the United States, particularly in cities with a sizable Thai population such as Los Angeles, Houston, Washington, D.C., New York, Chicago, and Atlanta, and it is well worth the hunt to find it.

For many *farangs,* Thai food is synonymous with the incendiary heat of chilies, and one of the most frequent comments about the cuisine is that it's very hot, if not at times too hot. Chalie is sensitive to this complaint and insists that well-prepared Thai dishes should be balanced, so that the spiciness of hot peppers is offset by the sweetness of coconut milk or palm sugar, the pungency of fresh herbs, the sourness of lime juice or tamarind, or the saltiness of *naam pla.* Too often in Thai restaurants in the West that balance is out of whack. In traditional home-style cooking, Chalie explained, the mother spiced the dishes mildly and offered small bowls of hot sauce on the side so that each person could fire up his or her serving to taste. Only when she thought she didn't have enough food for a meal would the heat be increased to keep the family from eating too much.

We were surprised to learn that the chilies so loved by the Thais are not native to Thailand at all but were introduced to the country by Portuguese missionaries, who brought them from

South America in the 17th century. Before that, the only peppers in Thailand were peppercorns, a fact reflected in their name, *prig Thai.* Peppercorns are still an important spice in Thai cooking, and the Thais are particularly fond of young, or green, peppercorns. In Bangkok markets the fresh green berries are sold still attached to their branches.

The unusual kapi, fermented shrimp paste, is the central ingredient in a class of foods that represent the very heart of Thai cuisine, the nam phrik, or chili-pepper sauces. The soul of Thai cuisine resides in the repertoire of nam phrik. These are purely Siamese recipes, and some have remained unchanged for many centuries. The ultimate compliment that can be paid to a Thai cook is to praise his or her nam phrik. Recipes for any given type vary so widely from household to household (and from restaurant to restaurant) that standardized quantification of ingredients is impossible, and cooks who have devised celebrated versions often keep the recipe strictly secret.

— Gault Millau:
The Best of Thailand

I marveled at how much more aromatic the fresh green peppercorns were than the brine-cured ones so loved by European and American chefs. What we consider an expensive specialty item in the United States, Chalie used with abandon, tossing clumps of peppercorns, twigs and all, into curries and soups. My favorite recipe utilizing green peppercorns, however, was for a concoction the Thais call a dip but that more closely resembles a relish or condiment. In this case the green peppercorns were mixed with garlic, sugar, dried shrimp, lime juice, and grated sour fruits. Chalie recommended it as an accompaniment for vegetables or grilled fish, but we found it addictive eaten straight with a spoon.

The Thais clearly took to the chilies that the Portuguese brought with them, and a myriad variety in different shapes, sizes, and colors overflow baskets in a riotous display in the markets. Although thin slices of fresh chilies appear frequently as a garnish, chilies are most often pounded into a paste with other aromatic seasonings. Depending on the type of dish it is headed for, the paste may include different combinations of such ingredients as the roots of fresh coriander plants, dried shrimp, shrimp paste, garlic lemongrass, and greater galanga. Chili pastes are the foundation of so many Thai dishes that it is no surprise to find huge conical mounds of them in the markets, in various shades of red, orange, and green. At least half the dishes we saw prepared in class, from curries to stir-fried noodles to soups, began with some form of chili paste.

"The secret to Thai chili or curry pastes is the pounding of the ingredients. You must break open the pores to bring out the flavors," explained Chalie to support his belief in the importance of the mortar and pestle. "A food processor does not do the same thing." Chalie was flexible on many other substitutions, but on this point he was adamant. He demonstrated the making of pastes with two different mortars and pestles. One was a deep, clay bisque bowl with a palm root for a pestle, and the other was carved from a solid piece of granite with a matching granite pestle. For those of us accustomed to modern, supposedly time-saving equipment, it was an eye-opener to watch the old fashioned mortar and pestle mash a mixture of garlic cloves, chilies, and lemongrass into an aromatic purée in no time.

What has long intrigued me about Thai food is its reflection of the unique way in which influences from neighboring countries have been adapted. As we tasted our way through five days of classes these culinary borrowings became clearer. From India came the curries, but, whereas Indian curries are based on spices, Thai curries are predominantly herbal, with the prevailing flavors of coriander root, lemongrass, chilies, and basil and only the occasional use of cumin, coriander seed, and cardamom. Reminiscent of Chinese cuisine are the stir-fried meats and poultry and the noodle dishes, but the addition of such seasonings as shrimp paste, lime juice, tamarind, and basil makes them distant relations. The Thais adopted *sates,* the skewers of grilled meats served with a peanut sauce, from the Malaysians, but instead of a dry marinade the Thais often combine the spices with coconut milk and let the meat marinate in the mixture before grilling it. The accompanying peanut sauce tends to be a touch sweeter and

creamier with the addition of coconut milk than the typical
Malaysian versions.

Thai cuisine was not new to me when I arrived in Bangkok,
although the food I ate at the school and in the restaurants was far
superior to anything I'd had before in the United States.
Interestingly, I sampled my first
Thai food at the New York
World's Fair in 1964. I accompanied friends who had lived in
Bangkok for several years, and we
had lunch at the Thai Pavilion. I
was eleven years old at the time,
not a typically adventurous age
when it comes to trying new
foods, but I remember particularly liking the fried-noodle specialty, which I now realize was
mee grob, sometimes referred to as the Thai national dish. Versions
of mee grob I've had since then in New York City Thai restaurants
have tasted overly sweet, a common problem due to the unfortunate belief that the American sweet tooth applies to savory foods as
well as desserts, and so I was eager to learn the proper method of
preparing it. Chalie confirmed that even in Thailand too much
sugar gets added to mee grob, especially in the quick versions hawked
in the markets. These simplified street concoctions bore no resemblance to the elaborate preparation we witnessed in the classroom.

Mee grob is a dish in which texture is crucial. Chalie explained
that the noodles should be crisp and crumbly, not crunchy. To
achieve this consistency he very briefly soaked the dried rice
noodles in water to seal their pores so that they would not puff
as they normally do when submerged in hot oil, then dipped
them in beaten egg as a further sealant. When the egg coating
had set, the noodles were deep-fried. The resulting tender-crisp
noodles kept their consistency even after a later stir-frying with
naam pla, rice vinegar, palm sugar, and a mixture of shrimp, pork,
and chicken.

The author's introduction to Thailand came, in fact, from her backyard childhood pal, whose father was in the Foreign Service in Thailand in the Kennedy administration. The two remain in contact, and Ms. Minifie's friend has returned to Bangkok to live.

—JO'R and LH

In a country blessed with a profusion of orchids, where people painstakingly string individual petals into elaborately patterned strands and necklaces and carve fruits and vegetables into a cornucopia of shapes, it is no surprise that aesthetics play an important role in the cuisine. "The Thais have always liked things to be pretty," explained Chalie. For novices and professional cooks alike, the inventive presentation of each dish made the classes especially worthwhile. For instance, to *gaeng rawn,* a simple bean thread noodle and vegetable soup, we added little bundles filled with the surprise of ground pork or vegetables and tied with a lily blossom. *Guay tiaw paad Thai,* a stir-fried noodle dish, was served enclosed in a thin egg sheet and decorated with red chilies. The monotone *mee grob* was mounded in an elegant and edible fried noodle basket, which looked impossibly complicated but was actually made easily with two metal bowls and a large deep-fryer in much the same way that French potato nests are formed. Delicate egg lace, created by drizzling beaten egg through a bamboo strainer into hot oil, was laid carefully over the *mee grob* and topped with red chilies and slices of pickled garlic and lime to create a spectacular-looking dish from humble ingredients.

In order to enhance our artistic appreciation of the cuisine, a skilled Thai fruit and vegetable carver led one afternoon session. We watched in awe as a lovely young woman with lightning-speed dexterity transformed a platter of fruits and vegetables into fanciful shapes and blossoms. A piece of rosy-red papaya took on the lines of a curvaceous leaf, a carrot metamorphosed into a partially shucked ear of corn, and a whole watermelon became a large blossom. The methods she used were simple, and yet the results were visually effective. I must admit that our first attempts to copy what we'd seen demonstrated were pathetic, proving that it wasn't as easy as it looked, but by the end of the morning we had made some passable creations. It was the most exciting class of the week for me. I saw so many new possibilities for garnishes that I couldn't wait to try the same tricks on other fruits and vegetables at home.

Given the exciting blend of flavors in Thai cooking and the artistry of its presentation, it is no wonder that European and

American chefs are making a beeline to Thailand. There is much to be learned in this magical spot in Southeast Asia, whether one is interested in duplicating an exact dish or in using the delicate balance of spicy, sweet, sour, and salty flavors as a springboard for new creations. Considering how richly satisfying this cuisine is, the Thais, whose thin physiques belie their appreciation of good food, provide food for thought for all the Western world.

Kemp M. Minifie, senior food editor of Gourmet Magazine*, has been a fan of Southeast Asian food since her first bite in 1964.*

✳

Restaurants in Chiang Khlong occasionally serve *pla buk,* a monstrous type of catfish considered the largest of its kind in the world. *Pla buk* can grow up to three meters in length and weigh over 300 kilograms, making it the undisputed monster of the Mekong. The fish is praised for its white, succulent meat, which tastes like milk-fed veal and guarantees long life to all who eat it.

The process of catching *pla buk* begins when local priests invoke dock-side prayers to summon the spirits of the legendary fish and bring good luck to the fishermen. Fishermen then set out in sleek pirogues on 24-hour fishing shifts, only returning after a successful catch. A successful expedition is celebrated with bottles of Mekong whiskey and all-night parties; a single catch can pay for a new boat or provide for the children's education.

Sadly, the *pla buk* is an endangered species. Earlier this century, *pla buk* (*Pangasianodon gigas*) were plentiful and could be captured from the Tonle Sap in Cambodia to Th Li Lake in Southern China. Overfishing, however, has severely reduced their numbers to the point where just a few dozen are now caught during the April-June spawning season. The Thai Fisheries Department has recently taken steps to save the fish by initiating a strict quota system and conducted an ambitious breeding program at nearby Ban Had Khrai.

—Carl Parkes, *Thailand Handbook*

ANTHONY WELLER

✦ ✦ ✦

Wat Massage

He kept all his clothes on. So did she. It was
the best massage in Bangkok. Really.

THE BEST MASSAGE IN BANGKOK HAS NOTHING TO DO WITH A
lissome naked Thai beauty lathering you to distraction using
every inch of her skin and the only soap pad nature has endowed
her with.

Rather, it takes place with no privacy, in daylight, and both of
you keep all your clothes on. Though not as profound a religious
experience as is the famous "body-body," this dry alternative occurs
under the incurious gaze of hundreds of Buddhist monks.

It is available daily, 7:30 to 5:00, in one of the largest temples
in Bangkok: the *Wat Po* (Temple of Enlightenment). A Thai
temple is characteristically a series of courtyards littered with
gingerbread pagodas and chanting shaved-headed novitiates. The
Wat Po also has tables of fake Rolex watches, at ten bucks each,
plus the Reclining Buddha, the biggest in Thailand: nearly half a
golden football field of him, counting the mother-of-pearl feet,
smiling as if he has just received the finest Thai massage. On a recent morning I paid my respects, then went to the next courtyard
to do likewise.

Having heard about Thai massage traditions going back twenty
centuries, etc., conferring the same beneficence on the giver as the

receiver, etc., I was with barbarian ignorance prepared to find that the saffron-robed monks themselves do the kneading. This, of course, is not the case. But the Wat Po School of Thai Massage—found in two screened-in, slant-roofed enclosures—has been the finest in the country for at least three decades. Eighteen hard beds are laid side by side in each room; fans keep the humidity and heat at bay.

Nearly all the beds were occupied by barefoot, clothed bodies being gently bent, pressed, and squeezed by barefoot, clothed masseurs. Both sides of this corporeal tug-of-war consisted of both sexes. My hopes for a pure massage, with no impure overtones, were dashed when (after paying my 140 baht [about $6]) I was introduced to my masseuse. Instead of some wiry Thai, I was assigned a slender, gorgeous young woman named Mon, with big dark eyes and long black hair.

Thai massage is based on the theory that invisible lines of force run through the body. Pressure is never exerted on the bones; rather, the muscles are worked and released, after a slow loosening. Another technique involves cutting off the circulation entirely in one area for a minute. Movements and stretches are always gradual, so you wind up in positions such as "the reclining cobra" without any strain.

One common and dangerous maneuver is to push firmly on both femoral arteries of the client for several minutes and then releasing the pressure suddenly. This results in a flushed feeling in one's legs. Embolic phenomena (blood clots) and sudden obstruction in the leg arteries, particularly in older persons, have been reported as a result of this practice.

—Henry Wilde, M.D., Supawat Chutivongse, M.D., and Burnett Q. Pixley, M.D., *Guide to Healthy Living in Thailand*

It was astonishing how much pressure Mon could apply. At times she simply leaned on me and seemed to weigh as much as a truck. She would tug one bent leg up easily and give a disarming smile; then suddenly, 10,000 pounds would be painlessly brought to bear on a tight muscle I'd never known existed. She would rock back and forth on my limb for a moment with the pressure on, then move elsewhere. It was less

like a massage than like a very thorough engine tune-up administered by a highly skilled mechanic.

After my legs, she went to work on my back, treating it like a
crossword puzzle, clambering up and down and across, leaning,
walking, kneeling, and squeezing with her toes, fingers and heels,
all at the same time. Eventually she took my arms, which by now
had little fight left, and stretched them until they were fifteen feet
long. Then she went to work relaxing my skull and kept up a
sing-song, twittering conversation in Thai with the masseur two
feet away, who was giving a comatose Dutchman the 100,000
pound treatment. Did I look soft? Was that why I'd been given
this slip of a girl rather than someone who'd treat me like a twist-
off cap? Anyway, the massage school was the most relaxing place
in Bangkok; I left invigorated, not exhausted.

Anthony Weller is a writer and poet who lives in Gloucester, Massachusetts.

✳

Life is impermanent. This key Buddhist tenet applies to success, wealth,
love, and happiness and Thais order their lives by thinking, not in straight
lines, but in cycles. The turning wheel that places one at the top can just
as easily roll over and crush one later in life. In a society in which one's
success depends as much on communal support as on personal merit, one
does not gloat over fallen enemies; he may himself someday need help rising from the ashes. It also reflects pragmatic recognition that fate is capri-
cious; cretins could regain their prominence and recall the snub.

—Steve Van Beek, "Thailand Notes"

✦ ✦ ✦

Paradise Found,
Paradise Lost

*Another heaven on earth can be found in the Gulf
of Thailand, desperately trying to stay one step
ahead of developers—and the rest of us.*

FOR SOME TIME NOW THE WORD'S BEEN GOING ROUND AMONG the tie-dye brigade, those ragamuffin gypsies who drift from one discount Eastern paradise to the next, from Goa to Bali to Lake Toba: another place to be is Ko Samui. And as soon as one descends from the heavens onto this coconut-palm island set in the Gulf of Thailand, white strips of deserted beach lining its shores like racing stripes, one can see why.

The airport itself is just a group of thatched huts, without windows or walls, lit up by the song of birds who chirp in cages hanging from its roof. The security area consists of a single, gently smiling man. A Buddhist spirit house guards the entrance. And while a couple of Danish freaks are unpacking the cat they've checked in as luggage, a Thai girl offers you a bus into town. Outside, the spare tires of the Suzuki jeeps resting in the sun are wrapped in yin yang covers.

The first thing to greet you, on departing the airport, is a fifteen-foot Buddha, looming high and serene above the sea, blue waves lapping against the bottom of his temple. Nearby the signs point to a Meditation Institute. All around, the beaches are clear and white and empty. Monks in saffron robes and women in lampshade hats flash past across the green. The jeep bumps along unpaved roads littered with the husks of coconuts. Here and there, on trees someone has inscribed "Have Mercy." Elsewhere hand–painted signs offer "Ancient Massage" and "Snooker" and even (in front of one unprepossessing hut) "Family Zoo." A red banner declares, in Chinese, "A new spring is coming! Rejoice!" Truly, one feels as if one has landed in some enchanted forest, a Buddhist arcadia 300 miles south of Bangkok and a million miles from care.

Of the roughly 80 islands scattered across the clear blue-green waters of the Gulf of Thailand, Ko Samui is the most well known. Its first great blessing is its relative seclusion. Until 1989 it could not even be reached by plane. Its second is that it offers all the native— and increasingly famous—blessings of Thailand: an exceedingly attractive and gracious people; delectable food; First World facilities at Third World prices.

With its golden temples and go go bars, its water markets and opium tribes, its jungles, beaches, and shopping malls rich with rubies, silks, and statues, Thailand has become as polished and satisfaction-guaranteed a tourist market as exists today, an irresistible sensual wonderland with a gift for giving pleasure. Inevitably, too, it has become a victim of its own considerable charms. As 13,000 tourists come pouring in each day, Thailand has been losing idylls almost as fast as it develops them. The island of Phuket is now afflicted with a Club Med and rows of high-rise hotels; Pattaya has become a bloated red-light district by the sea. Increasingly, therefore, more and more people are beginning to settle—and settle, and settle—on Ko Samui. That is a heavy burden, of course, to lay on a 154-square-mile island that is, essentially, just one thick forest of coconut palms ringed with pristine beaches. Until recently, at least, nearly all the island's 32,000 residents were coconut farmers and fishermen, and its main product was the 2 million coconuts it ships each month to Bangkok (many of them picked, no doubt, by graduates of the "Monkey Training College" you can see advertised along the country roads). Even now, much of the island still sways to a lazy hammock rhythm; there is nothing much to do but read, relax, and listen to the sighing of the surf.

Although there are seven or eight principal beaches in Samui, the setup at nearly all of them is the same: a row of simple, clean, thatched bungalows, lined up beside the beach, within whispering distance of the sea. Some of the cottages come equipped with bathrooms and air conditioning, others with nothing but hammocks and six-dollar-a-day price tags. Nearby are little settlements to take care of all one's unworldly needs: a paperback exchange, a lazy garden restaurant, a shop for buying incense or bikinis, all with the natural, easy camaraderie of a baby Bali. All a visitor has to do, really, is select his fantasy—Is he hippie or hedonist? Does he want action or quiet?—and then settle down on the appropriate beach.

The rest is pure leisure, set to a rhythm as gentle as the waves. One of the great blessings of Ko Samui is that it offers almost no diversions save for some laid-back windsurfing. There are a couple of waterfalls and a temple or two, but these can be seen in a single afternoon from a rented motorbike or jeep. Occasional claims are made for the cultural value of Thai boxing, and once, as I drove along an empty road, a Thai man pointed to two torpid water buffaloes standing in the trees, and announced, "Buffalo fighting stadium!"

If ever you have any pressing needs, you can always travel to the bustling little port town of Na Thon, which features all the conveniences you could want: tattooists, ear cleaners, Scandinavian food, and mannequins with neon eyes.

Mostly, though, Ko Samui is a place for escaping need, and lapsing into a simple island fantasy of food and rest. A lazy game of Ping-Pong in the shade. A waitress rocking on a swing between the palms. The smell of incense from a local shrine. A topless Swedish girl in fez and blanket sashaying down the empty beach. The occasional thunk of a falling coconut. A sign behind the bar saying, "You can't change the past, but you can ruin a perfectly good present by worrying about the future." And as you walk around a corner in the magic light of dusk, there, all of a sudden, you may find a Crusoe island, a boy and girl stretched out on it alone, unclothed, like Adam and Eve returned to the Garden.

Traditionally, the majority of Samui's visitors have been young Europeans seeking out quiet places in the sun—girls with top-knots, boys with dangly earrings, eager to undress and to unwind. (Most of the heads one sees here are blond.) Many of the island's facilities still flaunt their ironies, and their countercultural defi-ance of all bourgeois comfort. The Swiss Country Club is a se-ries of tiny huts, and World Bungalows offers "the Great World Tourist Information Center." One little shack calls itself the Beverly Hills Café, and the Hilton Garden Resort is no misnomer if you delete the first word, and the last.

> *Impermanent are all conditioned things. Unsatisfactory are all conditioned things. Not-self are all conditioned things. This is the Dhamma taught by the Buddha.*
>
> —Tim Ward,
> *What the Buddha Never Taught*

But as Thailand has become the leading tourist hot spot of Southeast Asia—the number of its annual visitors surging from one million to five million in just five years—Hilton hotels do not seem so implausible. The Danish couple's parents can now stay just around the bay from their children in a resort like the Tongsai Bay Hotel, whose red-roofed, white-stuccoed Mediterranean villas are scattered across a hillside thick with brilliant orchids and hibiscus. Everything is silent save the chirping of a bird. One could almost believe oneself in some sunlit pocket of Sardinia, except that every detail here is touched with the lovely Thai gift for design. Silver salvers of fruit—lichees, melon, and papaya—in every room, with flower scented finger bowls. Clusters of flowers streaming out of sea blue pots, and fresh asparagus for breakfast. Mandarin orange juice that tastes as if it just fell off a tree in Eden. A book of Buddhist proverbs by one's bed. And, on every side, the supple courtesy of slow-moving sylphs waiting to cater to one's every need.

Everything the Thais touch, they turn to seduction, and Tongsai Bay, with its scarlet tropical umbrellas and its cool wicker chairs, is graced with all the country's vaunted sense of elegance.

The main problem with Samui, in fact, is simply that it is so paradisiacal—and that it is the nature of human nature to wish to discover and develop paradise. (The Thais, moreover, are particularly adept at marketing their charms.) Thus, the poor man's utopia is fast becoming a Burgermeister's dream—the "German Riviera," a friend of mine calls it—and one can almost see Samui develop before one's eyes, as quickly as the photos at the 23-Minute Film Center in Na Thon.

> *I*n Thai, the third person singular or plural that can be used for farangs or other nationalities, is mun, "it." It's not, "he" or "she," "his," or "hers," or "they." It's "it" the whole time. When we talk Thai and we want to refer to you in the third person, we call you "it."
>
> —Kukrit Pramoj,
> *Kukrit Pramoj: His Wit and Wisdom*

Already parts of the island are awash in banners advertising new reggae bars, fancy discos, or "Kick in the Bollocks" cocktails (two for the price of one), and the stillness of the coconut groves is broken round the clock by the relentless sound of drills and banging hammers. And already the island's two busiest strips of beach—at Chaweng and Lamai—are bristling with beer gardens, V.D. clinics, and "cobra shows." Amenities are beginning to take the place of pleasures. Whole clusters of bars are cropping up each week with typically insouciant Thai names (No Problem, Good Friend, Why Not?) and a surplus of young girls on hand. And at night, amid palm trees strung with lights, restaurants vie for customers by showing "V.D.O.s" such as *Mutant on the Bounty*. (Hardly had *Batman* hit the screen than a high-tech new singles bar was bouncing up, all in fluorescent green and purple neon, called the Bat Cave.)

"Last year $6, this year $60," exults a local sharpie, handing out cabana brochures and insisting *"nicht so teuer"* ("not so expensive") to some German tourists off the boat. "Next year $150. Everyone much change. Before, family-style. Now, better service, clean room! Air-condition!"

It is precisely that intimation of the Ghost of Samui Future that is sending more and more visitors, these days, to the neighboring island of Ko Phangan. Phangan is still Samui five years ago, and four times cheaper. There is no airport yet, and electricity only in the evenings (from 5:30 till 11, they say, but you wouldn't want to set your digital clock by it). Where the bungalows in Samui these days boast upscale, Miami Beach names—Tropicana, Coconut Grove, Casanova's—those on Phangan are still called Sun Dance, Moonlight, Half Moon, Green Peace, Sea Flower, and Serenity Hill. In Samui the ad hoc signs for pub crawls are nailed to trees; in Phangan the notices for full moon parties are simply painted on the bark in happy children's pastels.

Phangan, therefore, is still a place where time moves slowly, and girls weave baskets in the shade. Water buffalo leading wooden carts pad placidly along the sea, and children engage in languorous games of badminton (without any nets). In the distance is the faint tinkle of temple bells. A little boy sports a t-shirt—apt, for once—that assures, "I may be slow, but I'm good." In Phangan I slept for four dollars a night in a bungalow supplied with two pillows decorated with pigs, rhinos, and elephants, and the slogan, "Let's Go Now." When I wanted to go to town to post a letter, I hitched a lazy ride on a fisherman's boat, and then on the back of one of the motorbikes that serve as the island's taxis.

Phangan is a place for aimless wandering. Monkeys hop and skitter across the paths. Gnomic chunks of wisdom adorn the trees. ("Do not stare too close at a buffalo ear-hole.") People leave messages on bulletin boards that say, "Sorry I couldn't communicate very well. I wasn't really 'awake' the whole time I was on the island."

Follow a steep path, up and up, around a hill, and you come upon a whole group of cottages at the tip, and top, of the cape, the ocean on three sides. Down below, the hidden Lighthouse Bungalow has an entire beach to itself, a slow, empty place, where ponytailed fathers, naked, lead their toddlers by the hand at sunset, and two-tone lizards slither through the grass. Nothing seems to stir here. One hut contains a shower, one hut a meditation center. That is just about all.

Not surprisingly, perhaps, this charmed tropical forest is quickly being colonized by hippies—or, at least by that moveable feast of global villagers always on the lookout for the next ideal. Many of them stay here for a month, or year, and already their loose, free-floating community has begun to set up its polyglot amenities—iced Ovaltine, the finest pastries this side of Nepal, chimichangas, and nut casseroles. Explanations of the chakras hang from trees, next to ads for "Tai Ch'i Shoes—7 different kinds available." Bare-chested longhairs sit in cafés, sipping lemongrass tea and reading Krishnamurti, *The Magus,* even Ovid. And every afternoon in a clearing near the beach, there is a kind of tribal gathering, and everyone—iridologists, turquoise jewelers, Dead Head jugglers, and musicians—gathers in a swirl of beads and bangles to trade rare goods and tales. Phangan is the place where the dreadlocked Swede who used to play Dylan songs on the streets of Kyoto ended up, along with the shaven-headed shiatsu girl from Angola.

Ko Phangan is not, then everyone's cup of herbal tea, but it does offer the gentlest and least intrusive life imaginable: an Indian Summer of Love. And there are worse things to do than just sit in one of the restaurants serving "no name with vegetables," and take in the passing scene. Tanned Israeli soldiers talk of the *intifada,* from which they have just come, while white-robed nuns shine with an unnatural glow.

Trust fund dropouts from the Upper East Side discuss Kali and Long Island, and meditating matrons from Montreal pull out the envelopes on which their short-time German boyfriends drew nude pictures. Brits sit back and take it all in sardonically.

At night bleary-eyed blonds with silly smiles recline on cushions around a low table, munching "special mushroom" omelettes and looking at one another dreamily. What do you do for a living? I asked an Aussie girl. "Oh, I sell battery-operated panda bears on the streets of Tokyo," she said carelessly. "Set up a couple of speakers, put on some Milli Vanilli, wave the bears about, collect $300 a night."

Ko Phangan is not, thankfully, all peace, love, and understanding; it is, in a sense, too unspoiled for that. One golden twilight, as I wandered from the sunrise to the sunset beach, I saw a huge circle of men gathered on a hillside shouting and screaming and howling.

I wandered closer, and began to guess what was going on when I saw other shifty men squatting around the hill, cradling cocks.

Closer still, around the cockfight itself, everything was a frenzy of waving and shouting and urging. Rarely have I seen so rough and wild a scene. Men with the red eyes of lifetime bong smokers, men so old their cheeks were sunken, men with evil scars across their cheeks. A reek of Singha beer. The fighting cocks pecking one another like angry lovers, while a fat man in shorts with a gold pen, and a thick gold bracelet, waddled around, calling out for bets.

A whistle blew, the keepers grabbed their birds and ran, furiously, to a clearing. The crowd followed in a disheveled mass. The guardians set their fighters on the ground, swabbed them frantically, poked feathers in their ears and down their throats, smoothed their wings with the attentive care of Porsche owners. Elegant women sat on wooden benches waiting for the next fight.

But soon the darkness fell again, and the moon was silvering the sea. Wind chimes sang across the dark. The sound of a guitar carried from a distant beach. In the soft tropical breeze the island was so tranquil, so transporting that one hardly need consult the fortune-teller who sits in the shade of Samui's Big Buddha to know that as soon as Samui is full, people will be talking of Ko Phangan, and then, and then…why not?

Pico Iyer also contributed "Love in a Duty-free Zone" to Part One.

✳

Thais give *farang* a wide berth, as one might a large muddy dog.
　　　　　—Charles Nicholl, *Borderlines: A Journey in Thailand and Burma*

JOHN HOSKIN

⋆ ⋆ ⋆

The Alms Bowl Village

*Saffron-robed monks with their alms bowls constitute
one of the most enduring images of Thailand.*

ALMS BOWLS, INTO WHICH PEOPLE HEAP RICE AND OTHER FOOD
offerings, are quintessential to the daily rituals of monkhood, virtual extensions to the monk's body. They are not begging bowls,
for the monk does not beg, rather in accepting alms he is allowing
the giver to make merit, a crucial concern in Buddhism.

One of the eight material possessions permitted a monk, the
alms bowl has been hand crafted for many centuries. Today machine production has largely taken over, though in one tiny corner of Bangkok the forging of bowls clings tenuously to the old
traditions. Tucked away in a tumbled down area off Bamrung
Muang Road, between Chinatown and the Golden Mount, is
Baan Baat, meaning literally "alms bowl village." Here an interre-
lated group of half a dozen families continue to produce hand-
made bowls.

Baan Baat is a throwback to the old days before Bangkok began
its metropolitan sprawl, when areas of the capital were designed
largely by the occupations they housed. Such identities have long
since vanished and Baan Baat is now an anomaly. It is scarcely a
quaint spot and by no means a picturesque one in its untidy
huddle of corrugated iron shanties nestling amid piles of rubble.

Only the lines of washing strung out to dry on bamboo poles lend a splash of colour to the otherwise drab scene.

Yet in this improbable location a score or so workers carry on the trade their ancestors established more than a hundred years ago. It was in the mid-19th century, during the reign of King Mongkut, Rama IV, that earthenware alms bowls, which were easily broken, began to be replaced by more durable metal ones. The new, stronger type of bowl quickly became popular and Baan Baat became established, flourishing as Bangkok's major supplier. Today it is the capital's only source of handmade metal alms bowls, though business has fallen sharply in decline in recent years.

In its heyday the "village" numbered about 100 families all engaged in the craft and the average production was some 400–500 bowls a day. Now the output is not even one-tenth of that. Nevertheless, all else remains much as it always has been and the handful of craftsmen—and women—presently working keep alive the cottage industry, performing the same tasks and using basically the same tools as their ancestors. It provides a living—just.

Alms bowls are commonly made out of steel (the brass lids are not produced at Baan Baat)

The rules governing the use and care of bowls were extensive and sometimes strange. Still, one could easily imagine the human foibles which led to the creation of these rules.

A monk must not look inside another monk's bowl.

A monk must not cover up the curry in his bowl with rice to make it appear he hasn't been given any curry.

A monk must not scrape the inside of his bowl with his fingernails.

A monk should not leave his bowl near a ledge or on the edge of a table.

A monk should not leave his bowl where it may be kicked.

The majority of these rules reflected a time when bowls were made of clay, not metal. A single moment of carelessness could produce unpleasant changes in such transitory and unstable objects. The Ajahn explained, however, that although the modern bowls could not be broken, the rules have been maintained so monks can develop mindfulness.

—Tim Ward, *What the Buddha Never Taught*

and, following long-held Buddhist principles, are comprised of eight separate pieces hammered and welded together. Thin strips are cut from sheet metal and beaten into curves. One long strip forms the bowl's base and curls up at either end to make the beginnings of the sides. Six other pieces complete the body of the bowl while an eighth is looped to form the rim.

Each segment is beaten and curved over a ball-shaped anvil attached to a short stem stuck in the ground; it looks curiously like a half-buried dumbbell. Shaded under crude corrugated iron shelters, these anvils mushroom around Baan Baat's working area to give the place its characteristic trademark.

In the fashioning of the metal strips teeth are cut along the edges so that the pieces can be interlocked and hammered together. Copper granules mixed up with a paste are then glued along these rough joins. After the bowl has been buried in a wood fire for a few minutes the copper melts, welding the joins in a rather crude yet effective fashion.

Craftsmen next hammer the squarish form to produce the bowl's rounded shape. The surface is then filed to give a smooth finish. Finally several coats of lacquer are applied and the bowl placed in a low heat fire to give it a black glaze. The entire process takes one person one day to complete.

Alms bowls at Baan Baat come in various sizes, though the standard models have diameters of seven to nine inches. Occasionally monster pieces with 24-inch diameters are made for holding sacred water at temples, though these are special orders. The finished products sell for 150-400 baht, depending on size and the quality of metal used. That compares to a cost of 40-70 baht for a machine-made bowl. Profit margins, however, are low and with the rising price of metal, production costs can be 75 percent or more of the selling price.

From Baan Baat the alms bowls are sold to retailers in the Sao Chingcha district which has long been the centre for shops specializing in the objects and offerings employed in Buddhist rites.

As with all arts and crafts in Thailand, alms bowl making has a *wai kru* ceremony in which the people of Baan Baat pay their respects to the leader of their community and to the spirits of past craftsmen. The ritual is held every year in April and, by tradition, always on a Thursday when for one day at least, the "village" assumes something of the vibrant atmosphere that must have typified it in more prosperous times.

The present 80-year-old elder of the community leads the ritual and presides over prayers at the spirit house. The villagers then gather to pay their respects while the old man acknowledges the gesture by placing a daub of fragrant paste on their foreheads. Traditional Thai dancers perform at the main spirit house and food offerings are made to the little individual shrines in each worker's home. Typically these spirit houses are made out of a pair of bellows used in forging. Adding a festive air to the scene are the pretty little flower garlands incongruously draped over the tools of the trade.

On a normal day Baan Baat is scarcely a hive of activity and production is carried out at a leisurely pace. How long it can continue is uncertain. "Most have just given up," commented the chairman of the Almsbowl Association of Thailand in a local newspaper article. "Many of the dealers at Sao Chingcha who used to be our patrons have turned to the mass-produced bowls. Cheapness aside, the alms bowl mass-producers offer a better deal by giving a few months' credit, while we ask for prompt cash."

He added that the days of Baan Baat were surely numbered. "Without a definite market in sight, we people around here, one after another, are just saying goodbye to this profession. The younger generation goes out seeking day labouring jobs to make ends meet."

The half-dozen craftsmen working when I visited Baan Baat on a Saturday morning were more optimistic. They proudly explained how hand-made bowls were of better quality and lasted longer than the mass-produced items. Because of this, they claimed, their products still found a market. While young men entering the monkhood only temporarily might choose the cheaper factory made bowls, the hand-crafted products were preferred by full-time monks, especially those belonging to the stricter Thammayut sect, founded by King Mongkut.

It is hard to say how genuine this optimism was, as mixed in with forthcoming answers to questions about the craft's process and background was a less than subtle sales pitch. Indeed, a few of the bowls are now and again sold as souvenir items and anyone passing nearby Baan Baat is likely to be invited in to take a look.

This could account for the optimism. "We are not worried about the future," said one bowl-maker. "We make enough money and there is a new generation coming up to carry on the craft. It's okay; people today are more aware, more appreciative of handicrafts."

There is no doubt that hand-made alms bowls are in danger of vanishing completely as factory products corner more and more of the market, and Baan Baat is now certainly a very pale shadow of its former self. But there is optimism and one hopes that it isn't ill-founded.

John Hoskin is a writer who lives in Bangkok.

★

I remember the Ajahn's warning never to speak to the givers of food. Once in the past a *farang* novice actually thanked a woman for a handful of rice. She was so offended she came to the monastery and told the senior monk she and her family would never give alms to the *wat* again. Devotees give to the robe, not to the wearer. They believe it is a ritual for the making of merit, for a better rebirth. If a monk thanks the giver, then by treating it as a personal favour, merit is not gained.

—Tim Ward, *What the Buddha Never Taught*

SOPHIA DEMBLING

✦ ✦ ✦

Take to the Hills

While trekking the hills and visiting hill
tribes have become commonplace,
the experience hasn't.

I KNEW, BEYOND A DOUBT, THAT WE WERE SOMEPLACE ELSE WHEN they killed the pig.

Our host grabbed it by a leg and, as it squealed with fear and pain, bludgeoned it with a piece of firewood. Then, holding its snout closed with one hand, he stepped on the hapless creature's throat until it suffocated.

This was to be our dinner.

This was not an adventure for the faint-hearted.

Our trek into the primitive villages of Thailand's hill tribes had started earlier that day in Mae Hong Son, a small, pleasant resort town near the border between Thailand and Burma (which now calls itself Myanmar).

For three days and two nights, my companion, Mary, and I would leave behind showers, plumbing, electricity, and *farang* life. We would be completely dependent on our guide, Jack Saw, a member of the Karen tribe, as we explored the world of the hills.

Six hill tribes—Karen, Lisu, Lahu, Akha, Yao, and Hmong— have populated the Thai hills for the past 300 years. Each has its own language, customs, crafts, costumes, and beliefs. While there are Buddhists and Christians among them, most are animists and believe in spirits. Many aren't even Thai; they came over the mountains to escape Burma's oppressive government. It is a complex subculture, existing on the outskirts of modern life.

In just one day, we traveled far from picturesque Mae Hong Son and far from our very first Lisu village where a beautiful girl, perhaps twenty years old in a bright tribal costume waits for tourists to take her picture; an elderly woman stitches up brightly colored wristbands and purses to sell; and children know enough English to beg tourists "Five baht?"

The girl, says an obviously smitten Jack, is a "first-class girl"— both beautiful and a hard worker. Jack, a middle-aged widower, would gladly marry her if he could afford the 30,000 baht (about $1,200) her hand would cost him.

But after this village, the truck in which we're riding drops us off in a grim, dirt patch of a town—devastated by heroin, Jack informs us, and now controlled by the army—and we continue our trek on foot.

Our destination is the Red Lahu village where tribes will congregate this week to celebrate the new year. There will be music, dancing, and whiskey, says Jack.

But first, there is the climb. It is March, the beginning of the hot season. The thickly forested hills are tinged with brown. Wearing sneakers and hiking boots, carrying day packs with clean socks and underwear, fresh water, and some toiletries, we can barely keep up with Jack, who traipses along in an army jacket and flip-flops.

When we stop to admire the long, rolling view, he points out mountains that mark the border of Burma, the site of years of fighting between the Burmese and the Thais.

Between feeding us information about the area, Jack tells us stories of *farang* who have been robbed, raped, or murdered on treks. It is difficult to know how to react except to silently assure myself that I could easily hurt him—as with most of the people of Thailand, he is small and delicate.

After a couple of hours, hot, tired, and wearing the red dirt of the hills, we reach the village, a collection of wood-and-bamboo huts on stilts. Pigs, chickens, and threatening-looking dogs roam untethered. Small horses are tied up in the shade under the huts. Children—runny-nosed all—stare as we pass.

Jack brings us to our hosts' home, a tidy hut where we are served much-welcome hot tea brewed over a fire built in sand in the main room. It is dark and almost cool inside. The bamboo mats on which we will sleep are in one corner. In another is a shrine to the house spirits, a high platform with strips of pork and colored streamers. Sunlight filters through slits in the woven walls.

We drink our tea, lulled by the sounds of the animals—nosing about in the muddy puddles that form under every porch, where dishes are dumped and washed—and the voices of men discussing who-knows-what in their unfamiliar tongue. The family goes about its business tending the fire, children, and animals.

We take a walk around the village. Compared with others, the hut in which we are staying seems to indicate relative affluence, and our host's children are far cleaner than many of those who clamor to look through the viewfinder of my camera.

It is shortly after we return to the hut that the pig is killed. Our host—his lips stained black with the betel nut that many like to chew—walks around the rest of the afternoon with dried pig blood up to his elbows.

Thailand's hill tribes are sometimes described as peaceful people living in idyllic harmony with nature—something of a forgotten Shangri-La—but nothing could be further from the truth. Most are extremely poor and live in dirty wooden shacks without running water, adequate sanitation, medical facilities, or educational opportunities for their children. Illiteracy, disease, opium addiction, and deforestation are other problems. Uncontrolled erosion and soil depletion have reduced crop yields while land, once plentiful and rich, has become scarce due to tribal overpopulation and the arrival of land-hungry lowlanders. Royal aid projects provide help and encourage alternative cash crops to opium, but tribal political power remains minimal since tribespeople are stateless wanderers, not Thai citizens.

—Carl Parkes,
Thailand Handbook

After whispered consultation we tell Jack, apologetically, that we don't eat pork. We do not tell him that we are afraid of becoming ill from meat prepared under such unsanitary conditions. He is flustered—he no doubt bought the pig and had it slaughtered for us—but fixes us a vegetarian meal.

Firecrackers have crackled all day in anticipation of the night's festivities. After dark, the party begins in a central spot in the village. It centers around a lantern-lighted altar decorated with streamers and three pig heads. Around this, the villagers dance to a tune in a minor key played on a multi-tone flute—the same dance to the same tune around and around and around. Occasionally, someone grabs a drum and beats on that.

The village headmen are young and solemn. One has an infant in a sling around his body. A little away from the dancing, men pass around the whiskey. The dance becomes more spirited as the whiskey is consumed.

New year's celebrations are very important to young men and women of marriageable age. Jack enjoys teasing two girls, fourteen and fifteen years old, who are dressed in colorful finery, their china-doll faces made up, their expressions solemn as they dance. They are ripe for marriage, as are many of the young men growing sloppy on whiskey.

We watch a while, then return to our hut to sleep. In the distance, the flute plays its mournful tune as the dancing continues into the night.

I wake early the next morning and lie quietly, watching our host's daughter start the day's fire on the wood stove, put a pot of rice up to steam, and scrub the wood floor of the hut with a damp rag. "The all-purpose rag," Mary and I call it, as it is used to wipe noses, faces, hands, floors, and feet. The flute music, which stopped for a while overnight, resumes.

When he awakes—with a hangover—Jack reveals that a dog bit him on the leg in the middle of the night. Our host has tied a piece of string around his wrist to ward off illness, but Jack seems skeptical. He accepts a bottle of antiseptic I offer. Still, he does not remove the string.

When our host family sees the medicine, they offer sores, fungal infections, and wounds for me to treat. I swab them all with the over-the-counter antiseptic. It is probably a futile gesture. Then I give one woman a gift of sewing thread, needles, and safety pins, which she carefully distributes among the other women gathered.

After breakfast and a wash in the communal spigot—shared with children hauling water to their huts—we press on.

We pass fields farmed by the Lahu village. All the tribes subsist on "slash and burn" farming, cutting down and burning the natural vegetation to clear the fields. When the soil is depleted, the tribe moves on.

Poppies are the tribes' primary cash crop. Some grow but don't smoke the opium, others do both. While opium addiction is a problem, says Jack, the introduction of its derivative, heroin, has been more devastating yet. A joint Thai-German government project encourages the tribes to grow other crops, but no mere vegetable can bring in anything near the profit that a good poppy harvest can.

Jack gathers a few poppies and cuts some slits in a seed pod from which a thick, white sap oozes. This is opium. We look but don't touch.

We hike through bamboo groves and teak forests and up to mountaintops. There is no point in taking photographs. The exotic, virgin beauty will not fit into 35mm. It is the scenery that begets religion.

Finally, we arrive at Jack's village, where his children live with his elderly in-laws and where he lived with his wife until her death, three years ago, from asthma. His father-in-law once was the village headman, and his hut is large, the main room is built entirely of smooth, dark teak.

This is a larger village than the last. It has a school and even a small store where we are able to buy warm bottled water and Coca-Cola.

But we are hot and tired and the combination of these factors, the strangeness of the adventure, and the barrage of primitive conditions, runny-nosed children, and squalor has started to wear on Mary and me. We sit on the porch, trying to smile at a filthy young woman, a dirty towel wrapped around her head, one dirty breast exposed, and her toddler daughter, also grubby and without pants.

And suddenly, we are overwhelmed.

We walk down to the river to wash. As we try to scrub the tenacious red dirt from our clothes, we decide to tell Jack that we're ready to go back, we have had enough.

But it is too late, he says. It's an hour's walk to the nearest town and the last bus leaves in 30 minutes.

We cannot face the porch again, so we sit down on a tree root in the packed-earth chicken yard.

And, rather than cry, we laugh.

We laugh about the pig and about the all-purpose rag and about mucus, which has become a recurring theme. We laugh at my white cotton shirt streaked with red dust, and our dirt-caked feet. We laugh at the grubby rice cake that Mary tasted when a little girl handed it to her the night before. When she handed it back, the girl threw it forcefully to the ground, indicating that *she* certainly wouldn't have nibbled the nasty thing.

We laugh at ourselves, two giant (to the villagers) *farang* sitting in the chicken yard laughing like loons.

We laugh until tears run down our faces and we are short of breath. And then we feel better.

As the sun starts to set, we join Jack's mother-in-law at the window of the hut to admire the peaceful view. She hawks and spits out the window. We do not laugh, although we want to.

Jack cooks us a chicken curry. He kills and plucks the bird, chops it up—bones and all—and throws it into the pot with savory seasonings. At each meal, he prepares far more food than the two of us can eat. It is probably intentional. Our hosts finish what we cannot.

We sit on the floor to eat and the children gather around us. I distribute several small boxes of crayons and drawing pads, and the children pounce, a semicircle of little, shiny black heads. They draw furiously while we watch.

A couple of older girls tell us the children's names and write them in Thai. They all make us gifts of drawings of flowers and houses and people, textured with the same kind of elaborate and complex patterns that decorate Thailand's temples.

Then Jack's little daughter and a bashful friend get up and sing and dance for us, their little hands like birds fluttering in the air.

Thank goodness we didn't leave.

The night is excruciatingly uncomfortable. The bamboo mats are hard and it is cold.

In the morning, we sit with the family around the stove, like *farang* families gather around the breakfast table.

Later, returning to the hut after washing up, we pass the village's three monks, walking single file on their way to the village's Buddhist homes for their food. They stop at one house and stand silently in a row as a little girl comes out, bows, and scoops rice into each of their bowls. Then they march on to the next house.

When it is time to leave, we shoulder our packs again and start trekking down the road. Just when we think we are too hot and tired to take another step, a truck comes along and we hop in the back with a group of Lahu boys on their way to town to buy whiskey for the coming night's new year's celebration.

The truck takes us to the town of Soppong, where we catch the bus back to Mae Hong Son, which now seems like a bustling city.

The day after returning to the United States from Thailand, I went out for breakfast in a suburban restaurant. Surrounded by women in makeup and tight jeans, men in sweatsuits, and plates laden with food, I knew—without a doubt—that I was Someplace Else again.

Sophia Dembling was born and raised in New York City, but at age nineteen discovered life west of the Hudson. She is a freelance writer who lives in Dallas and is the former assistant travel editor of The Dallas Morning News.

*

I spent four months working as a volunteer with the Karen tribe. I learned to speak their language and now know how they feel about tourism.

The Karen people already feel odd when they visit their local towns because they are so different from most Thais. When outsiders trek through their villages they feel even worse. The older Karens feel that this affects the young badly. They think it makes them start to see it as being "backward"; they want to have Western clothing and music in their villages; they may want to leave their Karen village to seek other lifestyles; they may try to copy what the Karen elders see as foreigners' "immoral" behavior.

Whatever the faults of organized tours, it seems that they are better than do-it-yourself tours as the Karen elders in a "trek village" can control the influence of the foreigners. They can also choose which parts of their culture to show.

The Karen people are very private and are likely to retreat when they see foreigners. They feel strongly about the way people dress, so travelers should not wear skimpy clothing when trekking.

—Jay Griffiths, Letter to the Editor, *Great Expeditions*

JEFF GREENWALD

✦ ✦ ✦

In the Andaman Sea

From tree houses in childhood to secret beaches in adulthood,
we all dream of hideaways. Phang Nga Bay's limestone
towers conceal such special places.

IT WAS THE TIME OF YEAR WHEN, ABOUT TO RUN OUT OF THOSE little soaps they give you in big hotels, I sensed I was due for another trip. Indeed, no sooner had the final sliver of "Jardins des Figues" disappeared down the drain than the telephone rang, bearing an invitation to visit the Kingdom of Thailand.

Two weeks later I was peering out the window of a jet—watching the surface of Phuket Island resolve from a hazy green mass into a welcoming landscape of palm trees and preparing, by way of the ocean, to get enviably clean.

This was my first visit to Phuket (pronounced Poo-ket) in nearly a decade. Memories of deserted beaches, Technicolor sunsets, and bath-warm waters beguiled me as I collected my luggage at Phuket International Airport. The island would have seen some changes, naturally, over the years; the huge airport, with its fifteen incoming flights a day, was certainly one of them. The others, I hoped, would be far less obvious.

Dense traffic between the airport and the southwest coast of Phuket quickly dispelled that notion. I sat riveted to my seat, barely able to watch as my shuttle bus to Karon Beach joined in a game of high-speed cat-and-mouse.

We finally arrived at my hotel, where a wave of *déjà vu* assailed me. Seven years ago, I had stood on the very same beach, watching a crimson sunset over Koh Poo, a pretty offshore island. Back then the locals were jumpy; Club Med had just announced plans to build a resort on the unspoiled crescent of beach. "I wonder," my traveling companion had remarked, "what this place will look like in ten years?"

Now I knew. Four huge luxury hotels had shouldered their way between the trees, and the beach was lined with chaises longues and umbrellas. Club Med, ironically, was the most tasteful resort of the lot: nestled into the southern corner of the beach, it was the only one that had made a bow to traditional architecture.

Fortunately, Karon Beach was to be no more than a base. What had brought me here, to the edge of the Andaman Sea, was the desire to immerse myself in Phuket's bath-warm waters. True, the land holds infinite diversions: an endless profusion of shops, bars, video arcades, and boutiques lined the Kata/Karon corniche, and the availability of short- or long-term "girlfriends" in this part of Thailand is legendary—if not notorious. But I wanted to spend my week developing an intimate relationship with the ocean; and Phuket offers some of the world's most popular water sports. It didn't take me long, however, to narrow the field.

> *Thinking about my yearnings and wantings, I recalled vividly the day at Wat Sraket when my teacher had pointed out that monks don't paint, write great novels, compose music, or create movie extravaganzas because these are forms of cravings or wantings. It was difficult for me to understand that writing a book was a craving, particularly when being creative was a coveted trait in Western society.*
>
> —Jane Hamilton-Merritt,
> *A Meditator's Diary*

Swimming, for example, would probably not be much of an adventure; Phuket has few sharks. And I happened to be among those who believe that all jet skis should be gathered into a pile, doused with gasoline, and burned. Parasailing, or whatever it's called, where they haul you into the air behind a boat, does not qualify as a water sport, since direct contact with the water's surface generally means that your ride, or your life, is over.

There remained, then, only two possibilities: sea canoeing in Phang Nga Bay and scuba diving at the Similan Islands.

"We're an expedition company that takes guests," John Gray, director of Phuket Sea Canoe Center, warned as he greeted me at the dock at Pho Bay. "We don't do white sand beaches."

Gray, 47, stood about 6-feet-2 in sandals and salmon-pink shorts. His long hair, reddish-blond and streaked with gray, was harnessed into a pony tail. Preparing for our trip he was assisted by Wanda: a large, bald, tattooed, and completely intimidating fellow who looked like Mr. Clean, but meaner.

"He's actually a beautiful guy," John assured me. "He's done all kinds of stuff. Even been in films; he played the heavy in *Sheeba: Queen of the Jungle.*"

Gray has his own story. He once lived in Hawaii, where he worked as the communications director for a cancer research center. "The great thing about working in Hawaii," he confided, "was that I didn't have to wear a tie."

Ten years ago he threw out his shirts as well. Gray started his sea canoe company in Oahu in 1983, established a branch in Polynesia, and is now gaining steam in Thailand and Vietnam. The thrust of the operation is different in each venue. In Thailand, he delights in taking his high-tech rubber canoes into *hongs:* open-air chambers (*hong* means "room" in Thai) hidden deep within the small islands of Phang Nga Bay. "The definition of a *hong*," John said, "is that you're surrounded, 360 degrees, by solid rock." Created by erosion and other natural forces, these *hongs* are accessible only through narrow, cave-like passageways that open and close with the tides—often in a matter of minutes.

Phang Nga Bay is one of the most beautiful spots in Thailand. Located in a crook of the Malay Peninsula, about 60 miles northeast of Phuket, the bay holds some 160 rock islands that jut out of the Andaman Sea at heights ranging from tens to hundreds of feet. Imagine those famous Chinese landscape paintings of Guilin, with their knobby, mist–ringed hills, and transplant that scenery onto the surface of the ocean. It's an astonishing sight.

By late morning we had arrived in Phang Nga Bay and anchored our mother boat—the *Ol' Lady*—near the cliffs of Koh Panak. After a miraculous lunch of spicy prawn soup, grilled fish, ginger vegetables, and Thai-style noodles with chili and chicken—all prepared, somehow, on the boat's single-burner stove—John supervised the lowering of the canoes. I'd expected that I would paddle my own; but the difficulty and danger of rowing into the *hongs* is a job for experts. I clambered into a bright yellow canoe, joined by a young Thai oarsman named Sadik.

As we approached Koh Panak, the island's architecture amazed me. It is a huge knob of limestone, freckled with trees and shrubs. The base—where island meets sea—is napped, like the back of a neck, and the overhang is draped with bizarre, drippy rock formations. I could see no entrance until Sadik turned the canoe and steered it directly toward an impossibly low cavern.

"You better duck," he advised. I lay straight back, hands clasped over my chest like a mummy in an Egyptian barque. The ceiling of the cavern—covered with razor-sharp, calcified oyster shells—passed inches above my nose. And then I clamped my eyes shut, because the sun was directly overhead.

We had emerged into the Land That Time Forgot: a dreamy, other worldly environment where the only sounds were the distant squeal of birds and the slow sloshing of our oars in the warm water. The sun bounced off the emerald water throwing Laserium patterns on the sheer stone walls. Mangrove trees rose up from the *hong's* sand floor, their roots tangled above the waterline like wooden webs. Sadik lifted the oars, and the silence was total—until I heard a low, beating sound to my right. It was a butterfly in flight.

An hour later, back on the *Ol' Lady,* the mood was one of subdued reverence. We sat at the dining table and listened, over horrible coffee, to John Gray's philosophy of life.

"My lifelong challenge has been—How do you improve the standard of living in Third World countries while maintaining ecological and cultural integrity?"

For John, of course, the answer is Sea Canoe: an environmentally savvy company that will ultimately be handed over to local owners. "I own only twenty percent of Sea Canoe," he said. "And I get outvoted at meetings all the time." When I asked for an example, he pointed to my cup. "Nescafé," he apologized. "I wanted drip coffee, but the others vetoed me."

At first, Gray recalled, Thai businessmen thought he was nuts. The only market they saw was for high impact tourist sports, or organized tours of the bay (one of Phang Nga's little islands was featured as a solar collector in *The Man with the Golden Gun,* and tourists throng to see this "James Bond island"). But Gray thinks Sea Canoe proves that a small, ecologically sound company can succeed, and he believes the trend will catch on.

Destruction of coral reefs is a great concern. Some are destroyed to facilitate swimming, and in the south of Thailand coral reefs are being blasted with home-made bombs by fishermen bent on an easy catch. As the coastline becomes fished out, the local fishermen have turned into boatmen and tour guides. The towns, meanwhile, have to cope with serious garbage problems—the collection services cannot handle increased garbage output. What is not collected is strewn around the communities, the beaches, or even in the water.

*—Michael Buckley,
Bangkok Handbook*

"I'd love to see the day," he said with a grin, "when Bangkok businessmen want to build a sea canoe instead of a jet ski factory."

Over the next two days we explored a dozen more *hongs,* carefully monitoring the tides. Each *hong* has its own window, a moment in time when the water level is low enough to allow a canoe through its entrance, but high enough so as not to expose a jagged bottom of scalpel-like stones and shells.

The *hongs* themselves differ in subtle ways. Some are virtually bare, like wells; others are full of bushes, mangrove trees, hanging vines, butterflies, and lizards that scamper across sand bars like overwound toys. There are monkeys living in some of the *hongs,* but we didn't see any. My favorite *hong* was more like a canyon than a room; we navigated a long, winding "river" through a deep gorge, where brilliant kingfishers flitted between the vertiginous walls.

For the climax of our sea canoe trip, John—tirelessly active—organized a night excursion into one of the *hongs*. It was nearly midnight before the tides were exactly right; then we crept into our canoes and paddled, with powerful flashlights, through a womb-like passageway into the preternatural stillness of the *hong*. It was magical. Above our heads, a circle of stars glimmered in the blackness: the water sparkled with phosphorescent plankton. It was perfectly, absolutely quiet.

I thought I heard a low, snarling sound. It grew in intensity, becoming a growl and suddenly a terrible roar. It stopped for a moment and then started again, echoing off the walls of the *hong*.

John Gray lay sprawled in his canoe like a beached seal, snoring at the top of his lungs.

Jeff Greenwald also contributed "Bite-sized Buddhas" and "The Burning Hills" to this book.

★

Phuket's terrain is incredibly varied, with rocky beaches, long, broad, sandy beaches, limestone cliffs, forested hills, and tropical vegetation of all kinds. Great seafood is available all over the island and several offshore islands are known for good snorkeling and scuba diving.

Comparisons with Ko Samui, off the east coast, as well as with other Thai islands, are inevitable, of course. All in all, there is more to do in Phuket, but that means more to spend your money on, too. There are more tourists in Phuket but they are concentrated at certain beaches—Patong and Kata, for example. Beaches like Nai Han and Karon are relatively quiet, in spite of major tourist development at both. Ko Samui is gradually starting to develop along Phuket lines but the feel of the two islands is different—Samui is much further out in the sea and as such gives one more a feeling of adventure than Phuket, which is connected to the mainland by a bridge.

—Joe Cummings, *Thailand - a travel survival kit*

SIMON WINCHESTER

* * *

Relics of Old Siam

In the much-visited ruins of Ayuthaya,
the former Thai capital, there is
a place most day-visitors miss.

FOUR HOURS UP RIVER FROM BANGKOK ON THE CHAO PHYA river—or perhaps sixty minutes, if you decide to risk your life in one of those pencil-slim, water-borne Concordes currently favored by Thailand's gondoliers—lies a most spectacular ruin, much visited but very little known. Ayuthaya was the capital of Siam for more than four centuries—from 1350 until 1767, when the Burmese sacked it and trampled everyone to pieces with their elephant cavalry. Now it is one of the great ruins of Asia, and as such it appears in all the tourist leaflets and is as obligatory a stop on a tour of Central Thailand as the Wat Arun or a live show in Patpong II.

But hardly anyone spends time in Ayuthaya. Each day, after luncheon, the great white boats from Bangkok slide up to the landing stages at Bang pa-In to disgorge their invading armies of package tourists, and at dusk the *charabancs* growl away with them in full retreat, leaving the old capital once more silent and deserted. Four hours appears to be the maximum permitted exposure to this most glorious display of Siamese history. To any but the most purblind visitor, it must seem that just as the tragic languor of the place begins to sink in, so a motor-horn barks and a guide bellows some instruction, and you are summoned away.

Yet it is entirely possible to stay a while in Ayuthaya—possible, inexpensive, delightful, and, for anyone attempting to understand the complexities of Thai history, eminently desirable. But to do so you have to make a show of your independence—ignore the persuasive arguments of the Bangkok boatmen (though by all means take up their offers for lesser journeys, to the Grand Palace or the Floating Markets) and insist, though they will advise you otherwise, on a northbound bus, train, or car. Travel up from Bangkok early one evening; the plains are dull, so there is no need to go by daylight. Take dinner at a café in the bustling little country town which is the sole living remnant of the old capital, and rise before the sun and *then* take a local boat. (A word of warning, drawn from the bitter experience of others: if you were incautious enough to allow the café-owner to flavor your curry with too much of that murderously hot green chili known as *prick kee nu,* you will have risen long before dawn. So it is as well to demand, in a town that entertains so few *farangs* to dinner, that the chefs go easy on the peppers.)

I took my boat, a slender "long-tail" with its propeller set on a pivoted stem to help avoid the floating clumps of water-hyacinth, just before dawn. When King U-Tong established Ayuthaya in 1350 he chose a site at the confluence of three rivers—the Lop Bur, the Pasak, and "Thailand's Mississippi," the Chao Phya—and then had a small canal constructed to turn his city into an easily defensible island. island, lozenge-shaped, two miles by one, is itself incised by dozens of narrow *klongs,* or canals—meaning that a boat, and especially a narrow boat, is an essential means of exploring the city.

I found mine moored behind my hotel, the steersman puffing contemplatively on a ragged cheroot. He agreed on 25 baht—a dollar—an hour, and once the deal had been struck and the cheroot tossed away, declared himself proud to be able to show me the city that 16th-century wanderers called the most beautiful in the East. "They said it was like your Venice," said my boatman, who was called Mr. Sak. "Many canals. Much water. Many lovely buildings. But so many are knocked down by the Burmese. You have to imagine what it must have been like before the Burmese came."

Ayuthaya was a mere vassal state during the closing years of that most glorious and idyllic period in Thai history, the age of the kingdom of Sukhothai. The kings who ruled from Sukhothai are regarded even now with nostalgia and reverence—they were deeply religious, kindly, learned, accessible, paternal figures, men whose wisdom brought a golden era to Siamese history. But they were ultimately weak rulers, and down in Ayuthaya a new class of more martial figures began to assert themselves. By the mid-14th century these men had seized power from the pious monarchs of the north. The kings of Ayuthaya, the so-called "Lords of Life," were quite different. They ruled as absolute monarchs, ambitious and nationalistic men who ran disciplined and ruthlessly organized courts: a strict ban on "amatory poems," amputation for anyone who kicked a palace door, a code of laws laying down that errant princes could be beaten to death by means of sandalwood clubs drummed against the napes of their royal necks.

The island-city built by the thirty-three Ayuthaya kings during their five dynasties and four centuries was appropriately regal in scale and style—a mix of architecture that managed to be both bombastic and reverential. There were huge palaces, wide moats, magnificently expensive temples, towering *prangs,* whole forests of brick *chedis,* endless rows of Buddhas and icons in gold and jadeite and marble. The Dutch, the French, the British, and the Japanese were in Ayuthaya too. King Songham had permitted his cities to be used as entrepôts, and there was a bustling trade in silk, spices, hides, teak, tin, and sugar. The traders built their embassies and houses and, in the case of the Dutch, a huge cathedral. Ayuthaya at its zenith had all the trappings of a major world capital, and was respected and admired by everyone who visited it.

But it was not to last. The Third Burmese Empire had designs on the Thai fiefdom in the south, and Ayuthaya came under attack—first by King Alaungpaya in 1760 (though he withdrew, having been injured by his own cannon-fire), and then again, and fatally, by Alaungpaya's son Hsinbyushin in 1767. The city was under siege for more than a year before the Ayuthayan guards gave up the struggle and the Burmese poured into the city on their

squadrons of battle-elephants. Then, in an act of collective vandal-
ism that is almost unmatched in Asia, they set this lovely old capital ablaze, ruined its palaces and forts, and melted every ounce of
gold from every Buddha and icon in sight. By the end of the year
the place was a total ruin, only
the stumps of its temples and the
foundations of its palaces remaining for the jungle grasses to
reclaim.

*I stood frequently in admira-
tion of the strong great city,
seated upon an island round which
flowed a river three times the size
of the Seine. There rode ships from
France, England, Holland, China,
and Japan, while innumerable
boats and gilded barges rowed by
sixty men plied to and fro. No less
extraordinary were the camps of
villages outside the walls inhabited
by the different nations who came
trading there, with all the wooden
houses standing on posts over the
water, the bulls, cows, and pigs on
dry land. The streets, stretching out
of sight, are alleys of clear running
water. Under the great green trees
and in the little houses crowd the
people. Beyond these camps of the
nations are the wide rice fields. The
horizon is tall trees, above which
are visible the sparkling towers and
pyramids of the pagodas. I do not
know whether I have conveyed to
you the impression of a beautiful
view, but certainly I myself
have never seen a lovelier.*

—Abbé de Choisy, a Jesuit priest,
French diplomat in Siam in 1685,
and once famous Parisian
transvestite, quoted by
William Warren in *Thailand,
Seven Days in the Kingdom.*

But Thailand herself was to
survive the assault. A young
general, Phya Tak Sin, escaped
the siege, set up a temporary
headquarters on the Gulf of
Siam and some months later
traveled back to drive the
Burmese occupation garrison
out of the capital. The devastation he saw was too terrible: he
spent barely a night among the
ruins before leaving for the
south, for the riverside town of
Thonburi and the place they call
"the village of wild olive
groves"—Bangkok. But that is
another story. While Bangkok
was to grow and prosper,
Ayuthaya was to moulder and
decay in the steamy heat of the
tropics, waiting for its rediscov-
ery as a treasure-house of old
Siam.

Old Mr. Sak steered me
slowly down the Pasak River,
under the single road bridge
that is Ayuthaya's only physical

link with the outside world. Even at dawn the river was busy. Long trains of huge old rice-barges lumbered by. Fisherwomen cast nets, and sat smoking cheroots as they waited for them to fill. A boatload of young Buddhist monks, all in their deep red robes—one shoulder bare, as is the Thai custom—flashed past on the way to worship at a *wat* nearby. Their driver gunned his Evinrude to show off, and the monks stumbled over each other as the prow rose from the water. But they grinned and waved. Such a cheerful religion, Buddhism—so very little that is solemn.

We stopped at a temple, the Wat Phanan Cheong, which was built a few years before Ayuthaya herself and has long been popular with the local Chinese. The Buddha is almost unbelievably large—so tightly jammed inside the temple that it appears to be supporting the roof. Even at this hour the temple was full. Old ladies were lighting incense tapers, men were pasting tiny offerings of gold leaf on to the Buddha's feet and shins, schoolchildren were bowing low and reciting their morning mantras. Outside I paid ten baht for a tiny caged bird, and set it free above the river to carry my wishes where they might be answered.

(After flying a few circles, the bird went straight back to its mistress, who re-caged it and sold it again ten minutes later. She did the same with terrapins and, said the ever-skeptical Mr. Sak, made a small fortune doing so.)

Beside Phanan Cheong is a small Shinto shrine and a little cemetery—the remains of the Japanese community that once thrived here. But when in 1682 the *shogun* refused to recognize the usurper Prasattong as King of Thailand, the Japanese were murdered, or fled. To modern Japanese the tombs are holy relics, revered as war graves, and they are carefully tended by their Thai guardians.

A clockwise progress along the river—the way Mr. Sak insisted on taking me each day—leaves the old city itself on the right bank. I would stop the boat every few yards and walk, or paddle up along a tiny *klong,* to see the various ruins within. Some are magnificent; the Chandrakasem Palace has been turned into a most agreeable museum, and the Wat Raj Burana has been splendidly restored with huge *prangs,* superb gateways, rows of *chedis* standing on freshly mown lawns. The old royal palace, Wang Luang, was totally destroyed by the Burmese; but close by its foundations is the marvelous line of the three identical *chedis* of the Wat Phra Sri Sanphet, as dignified and harmonious an example of Buddhist temple-building as you will see anywhere in Asia.

The huge Buddha at Phra Sri Sanphet is even more impressive than that at Phanan Cheong, and the throngs of the faithful are greater, their devotions louder. But this is where the foreign tourists tend to start their wanders (the boats from Bangkok arrive around 1 p.m.), and it can become unbearably crowded. There are souvenir stalls, too—an eruption of commerce that sits uneasily against the tranquillity of other ruins nearby.

Pleasant hours can be spent wandering in the old city itself. One can start at the island's western end, at the monument to the heroic Queen Suriyothai. (In the great battle with the Burmese in 1549 the Queen, a great feminist, dressed in men's clothes and fought, on her elephant, alongside her King. In one memorable cavalry charge she saved her husband's life, but died in so doing. The *chedi* that holds her ashes is one of Thailand's most sacred.) And one can finish at the east, by the Phom Phet fortress, or the attractive Wat Suwan Dararam, a place which is quite lovely at dusk as the monks, framed by the magnificently restored columns and frescoes, chant their plain song devotionals. And then, being nearby, one can dine at a floating restaurant on the Pasak River: there are two beside the Pridi Damrong Bridge, and the road home.

However my own preference in Ayuthaya is for the unrestored, the ruins *sensu stricto,* where some of the sadness of the saga of the capital remains embedded in the stone. To see such a place one is forced to look at the river's left bank, not the right. My own favorite—somewhere that tells the essence of the Ayuthaya story, I like to think—is beside the old Dutch cathedral of St. Joseph (which still stands, and from which you can hear Christian hymns on a Sunday morning, sung in Thai.) Called the Wat Chai Wattanaram, it is a place of silence and forlorn beauty on the bend of a river. There is a mighty *prang,* covered with foliage, with small bushes growing from its cornices and parapets. A single Buddha looks down from a pedestal. Surrounding the *prang* are the subsidiary *chedis,* all more or less intact but weathered like ancient stalagmites, the brown of their stones rendered green by the plants clinging to every horizontal surface. There are dozens of headless Buddhas, still sitting in contemplative attitudes, still somehow radiating peace, still somehow managing to look beatific and even forgiving to those ancient vandals to whom they fell victims.

Cattle wandered through the ruins and small black pigs rooted among the tussock grass. Flocks of brilliantly-colored birds rose in alarm from the recesses of the old stones, like sudden rainbows and bursts of fire. Lizards lazed in the sun, prompting Mr. Sak to wonder if there might be snakes in the deeper grass. He may well have been right. There was no one else in the grounds of the temple; boats no longer stopped here. The whole place had returned to the jungle, swamped in a green and feral wilderness beside the slow river.

It was like a lost city, somewhere which had slumbered for centuries, unvisited and undisturbed. Indeed, I thought, Wat Chai Wattanaram looked today as Ayuthaya itself must have looked before it was rediscovered and placed foursquare on all the tourist maps. It was perfectly quiet that morning but for the chatter of song-birds as I stood beside the river, gazing at the wrecked spires and domes and all those ranks of statues…despoiled, but still serene.

Two hundred years ago all of them—statues, temples, monuments, tombs—were intact. But then the Burmese elephant-squadrons made their final attacks, the fire-boats crossed the river, the soldiers from the North began their final rampage and the era of Ayuthaya was over. Elsewhere, where temples and palaces have been restored, the sights are impressive. But in this temple, above all others, the sense of deep and abiding tragedy—the real sense of Ayuthaya—remains. On this one spot beside the river stands a poignant reminder of the troubled history of the Thai people and their land. It is a discovery that the average day-visitor will never experience; but it is one well worth making, an essential way-station on any serious progress through the story of Siam.

Simon Winchester is the author of The Sun Never Sets, Korea, River at the Center of the World: A Journey Up the Yangtze and Back in Chinese Time, *and* Pacific Rising, The Emergence of a New World Order, *from which this was excerpted. He also makes TV documentaries and is chairman of InterOptica Publishing Ltd., a company that creates interactive multimedia products.*

★

Don't be shocked to see women holding hands with other women when walking down the streets and men walking with their arms around each other; however, men and women never touch each other and travelers should avoid any public display of affection.

> —Elizabeth Devine and Nancy L. Braganti, *The Travelers'
> Guide to Asian Customs and Manners*

JOHN REMBER

* * *

Highland Carnival

The author finds sanuk *in
ancient Chiang Mai.*

CHIANG MAI IS THAILAND'S FOURTH LARGEST CITY, AND YET, next to Bangkok, it isn't a city at all. The capital has 6 million inhabitants, while Chiang Mai is home to only 160,000. In the last decade or so Bangkok has become one more borough in a huge ocean-orbiting metropolis that includes Los Angeles, Seoul, Tokyo, Seattle, and Sydney. But Chiang Mai province still provides glimpses of rural Thailand, of old Thailand, of 800-year-old temples, small villages, and rice fields where monks in saffron robes walk the berms between electric green paddies.

Less worldly, less driving than Bangkok, this old city of the north, founded in 1296, has grown and shrunk and grown again over the centuries. A large part of it still sits inside a square of ancient brick ramparts, crumbling and broken, edged by a moat a half-mile on a side.

You can travel the 427 miles north from Bangkok to Chiang Mai by air—and most visitors do. But you can also get there by train, or by bus as I did. It is not the safest or most convenient way to go—the two-lane roads the buses travel are narrow and winding, and there are occasional dramas involving oncoming rice trucks. But there was wonder in the journey north through

173

a flooded green landscape gazed upon by great hilltop statues of Buddha.

Some of those statues were new two- and three-story figures, painted bright colors, and surrounded by the gilt columns of temples. But the older ones more often caught my eye, statues pitted and time-blackened and crumbling, statues that had kept watch on rice fields for seven or eight centuries. Wars had been fought under their smiles. Unmoved, they had seen kingdoms come and go. Thirty generations of monks had draped the huge figures with saffron banners.

In the small towns, teak buildings, swaybacked and angular as old horses, stood here and there behind tile-faced commercial banks and concrete restaurants. Everywhere, I saw Thai spirit houses—tiny temples on pedestals that shelter and propitiate the forest ghosts displaced by human habitation.

It was a magical trip, and by the time the road began to wind up into the mountains that surround Chiang Mai, the city had taken shape in my mind as the gilded capital of one of those vanished kingdoms. Taxes and tribute had passed over the mountains I traveled through. Teak for temples and palaces had been carted over the roads I followed. Architects and scholars, some of them 700 years dead, had practiced their arts in this city.

I knew that the Old City inside the walls was home to temples, shrines, and museums. Here was the marketplace for the diverse hill tribes of the Golden Triangle region (once the crossroads of trade between Laos, Thailand, and Burma). These aboriginal peoples— Akha, Lahu, Lisu, and Hmong—had migrated centuries ago from Tibet and China to the steep limestone mountains of Northern Thailand. I knew it was a place where pedicabs, banned from Bangkok because they slow the flow of traffic, still silently moved along the streets. I imagined it was a place where ghosts still lived in their own homes.

And so I was not prepared for Chiang Mai. A few hours after I hit town, I found myself at the night bazaar, in a built-over section of the new city that lies between the old walls and the river. From my hotel I walked along streets noisy with the snarls of *tuk-tuks,* which sound a bit like a chain saw attacking a tin roof, the blaring horns of truck drivers and the mutter of motorcycles, in addition to sirens, shouts, and rattles. I refused a dozen offers of taxi rides, looked into store windows full of running shoes and microwaves, and walked past restaurants advertising hamburgers and banana splits.

In the bazaar itself, the sound systems of three or four pirate cassette stands pounded away as members of the hill tribes, in full costume, hawked their wares: hand-embroidered quilts, bags, backpacks, jackets, pillowcases, and tablecloths. Lowland Thais sold lacquer ware, beaten silver, small bronze statues, silks, wood carvings, painted umbrellas, and Burmese wall hangings. On the sidewalks, tables were laden with fake goods: Gucci vinyl, Taiwanese Rolexes, shirts bearing the labels of Lacoste, Dior, and Chanel. Street vendors sold Mekong whiskey by the drink as well as steamed bread and barbecued strips of pork on bamboo spits. Tourists from everywhere—Sweden, Japan, Saudi Arabia, South Africa, India, Italy, Germany, France, and Hong Kong—crowded the stalls, sidewalks and streets. Words from a dozen different languages came alive, began to collide, ricochet, fuse, burn—and turned to laughter in the night.

The Lisu, Thailand's premier opium cultivators and the most culturally advanced of all hill tribes, are an outgoing, friendly, and economically successful group of people. While most hill tribe villages are poor and dirty, Lisu villages are often clean and prosperous, loaded with sewing machines, radios, motorcycles, and perhaps a Datsun truck. Terrific salespeople, they enjoy setting up stalls and selling their handicrafts in Chiang Mai's night market.

—Carl Parkes, *Thailand Handbook*

This Chiang Mai I had come to was a carnival. Giddiness floated in the air, and glee gripped visitors as they cashed in yen, marks, and greenbacks for wads of crimson and purple bills. Whole streets had become festivals of neon.

Other festivals were in progress. In hotels and cultural centers across the city, troupes of traditional Thai dancers performed to the weirdly percussive music of old Thailand. Audiences sat around low tables, leaning against hard triangular pillows called *mon khwan,* while they ate a *khantoke* dinner—Northern Thailand's traditional cuisine of barbecued chicken, sticky rice, and curry stew—and watched the sinuous moves of dances choreographed a millennium before.

In the nightclubs that line the strip across from the Old City's Thapae Gate, Led Zeppelin and Grateful Dead tunes were performed by brilliant guitarists and drummers—and by singers who had learned their lyrics a phoneme at a time. In some of those same clubs, bar girls sat at tables, drinking $2 instant coffee and practicing English with Germans, Italians, and Japanese.

Chiang Mai can be an overwhelming experience for a visitor who comes into it lulled by the serenity of rice fields. My first night there, I collapsed at midnight into my bed at the Montri Hotel, tired but unable to sleep. The downtown tour had left me with images that did not fit well together. After a thousand repetitions, the Klee-like designs of hill tribe embroidery had begun to explode against my eyes. The American music had become too loud, too jarring.

Confused by my sudden plunge into the noise and light of a full-tilt tourist industry, I had left the markets empty-handed, convinced that the ancient hill tribe designs had been overproduced, handcrafted or not, that lacquer ware might have looked all right in a world without plastic, and that even the ersatz Rolexes, at $30, were too expensive to take home to the children of friends.

The Montri itself contributed to what was, by then, an acute case of overstimulation. I had meant to save money by staying there, and indeed I did. But while my room was clean and the shower had hot water, I was trying to sleep right above the kitchen, and garlic fumes had wafted up around the pipes in my bathroom. Going in there was good for the sinuses, bad for the eyes. Noise from the Thapae Strip—the horns of taxis, the bass notes of rock and roll bands, the shouts of drunken tourists—came in through my window. *I've got bus lag,* I said to myself. Sometime in the early morning hours, sleep finally came.

The Montri might be a cheap hotel, but its restaurant serves the best cup of coffee in town. I made my second foray into the city late the following morning, after drinking five thick black coffees and reading the Bangkok *Post*. I walked out into warm February sunlight.

Chiang Mai has the easy morning atmosphere of a place that stays up late. Along the moat north of the Thapae Gate, grassy banks provide small secluded places to sit. I found one and gazed down the line of trees to a brick corner of the old wall. The water was quiet, except where the fine high spray of fountains rippled the surface. The vistas seemed European rather than Asian, at least until a single fisherman began to walk slowly along the inner bank, holding a bow and shooting a tethered arrow at any carp careless enough to let a fin break the water.

This small scene lingers in my memory. Behind that suddenly loosed arrow and the arc of line that followed it half across the water, I began to see a different city. The night before, I had wondered if the ancient capital of the Lan Na Thai, or "Kingdom of a Million Rice Fields," had not been transformed into just one more late 20th-century stop for exotic goods to display in cultural trophy rooms. The sudden thrashing of a carp in still water ended that line of thought.

In the afternoon I rode in the back of a *songthaew*—one of the small covered pickups that are used for passengers in much of rural Thailand—up Doi Suthep, the 5,500-foot peak that provides a majestic backdrop to Chiang Mai's skyline. Its top is crowned by the ornate roofs of Wat Phrathat Doi Suthep, a 14th-century monastery that overlooks the city. It is a 40-minute ride to the base of the great serpent-flanked stairway of 290 steps that lead to the central temple. Once there, I found myself in the midst of a great crowd of Thais and foreigners. We

The first thing to remember is that our temples are based on the sacred Buddhist texts known as the Traiphum, which describe heaven, earth, and the netherworld. Our temples are designed to resemble heaven as closely as possible, so that we can ensure an intimate harmony between heaven and the more immediate world of our land and its people.

—Abbot of Wat Doi Suthep, quoted by Jeffrey A. McNeely and Paul Spencer Wachtel, *Soul of the Tiger* made the climb, paused for soft drinks at the small stand at the top of the stairs, took off our shoes and walked into the cloister. Foot-worn stone floors led past what were once bronze statues of the Buddha, now near-featureless mounds of gold leaf, their sculptors' art obscured completely by the microscopically thin, inch-square offerings of pilgrims. Other, larger statues filled niches and rooms off the central plaza of the temple.

From a parapet facing east, you can see the buildings, streets, and trees of Chiang Mai and its surrounding villages. This is a Buddhist city. Everywhere I had gone in it, I had seen monks, studying English in open-air classrooms, hitching rides on motor-cycles, or gazing impassively at the goods in the markets.

There are more than three hundred other temples below the one at Doi Suthep (the city's highest). Besides Buddha images, many temples also give space to Hindu and animist deities. Sculpted demons, the more modern of them wearing wrist-watches, scowl behind temple gates. Murals and statues dramatize the ancient myth that pits the *garudas* (birdlike creatures), who rule the air, against the *nagas* (serpents), who rule the earth. There on top of Doi Suthep, I knew what it meant to see with the eyes of a *garuda*.

Back at the bottom of the stairs, I found a woman who sells pairs of sparrows in tiny bamboo cages. I paid a few baht to release two birds.

A culture that accepts motorcycles and forest spirits, *nagas* and *garudas,* bow-fishing and Led Zeppelin, also accepts the traveler, makes him feel welcome, bids him stop, slow down, and look around. I spent a week in Chiang Mai, staying quite comfortably at the Montri (after I'd changed to an air-conditioned room far from the kitchen).

I took a couple of tours out to the factories that line the road to Sankampaeng, a handicrafts village eight miles east of town. There, in small adjuncts to factory outlets, artisans create teak landscapes, silk cloth, dolls, wall hangings, elephant-skin boots, silver bowls, statues, and jewelry. Six-foot umbrellas are made and painted before tourist audiences. Child artists demonstrate the intricacies of producing lacquer ware, step by painstaking step. Tables, chairs, and beds—heavy, solid teak designs that recall an age when trees were thick and wood-carvers thicker—crowd showrooms.

There is a danger in factory tours. *Tuk-tuk* and taxi drivers will offer to take you on one without charge, because the factories pay them ten baht for each tourist delivered to their doors. And once you're there, people try to sell you things you don't need. I must confess I bought some—a silver bowl, a teak duck—and I'm glad I came home with them. But for a while, carrying them around town in bags that were already bulky, I wondered about my shopping wisdom.

I had better luck back at the night markets. I realized that the quilts, embroidery, and hand-weaves of the hill tribes, once taken away from clashing colors and crowded stalls, become beautiful. Hand-stitched quilts for $50 and loomed wall hangings for $20 are particularly good buys. And mailing home a package from the Chiang Mai post office took care of most of my purchases, though the duck remained with me throughout my stay.

But it is not the goods of Chiang Mai that characterize the city. I remember a late night at the Six-Pole House, a restaurant and nightclub in a restored century-old teak warehouse, on Charoenrat Road across the river from the Old City. A Thai rock band was tearing into Olivia Newton-John's "Let's Get Physical." When the song was done, a young Canadian, carrying a clarinet case, walked to the bandstand and asked if he could join in. He stepped up to the microphone, and the audience—half Westerners, half Chiang Mai University students—heard him play a Benny Goodman arrangement of "April in Paris," then "Take the A Train," then.... But the band wanted to play rock and roll. The clarinet went back into its case, the Canadian stepped down, and the old walls began to shake to Creedence Clearwater's "Born on the Bayou."

I remember this scene because the young Thais who made up the band were having a good time picking and choosing from a whole worldful of music. It wasn't that they didn't like Benny Goodman or couldn't play a polite backup to a young foreigner. But they were there to rock out, and they had the aggressive confidence of people who have a culture that can assimilate alien art forms and technologies and still remain intact.

This flexibility is not part of hill tribe cultures. In the middle of my stay I arrived late one afternoon at Chiang Mai University's Hilltribe Research Center. I knocked, having finally found the way northwest from town to the campus, past uniformed soldiers at the gate, through a maze of buildings and roads, to the center's closed door. A woman opened it.

"We're closed," she said, and smiled. "But you can come in."

Inside I wandered through a small museum that shows the traditional costumes of ten hill tribes. Baskets, wooden tools, and fantastically ornate silver jewelry—all specimens of items sold in Chiang Mai's antique shops—surround life-size wooden figures in tribal regalia. I thought of American Indians, of ways of life that did not fare well when they met more aggressive cultures.

In the hills around Chiang Mai, trekking companies have introduced the tribes to the money and clothes of tourists. (The witch doctor of one tribe wears a hooded Yale sweatshirt.) These people sell baskets and traditional clothes to antique dealers, since such items have given way to plastic buckets and blue jeans in mountain villages. The Thai government has suppressed opium growing, a prime source of income for many of the tribes, and has begun an assimilation program that is bringing people out of the mountains. A way of life is being lost. Tragedy lies in the carved faces of those museum figures. I lingered with them until the staff of the center told me it was time to lock up. Back in the night markets, members of the hill tribes were opening their booths and stalls, getting ready for the night's onslaught of buyers.

If there is tragedy in the air of the Hilltribe Research Center, it does not reach the food markets and restaurants of the city. For Chiang Mai, if nothing else, is a wonderful and comic celebration of food and drink and the good life that goes with them. The city's expatriate restaurateurs offer French, Italian, and German food—most of it good.

But Thai food is wonderful. You can try Northern Thai cooking—hot, full of incandescent peppers and fresh vegetables, spiced with lemon grass and lime and ginger—at storefront cafés and elegant restaurants all over town. Particularly good are the noodle dishes, fresh vegetables, Burmese-style curries, and anything—pork, shrimp, fish—doused with the local pepper sauce.

North of the night markets and squeezed into a grid of narrow streets is a great open-air market of farmers, fishermen, frog-sellers, and noodle-makers. Stalls sell sardines steamed in curry and wrapped in banana leaves, fish heads, a half-dozen colors of rice, live starlings, bamboo shoots, eight kinds of peppers, strange tubers, swimming catfish, hulking chunks of beef, breadfruit, pomelos, baby squid, dried and pressed fish, bundles of shallots, small haystacks of noodles, crabs, cheeses, mushrooms, bird eggs, and swimming eels. And those are just the items I could identify. There is much more—steaming bathtub-size woks of food, all of it new, all of it disturbing to a palate trained by American fast food.

But a week of eating in Chiang Mai cured me of any apprehensions I had had in its food markets. I walked to shrines and ate, visited temples and ate, wandered through museums and ate, listened to music and watched dances and ate—at food stalls and storefronts, as well as at restaurants near the hotels.

Toward the end of my stay, I was sitting in the Roof Garden Restaurant, an open-air fifth story dining room just across from the restored Thapae Gate. From there, I could see my hotel and the serrated brickwork of the gate, dark against the sunset. Above them, to the west, golden light shimmered around the edges of the broken-topped pagoda of Wat Chedi Luang in the Old City. The temple towered above the trees, ruined but majestic; once it was 260 feet high, before an earthquake toppled it in 1545. The sun, bright red and huge, sank into the ridges of Doi Suthep.

This is the image I most remember when I think of Chiang Mai. The city had changed after a week—and had emerged from under its carnival garb. I had begun to feel its peace, to sense its deep history and its connection to a way of life not tied to day-to-day concerns.

I have forgotten the Thai names of favorite foods, and some of the souvenirs I bought in the night market have disappeared—gone to friends for birthdays or weddings. But I still remember that sunset over a ruined pagoda, in a city under a mountain, half a world away.

John Rember lives in Stanley, Idaho. He is writer-in-residence at Albertson College, Caldwell, Idaho, and is the author of two collections of short stories, Coyote in the Mountains *and* Cheerleaders from Gomorrah.

★

The Western idea that a white elephant is an object which is not only valueless to its owner but is also a real burden seems to spring from an account of court life under the ancient kings of Siam. In those days of numerous concubines and a libidinous king, the story goes, there were so many offspring, nephews, and cousins vying for official state appointments that the king had to be creative to come up with sufficient titles to go around. He devised the position of Keeper of the Sacred Royal White Elephants and gave a relative a position of trust and honor by making him responsible for the care, feeding, and costuming of the pampered animals, all to be paid for out of the keeper's own purse. The keeper soon found himself penniless as a result of being forced to support huge and economically unrewarding animals which, as the sacred possessions of the king, had to have only the best of everything. Thai historians insist that this story is apocryphal, but knowing the keen Thai sense of humor and the Asian way of getting the upper hand through a smile-clouded subterfuge, it is not unlikely that at least one Thai king had had his fun—and maintained his elephant entourage—in this way.

　　　　—Jeffrey A. McNeely and Paul Spencer Wachtel, *Soul of the Tiger*

MORRIS DYE

* * *

Cycling Rural Thailand

*A cyclist at home, the author pedals the
hills of northern Thailand.*

THE APPEAL OF MOUNTAIN BIKING IS A LITTLE HARD TO EXPLAIN TO
someone who isn't already hooked. Of course part of the attraction is the simple pleasure of being in the great outdoors and
inhaling great gulps of negative ions as you roll through a pretty
natural setting. But off-road cycling is definitely not like taking
a peaceful, meditative walk in the woods. Nor is it generally a
means of getting from one place to another—most mountain
bikers I know are not going anywhere in particular...they're
just going.

A big part of it is the joy of physical exertion and of reacting
to the randomness of the trail; in that sense, mountain biking is
a lot like skiing or dancing. It is a serendipitous game of give and
take between cyclist and terrain, with the bicycle as a facilitator
and mediator between the two.

These various elements came together in perfect harmony one
morning during a ride with two companions along the left bank
of the Maekok River in northern Thailand. We were part of a
group of twenty cyclists participating in the kind of cushy, full-
service bike tour that has become so popular in recent years.

When we arrived at the 14.2 kilometer point on day six of our nine-day itinerary, where the detailed route instructions said, "Maekok River. Hut on the right. Cross river by dugout canoe," we decided to follow an enticing little dirt track that veered off to the left just before the river crossing.

The path wound its way up and down through sunny meadows and patchy woods, with occasional glimpses of the Maekok and not a soul to be seen. Soon we arrived in a remote riverside village that seemed all but deserted. The village was a study in earth tones—a brown dirt road, a dozen or so brown huts made of wood and thatch, tall brown trees arching overhead, the mud-brown Maekok flowing silently below in the growing heat of the day.

A few women peered out from the shadows of their homes to observe our unlikely arrival, the silence broken only by the occasional passage of narrow wooden longtail boats powered by outboard-mounted automobile engines with long propeller shafts screaming out behind.

Past the village, the trail dwindled to a narrow track that led us on an exhilarating up-and-down jaunt through a grove of banana trees, through already-harvested fields of corn and rice, and finally to an uncultivated part of the riverbank where the trail divided, then subdivided, and finally brought us to a halt on a steep, impassable footpath surrounded by dry, yellow grass.

It was the kind of ride that leaves you hot, tired, dirty—and grinning uncontrollably from ear to ear because you know you're about to do it all over again in the reverse direction.

Back at the river crossing, we loaded our bikes, one by one, onto a narrow dugout canoe and paid the local ferry-man ten baht apiece to paddle us to the opposite bank. From there it was a short ride to a lingering lunch of noodle soup and beer at a small riverside food stall with other members of our group. By this time, lethargy had set in along with the midday heat, so we chartered a couple of longtail boats to carry us and our bikes back to our starting point, a hotel in the town of Tha Thon near the Burmese border.

Our journey in Thailand was typical of a proliferating species of package tours based on a simple formula: you love cycling and you love to travel. Pay a couple thousand dollars, and with minimal hassle you can do the same thing you do every weekend, but in an exotic and unfamiliar setting—say the Yucatan Peninsula, or the English Lake District, or the hills of Southeast Asia—with plenty of logistical support in the form of previously researched routes, pre-booked accommodations, luggage transfers, a support van, and local guides.

Our basic route, which covered about 30 to 60 miles a day, was mostly on pavement—sometimes on busy, smoggy highways, but more often on relatively quiet country roads—with options for off-road side trips along the way. Much of the route passed through more or less flat agricultural land, but the itinerary was not without hills, some of them long and steep. For less experienced cyclists, there were various options built into the itinerary (including the option of riding in the support van) to make the tour more accessible.

We gathered at a marvelously funky resort on the outskirts of Chiang Mai called the Chiang Mai Lakeside Villa, a complex of picturesque wooden cottages set around a large pond where a boat-like restaurant served exceptionally good Thai food. Chiang Mai is the biggest city in northern Thailand, and also the primary entry point for tourists in the region, so our first day of cycling presented us with rather a lot of traffic and an amusing assortment of roadside attractions: a snake show, an elephant show, butterfly farms, orchid farms, craft emporiums, and a quite unbelievable flower garden on the grounds of the Erawan Resort, where we stopped for the night.

After dinner in the garden that evening, the Erawan treated us to an amateur "folklore" performance in which various young staff members from the resort played a bit of traditional hill tribe music, folk-danced in crude costumes, and then started lip-syncing to recorded Thai syntho-pop tunes. The soirée quickly degenerated into a kind of disco party at which I got my first-ever marriage proposal, from a 27-year-old member of the resort staff who wanted nothing more than to accompany me home to America. I declined the invitation and turned in early.

So far this had hardly been an introduction to traditional Thai culture but an entertaining jaunt through a highly developed vacationland frequented by foreigners and middle-class Thais from the south. But as we continued cycling over the next few days, we passed out of the shadow of urban Chiang Mai and into the more rural and culturally diverse hill country of the far north.

Before we got there, however, tragedy struck: as we coasted downhill from Erawan, one of the more agile and experienced cyclists in our group lost control of his bike on some gravelly pavement, slammed into a cement post and landed in the ditch by the side of the road. He was rushed off to a hospital in Chiang Mai for surgery to repair a broken hip and a broken femur. It was the kind of accident that could happen to anyone, and it served as a healthy reminder to wear a helmet and to take it a little easy when riding in an unfamiliar environment.

> *One of Thailand's chief accomplishments in the war against HIV transmission is that the medical blood supply is now considered safe, thanks to vigorous screening procedures.*
>
> —Joe Cummings,
> *Thailand - a travel survival kit*

Humbled by that incident, we continued cycling through flat, dry agricultural land past the towns of Mae Rim, Mae Malai, and Mae Taeng, and then into sparsely populated rolling hills covered with rice fields and teak forests. About 65 miles from Erawan—the longest ride on the itinerary—we arrived at the Chiang Dao Hill Resort, another cottage complex with extensive gardens. Here we would spend two nights, allowing time the next day for a memorable off-road excursion to visit several hill tribe villages.

In the past ten or fifteen years, visits to hill tribe villages—which are known for their colorful styles of dress and intricate handicrafts—have become popular among Western tourists, who trek into the hills with local guides, sleeping in grass huts and taking pictures of exotic costumes—and sometimes smoking opium with the villagers. Predictably, the practice has been institutionalized to the point that the most accessible villages have transformed themselves into tourist bazaars where women and children in native dress aggressively demand money in exchange for photo sessions and peddle carbon-copy craft items with all the charm of car salesmen.

On day four of our tour, we cycled out of the Chiang Dao Hill Resort, and a short way up the highway turned onto a dirt road that passed through fields of corn and banana trees, gaining altitude beneath a row of craggy pinnacles. A few miles from the highway we arrived at Hoi Jaken, a fairly modern village inhabited by a mix of Thai and Lisu people. We happened to arrive on the day of a nationwide children's celebration, and an open field by the road had been set up as a kind of carnival with special games and shows for the kids. The passage of sweaty foreigners on mountain bikes only added to their fun, and we were soon surrounded by curious onlookers who interrupted their festivities to enjoy this unexpected spectacle.

After entertaining the crowd for a time, we continued into nearby Doi Ngan, an adjacent Lahu village that was all but deserted this day—very likely because everyone was at the party in Hoi Jakan. From there the dirt road dwindled down to a smaller trail that passed through a pleas-

Another popular way to explore northern Thailand is by motorbike, easy to rent in Chiang Mai. Show respect for the local people by cutting your engine and gliding in quietly when you enter a village.

—JO'R and LH

ant forest where teak leaves the size of dinner plates dropped noisily to the forest floor, and where the sun shining through the branches scattered a mottled glow over the ground.

A few miles into the woods we reached the end of the road at Bon Nong Kam, a remote Lisu community nudged up against the base of a steep hill that made further cycling impossible. This village showed little evidence of modernization, except for an odd mix of Western and traditional Lisu clothing; most of the men were in slacks and button-front shirts, the women and children in brightly colored smocks. The houses (perhaps 25 or 30 in all) were simple wooden structures with floors three or four feet off the ground, walls of woven bamboo, and roofs shingled with leaves.

Unlike just about every other village we visited, there was absolutely nothing for sale in Bon Nong Kam. The adults seemed a little wary of our presence, though not unfriendly, while the children were amazed and delighted at the sight of so many *farangs* on bikes; they quite enjoyed staring at our strange-looking outfits, begging half-heartedly for money and hamming it up for our cameras.

The visit left me feeling at once fascinated, delighted, and a little sad for although it was interesting to get a glimpse of hill tribe life, and although the bright smiles of the children left me giggling right along with them, I wondered what sort of problematic impressions we might leave as we passed through with our high-tech bicycles and expensive industrial toys.

These people, would-be nomads in an age of private property, were caught in an all too common no-man's-land between age-old traditions and the encroachment of the industrial world. I longed to learn more about their way of life, and to share with them my views on the complexities of ours, but since we had no language in common, playing with the children was about the only means of communication we shared. After an hour or so we waved good-bye and rolled back down the hill the way we had come.

After leaving Chiang Dao, we continued on to Tha Thon and stayed there for two nights, with another successful day of off-road riding in between and a short excursion to the Burmese border. This remote checkpoint, less than a mile from our hotel, was nothing more than a couple of crude shacks on a dirt trail by the river. The smiling border guard posed proudly with his pornographic posters and a large machine gun recently issued by the Thai military.

That same afternoon we could hear shells exploding occasionally just across the border, and there was talk of factional violence involving a militia group commanded by Khun Sa, an opium warlord who controls that part of Burma. The fighting is said to spill over into Thailand on occasion, but local *farangs* assured us there was nothing to worry about.

The next day we loaded our bikes onto longtail boats and motored downriver to Chiang Rai, with a stop for a gimmicky but fun elephant ride through the hills and a short trek to an opium poppy field kept by two elderly addicts. And on our last day of cycling we rode from Chiang Rai about 60 miles north to the Golden Triangle Resort. This large modern hotel sits incongruously at the confluence of the Sop Ruak and Mekong rivers, at a point where the borders of Thailand, Burma, and Laos all come together. Then on the morning of the ninth day we packed away our cycling clothes and boarded a chartered bus bound for Chiang Mai.

The tour ended where it had begun, at the Chiang Mai Lakeside Villa, full circle on a mountain bike through northern Thailand.

Morris Dye is a San Francisco Bay Area writer, editor, and Web site producer specializing in travel and outdoor recreation. He is the former associate travel editor of the San Francisco Examiner, *and he has produced interactive Web-based programming for America Online and Microsoft's San Francisco Sidewalk.*

*

Leaving China, the Mekong slides between Myanmar and Laos, serving as the border, then touches Thailand. Here—where these three countries meet—lies the heart of the fabled Golden Triangle, where most of the world's opium is harvested and processed. It has long been an area of warlords and armed mule caravans carrying bales of opium paste.

When I reached Sob Ruak, a Thai hamlet on the Mekong at the very center of the triangle, I found not mule caravans but big, shiny buses and European tourists. On the hillside stood two resort hotels; a third was under way on the Myanmar shore.

The Thai military had pushed the drug refineries and mule trains out of the area. To replace the opium economy, tourism. Visitors fly from Bangkok to Chiang Rai, 40 miles south of Sob Ruak. They then bus here. Between November and May—the dry season—the two resort hotels are fully booked.

"It's the infamy of the place that draws them," said Marc Cremoux, the dapper French manager of the Baan Boran, one of the hotels. "I hear my visitors say, 'This is where the drugs come from.' People think they're having an adventure, even if they are staying in a five-star hotel and riding in air-conditioned buses."

—Thomas O'Neill, "The Mekong," *National Geographic*

JEFF GREENWALD

* * *

The Burning Hills

Going to northern Thailand can challenge your
conscience, as well as your assumptions
about culture and travel.

LANDING IN MAE HONG SON, MY FIRST IMPRESSION WAS THAT we'd arrived during a solar eclipse. The sky was brownish gray, and an unnatural stillness lay upon the town. I stared at the sun: a persimmon billiard ball suspended above jungle-covered hills. From the hills themselves, columns of thick smoke rose into the air.

"Burning season," explained Boy, the young Thai guide whose awkward nickname made me feel like a Southern plantation owner whenever I addressed him. "The villagers burn the woods to plant rice in the rainy season. Too smoky."

I smelled trouble. Mae Hong Son, mere miles from the Burmese border in Thailand's mountainous northwest, is famous for spectacular scenery and expansive vistas. I'd long fantasized about visiting this part of Southeast Asia, of trekking between tribal villages, drunk on the high-grade oxygen exhaled by a thousand square miles of jungle. Today, though, taking a deep breath was like smoking a pack of Chesterfields. I could barely make out the closest hill—which seemed, actually, to have a big Buddha on top of it.

"That is Wat Doi Khong Mu," said Boy, following my gaze. "Would you like to go there?"

"Why not?" We left the airport and were greeted by Duang, our high-spirited driver, who lounged against the fender of a battered old Land Rover. I couldn't guess Duang's age, but he would have looked a lot younger if he had more teeth.

We drove two or three miles up the nearby hill, where the venerable old *wat* overlooked the town. The large Buddha I'd spied from below was made of plastered cement, and brightly painted. He was standing, palm raised in a gesture of blessing. Higher still, on an adjoining hillock, microwave towers beamed their equally sacrosanct signals toward the village. Boy strolled to a point overlooking Mae Hong Son. Though an opaque haze obscured the valley, I could imagine how spectacular the view must be the nine other months of the year.

"In the winter," Boy sighed, "it looks like a Japanese painting." I nodded wistfully, counting the spots on the setting sun.

Mae Hong Son has long been considered the Thai version of the Middle of Nowhere: a remote and relaxed hill town that in winter provides a welcome escape from Bangkok's unrelenting heat. It still recalls, for some travelers, the Wild West; the town remains a way station for traders from

The Thais call it the City of Mist, but its proper name is Mae Hong Son, and along with being the capital of Thailand's northwesternmost province—hard by the border of Myanmar (formerly Burma), and six hundred miles from Bangkok—it also boasts the kingdom's most spectacularly rugged terrain. Everywhere there are densely forested mountains, so many that four-fifths of the province is on a slope of at least forty-five degrees.

Despite its beauty, Mae Hong Son remained cut off from the outside world, and rare was the Thai traveler or trader who dared the trackless trek from Chiang Mai. It was not until World War II that even a semblance of a road led in or out of Mae Hong Son, and the one constructed then (by the invading Japanese) was a twistingly narrow dirt lane that one downpour made impassable. Finally, in 1968, a paved road linked Mae Hong Son with Chiang Mai and beyond.

In 1990, Mae Hong Son was a make-believe CIA air base in an alleged comedy entitled Air America.

—Robert Sam Anson, "The Bridge on the River Pai," *Condé Nast Traveler*

Burma and a relay point for opium being smuggled out of the Golden Triangle.

After returning to the temple I wandered down the main street, throat parched, stopping every few yards to gulp down a soft drink. Boy and Duang, meanwhile, downed bottle after bottle of Lipo-Vitan, a tonic that I imagined to be the Thai equivalent of "smart drugs." When I asked where the drink's enhancement qualities worked, they laughed uproariously and pointed, but not at their heads.

After walking a few blocks I found an amazing junk and antique store, crammed floor to ceiling with a bizarre inventory: used motors, opium weights, saddles, temple bells, grandfather clocks, samurai swords, Buddhist begging bowls, beautiful Burmese prayer books, and exquisite wooden Buddhas.

"Where did these come from?" I turned one of the gilt figures in my hand. There were dozens of them, all different.

The owner tore his eyes away from a television show just long enough to regard me with annoyance, and shrugged his shoulders. Boy led me aside. "From Burma," he whispered. "Thieves loot the temples and bring the things here to sell. Not so good, I think."

By the time we left the shop it was quite dark. We backtracked a block to the all-night market where quick, simple Thai dishes were being concocted at lightning speed beneath fluorescent tubes.

We had a fast, delicious meal. The total bill was roughly $2.40. After dessert of fresh fruit salad, Boy handed me a typed itinerary that detailed our plans for the next day. These would include "a ride along the Pai River, an hour drive along a bumpy and dusty trail through the jungle, continued on another hour by Jumbo (without jet) to the frontier village of amazing Pa Dawng (long necks)."

I didn't even try to make sense of all this, but returned to my air-conditioned room at the Tara Hotel, where I spent half the night trying to figure out how they'd folded the cloth napkins next to my complimentary fruit platter into miniature pagodas.

The next day dawned deliciously cool, with welcome rain clouds in the sky. "They're not rain clouds," Boy laughed. "Just smoke from early fires. You wait and see."

We began our day by driving to nearby Pai River and boarding a longtail boat. It was a lovely morning. Families scrubbed their clothes on the riverside, and men set up fishing traps suspended from poles bridging the current. Work teams dredged the shallows with pails, gathering sand and stones for construction projects. We passed through rapids, driving upstream into white water. After a half-hour or so, it occurred to me to ask Boy where we were going.

"Nowhere," he responded frankly. "All tourists in Mae Hong Son must do this. Duang will meet us at the end."

"And then?"

"The Pa Dawng village."

The Pa Dawng, known in the vernacular as "long-necks," are a tribal group of ethnic Burmese who have fled over the border to escape oppression at the hands of Burma's ruling junta. Visiting such hill tribes, I gathered, is the big attraction in northern Thailand. All along the streets of central Mae Hong Son, travel agencies display brightly painted signs advertising one-, three-, even fourteen-day treks into the hills, with overnight visits to Shan, Lisu, Karen, Lahu, and Pa Dawng settlements. The Pa Dawng, with their unusual custom of elongating women's necks with stacks of heavy brass rings, are the most exotic—and photogenic—of these tribes.

About an hour's drive out of Mae Hong Son we arrived at Naisoi, a Shan village. It was clean and simple, with elegant homes perched above the ground on poles. Each house had woven cane walls and an elaborate gate entering into a front yard.

Naisoi was a quiet, easy place—much as I'd first imagined Mae Hong Son would be. Butterflies flitted between fragrant shrubs, and a narrow river gurgled beneath a wooden bridge. Outside the local *wat*, three children ran among the trees, playing with strange noise-makers: long sticks with buzzers on the end.

As I approached, I realized that the "buzzers" were actually live cicadas. The ends of the sticks were coated with a sweet, sticky substance that attracted the bugs. At first I thought the children caught the cicadas for fun, for the loud buzzing sound they make. But they quickly removed the insects into plastic bags and ran off to catch some more. Boy later informed me that they'd be fried up as snacks.

In a local restaurant, I scrutinized my lunch as Boy spoke with some Thai soldiers. Finally, he called me over.

"We won't be able to spend the night in the Pa Dawng village," he explained. "There's trouble on the Burmese border, less than two kilometers away. Tonight there may even be an invasion; the Burmese army might come after the long-necks."

"It's funny," he reflected. "There's no fighting at all in the wet season. In the winter, everybody drops everything they're doing to grow opium poppies. Then in the dry season, they fight. It's like a game."

From Naisoi, all roads lead to the Pa Dawng village—or so say the local signs, emblazoned with bizarre caricatures of giraffe-necked humans. I was quizzical, then, when Duang pulled over and Boy signaled me to get out of the Rover.

"What's this, Boy?"

"We must ride an elephant."

Boy and I walked to a clearing, where a man crouched disconsolately next to a wrinkled old pachyderm. After some minor acrobatics we were safely seated in the rickety *howdah,* and we set off along a dirt track leading through the jungle. At first I thought we were going directly to the long-necks village; but Boy informed me that the elephant ride was merely another scenic diversion, part of the usual tourist itinerary. My well-meaning hosts were clearly eager for me to partake of every nuance of the Mae Hong Son experience.

This one, unfortunately, sort of backfired.

The elephant was lazy, and the day was hot. Every third step, "Jumbo" veered hugely into the woods, oblivious to his driver's hoarse commands. Each time he did so, Boy and I were thrust into the limbs of nearby trees, encounters which left us scratched and covered with red stinging ants.

Ultimately the beast simply stopped, lifted his proud trunk high, and showered us liberally with dust. This said, he stood his ground. Whether goaded, coaxed, or even stuck with a bamboo plank, the elephant would not move. The driver finally dismounted, attached a hook to the elephant's ear and led him down the trail like a petting zoo pony. Large was my relief when, after an abrupt shortcut, we came upon the Land Rover and the implacable figure of Duang smoking a cigarette beside it.

Duang winked slyly as he held open the door of the car. His lack of English was more than compensated by his mastery of the droll regard. I climbed in and we set off bouncing along rough dirt roads and sloshing messily through rivers. The ancient Rover bucked like a mule.

"Duang," I said, "this car… it's old…not so sturdy…many noise…"

"Numbah One!" Duang hollered, thrusting a gnarled thumb, pointed skyward, in my face. "Body no good. Nevah break down." He slapped the dashboard—what was left of it—as if to console the vehicle. A bolt flew out from somewhere, striking me painfully on the knee.

It is a popular belief of the Thai in general, that apart from human beings, certain animals such as elephants, horses and ponies, buffaloes, oxen and cows, and certain inanimate things such as carts, rice, and what-not have in them each a khwan *too. For the welfare of any animal or thing mentioned and also for the welfare of its owner, a certain rite is performed on special occasions. Such a rite we call in Thai* tham khwan. *Literally it means "the making of* khwan." *The* khwan *of a human being also has its ritual* tham khwan, *which is a sort of confirmation sacrament.*

—Phya Anuman Rajadhon, *Some Traditions of the Thai*

Boy and I were greeted at the entrance to the Pa Dawng village by Silver, a beautiful and sophisticated Shan Burmese woman in her late forties. She collected my entrance fee—about $12, which ostensibly goes to the Burmese resistance—and led us into the settlement. I counted about twenty thatched huts with shaded wooden porches and woven cane walls perched on the dusty hillside.

We wandered up the hill toward the huts. The long-neck women sat on their porches, weaving, working, or nursing babies. Their rings appeared at once beautiful and oppressive, a decorative burden that seemed out of place in the late 20th century.

The Pa Dawng village has long been a huge attraction, and many of the young girls have pictures of themselves—clipped from glossy travel magazines—plastered on their walls. At one hut, a woman named Mu Pong was manufacturing the traditional rings; they are actually spirals of brass, like polished car suspension springs. Boy tried to lift one with his foot, and howled at the weight. A good coil runs some ten pounds, and the women wear them on their legs and arms as well.

Farther on we were introduced to another Mu Pong, who holds the village record for neck rings: 24.

"What does this mean?" I inquired of Silver. "Is she the wealthiest woman in the village. Is she the headman's wife?"

"No." Silver shrugged. "She was born with a long neck to begin with."

A girl's first rings, explained Silver, are put on at the age of five and increased in number until the girl reaches her early twenties. Rather than elongate the neck, they actually push the collarbone down. As a result, the neck muscles grow quite weak; if the rings have to be removed for medical reasons, the neck must be supported by a brace.

"You know," I suggested to Silver, "the village could charge twice as much money if the men wore neck rings, too."

"No, no, impossible!" she cried. "Only the dragon has a long neck." In Pa Dawng mythology, she explained, the women symbolize dragons—and the men are wind. What's more, I was told, only girls born on a Wednesday during a full moon can wear rings. This was hard to believe as every single woman in the village seemed to be adorned.

Our most memorable visit was to the home of Ma Nang, who brought out a crude, four-string guitar she had carved herself. Ma Nang sang us a haunting love ballad in her strange, stretched voice, and treated me to a beautiful smile. I tipped the musician twenty baht, which she folded into the hollow beneath her neck rings.

Boy and I were denied permission to stay overnight, in spite of my earnest pleas. "It's too uncertain," Silver apologized. "The fighting is too close by. Every evening we have to pack our things and be ready to leave in an instant."

Our brief visit to the Pa Dawng village left me with mixed feelings. Some, chafing at the admission fee, have called the place a "human zoo"; but I had enjoyed meeting these unique people. The women were very happy to show off their long necks, and I was very happy to see them. What bothered me most was the fact that, since the rings go on at the age of five, the girls never had a choice about it. Then again, I wasn't consulted about my own circumcision, either. For the Pa Dawng villagers, at least, the neck rings provide a living—and these are trying times for ethnic Burmese.

Shortly before sunset, we took our reluctant leave, stopping to have a cup of tea with Silver. Through her window I watched the women bathing in the village stream, using fistfuls of grass and cold water to polish their burdensome jewelry to a high golden luster.

We began our final day in northern Thailand with a visit to Wat Chongkham, an elegant temple located in the center of Mae Hong Son itself. After paying my respects to the resident Buddha, I entered an adjoining museum, where a series of wooden statues graphically illustrated the inevitable pitfalls of human existence. A hand-lettered sign drove home the point:

> The Circle On Life
> With the old people, illness
> people, after than, get dide,
> so what going on.

I contemplated this in silence as we boarded the Rover and began what would be a six-hour drive to Chiang Mai, where a night flight would return me to Bangkok. Though it was still morning, the air was devilishly hot; the air vent felt like a blow dryer.

Along the highway we overtook huge lumber trucks loaded with felled trees. Burma's beautiful teak forests, I was told, are being sold off, at bargain-basement rates, to Thai industries. Sometimes the profits from these teak sales help arm Burma's military dictatorship; sometimes the Karen rebels themselves benefit from the trade. The teak is milled in Thailand, and the finished products are sold worldwide.

Yet even as we passed these trucks, half a dozen army tanks—amazingly fleet for their size—rumbled down the road in the opposite direction. I noted a conflict of interests here. The Thai government is taking obvious pains to keep the border war from spilling over into its territory; but it doesn't forbid opportunity, while it lasts, of striking a bargain on rare hardwood.

Continuing toward Chiang Mai, we stopped at the Fish Cave, a famous local shrine. A short walk through a lovely green park brought me to a little grotto, sheltering a golden statue of a saint. Below the grotto was a deep natural pool, filled with beautiful iridescent carp. They hung in the clear water like apparitions, and I found it easy to believe they were sacred. But why were they all clustered right here, in one spot?

The reason became obvious as a troupe of Thai tourists came marching up. After reciting brief prayers they began to hurl offerings into the water: giant prawns, whole cabbages, and dozens of hardboiled eggs, dumped from huge plastic bags. The fish, sacred though they might be, were not above an old-fashioned feeding frenzy.

Our final stop was at Tham Lod, a celebrated cave some forty miles northeast of Mae Hong Son. Fork-tailed swifts flew from the gaping entrance as we approached, accompanied by a lamp-bearing guide. Our tour of the cathedral-like interior consisted of appropriate activities, such as stumbling about in the darkness and bumping into stalagmites and stalactites.

Tham Lod is enormous, at least a third of a mile long, with a river coursing through its length. By the time we approached the exit I was genuinely impressed by how eerie and otherworldly the place was. Beams of smoky light filtered in through the huge maw, illuminating the dark water. It looked exactly like a scene from *Journey to the Center of the Earth*.

By the time we emerged it was late afternoon. Smoke from the day's fires had spread like a dome across the sky, magnifying the spring heat. I would have gladly spent the rest of the day back in the cool silence of the cave or the breezy interior of the *wat*.

As we made our way back to the car I spotted an austere dormitory on a nearby hillside. It was a monks' retreat. Just a few yards away, I realized, devout Buddhists were sitting in isolated cells, deep in meditation. It seemed like the right idea: find a shady little place that the heat could not reach, settle down and cultivate an inner clarity that no amount of slash-and-burn agriculture could obscure. Someday, perhaps, I'd find myself in one of those little cells; meanwhile, there was the Land Rover waiting.

Hours later, as we crested a range of hills, I pensively puffed on a Burmese cigar that I'd bought at the market in Mae Hong Son. I wouldn't know a good cigar from a flying saucer, but after three puffs I was ready to be rid of this one. But what to do? The Rover had no ashtray.

"Throw it out the window," Boy advised.

Out the window? A lit cigar? No, no, I couldn't. But after one glance to the side, I did so without hesitation. The woods, you see, were already on fire, and smoke was billowing into the air. I fixed a bandanna over my face and found my notebook.

"If you're planning a visit to northern Thailand in the early spring," I wrote, *"don't.* Visit in the rainy season when fantastic clouds sail over the hilltops and waterfalls cascade in thunderous sheets of water. Visit in December, when the air is crisp and opium poppies wink seductively among the trees. But do not visit in mid-March or April, when fires bloom on every hillside, and the sky is the color of onion soup."

We hurtled on through the miasma, arriving at sunset in the nuclear winter of Chiang Mai.

A Pa Dawng Postscript

After I wrote about visiting the Pa Dawng, a number of people—including some close friends—took me to task. "Whether you intend to or not," they said, "you're helping to perpetuate an exploitive practice."

My friends' arguments, at first purely emotional, were given credibility by a GlobalQuest Feature Service story by Jane Ellen Stevens. In her story, Stevens raised three specific points:

• The Pa Dawng are Burmese refugees who, because of Thailand's unwillingness to help them, are not eligible for assistance from the United Nations. Several years ago Thai entrepreneurs, seeking to exploit the plight of the Pa Dawng, offered them the opportunity to earn tourist dollars by donning neck-rings—a once-traditional practice they had abandoned years ago.

• Tourists who visit the Pa Dawng settlements near Mae Hong Son are being misled by local guides—and by the Pa Dawng women themselves. Pa Dawng women have not been wearing the neck rings since the age of five; some put their rings back on just three or four years ago.

• The rings can cause physical deformities as severe as those created by foot-binding or female circumcision. A traditional punishment for adultery, the article notes, was to remove a woman's rings and allow the neck to flop over, suffocating the woman.

I won't debate these arguments. There may be some validity to all of them (although I am still not convinced that wearing the neck rings is as painful, immobilizing, or oppressive as either foot-binding or clitorectomy). Nor do I intend to defend my research; I spent just one afternoon in the Pa Dawng village, and it's certainly possible that I was misled as easily as any garden-variety tourist.

I do feel, however, that there's something rather self-righteous about declaring, from the aerie of political correctness, that the Pa Dawng are cultural victims. Unlike many ethnic Burmese, who were massacred under Ne Win's murderous regime, the Pa Dawng managed to escape across the border to Thailand. It may be true that, at present, for economic and/or political reasons, Thailand refuses to help its Burmese refugees. If this is a fact, the Pa Dawng face two choices: they can return to Burma, and face ethnic genocide; or find a way to abide in Thailand until world attention motivates the Thai government to give them the aid they require.

Travel writing is usually viewed as romantic, but doing it for a living quickly makes a realist out of you. It's a thin line, sometimes, between opportunity and exploitation. For me, the bottom line is that the Pa Dawng were *offered* a choice of reviving their neck ring tradition for income. While dire straits may have compelled them to do so, it's extremely patronizing to deny them either responsibility or credit for their decision. These are not helpless primitives who, enticed by a few shiny coins, sold themselves into cultural slavery. They are pragmatic people, and survivors. Though their compromise can be perceived as uncomfortable and even degrading, one must allow that they have made their choice for a reason. The situation on the Thai/Burmese border stinks, but any outrage directed at the Pa Dawng's survival tactic had better be accompanied by an alternative solution. Meanwhile, similar choices—by people who must perform dangerous or uncomfortable work in order to feed their families—are being made in this country as well. (I do find it admirable that the Pa Dawng women's "occupation"—unlike hotel work, PC-board assembly, or sneaker sewing—allows them to spend most of the day with their children.)

I enjoyed meeting the Pa Dawng women. They are dignified, articulate, and funny. And the fact that their walls were peppered with self-portraits from magazines and newspapers indicted, at least to me, that they aren't ashamed of their lifestyle. I did not, and do not, feel it is my place to either damn or pity them for the decision to turn a possibly arcane tradition into a lucrative tourist attraction.

Nor do I feel the situation is without larger value. My sincere hope is that the debate over the Pa Dawng will focus attention on Thailand's role in the refugee crisis—and lead, ultimately, to a regional solution. For if there is an ultimate goal here, it is not the elimination of neck rings; it is the day when all ethnic Burmese can return to a free Burma.

Jeff Greenwald also contributed "Bite-sized Buddhas" and "In the Andaman Sea" to this book.

★

"How big is a stick?" Ajahn Chah once asked his disciples. "It depends on what you want to use it for, doesn't it? If you need a bigger one, then it's too small. If you need a smaller one, then it's too big. A stick isn't big or small at all. It becomes so as a product of your desires. In this way, suffering is brought into the world."

—Tim Ward, *What the Buddha Never Taught*

BETTY MCLAIN

* * *

Slime and Punishment

*An arduous experience is often
the most memorable.*

SMITTY AND I ARE HANGING OVER THE WOODEN BASKET DESIGNED for one small Thai. Our backs and knuckles ache as we squeeze the rails. The mammoth hairy elephant under us does a nimble tango straight up the waterfall. The four-hour ride is a feature of our trek to become one with the primitive hill tribes of northern Thailand. For six days we sleep in various huts, help winnow rice, wash in rivers, boat down the river separating Thailand from Burma.

For me it is an "Outward Bound" experience that I am determined to complete. I am the slowest of our group of eight. Our guide, Eckisid, moves swiftly through the jungle on thonged, sure feet. He spots a cobra in our path and beats him to death. Smitty is the victim of leech bites. I struggle through the twenty-mile, eight-hour walking day up 1,000-feet elevation, then 1,000 feet down, carrying a borrowed, World War II rucksack that digs into my shoulders.

For five nights I do not sleep. I learn about being cold all night—hungry, thirsty, dirty. I listen for the night sounds inside our bamboo hut on stilts; the village opium smokers puffing by candlelight in the adjoining room, the young New Zealand couple making love next to me, the pigs rustling about a human squatting outside near our hut (how I hate these aggressive pigs who cannot wait for our excrement to fall!), the chorus of roosters, animals, villagers pounding their rice at four in the morning. We see the wild marijuana and the Thai-Burmese black market of smuggled teak.

This jungle trek unites us as a group with our sensitive, peace-loving guide as its head. We come to love him, as well as Shozo, a young Japanese with a serious speech impediment. He enchants the village children with international language: the folded paper crane.

This trek is the most exciting experience of my life, and the entire week, including food, boats, and all, costs less than dinner out back home!

Betty McLain sent this journal entry to Rick Steves and John Gottberg for inclusion in their book Asia Through the Back Door.

★

Trekking out of Chiang Mai is neither as cheap nor as straightforward as it used to be. There are still some excellent treks to be had, if you deal with the right people. But to deal with the wrong people is to court disaster. Recently, there have been too many cases of over-trekked areas and inadequate service from trek companies. This produces the following kind of situations:

- All we got to eat for three days were hardboiled eggs—with baby chicks inside them. They were so well disguised by the sugar coating that we munched quite a few before realizing the truth.
- Our guide was out of his head on opium. The village chief gave him a pipe of peace, and the two of them spent the next 36 hours horizontal. Come to think of it, we hardly ever saw the guide in an upright position—even on an elephant.
- Our bamboo raft disintegrated in the middle of the river. Our guide and two old ladies were left dangling out of a tree. The next day, our elephants stampeded off into the jungle.

• We arrived in a village to find a party of package tourists already there—all clicking away with Nikons and peering into private family huts. It was like a human zoo!

Good trek companies come and go, and your best recommendations will always come from speaking to other travelers.

—Frank Kusy, *Cadogan Guides: Thailand*

E. M. SWIFT

* * *

Sport in the Land of *Sanuk*

*What is Thailand's favorite sport? If it
isn't fighting (fish, kites, bulls, boxers),
it must be wagering.*

I BEGAN TO SUSPECT WE WERE IN FOR A FAIRLY UNUSUAL TRIP
shortly after the visit to the snake farm. A man there had leaped
into a pit with three deadly cobras, caught one in his left hand and
another in his right, and then while holding those two squirming
vipers aloft, put his face inches in front of the third. Serpent and
man bobbed and feinted at each other—cobras apparently have
poor depth perception—until with a sudden thrust the man
crashed his face against the snake and, because the snake was on the
cement floor, against that as well. The man wriggled there as if
stricken, gathered himself, then rose to his feet in triumph. To the
relief and the disgust of the spectators—most of them tourists—he
now had the third cobra in his mouth. His teeth grasped the back
of the snake's hood while its tail lashed him across the chest and
shoulders. The proud man circled the pit, posing with the snakes
for pictures.

Back in our river taxi, one of the ubiquitous, long-tailed
motorized gondolas that navigate Bangkok's canals, I asked our
guide, "Have you ever been face-to-face with a cobra?"

"I killed many cobra." James replied without bragging. James'
real name is Chamnong Tongkaew. He asked that we call him

James though, because he likes James Bond. One of the Bond movies, *The Man with the Golden Gun*, had been filmed in Thailand.

"In the rainy season, after flooding, cobra come inside my house," James explained. "Have nowhere else to live. Dogs help me. They bark and block the door. I use stick. I try to use my hand like the man in the snake farm, but is very difficult. I use stick. Cobra very good to eat. Old saying our country: Mongoose, he eats cobra. Cobra, he eats rat. Rat, he eats rice. But Thai people—we eat al-l-l of them."

James sensed our queasiness. "Not city rat," he assured us. "Rice paddy rat. Is very good. Better than chicken. Not as good as cobra. You will have some before you leave. But you maybe will not know it." James smiled his wonderful smile as the river taxi continued its lazy tour of the filthy, fascinating *klongs*. My wife, Sally, pointed out a lovely private home tucked among the wooden huts and salt barges–turned–houseboats. "Yes, very beautiful," agreed James. "Owner must be corrupt."

Sports in Thailand. That was the idea. Go to Bangkok, poke around the countryside, paddle through the *klongs* and find out what the Thais like to do for sport. Over the centuries people have come to beautiful, exotic Thailand looking for many things. Few have left disappointed. Between the 16th and 18th centuries, when Thailand was known as Siam (the name was changed in 1939 when Premier Pibun Songgram sought to expand his country's borders to include all Thai-speaking regions), the Burmese came looking for riches and slaves. In the mid-1800s the

At sunrise I had taken an early bus to the Chin River and unpacked my kayak on a landing by 6:30 a.m. Everyone else appeared to be up to make the most of the cool morning hours. As I removed the frame sections and unrolled the canvas hull, I noticed local Thais were not self-conscious about staring. As if in a trance, they stood in a circle around me until I motioned one person to help. I suddenly had smiling faces and helping hands all around. It became a pattern wherever I visited in Thailand that local people, at the slightest sign of friendliness, would offer to help assemble my kayak.

—Peter Aiken,
"Thai Waterways"

Chinese began a steady immigration, seeking opium and opportunity. At the same time European traders were arriving, hungering for rice, silk, teak, and tin.

The Americans did not make their presence felt until the Vietnam era when thousands of R&R-seeking GIs sought out a particular section of Bangkok known as Patpong looking for go-go girls and sex. More recently tourists of all nationalities have come to Thailand for its superb shopping, mouth-watering food, scenery, temples, festivals, royalty, and—above all—charming, hospitable people. But to come in search of sports?

"This is a most unusual request," said James, upon being told of our mission. "I must make some phone calls."

James called us the next morning to say that we had missed by a week the elephant festival in Surin, a day's train ride from Bangkok. The event is a two-day rodeo held each November in which trained elephants run races, roll logs, and play soccer. And 100 soldiers challenge an elephant to a tug-of-war.

It would have been an interesting spectacle, especially because elephants have played an important part in Thai history. One of the nation's most famous battles in the town of Nong Sarai in 1593 turned in favor of the Thais when King Naresuan met and killed the Burmese crown prince in a duel on elephant-back, ending 30 years of Burmese rule. Mongkut, King Rama IV, after whom the king in *The King and I* was modeled (because so much of it is imprecise history and derides the king, the movie is officially banned in Thailand), once offered to send Abraham Lincoln a herd of elephants to help stem the Confederate tide during the Civil War. Honest Abe declined.

We had asked James to check into kite fighting, but here, too, we were out of luck. During the windy season between February and April, the Thais fly brightly colored kites of all shapes and sizes playing a game with them that amounts to an aerial battle of the sexes. There are teams, referees, national championships, and heavy wagering on each fight's outcome. Of course, the Thais would bet on raindrops running down a windowpane. They, like the Chinese, are gambling devotees. The idea is for the large male kite, the *chula,* to clasp the smaller female kite, the *pak pao,* in its bamboo talons. As you might imagine, this is not an easy task requiring teams of as many as twenty men to handle the massive (up to 25 feet) *chulas.* The *pak pao,* meanwhile, flits and dances gaily beneath its suitor endeavoring to fly up and loop its line around the *chula's* head causing the larger kite to plummet to earth.

James did assure us that we could see as much Thai boxing as we wanted and we arranged to do so that night. Thai boxing, the most famous of the indigenous Thai sports is not just kick boxing. Elbows, fists, and knees are part of the arsenal, although biting, spitting, hair pulling, and head butting are penalized. *Muay Thai,* the proper name for the sport, was originally taught to Siamese soldiers for use in hand-to-hand combat—which explains the anything-goes nature of the rules.

There are two permanent boxing stadiums in Bangkok, the Rajadamnern and the Lumpini, which generally hold fight programs on alternate evenings. Ringside seats are primarily filled with *farangs.* The true fight fans are back a few rows standing waving fistfuls of baht while shouting out odds that change with each solid blow. "Four to five! Four to five." (Thug! Whack!) "Eeeee! Three to one!"

The fights we saw were, for the most part, bloodless affairs. In sixteen bouts over two nights only two ended in knockouts. *Muay Thai* fighters are small—70 percent of them are either fly-weight (112 pounds) or bantam weight (118)—and many are barely in their teens. "We call ourselves the small chilis," James said, referring to Thai boxers. "The smaller, the hotter."

The evening was a wonderful spectacle. Before each bout the boxers performed an elaborate warm-up dance, called the *wai kru,* which served the dual purpose of loosening the muscles and getting the *Muay Thai* spirits on one's side. Each fighter, in his own highly specialized way, would pay homage to the elders of the *Muay Thai,* men like Nai Khanom Tom, the most famous Thai boxer in history, who, in 1774 as a prisoner of war, defeated ten Burmese boxers in a row to earn his freedom. Often a boxer would encircle the ring with his glove on the top rope to ward off evil spirits.

Some wore amulets around their arms; others wore headbands to hex their opponents.

Strolling along a side-street late that first day we saw a group of young men who had just gotten off work, kicking a woven rattan ball into the air on a school playground. We had heard about this game, called *takraw,* but had not seen it in Bangkok. Now we began to notice it in every playground or schoolyard we passed.

Takraw is, essentially, volleyball with the feet. Three players stand on each side of a 5' 2" high net. Games are played to fifteen. The only time the hands are used is during the serve, when one player is allowed to pitch the ball back to a teammate, who kicks it over the net to start the point.

The agility of the *takraw* players was amazing. Every player could spike the ball with his feet, sometimes doing a full flip afterward to land upright. The best players were so skilled they could take a spike with a foot, and then bunt the ball over with their heads.

There are other versions of the game. In basket *takraw,* three baskets, or nets, are hung some twenty feet off the ground, and players try to kick, head, knee, or elbow the ball through. In the simplest form of *takraw,* a group of players simply tried to keep the ball aloft, showing off trick shots and not keeping score. Thais are individualists with a loose, cheerful approach to team sports. *Thai,* in the Thai language, means "free" and that is very much the spirit that prevails.

The Thais also favor diversity, not specialization, in their sports programs. At Chiang Mai's Hoa Phra Secondary School, we were told that seventh-graders learn table tennis and gymnastics. In eighth grade, students are taught *takraw,* soccer, and *krabi*—an ancient sword-fighting technique. The swords for these thirteen-year-old boys and girls are made of bamboo. In the ninth grade the children learn basketball, volleyball, and track and field. The sessions we attended were organized but not too disciplined. Giggling was a perfectly acceptable way to react to a missed layup or a bamboo sword to the belly.

During recess we noticed one final activity of interest; the kids were playing tag with their feet. One lad stood in the middle of a circle of his classmates while the others jumped in and out teasingly. When the boy in the middle managed to swipe one of the others with a kick, the two exchanged places and the game began anew. For a society that considers the foot an extremity of exceedingly low esteem, the Thais certainly employ it a lot for amusement.

From Chiang Mai we flew down to the island of Phuket in the Andaman Sea. Only a few years ago Phuket was considered an undiscovered paradise, but paradise has been found and taken over by sun-hungry Europeans, particularly Germans, who have changed the ambiance just a little. For sports there are golf and tennis and various water activities. In Phuket the only Thais one sees are in bow ties carrying *mai-tais*.

Old pal James found us a bullfight in the mainland town of Chiang Di, however, a three-hour drive from Phuket to the eastern side of the peninsula. Bullfighting in Thailand, he told us, was not at all like bullfighting in Spain. The bulls fought each other, no one died; much money was bet. The action was spellbinding. James assured us we would be the only *farangs* in attendance.

We rose at dawn and, taking leave of our beachfront hotel, crossed the bridge to the mainland. In the distance we could see the lights of the squid boats plying the Andaman Sea. On the coastal highway we passed sheer and bizarre limestone formations jutting up from the sea. These, too, had been features in *The Man with the Golden Gun,* and one formation, called James Bond Island, is now one of Thailand's most popular tourist attractions. Heading inland, we drove through miles of rubber plantations, watching workers as they gathered the buckets of sap. The sap was poured into bath-mat-sized sheets of raw latex that were then hung from rails by the roadway to cure in the sun like great slabs of mozzarella cheese.

At the bullfight we were greeted by a striking billboard depicting a white bull and a black bull squaring off before a sack of 200,000 baht. This was to be the featured event. A full day's admission (fifteen fights) was expensive for the locals, so the rambutan trees overlooking the back fence of the bullring sagged with spectators sitting shoulder to shoulder. Midway through a particularly exciting contest, fifteen of them plummeted ingloriously to the ground when one of the branches snapped.

The fighting bulls, Brahman strain, were matched by size. Before each fight the referee thoroughly washed both bulls, particularly the horns, to discourage the sort of hanky-panky that seems inevitable anytime men gamble on animals. Some trainers, we were told, used the trick of rubbing essence of tiger on the shoulders of their bull, so that the opposing bull would smell the tiger, become afraid, and run away.

After the bulls were washed, their faces and shoulders were smeared with bananas, the natural oil in the fruit protecting the bull's skin against chafing. And a powerful lot of chafing was to follow, for the bulls fought not by making long, fearsome charges at each other, like rams, but by butting their heads together and pushing like football linemen. The struggle was primordial. As the animals braced and heaved in the center of the dusty ring, their muscles gathered like waves. And each step forward, each step back, changed the odds in the fight. A fight ended when one bull, sensing his opponent was stronger, backed off and ran away.

The longest fight we saw lasted 45 minutes. The shortest ended in a matter of seconds. Afterward, the handlers pounded the bulls' muscles to relax them and doctored their scrapes and gouges by spitting soda water into the open wounds. Judging by the bulls' reactions, this was their least favorite part of the day. The handlers, who literally had to take the bulls by the horns and press their lips into the raw, sore flesh of the still-sweating behemoths, seemed none too fond of it either.

As James had promised, we had been the only foreigners there, and the experience was exhilarating. People had moved to offer us their seats and shared their chili-covered grapefruit with us. They had explained through interpretation and sign language the betting procedures, the ebb and flow of the fights, and which bull was doing better and why. Fathers were there with their sons as fathers and sons in the U.S. spend Sundays together watching football.

Two days later we left touristy Phuket and returned to Bangkok.

We were staying at the Regent Bangkok, a few blocks from Lumpini Park, and early one morning, I got up for a jog. The park, to my surprise, was packed with thousands of people at 6 a.m. Joggers crowded the track. An aerobics class was being held in the shadow of the statue of King Rama VI. A group of elderly people practiced the balletic martial art of *t'ai chi ch'uan*, moving so deliberately that they looked like flowers opening with the dawn. Another large group of older people was spread out on a knoll in semi-disarray, a sort of human Stonehenge, hands on hips, bending at the waist, wailing like banshees. Sweaty jog gers, into a more contemporary form of exercise, would trot past. The old folks on the knoll would let out a howl and 50 tired runners would burst out laughing.

There were three badminton games in progress, a man was swinging a sword, a golfer was practicing chip shots, some boys were playing soccer, and a group of Thai boxers were shadow-boxing. Because of Bangkok's oppressive heat, of course, dawn is the ideal time to exercise.

James wanted us to see one final attraction, a Siamese fish fight, but it seemed they were only held on the weekends. We would be gone by then. So we decided to hold our own. When James was a boy, he had found his fighting fish by going down to the rice paddies and scooping them up in his hands. The females, which he could identify by a white mark

Henk [an expatriate Dutchman] drove us down a narrow alley to avoid the traffic jam on Phya Thai Road. We crawled through soi after soi, each one crowded with shops spilling into the center of the alley. Lights glared over tables filled with cloth-ing, bolts of fabric, watches, and hardware; food stalls lined every curb, steam rose from cooking pots, and the smells of grilled meat wafted on the thick air. Music blared, and people were every-where, doing business, hanging out, laughing with friends, passing the time, all part of the driving energy of the night. Guiding the car slowly through the melee, gazing through the windshield with a sweaty rapture on his face, Henk said suddenly, "This is why I live here! There is so much life! You would never find people out like this in Holland."

—Larry Habegger,
"Eating the Wind"

on the fin, he returned to the water. Only the males will fight. Then
he and his friends would get together and bet on the outcome.
Kids in Thailand also stage cricket fights and beetle fights and in
rural areas, we had seen them playing pitch-penny with washers and
wagering rubber bands, which they wore on their arms by dozens
like prized jewelry.

We did not have the time or inclination to seek out a rice paddy,
so we took a taxi to the local pet store which sold fighting fish for
$1 each. They were easy to spot. Each required its own separate
plastic baggie, filled with a little water. The baggies floated on top
of the goldfish aquarium by the score. Had the fighting fish been
turned loose, the owner told us, they would have torn each other
to ribbons. They seemed harmless enough to look at, about the size
of a thumb and murky brown or gray in color. We purchased nine
of them plus a baggie of mosquito larvae to sustain their strength.

The fish customarily fight in round jars so there is no hiding
in corners. We bought two of them, plus four containers of unpu-
rified water. While setting everything up back at the hotel, James
told us to be careful not to put the fish within sight of another or
they would mash their faces against the glass in an effort to attack.
The same was true if you put one in front of a mirror. He would
butt himself into submission. It was difficult to believe that this
innocuous-looking little creature before me was so full of anger
and aggression.

And then the battle. For the next four hours we fought these
game little roughnecks. When they first faced each other in the
jar, the fish literally lit up. Their dull colors immediately flushed
to iridescent crimson, emerald, or aquamarine. Their fins flared
out as they circled. Then, finally, they attacked.

It was not as vicious as we had been led to believe. No fish
was torn to ribbons. Shredded a little, perhaps, at least around the
fins, which was the primary focus of attack. Sometimes one would
latch onto another's gill which seemed to be an effective hold.
And often the two would become clamped in a liplock, turn
upside down, and fight that way for a while. When one had had
enough—the fights seldom lasted more than ten minutes—it

would suddenly back off, lose all color, turning almost completely white, and swim away. Then, as had happened with the bulls, the victor would follow the vanquished around the jar without attacking. Bets were paid. The fight was history.

Two fish remained undefeated. One was a favorite of James, a pig with fins, a blue monster the size of a big toe. The other was mine, Rama I, a green tiger with a lifetime 4-0 record. I wouldn't put him in against James' pig. One thing I had learned from watching the bulls and fish was that the big guy eventually won. He would wear down the smaller, quicker opponent with the great big heart. Every time.

James took his monster home with him. I had a feeling that it would make the rounds that weekend at the local fish-fighting hangout. We flushed the losers down the toilet with enough mosquito larvae to sustain them, if they were lucky, for months. As for Rama I, I put him in a jar, took a taxi to the *klong* and dropped him in beside a water-hyacinth. It was only fair. Like the great Thai boxer, Nai Khanom Tom, the man who had defeated ten Burmese, that fish had earned its freedom. Thailand, after all, means "land of the free."

E.M. Swift is a senior writer for Sports Illustrated. *He lives in Carlisle, Massachusetts, when he's not traveling.*

✳

"*Kriangjai*" denotes reluctance to bother someone of higher status with a petty matter. Or upsetting someone with bad news. Thus, an underling may neglect to tell his boss the water pipes have burst and flooded the basement because that would upset him. Worse yet, it would make the underling the bearer of bad tidings and thus reflect badly in his boss's eyes. Much better to let someone else tell him or let the boss discover it himself.

—Steve Van Beek, "Thailand Notes"

PART THREE

GOING YOUR OWN WAY

SUSAN FULOP KEPNER

* * *

Mein Gott, Miss Siripan

*Learning a tonal language such as Thai is a
challenge under any circumstances, yet
not without unexpected rewards.*

THERE ARE SEVERAL REASONS WHY PEOPLE STRIVE TO BECOME
fluent in the local language when they go to work in a foreign
country. One is sheer intellectual curiosity; another is the fear of
being left out of a conversation just when it is getting interesting.
Driven entirely by the latter motivation, the first thing I did when
I went to work in Thailand was to look for a language tutor.

Miss Siripan came highly recommended by my next-door
neighbor Mallika. Mallika's version of English was unique and inno-
vative. Much later, I would undersand the reason: her self-taught
English was ingeniously—and directly—translated from Thai.

"I tell you true, Mrs. Su-san, Miss Siripan not can teach you
Thai, not have a day you learn, for sure. This woman better from
every Thai teacher."

True, Mallika went on, Miss Siripan wasn't *exactly* Thai. But she
was practically born in Thailand, and if the boat from China had
gone a little faster, she would have been. "This is the fault of Miss
Siripan?"

Certainly not, I agreed.

Miss Siripan had a Thai name and she spoke perfect Thai, and
she had taught herself both German and English. Miss Siripan

was the smartest person Mallika had ever met. "Never mind what people say."

What did people say?

Mallika waved her hand dismissively. "About how she crazy, about how she a mean woman. She just like a determine woman, that's all, she perfect for you learn talking like a real Thai."

I shall never forget the day Miss Siripan first appeared on my front porch. She stood framed by the screen door, a gaunt woman of about 35 with a fierce, square smile and enormous sunglasses that she never removed. She introduced herself in a startlingly high-pitched voice that rose imperiously at the end of each phrase.

"I have taught many Americans," she said. "Most are dummies. Expecially the men, to my experience. But the women are more lazy, to my experience. What are you thinking about that?"

"Well, I…"

"Never mind. Why are you not inviting me inside your house?"

"Oh, I am sorry. Whatever can I be thinking of…"

"How do I know?"

I opened the door. Miss Siripan slipped out of her shoes, as one always does in Thai homes, strode through the living room, into the dining room, and sat down at the head of the table.

"Sit down, Mrs. Su-san," she gestured graciously. "Thank you. If you are lazy or a dummy, I will not teach you. If you tell a lie to me, I will never come back. If you wish to learn Thai language you must read Thai. Not what you call pho-ne-tic. *Pho-ne-tic* is not good. Make you talk so nobody can know what you say. I teach you Thai alphabet. You talk Thai like a Thai people, not like pho-ne-tic."

"Frankly, Miss Siripan, I thought that perhaps—"

"You perhaps nothing. You want to learn Thai from me, I must be proud when somebody hear you."

She dug around in her huge handbag, finally coming up with a Thai primer. On the first page she pointed out the first letter of the alphabet, *gaw,* which looks like "n" and is equivalent to a hard "g." Above *gaw* was a picture of a big black chicken, *gai.* *Gaw* is for *gai,* just as "a" is for "apple."

"Look at *gaw*," she commanded, tapping one dagger-like fingernail on the chicken's beak. "American pho-ne-tic say this same 'k' so maybe you go around and never know is *not* same 'k.' Is sound *gaw gaw gaw*, not *kaw kaw kaw* like crow. You want forever say *kai* instead of *gai* when you try to buy chicken and market woman think you say *kai*-egg from letter *kaw* but you only know American pho-ne-tic so you never hear any difference, and Thai people think you not know what, Mrs. Su-san?"

Thai consonants

ก ข ค ฆ ง จ ฉ ช ซ
ฌ ญ ฎ ฏ ฐ ฑ ฒ ณ ด
ต ถ ท ธ น บ ป ผ ฝ
พ ฟ ภ ม ย ร ล ว ศ
ษ ส ห ฬ อ ฮ

Inside me, a tiny voice was saying, "If this woman is still here in fifteen minutes, you will have agreed to anything."

The mesmerizing tap of Miss Siripan's amazing fingernail on the chicken's beak continued. "Repeat after me this one sentence." She slowly pronounced a series of sounds, I strained to pronounce them. No mynah bird could have done better.

Thai vowels

–ะ –า –ิ –ี –ึ –ื –ุ –ู
เ–ะ เ– เ–อะ เ–อ
เ–า เ–อะ เ–ียะ เ–ีย
เ–ือ แ– ะ แ– โ–ะ
โ– ใ– ไ–

Why did I try so hard? Was it because I hoped to vindicate my countrymen (dummies) and women (lazies)? Or because I could not—for reasons I couldn't begin to understand—bear to disappoint Miss Siripan?

When I finished, there was a long silence, the first since her arrival.

"Mein Gott!" she exclaimed in a stage whisper, then grasped my hands with excruciating force. *"Mein Gott,* Mrs. Su-san, you have ear! I can't believe it, I finally got a student who hears Thai language. All many damn dummies and lazy women and now, now I am luckiest Thai teacher in Bangkok. You know what you said, Mrs. Su-san?"

"Something about a chicken?"

She roared with laughter and wiped her eyes. "Never mind damn chicken. I just fool you about that. You said, '*I will write Thai language.*'

Fifteen minutes had not passed. She had hooked me in three.

"Today I tell you twenty letters," she continued, now triumphant. "You say after me until you perfect, then you write one hundred times each letter for homework. I come back tomorrow with more books."

An American study in the 1970s found that American speakers were best able to pronounce Thai sentences after consuming one ounce of alcohol.

—Michael Buckley,
Bangkok Handbook

"When will you expect me to have written the twenty letters one hundred times?"

"Why you not listen to me? I said I come back tomorrow. Every day, twenty letters. On fourth day, finish all sixty-four alphabet letters and feel pride and happiness. Then for two weeks practice five tones of Thai language, and make one hundred sentences every day. Then for two months read newspaper and make vocabulary. Then you will be a Thai-speaking person." She sat back and smiled. "Not one hundred percent, but I won't have to be ashamed when somebody hear you."

The weeks passed. Hour after hour, day after day, I copied, memorized, repeated sounds. First letters, then words, then the five tones of the Thai language which are as important as the alphabet itself. To change "horse" to "dog," or "wood" to "new," nothing was required but the rise and fall of the voice.

Three months passed. Then one evening as I stared at the dozens of sheets of homework filled with columns of scribbled words, I was overwhelmed. I had completed only 64 of my mandatory 100 new sentences for the week. My mind was empty. I didn't want to learn anything. I quit, and I didn't *care.*

But the next evening, when I heard Miss Siripan walking up the path, suddenly I cared very, very much. The quite justifiable speech I had rehearsed 20 or 30 times had become a mouthful of ashes.

There was only one sensible thing to do, and I did it. I ran upstairs, locked myself in the bathroom, and told my servant Anong to tell Miss Siripan that I was quite, quite ill.

I had *told a lie.*

Cowering in the bathroom, I heard Miss Siripan speak sharply to Anong. The terrified Anong whimpered in reply and scurried away. Then came the steady pad, pad of Miss Siripan's bare feet on the stairs.

"Mrs. Su-san," she shouted. "You not sick. You not finish sentences. True or false?"

"I…please, not today."

"You see! You afraid make more lies."

I hated myself for the sniffling, squeaking noises that were escaping through the bath towel.

"Sounding like a mouse, Mrs. Su-san," Miss Siripan said. She laughed, softly for her, and said, "I know you are not a dummy, not lazy. Maybe I make too hard for you. I come back tomorrow. You make only, maybe fifty sentences. But no more lies."

"Thank you," I whispered through the door, but didn't unblock it. "I promise I will never lie to you again."

"Stop that mouse crying. Stay in the bathroom so you not have to look at me and lose your face."

Her footsteps faded away, the screen door banged shut. I watched the second hand on my watch go around twice, then unlocked the door. Ever afterword, I would understand the subtle give-and-take of "saving face."

In another month I was truly reading, writing, and speaking Thai. Not 100 percent, but Miss Siripan did not have to be "ashamed for somebody to hear me." Her joy in my progress was almost embarrassing. But my ability to hold up under her will, what had become her total domination of my life, was crumbling. And so I grasped at a feeble excuse, in an attempt to pull away.

"Miss Siripan," I began, keeping my eyes fixed on the newspaper I had been reading aloud to the steady tap-tap of her fingernail. ("Mrs. Su-san! *Thai* rhythm. *Thai* rhythm.") "Miss Siripan, there's something I have to tell you. Really, it's good news."

The tapping stopped abruptly.

"I got a promotion at work." This was true. Whatever excuse I used, it would have to be at least grounded in the truth. "Of course, I'm *thrilled,* and I'm sure you know that a big part of it is all you've done for me."

Silence.

I began babbling. "This will mean I have to work a lot more hours—actually, I'll probably rue the day I got promoted—and I—I hope you will undertand but I am just going to *have* to take a break from studying Thai for a while. Of course, it won't be permanent. I mean, I think I just need a few months."

Miss Siripan sat perfectly still for a moment, then rose slowly from the dining room table with an unbearable smile on her face.

"This is not about promotion, is it? Say so, Mrs. Su-san. *Do not tell a lie to me!*"

"I did get a promotion. I have never lied to you since—since that one time. Oh, Miss Siripan. Please, please *try* to understand."

She began stacking her books neatly. Then she reached swiftly across the table and clutched my shoulders. The force of her grasp was painful. And then, with one awful sob, she snatched up her books and her handbag, and fled.

I did not hear from Miss Siripan for an entire year. During that time, I studied with a friend's auntie who was eager to introduce me to Thai literature. Khun Sangworn was a soft-spoken, lovely lady who amused herself by translating French novels into Thai. Every few years she would take a coterie of young Thai ladies on a cultural tour of Switzerland, France, and Italy.

If Miss Siripan had been, as Mallika described her, "not exactly Thai," Khun Sangworn was quintessentially Thai. The contrast between my first teacher and my second was indescribable.

The first time Miss Siripan came back to visit, she was friendly and polite, and made no mention of our lessons together. Although she made clear that she knew I was studying with someone else, we both smiled our way through the conversation, saving each other's face.

Every month or so thereafter, she would drop in unexpectedly for tea. Occasionally she would correct a slip in my Thai, we would laugh, and the sense of strain would fall away. But eventually the visits stopped. I wrote, and my letter was returned "addressee unknown."

I never saw Miss Siripan again.

Over twenty years have passed since I sat across a dining-room table from that remarkable woman, learning to speak Thai with a faintly Chinese-German accent, and reading newspaper articles aloud, frequently interrupted by her high, sharp voice and her shattering laugh.

"Mrs. Su-san, wrong, wrong, wrong! Why you make word for 'revolt' sound like word for 'shrimp paste'? Some revolt. Maybe Mrs. Su-san wants to say about those revolting people. 'Let them eat shrimp paste!'"

"I beg your pardon?"

"What, Mrs. Su-san never study French Revolution?"

The excellent Susan Kepner has also translated and written an introduction to Botan's Letters from Thailand, *which deals with the life of the Chinese minority. Of all the countries of Southeast Asia where Chinese have settled over the last four centuries, it is only in Thailand and to a lesser extent the Philippines that they have been accepted and even assimilated.*

—Richard West, "Royal Family Thais," *New York Review of Books*

"It's not revolting people, Miss Siripan. It's *rebelling.*"

"What is revolting?"

"Actually, shrimp paste is revolting. It smells."

"What you expect? Smell bad because it get old, and smashed with salt."

"Right. So I don't want to eat it. I *rebel...*"

Revolt is ga-*bot*...shrimp paste is ga-*bi*...Never to be forgotten.

I remember particularly one day toward the end of our lessons together, when she appeared with those other books.

"Mrs. Su-san, you speak pretty good Thai now. I have taught you because I had an intelligent idea. If American can read Thai alphabet and make all sounds fluently, that American can use Thai for something important. Here, you copy this."

She scribbled something on a sheet of paper and pushed it toward me.

"But, Miss Siripan, this is a *Chinese character!* What does this have to do with my Thai?"

"Ha, ha! Perfect Thai alphabet with vowel and tone can make pho–ne–tic way for learn Chinese one hundred percent better from English pho–ne–tic for Chinese. English pho–ne–tic smell for learn Thai, smell worse one hundred times for learn Chinese. Make you speak Chinese like I not know what—

"Oi, Mrs. Su-san! You crying? You going to lock yourself in bathroom again?"

She smiled, but then, sensing my mood, she asked, "You angry, Mrs. Su-san?"

"It isn't a matter of angry—I mean anger. I guess I just can't cope with this—this idea of yours."

"Cope?" she frowned. "I do not know this word, *cope.*"

"It means—well, I just can't begin to manage the idea of studying Chinese at this point."

"Ah." Her expression relaxed. "*Manage.* I know about *manage.* Never mind. I manage. You write."

No, Miss Siripan. I wasn't angry. Not then, not now. Wherever you are, I hope you have a student who does not tell lies, and who has an ear, and who, *Mein Gott,* will remember you as fondly as I do.

Susan Fulop Kepner teaches at the University of California, Berkeley. She has translated the novels Letters from Thailand *and* Child of the Northeast.

★

Do you want to say "I love you" in Thai?
"*Phom*" always means "I" (male)
"*Dii-chan*" always means "I" (female)
"*Chan*" can mean "I" (male or female)
"*Khun*" and "*thoe*" both mean "you" (male or female)
"*Chan rak thoe*" for "I love you" is far more common than "*Chan rak khun,*" since "*khun*" is rather more formal in the context of such intimacy.

—Joe Cummings

KAREN L. LARSEN

* * *

Farang for a Day

*Stagefright isn't the only thing that melts
in this meeting between a teacher from
Montana and a class of 200 students.*

THE FADED GREEN VAN WORMED ITS WAY THROUGH THE BANGKOK
streets lined with shops all filled with an infinite variety of goods
oozing out of the cracks and spilling onto the sidewalks. As we
drove across the Chao Phya river, the discussion in the van, alternating between Thai and English, flowed from my life in Bangkok
fifteen years ago to what I was to encounter at Wat Noi Nai,
where I'd teach for the day.

As we turned down the small *soi* lined with fenced houses and
an occasional open-air restaurant, I was exasperated to learn I'd be
facing a morning and an afternoon class of two hundred students
each. The Thai teachers calmly told me I could teach the students
a game or do conversation with the classes—whichever I liked.
"Two hundred students? A game? Conversation to two hundred?"
I thought, "And in *one* class? This is crazy." Before I had time to
reconsider my decision to come here for the day, I was told how
fortunate the school felt. "We haven't had a foreign teacher for
many years. Our students will be so lucky to have you today.
We're so pleased and fortunate." How could I turn back now? I
was their *farang* for a day, some students' only contact with a native
English speaker. Two hundred students or not, here I was.

Entering the school compound, I noticed the field in front of the flagpole filled with endless rows of students dressed in stiffly starched, sparkling white shirts and navy blue pants or skirts. All eyes darted in my direction as my hosts escorted me from the van through the heat and humidity to the English office building. The director was announcing over the intercom that today was special because a *farang* would be teaching. I laughed to myself, feeling proud to be considered special and yet knowing I could never give them as much as they thought.

The number two hundred kept running through my mind. I quickly reviewed my past three weeks as an American Field Service Exchange Teacher. At Suan Suanantha in Bangkok, I had survived teaching classes ranging anywhere from thirty-five to sixty-seven students. I had spoken of American life, Montana and its wide open spaces, Joliet, the school and the students there. But with two hundred students? How was I to pass around the picture of my house (You live alone here? Why isn't there a fence around it?), a school bus (It's free. No charge, you mean?), the Joliet cemetery (Bodies are buried there?)—all oddities to Thai students. It would never work—What would I ever do with a class this big?

Before I could decide, my thoughts and fears were driven aside. I was shuffled off to the English department and introduced to teachers who crowded around me as young children around a new toy. Ushered to a desk, I was offered Coke and exotic Thai fruits of rambutan and mangosteen. Two fans were placed to keep me cool, and everyone wanted to know if their special visitor was comfortable. "Do you need more Coke?" "Would you like to go to the bathroom?" "Do you like this kind of fruit? Can we get you another kind?" With all this Thai hospitality and fuss, I hardly had time to think of the class of two hundred awaiting my arrival in a few minutes.

K̆wàa tùa jà sùk, ngâa kâw mâi.
"Before the peanuts are cooked, the sesame (seeds) will have burned."

—Thai proverb

"Come. It is time." I wasn't certain whether I was being led to a death squad or an arena filled with fans, but I quickly followed along behind the Thai teachers who proudly led me to the auditorium. On my entering, the idle chatter among the student's turned to "ooh's" and "ahh's"—once again I felt like a queen or a rock star. Slowly I fell into the cushioned seat offered me, for I was overwhelmed with all the attention. I thought, "What am I going to do?" Again, I heard how fortunate the students were to have me to talk to them, and then came my introduction in Thai. I walked up to the podium where fans and ice-cold Coke awaited me once again.

As I looked out over the ocean of students, my heart melted. Could it be the sweltering heat and humidity of Bangkok that was doing this to me? Or could it be my nervousness in facing all these students?

Drawing in a deep breath, I began what had become a routine—my name, what state I was from as well as telling where Montana was since it is relatively unknown in Thailand, my occupation, and my life in Thailand fifteen years ago. Then came the photos and folders about Montana, Joliet, Yellowstone National Park, Old Faithful, and, naturally, Christmas and snow storms. I wondered how much of all this the Thai students were comprehending. The faces still shined with the heart-warming Thai smiles; their eyes stared unbelievably at the snow, the geysers, the wide open spaces, and the unfenced houses.

Oh, how I would like to take each and every one of them back to America to show them all these things in person. It seemed so unfair for me to be sharing their world of *klongs, wats, ngok rongrien* (rambutan), and *talaats* (markets)—and all I could offer them were pictures and folders. But never once was there any show of displeasure—only hunger for more, more pictures, more spoken English, more stories, more of the *farang*.

Reluctantly, I asked for questions, for knowing the Thai classroom and Thai students I was afraid there would be none. I looked out over this sea again to see if there were any movement. None—only those smiling faces and shining eyes staring up at me.

Again, I begged for questions. Only after telling them they could ask in Thai did I finally get a response. Then came the bombardment of the nine questions I had been asked so often over the past weeks. How old are you? Are you married? Do you have a boyfriend? What do you think of Thailand? What do you think of Thai people? What Thai food can you eat? What Thai fruit do you like? Can you eat durian? And the last and most often asked: Can you sing a song?

Finally, I would smile and say, "No, I can't sing, but I do have a tape of some American songs for you." That always brought the end to any sort of lesson, for the Thai students love to sing or just listen to songs, especially "Old MacDonald." The "quack, quack" part always brought laughter and cries for "one more time, one more time." They struggled through "Bingo" until the clapping and leaving out the letter became routine, while I struggled with the fact that everything I did was being videotaped. Hearing two hundred students singing "B-I-N-G-O, B-I-N-G-O, B-I-N-G-O, and Bingo was his name-o," was amusing, but the highlight was yet to come.

With about twenty minutes left, I fast forwarded the tape to "Skid-a-ma-rink-a-dink-a-dink." Slowly going over the words and having the students repeat each syllable, then each word, then each line, I rewound the tape as fresh Coke was again delivered to the podium. I quickly took a drink to clear my dry throat and asked the students if they were ready. Following the words written on the blackboard, the students loudly sang along to the tape. On the third time, I turned off the tape and looked out over my ocean of students again. My eyes filled with tears as all 200 shining, smiling Thai faces looked up at me and sang "Skidamarinkadinkadink, skidamarinkadinkadink, we love you." How could I ever leave students who were so eager to learn, who were so eager to please their special guest, who were so eager to drink in all a *farang* could tell them?

After the usual "thank you, teacher," with students standing and placing their hands in a *wai,* the show of respect, I gathered my well-fingered photos and folders, received a thank-you gift of pink lotus flowers from the school's director, and stepped off stage. My rock star routine was over, or so I thought. Within minutes about a hundred students with pens, pencils and papers gathered around me. They wanted my name and address, and some without paper requested I sign their shirts or handkerchiefs. It didn't end there—next came the handshakes, about fifty to sixty. Several students handed me gifts of *champoo* (a rose-apple fruit), book-marks, and *kluay hom* (one of the nine types of Thai bananas). I was beginning to think I'd never be able to leave the auditorium, but at last the line ended.

As I made my way through the parted sea, one young Thai stu-dent came running up to me. I held out my hand, thinking she wanted to shake hands. She slowly shook her head from side to side, looked up at me with warm, smiling eyes, and said, "I love you." Dropping the photos and folders to the floor, I quickly grabbed her in my arms and held her tightly, repeating, "I love you." My eyes swelled with tears, my heart melted.

Back now in Montana, each time I recall this particular mem-ory of my summer stay, my heart twinges. Not from the heat and humidity but rather the warmth, hospitality, and love shown by the always-smiling Thai students.

Karen L. Larsen used to teach at Joliet High School, Montana, but seems to have moved on. Perhaps she was drawn back to Thailand, or has taken her skills to another foreign land.

✳

Buddhism has not been kind to women. Although there is evidence that they once were ordained as monks, none exist today. The logic employed to bar them from the priesthood is specious. No less an authority than Kukrit Pramoj (found elsewhere in this book) argues that a nun can only be ordained by another nun. And since there are no ordained nuns, there is no one to anoint a new one. A woman may wear white robes and live in a nunnery but does not enjoy the same respect as a monk. She achieves grace through men. Thus, when a man takes vows as a monk, he earns merit not only for himself but for his female relatives. Among his vows is one of chastity which means he cannot touch a woman, not even his

mother. Foreign women are advised to avoid brushing against them, even
in crowded buses, for fear of compromising their vows.

—Steve Van Beek, "Thailand Notes"

KEVIN MC AULIFFE

✦ ✦ ✦

Bridge to Yesterday

*Movies can derive from real experience, but they create real
experience too. For the author, the reality behind a
movie and the reality it created for him meet.*

I WAS EIGHT YEARS OLD WHEN I FIRST SAW *THE BRIDGE ON THE
River Kwai,* and I've seen it twelve times since. I never tire of
watching William Holden desperately splashing across the water
through a hail of Japanese bullets, or Alec Guinness, eyes rolled
back, dying and dynamiting his creation in the same indelible in
stant. With damp palms and racing pulse, I may yet see my favorite
war movie another dozen times.

Director David Lean's 1957 epic affected millions of other
viewers, some of them no less *Kwai*-struck than I. Pierre Boulle's
best-selling French novel,
on which the film was
based, goes on attracting
new readers. Still, few today
realize that the Kwai fiction
is actually fact—there was
indeed such a bridge dur-
ing World War II.

The movie that rivets
me was imaginary mainly
to the extent that Lean

The Bridge over the River Kwai

233

shot it in Sri Lanka, a thousand miles from its wartime origins. As soon as I first learned this, I began musing about the real Kwai, the real shooting location as it were, and I dreamed of someday exploring whatever ruins survived.

My reading informed me that the wartime bridge spanned the banks of the Kwai in a town called Kanchanaburi, in the interior of Thailand, about 80 miles northwest of Bangkok. Japanese military planners saw this place as ideal for spanning the river and completing a strategic rail link between Rangoon and Bangkok. To do the job, the Japanese turned 30,000 Allied POWs and 100,000 Asian civilians (mostly Chinese and Malay coolies) into slave laborers. More than half were worked to death under hellish conditions.

In real life, no commandos trekked through the jungle to blow up the bridge; but Allied bombers, after repeated attempts, finally destroyed it in 1945. After the war, Thailand reopened the rail line as far as its remote hill country—and restored the bridge on the river Kwai.

It is still there, still operating—which meant, when I recently planned a solo trip through Asia, that I really had no choice. I had to find and see the real bridge for myself.

In 1977, local Buddhist monks opened a museum on the site of one of the POW camps; a few travelers with wartime memories have since made their way to Kanchanaburi. But only recently has the Thai Government recognized the historical (and tourist) value of the place. Indeed, the travel agent who booked my hotels in Asia tried to convince me that it would be impossible to see the bridge on my own, much less go there and return the same day.

As it turned out, I had ample time not only to visit Bangkok's Grand Palace and Wat Phra Keo Temple, but also to take a bus from the city out to the bridge and back—all in one day.

Buses for the two-and-a-half-hour trip are plentiful. Air-conditioned coaches depart every hour directly across from the local railroad station on Charansanitwong Road in the Thonburi district. Regular buses leave every fifteen minutes from a terminal two blocks south. At current exchange rates, either bus is far cheaper than a taxi ride across Bangkok. And both stop at Nakhon Pathom, where you can walk into Asia's tallest Buddhist pagoda, then simply board the next bus to resume your journey.

In Kanchanaburi, I found a modern provincial capital of 50,000 people, surrounded by lush green hills. The Japanese used it for their construction headquarters and POW camps. Following the bilingual street signs along Saeng

Railroad buffs can take the train to Kanchanaburi, then take a local across the bridge to Nam Tok.

—JO'R and LH

Chuto Road, the town's main drag, I quickly found the Tourism Authority of Thailand office, received directions, and walked another five minutes to the War Museum along the river banks.

The museum is a reconstruction of a typical bamboo barracks for POWs. Inside, vintage photos, mementos, news articles, and prisoners' reminiscences graphically describe the barbaric treat ment its inmates endured. Among the prize military curios on display: an undetonated bomb dropped by a B-24 in a vain attempt to knock out the bridge. An American traveling alone notices other Westerners, but the noisy bustle of conducted groups is mercifully absent. Postcards, t-shirts, and bric-a-brac are quietly for sale, but the town is refreshingly devoid of tourist traps. And one can't help noticing something else—Asian ambivalence about Japan, as when the museum juxtaposes its vivid documentation of wartime atrocities with a plea "not for the maintenance of hatred among human beings especially among the Japanese."

A short walk along the river yielded my first view of "modern" Kwai—pagoda-topped huts poking through the vegetation, motorized *sampans* chugging past, floating concession stands on wooden pontoons selling Pepsi and myriad Asian thirst-quenchers that I eagerly tried as the temperature topped 105 degrees.

Given the heat, I hired a guide. It was a good move. For one thing, Kanchanaburi has become urban, devoid of whatever shade it once had, and most "Death Railway" sites are several miles apart. For another, tourism has not yet soured people here—they can be bargained with, minus the hostility that pervades other places.

Veins popping as he propelled us uphill on his trusty *samlor*, my guide pedaled me to Chung Kai, smaller of the Allied cemeteries, and then to the imposing Kanchanaburi War Cemetery outside town (7,000 Allied POW graves, beautifully arranged and maintained). Farther along the road, he pointed out the surprisingly unheralded cemetery for the many more Chinese who died. Somehow, the scruffy look of these graves—Buddhist spires and idiogram inscriptions wedged together in the dirt, underbrush poking through in spots—was more moving.

Next he took me through cliffside streets (named for the countries whose nationals worked on the railway) to a cenotaph erected by the Japanese—in memory of all who died there, on both sides. That Asian ambivalence again: no signpost whatsoever marked the way to the Japanese cenotaph.

Finally, we reached the bridge itself: not the wood and bamboo edifice of the movie, but the *real* bridge on the river Kwai—thick wrought iron, steel tresses, concrete stanchions. With its black beams and rivets glaring downriver in the sun, this ominous bridge asserts, even if you don't know its history, that it *has* a history.

A plaque tells how and why the Death Railway was preserved. Nearby, one of the first locomotives to make the Rangoon run sits on display. Wooden slats permit easy walking across the span, affording long, graceful vistas of the river. But this is still a working bridge, a fact I realized when I saw a yellow diesel coming out of the mountains, headed straight for me. Fortunately, I hopped onto one of the original guard lookouts, a sort of wooden porch, and duly photographed the train as it passed by.

I followed the track upcountry a bit, then doubled back, keeping in mind that where I stepped, men had died in agony. Other Westerners appeared to be doing the same. Back at the station, two young New Zealanders introduced me to an impressive old man— Trevor Dakin, a former Canadian POW. Dakin was celebrating his 70th birthday by standing on the bridge that, as a 23-year-old, he had been forced to build. He had no camera with him, so I took his photo, and listened as he discussed his life. Wife dead, children grown, he had immigrated, married a Thai woman, and now lived with her on the hill overlooking this spot. And here, where he had survived the most intense experience of his life, and so many of his youthful buddies had not, he would pass the rest of his days. "I'll never go back," he said. "This is my home now."

The sun was setting. My guide (whose labors had cost all of $6) took some final shots of me, then negotiated my ride back to town aboard a cigarette boat owned by a friend of his. In minutes I was streaking past the bungalows, docks, floating restaurants, and other signs of life along the river, looking over my shoulder as the big black bridge receded into the distance.

I had done it. I had actually seen the bridge on the river Kwai— the real thing. But I'd done more than satisfy a long-standing passion. I had encountered the legacy of World War II in a way I never could have otherwise. And I'd seen for myself how, deep in the Asian countryside, life was reclaiming a site where once death had ruled.

Kevin Mc Auliffe is a speechwriter and the author of The Great American Newspaper: The Rise and Fall of the Village Voice.

✦

About 10,000 snake bite injuries are reported in Thailand annually...Unprovoked attacks by snakes are rare. Most bites in Thailand are the result of stepping on the snake and many bites occur at night...The danger of snake bite is generally exaggerated and Bangkok's traffic poses a far greater danger than snakes and tropical disease combined. There are probably less than 100 annual snake bite deaths in Thailand with a mortality rate of 0.2 percent per 100,000 people. The rates are much higher in Burma (3.3 percent) and Sri Lanka (16 percent). India alone has some 20,000 snake bite deaths annually. The United States, for comparison, has 45,000 snake bites per year of which 7,000 are by poisonous species. About 10 annual deaths are reported.

—Henry Wilde, M.D., Supawat Chutivongse, M.D., and Burnett
Q. Pixley, M.D., *Guide to Healthy Living in Thailand*

* * *

The Spirit Likes
a Little Blood

Having just spent time as a lay monk in a Buddhist
temple, the author returns to the city and is
drawn into perplexing relationships.

I WAS INVITED TO A ROOFTOP BARBECUE IN BANGKOK, MY FIRST social event with other foreigners in many months. Party chitchat felt awkward, a grueling ordeal after the silence of the temple. There I met Tham, a rich Thai businesswoman, who took me under her wing, perhaps because she had spent many years in the States becoming Americanized and felt a certain kinship with me in my attempt to immerse myself in a foreign culture. We danced together for most of the evening. She had almond skin, and thick black hair that fell like silk to her shoulders. Her mouth held an enigmatic Thai smile, her eyes a very American-like determination to get what she wanted.

"How long are you staying in Bangkok?" she asked.

"Just a few more days," I replied. "I've almost finished my rough draft. Soon as it's done, I want to get back to the wild. Probably I'll head for Sumatra. Big cities don't do much for me.

"Bangkok can be pretty wild."

I shrugged. "I haven't seen much of it, I guess."

"Stay a while." She touched my arm. "We can have fun together."

Tham took me to Bangkok discotheques, sacred temples, shopping centers, the royal palace, and not-for-tourist Thai restaurants that did not know the meaning of the words *mildly spicy*. She owned a hundred silk dresses and bought jewelry for sport. She traveled first class or by chauffeured limousine and received the kind of respect paid to royalty—even from her family members who came from the village to visit her luxury apartment.

Her estranged husband and business partner was a former CIA operative. They had met in Bangkok during the Vietnam war. James Bond, she called him, scornfully. She had used his influence to get herself a student visa to America. Years later they married, mostly due to his persistence, she claimed. He'd quit his job and set up operations as a middleman for foreign businesses seeking major public-works contracts with the Thai government, basically arranging bribes and keeping potential deal-makers entertained. In Bangkok, that meant frequent visits to the massage parlors of Pat Pong. It stung her deeply that James included the receipts for such services rendered to him with the lists of business expenses that Tham processed every month. She described him as insensitive, jealous, and brutal, but refused to divorce him until their business paid off with a major contract. Until then, buying jewelry served as a form of insurance and revenge. She could only tolerate her situation, she explained, because James was almost always out of the country, setting up deals in Singapore and Hong Kong.

> *Thai police explained to somewhat startled [American] agents that professional Thai criminals sometimes insert pearls in their foreskins as a boast of incarceration. A hardened convict with a number of long sentences behind him may have a ring of pearls encircling his penis.*
>
> —James Mills,
> *The Underground Empire*

Tham's son's birthday was approaching, and she had decided to celebrate it in the traditional Thai manner with her extended family in their village, near Petchaburi. She planned to invite local dancers and puppeteers to put on performances for the child. She assured me such an intimate Thai occasion was an opportunity not to be missed, and invited me to join them.

The town of Petchaburi had, per capita, the greatest number of Buddhist temples and violent crimes—murders, rapes, and robberies—in the whole of Thailand. It was also famous for the multitude of syrupy sweet pastries and confections that its cooks produced. Serenely spiritual, unpredictably dangerous, cloyingly sensual, Petchaburi seemed as quintessentially Thai as the Siamese fighting fish for sale in the town's main bazaar. Exquisite males floated in their individual bowls like suspended rubies, sapphires, and emeralds, nearly motionless save for the gentle rippling of their silken veils. Between the bowls the merchants had placed cardboard dividers so the fish could not see each other. When a potential customer showed interest in a particular fish, the divider would be removed. The males on either side would flare their fins, flashing colors of sunset and blood in preparation for the lethal battle so essential to the mating ritual of the species. No wonder betting on bloody fish fights—the perfect melding of violence, sex, and beauty—had become a national sport. When the divider dropped back into place, the combatants' fins wilted instantly. Once more they became tranquil gems floating in isolated bubbles of glass.

Situated on the western rim of the Gulf of Siam, four hours from Bangkok, Petchaburi missed out on most of the foreign tourist trade. Packaged tour groups could surfeit themselves with Thai exotica and glittering souvenirs in the capital without ever having to stray far from their five-star hotels. The most ardent of *dharma* bums could slake their spiritual lusts with the shrines and pagodas surrounding the City of Angels—or else head north or east, as I had done, for the ascetic life of a forest monk. Those seeking the worship of the flesh headed east along the coast to Pattaya, a vast expanse of brothels, massage parlors, and go-go bars, poorly disguised as a city. Trekkers passed up the wild hills west of Petchaburi, preferring instead to frolic in the opium gardens of the Golden Triangle, while those in search of the perfect beach drove past Petchaburi's gray sands on their way to the sprinkled-gold islands in the south. A neglected city, filled with its share of wonders but cursed by an inconvenient location, Petchaburi's only benefits from Thailand's nationwide tourist boom were candy orders from the capital and the occasional bus robbery.

Tham and almost-eight-year-old Sammy had gone ahead to Petchaburi by car, while I took the westbound express coach a day later. Thai coach rides were as alien to me as space travel, with their huge, high, shiny interiors and air-conditioning set just above freezing, as if it were a luxury to shiver when the outside temperature hovered halfway to the boiling point. Each coach had a uniformed stewardess who dispensed blankets and iced drinks, moist towelettes and snacks. I expected ours to demonstrate the use of oxygen masks in case of an emergency. As we crawled east out of Bangkok, huddling in our blankets and sipping chilled lychee juice, the driver turned on the video screen mounted in the front of the bus. Careful consideration had been given to the placing of the screen so that the driver could watch the movie while he drove.

The film was a bloody tale about Thai army commandos fighting a band of communist terrorists holed up in the jungle. This public airing to a captive audience seemed as insensitive as showing *Texas Chainsaw Massacre* on a school bus. At one point, the terrorists had taken several commandos captive. They buried one up to his neck in sand and left him to fry under the noon sun while his bound companions looked on. The head terrorist, a huge bearlike man with a shaggy black beard and tiny eyes, emerged from his tent, saw what his henchmen were doing, and exploded into a rage. Amateurs! No imagination at all! He stormed back into his tent, came out again with a razor, soap, and a small glass bottle. He ordered a bucket of water dumped on the sun-crazed man's head, soaped down his hair, and shaved him clean to the scalp.

Kneeling down to show the buried man the straight razor, still dripping suds, the terrorist sliced open the top of the prisoner's skull as if splitting the skin of a melon. The captives on the bench wailed while their companion shrieked in agony. To the Thais, the head is sacred. Even the accidental touch of another's crown is an act of great indecency, for the head houses the soul. Horror filled the prisoners faces as their companion's ineffable spiritual essence was cracked open, exposed, and made vulnerable before the grinning

Thailand is in fact a very violent society, as one can tell from the lurid crime stories in the Thai newspapers. Packing guns is a common way of displaying machismo. Hired killers, one is told, are cheap in Bangkok, and seldom unemployed. Terrible stories did the rounds: Foreign homosexuals were stabbed to death in their hotel rooms. Rural policemen were accused of kicking the victims of a traffic accident to death to get at their valuables. A man in the Bangkok building where I did some writing blew his girlfriend up with a hand grenade. Many crimes appear to involve trickery of one kind or another. During my visit, the police arrested a group of robbers who went around disguised as monks. Tourists often fall victim to a notorious gang of transvestites.

In a book about Siamese folk tales, written in 1930, Reginald LeMay commented that "the Siamese are realists. This is a very wicked world, and everyone is trying to get the better of you in some way or other. Your only means of protection is to be cleverer than your neighbor, and if you gain a reputation for being alert and keen in your business dealings, you will be looked up to and admired. There is little sympathy wasted on the dupe...."

—Ian Buruma, *God's Dust: A Modern Asian Journey*

bear. The bearded one knelt down again and showed the man the bottle. Sulfuric acid. Slowly, he poured the contents into the slit in his victim's steaming skull.

I covered my eyes, revolted, sickened at this depiction of the murder of the soul. Would the victim ever reincarnate? Or had his spirit been eradicated from the human realm as surely as an *arahant's*? Thai mothers and children munched sweets and sucked lychee fruit while the movie continued. Finally the bus dropped me by the side of the road at the outskirts of Tham's village. I plunged into the dust and heat 40 degrees warmer than the icy interior of the bus. Tham was waiting for me, as arranged, under a covered bus stop. Her silk business suit had been put aside in favor of a purple sarong and a simple white blouse. "You look sick," she greeted me.

"I have a headache from the bus."

The family's rambling wooden house sat back from the road, surrounded by bushes, papaya trees, and bamboo. A wrecked car, a flower garden, and some rusted machinery parts decorated the front lawn. Inside, Tham introduced me to a dozen relatives who floated aimlessly in and out through a large, airy common room. Tham's mother had been working in the kitchen, shredding coconut and squeezing out the milk for Sammy's birthday feast. She wore only a sarong and a brassiere—the latter a proudly displayed sign of affluence for women of her generation in rural Thailand. Her arms were long and sinewy, the fingers tough. She had a handsome face with a strong jaw and a gravelly voice that muttered a curt greeting. Mother made her living as a cook selling homemade lunches at the local police headquarters. The outdoor kitchen area, covered with a rusted tin roof, sprawled along the entire side of the house. Twined strings of garlic and dried chilies hung from the beams next to suspended baskets of dried mushrooms, aromatic leaves, and spices. Huge steel pots with blackened bottoms lay on the table next to a large steel drum with a wood fire burning inside.

"I bought Ma a gas stove and had a room inside remodeled into a modern kitchen with shelves and Teflon pans," Tham told me. "But she never uses it. She stays out here, belching soot into the neighborhood, everything open to the flies and wind. I suppose I should be thankful she at least uses the refrigerator I bought her last year, if only for sodas and ice cream."

Evidently, the infrequent visits of the prodigal daughter back to her family home were more like hurricanes than a breath of fresh air. Mother never cleaned or dusted, Tham complained. Tham always spent her first day home with soap and water, scrubbing grime and sweeping dirt. She enlisted me to help rearrange all the furniture. Ma kept a dozen green vinyl chairs in two rows facing each other down the center of the common room with tables between them, as if set up for two competing teams in a spelling bee. Tham directed me to pull them into tasteful, intimate clusters. She plucked dust-coated plastic floral arrangements from their vases and replaced them with fresh-cut flowers. Mother retreated, muttering, to her outdoor kitchen, the one place Tham would not touch—though given the opportunity, she gladly would have bulldozed it.

The extended family seemed to treat Tham with a mixture of deference, envy, and a kind of confused resentment. The prodigal daughter had broken away from home and tradition, and had accomplished the ultimate fantasy, the impossible dream: she had gone to America, married an American, and come back rich. On her visits she dispensed electronic gadgetry and modern appliances like a visiting queen. She inquired as to their well-being and was quick to offer cash for repairs or medical bills. At least two members of her family had stayed with her in Bangkok, either to start school or to search for work. No one could accuse her of negligence, yet in keeping her mother, brothers, uncles, and cousins on the receiving end of her largesse, she had inverted the natural Thai hierarchy of status. For a daughter, submissive compliance to parents and male relatives was the natural order of things. But the steady flow of gifts and cash far beyond what was expected of a working daughter kept her family in the role of supplicants. Their social conditioning had virtually forced them to their knees.

The family doted on Sammy, who stood out from his older cousins with his freckles and green eyes. Despite his mixed blood, Sam's character seemed totally Thai. He was quiet, polite, observant, and, like almost every other male child in the country, spoiled by his mother. He delighted in the attention paid him in the village. In the city, he spent his days alone with a nanny in the apartment while his mother worked and shopped. At eight, he could speak both Thai and English fluently, and I found his company a delight. Many things puzzled him, though. His mother's responses to some of his questions merely schooled him in the Thai art of indirect answers. At times he withdrew, watched, and listened, brow furrowed and lips tight, as if sensing all too clearly that everything around him was laced with lies.

When we returned home from a late afternoon walk, Tham's mother and one of the women of the house were on their way out to visit a local healer to have pains in their legs cured. Tham suggested we go with them, thinking the encounter would interest me. The woman in question was called a *song,* the Thai word for spirit medium. She would go into a trance and the ghost would possess her, then offer advice and heal those who came to her.

The *song* greeted us at the front door. She was a soft, grandmotherly woman, well into her sixties to judge from her white hair and fleshy wrinkles that surrounded her gentle face. We followed her padding bare feet through the wooden house to a large central room, where three grandchildren sat watching a color TV in one corner. An elaborate spirit altar covered the far wall. Instead of the tranquil and sleek gold Buddhas I had seen in Thai temples, jungle-like wildness flowed from this multitiered shrine. It held over thirty miniature statues of monks, guardian deities, old bearded men, and tiny spirit beings with eight or more arms. A wooden sculpture with an elephant's head reminded me of the Hindu god Ganesh. Incense curled from a hundred lit sticks. Purple and pink flowers garlanded several of the larger figures and hung in streamers from the rafters. Vases containing both real and plastic flowers covered in the dust of burnt incense had been placed between the statues like faded trees.

The old woman shut the windows, darkening the room. She turned off the sound of the television set, but left the picture on for the children; it threw flickering colors across the gloom, reflecting off the altar. The *song* bowed before the altar, then put on a white linen shirt and a white sarong over her own clothes. She parted and combed her short hair back like a man's, then took a seat cross-legged in front of the altar. She closed her eyes. We waited in stillness until the woman gave a sudden violent shudder, bouncing a foot or more off the floor. Her eyes opened. Her hands reached down and put on a pair of heavy dark-framed spectacles. Looking up, she spoke to her guests in a male tenor's voice, strong and clear. The old hands unscrewed the top of a Coke bottle that smelled of whiskey and took a large swig of it. Pulling out a cigarette and lighting it, the *song* spoke to me directly. Who was this foreigner, and for what purpose had he come?

Tham explained that I had wanted to meet the *song* and although I didn't have any questions about myself, I did want to ask the spirit who it was, and why it came to possess this woman.

The spirit seemed pleased. Through Tham's translation the spirit said he was a Brahman god, a being from the heavenly *deva* realm who had been allowed twelve human lives to speak through over a period of three hundred years. This woman was his twelfth and final channel. For the past twenty years he had been working with her and had found her very cooperative. She donated money wherever he guided her, not thinking of herself.

I asked why the spirit came into the human realm like this. He replied that the human realm was his special interest; he liked to help those stuck in it. Through this woman, he was able to give advice, heal the sick, and encourage respect for the gods. He talked about his studies of religion and spiritual languages in his last earthly incarnation as a Brahman priest, before he ascended to the *deva* realms.

The *song* motioned me to come closer. The old woman's hands took my own. Through her thick glasses, the *song* squinted at my palm. "You'll succeed at whatever you try hard to accomplish," Tham translated. "But money slides through your fingers. I see a lot of travel ahead, but don't leave Thailand too soon. Don't be hasty! But do be careful or you may not be able to avoid a terrible accident."

The spirit said he wanted to talk more with me, but others had come to him with pressing concerns and he needed to attend to their needs. I moved back and watched Tham's mother walk to the front on her knees. The *song* probed her sore leg firmly; Ma winced under pressure.

"Something in your leg is twisted. It needs to be set straight," the spirit spoke.

Ma nodded, her face contorted.

The *song* breathed deeply several times, then took a large gulp of whiskey-cola. The old woman bent low to the knee, then sprayed the drink from her mouth all over Ma's leg. Ma crawled back from the altar, bowed gratefully. She rose shakily to her feet and limped home to prepare dinner.

The woman who had come with us from the house complained of a sore ankle. The *song* gave it a similarly rough probe, but no anointing with whiskey and Coke. Softly, the woman asked about her future. The spirit's palm-reading contained no encouragement. She had no job, only delays and disappointments, and was in love with a man who didn't love her. All true, Tham confirmed. The woman was in love with Tham's younger brother, who had fallen out of love with her and gone on to someone else. At least he'd been honest about it. But she had become a part of the family. While her ex-lover had moved to Bangkok, she still spent most of her time with his family. Nobody stopped her from trying to hang on.

A villager entered, interrupting the audience to ask the spirit for one piece of urgent advice. He had built a new house, and needed an auspicious date, quick, for the move.

"But your new house is not yet ready," said the *song* sternly. "How can you move, when you have not built a home for the spirits?"

The man's eyes fell to the ground. He stuttered. In many parts of rural Thailand, households keep a miniature spirit shrine outside, usually on top of a short pole. They look rather like birdhouses for the gods. Daily offerings to the local spirits are left at the door. By appeasing them, one ensures domestic good fortune. Ignoring them invites their neglect or even ill will. The man apologized profusely for his lack of spiritual etiquette.

"And in your present home," the spirit continued, "I see the inside *deva* shrine covered with dust, the fruit rotting, the candles unlit, all pushed into a small corner in a side room, instead of in the center where the gods can bless your family with good fortune…."

The man was sweating now, bobbing his head in meek agreement. When the spirit finished speaking, he bowed deeply, then rushed out, presumably to build a home for the gods as quickly as possible.

When Tham's fortune had been read, the spirit asked me to come forward again and ask more questions. I inquired, as politely as possible, why the Brahman-god chain-smoked and drank whiskey. Was this not hard on the old woman? The *song* nodded sagely. Such possession was indeed most taxing to the mortal body. He had to be careful to put just a tiny bit of himself into her.

Even so, her body needed the tobacco and booze to stay calm and relaxed. In fact, the spirit announced, today's possession had gone on longer than usual. It was time to depart. He needed to take good care of her, the spirit said with a smile, one hand affection-ately patting the other. We said cordial goodbyes. The woman shuddered as if having a violent fit. She removed her glasses, took off her white outer garb, and asked in her timid, grandmother's voice if we'd had a good conver-sation with the spirit.

"So what was your fortune?" I asked Tham that night while the family slept below us on mats in the common room. Tham had given me her old bedroom and had arranged a cot for herself beside Sammy in the room next door. She came in and sat beside me on the bed that night, wear-ing a Chinese silk robe that came down to just above her knees, deep blue with a red dragon em-broidered on the back. The dark wooden walls blended with the screened wooden windows and the black sky beyond; moist night air blew in, filled with the nectar from the blossoming trees that surrounded the house.

"I don't believe in fortunes," she said, gazing out into the dark-ness. "I make my own fortune."

"We sure go to enough for-tune-tellers."

For many Thais, spirits, or phis, both good and bad, figure prominently in every-day life. Homes, farms, rice paddies, offices, government buildings—even night clubs in Bangkok's red-light district—sport tiny doll-like houses where good spirits are said to reside.

"In Buddhism, there is nothing against this kind of belief," Mr. Chatsumarn says. "Before I go out, I tell my spirit to please take care of my house and kids for me. It's a kind of living together."

To avoid trouble, a spirit must live in its own abode, called in Thai phra phum, *and not in the real house. That means the spirit house, which usually sits atop a pole, must be comfortable and not fall in the shadow of the main structure. In crowded Bangkok, the spirit house often ends up on the roof. If the main house is enlarged, so is the spirit house.*

Among the status-conscious middle class in Bangkok, no longer is a spirit satisfied with only a one-pole house. Keeping up with the Joneses —Bangkok-style—means luring the spirit with a four-pole abode.

—Sheila Tefft, "Thai Spirit Houses," Christian Science Monitor

"It's for your interest," she shrugged. "If I believed in fate, I'd still be in this village. You don't know what it is to be a Thai woman. You get two choices: you can be miserably married or a whore. Nobody needs a fortune-teller to tell them that. But I escaped."

She opened her closet door and rummaged through old plastic-covered dresses to a box at the rear. She came back with a black-and-white photo album. We flipped through, looking at her girlhood pictures. She had always been gorgeous, the darling of the family.

"This is my first boyfriend," she said, pointing to a fleshy young Thai wearing dark sunglasses and smiling gallantly. A willowy young Tham pressed against his side. "He helped me move to Bangkok, away from my parents. They would never let me see him. He was several years older than I was, but I was in love and he meant the world to me. I worked in the city and never saw enough of him. I was glad to be free, but sometimes I wondered why we only made love in my apartment, why he never stayed all night, why I never knew where he lived. So one day I followed him from work, back to his house, back to his wife. I watched the children playing out front, and I knew my parents were right about him. But I knew he loved me too...."

She flipped the pages. I stopped her at a photograph of her and her boyfriend kneeling before a Buddhist monk in the middle of some kind of ritual. The boyfriend's smile had been replaced with a sullen, fearful look.

"Father insisted. It was never legal, only religious, for the sake of saving face in our village. It's not against the law in Thailand for a man to have two wives. They said I was lucky. But I could never...You don't know what happens to women in my situation. Usually the man gets away and the girl goes home to live with her parents. She doesn't care what they do with her anymore. They arrange a marriage to a nice neighbor boy. Soon the boy discovers her heart is broken, so he goes off and finds a pretty young girl. The wife has a baby, gives him all her love, spoils him, and he grows up just like his father."

I moved to put my arm around her in comfort. She played idly with my fingertips, gazing out the dark window.

"Some girls, the families don't take them back, or they're too ashamed—they run away to Bangkok and can only find work as whores. But not me. I made it to America, where you can build your own life. I had my own business. Sure, James Bond is a jerk, but I had lovers and I did as I pleased. They treated me well, they treated me well..."

"Mommy!" a small voice whined.

The door pushed open. I pulled away from her. Sam came in, rubbing his eyes.

"Sammy, what are you doing up?"

"I had a dream, Mommy. I was scared."

"All right, lover," she rocked him in her arms. "Now you go back to bed. Mommy will be in in a few moments."

At dinner the following night I met Tham's father for the first time. He'd taken early retirement from his job as a police officer to devote himself full time to alcohol. Ma had kicked him out of the house almost a decade ago. For years the family saw next to nothing of him. Recently, however, he had come wandering around again, sometimes appearing regularly for meals for weeks at a time. He looked half emaciated, with clawlike hands and thick nails yellowed by tobacco. Some of his teeth were broken or missing. His level, bloodshot eyes looked like those of a sick old lion slinking around the edges of the pride. After introductions, he pointed to my near-shaven head, then stroked his own naturally bald dome. When Tham explained I had recently been in a monastery, he grasped my hand warmly and pulled me to sit by his side. He grabbed Tham roughly by the arm, commanding her to interpret. She shook free and sat down, graciously, on the other side of him.

"You see," she explained, "when Father was young, he spent three months in a temple. Oh, it's nothing special. At that time, every young man had to do it, just to become respectable. A way of showing self-control and maturity. It showed you were ready for marriage. I can hardly believe it—now he's saying he's been thinking of going back to the temple for the rest of his life! He's the meanest son-of-a-bitch I know, and he's thinking of becoming a Buddhist monk! He says he wants to go there with you. I don't know. It's probably the whiskey talking."

"Tell him thanks for the offer, but I've just gotten out of one temple. It'll be a while before I'm ready to go into another."

"He says he'll wait for you, patiently."

Pa raised a glass of orange soda—he was forbidden whiskey in the house—and downed it with a wince. My interest in Thai trance channelers intrigued the old man. He recommended I visit a *song* several villages away who was so famous that believers came from Bangkok to have their fortunes told. He said a drinking buddy of his, a taxi driver, was a devotee of the *song*. He'd send him around in a couple of days, to take us for a visit.

Tham stood up to help with dinner preparations. Pa clutched her arm and tried to force her back down. He was clearly far from finished with our conversation. She tried to pull free, but he tightened his grip. Tham tore loose with a short, savage yell and glared at him, breathing heavily, her eyes filled with undisguised hatred. Ma stuck her head in from the kitchen, a carving knife in one hand, and a headless, bleeding chicken in the other. She hollered at the old man, pointing to the door with the red tip of the blade. He curled his claws into fists, made as if to stand, then fell back, staring glumly at the lines of the green linoleum. He looked over at me with doleful eyes, tried a weak smile, muttered something in Thai, and shook his head. The rest of the family smiled and resumed talking as if nothing had happened.

The cabby was an oily-haired man with a puffy face and polished white dentures. On the ride out to the famous *song's* place, he asked Tham for my opinion of spirit mediums, perhaps somewhat ill at ease about bringing a foreigner into the spirit's presence. I said it seemed quite logical that beings from another realm could speak through chosen individuals in this one, although in our society when a different personality, or multiple personalities, took over somebody's body, this was usually diagnosed as a mental disorder.

I sensed that much of my explanation was being left out of Tham's interpretation. It was hard to get across to the cabby just what I thought. If there were no truth to the *song's* predictions, the superstition would have died out long ago. That trance channeling occurred across many cultures seemed to me to indicate that something extraordinary was indeed going on. But maybe spirit mediums just tapped into our collective mind. Perhaps subconsciously they saw things that our societies had taught us to ignore. Some intuitive people may have been driven crazy by not being able to express what they perceived, especially in Thailand, where peace and harmony were valued much more highly than confronting the truth. Only a spirit from another realm, someone powerful and with lots of status, could speak some things out loud. A *song's* words thus became sanctified and mystical, and made the individual worthy of respect for his or her gift. At the same time, the medium was free of blame for his or her intuitions and their consequences. They didn't even remember any of it—a kind of socially useful, controlled craziness.

"Wait and see," came the driver's response. "The *song* will make you a believer."

The *song* came down the front steps of his house to meet us. He wore a sarong and an undershirt. A large, vigorous man with shiny black hair, a large nose, deep black eyes, and a wide, easygoing grin, he welcomed us in a friendly, loud voice and led us upstairs. His spirit room was large and bare except for an elaborate shrine that covered half the floor. In the center hung a portrait of a Thai army officer in traditional uniform. Plastic flower garlands framed the painting. Small idols surrounded it like a miniature spirit army. The perfume of wilting flowers was mixed with thick incense from twenty glowing sticks planted in a brass urn. Next to the shrine was a chair with rows of steel blades on the back, seat, and arms, the sharp edges pointed toward the flesh of anyone who would sit in it, ready to slice a victim like a loaf of bread. At the front was an altar. On top of it lay a pile of red silk and a sword.

Our host explained apologetically that the spirit had been uncooperative in recent weeks, refusing to possess him. Candidly, he admitted that the spirit felt that the *song* had been taking advantage of his position, misusing the offerings of devotees for personal gain. But wait and see, he suggested. Perhaps for a foreigner the spirit would make an appearance. The *song's* wife brought us plastic cups of cold water. Before leaving, she placed a spittoon by her husband's side. For an hour our host chatted amiably about the spirit—the best way to attract his attention, he whispered slyly. The spirit had been an aristocrat and a general during the ancient Burma-Siam wars, a brilliant strategist and a fierce warrior. Royal blood flowed through his veins, and he could command a thousand men to fight to their deaths just as blithely as order breakfast. Not an easy spirit to work for, the *song* complained.

Mid-sentence, our host gagged and let out a strangled moan. He leaned over the spittoon and dribbled into it. A spasm shook him. His eyes bulged and his face reddened as if he were choking and about to vomit. The cabby glanced at me and nodded. He smiled and began to arrange an offering of cigarettes, incense, and flowers on a tray. When the *song* stopped shaking, he stood up and put on the red cloth from the altar. It was a loose, flowing silk robe with trousers. He picked up the sword, stuck out his tongue, and pressed the flat of the blade against it. He rubbed the steel up and down until his face was smeared red with blood.

"The spirit likes a little blood," Tham translated the cab driver's whisper.

With mechanical, trancelike motions, the *song* then wiped the blood across several sheets of yellow tissue paper and laid the red-patterned prints on the altar. Finally he turned to us and spoke, a black blood crust darkening his lips. His voice was high-pitched and effeminate, devoid of the warmth and good humor of our host. His face seemed to have changed, becoming pinched and angular, the eyes squinty and darting.

"He says some of us are unbelievers," said Tham, "so he will prove himself to us before answering our questions."

The *song* marched to the throne of swords and sat down firmly on the steel blades. At his beckoning, we gathered around to watch. He smashed his arms against them and wriggled his back, bouncing up and down on the seat. Then, solemnly, he returned

⸺ the front of the altar. There was no blood, not even a rip in the silk. Before following him back, I pressed one of the blades with my thumb. It was no sharper than a dinner knife, but I would not have wanted to sit on it and bounce.

The *song* sat in a chair looking down at us, frowning. He crossed his legs. One foot jiggled up and down with a nervous twitch. His hands fidgeted. He lit a cigarette, blowing out smoke in quick little puffs. His voice whined peevishly as he received his offering from the driver, who had crawled close on his knees. The spirit seemed angry, for the man had not followed through with his previous advice on some matter. The cabby bowed low in repentance. The *song* stood up and retrieved the bloody sword from the altar. He dangled it point down over the devotee's head, then brought the point of the blade to rest on his crown. He chanted in a high-pitched, nasal drone, while the steel tip pressed against the thin flesh covering of the man's soul. I felt my palms sweat, fearful that we might see more blood. The driver knelt, motionless, until the point was removed without breaking the skin, then crawled back, humbly, to his place, his palms pressed together in thanks for so great a blessing. The spirit called me forward.

"Foreigner, what do you want?"

"For myself, nothing but to understand. Your host has told us you are a great Thai general. I'd like to ask, why have you troubled yourself with this world you have left behind?"

The *song* sat back, the spirit seeming genuinely flattered that someone had come to ask about him, rather than for favors and advice.

"You see," the spirit replied, "in the spirit realm, one sees many things clearly which cannot be seen by the living. A lot of misery is caused by lack of understanding. In past lives, I have caused a lot of killing—not that I regret killing Burmese. It was my duty. But now I like to help set people straight." The *song* looked around at us with a squint. "Of course, despite my wisdom and the difficulty of entry into the human realm through this lump of selfish earth, most visitors are too stubborn, too deep in the muck of their own ignorance to do as I say." He jiggled his leg and sucked on his cigarette.

"Now, foreigner, since you have come such a long way, here's some advice—something that may help you overcome your doubt: Your biggest problem is your mouth. Learn to think before you use it. Keep it shut, or it will soon get you into big trouble."

Tham asked if I should stay in Thailand longer.

"Only if he goes back to a monastery. Otherwise, there will be some danger! Now for your blessing."

Before I could move, the *song's* hand flew up toward my head. I caught the gleam of a metal spike concealed in his palm, I felt the steel point of it press against the top of my fuzz-covered skull. I held still, sweating in the heat, my heart pounding in my ears while the possessed and possibly crazy man chanted his ritual blessing through to the end. He pulled back the spike without drawing blood, a slight, superior smile curving on his blackened lips. I crawled back to my seat, grateful mostly that I had not wet my pants.

He spent twenty minutes with Tham, whispering in her ear. He pointed at me and when she shook her head, he scowled at her. When we left the place, her face had turned gray. On the ride home, she refused to talk.

That night in the upper bedroom, while the family lay asleep below, she confided that the spirit had accurately described her misery, the ugliness of her marriage, and her inability to find happiness despite her determination. He told her that her bad luck would never end until she removed the cause of it: a mole on the lips of her genitals.

"He's right," she said, almost weeping. "I don't know how he knew I have such a mole. It's Thai superstition. Sometimes a mole is lucky, sometimes a very bad curse. He says he wants me to come back, alone, so he can remove it with magic. But I can't, I won't, not alone with him."

"Well, can't a doctor remove it?" I said, reaching to put my arm around her.

"Surgery can't remove a curse," she shot back angrily, pushing me away.

"I thought you didn't believe in superstition."

She looked at me coldly. We sat on the bed in wretched silence. Outside the window, we heard a car roll over gravel. Tham moved to the latticework and peered down.

"It's James!"

"I thought he was in Taiwan!" I fought down panic. A fist pounded on the front door. Sleepy voices murmured below.

"He'll kill you if he finds you here. Into the closet, quick!" She threw my bag and clothing, then shoved me in with her old dresses sheathed in plastic. The door shut out the light as I crouched next to the box of photo albums. I heard Tham straightening the covers as footsteps were coming up the stairs. My time spent in Buddhist monasteries had ill prepared me for this. What if James, enraged, strode into the room and tore open the thin divider between us? Would we flare fins and spill each other's blood? Or would the former CIA man merely pummel my face as if it were a ripe papaya? Frantically I searched for other scenarios: he opens the door. I smile up at him and say, "Hello, I'm a closet monk. Been meditating in here for the past forty years." No: as soon as he enters, I spring out of the closet, tell him *I'm* with the CIA and he's under arrest. No: he enters, I open the door, speak in a calm voice, and say, "Look, this woman you once loved, she's hurting badly from how you've abused her. All she needs is some caring, some affection." He's enlightened. We all hug each other and cry, then join a monastery together and devote the rest of our lives to cultivating compassion. Yeah, that's the Buddhist way to escape being murdered by an angry husband.

But the peevish spirit's advice rang in my ears: your biggest problem is your mouth. Keep it shut, or it will get you into big trouble. So I held my breath and tried not to rustle the plastic sheaths around the dresses. James burst into the room.

"What the hell are you doing out here in Petchaburi?" he demanded angrily. "You got an office to run. I've been calling the last two days going nuts with no answer. A big client's coming to town. This could be the meeting that makes it, and there's no one to set it up! I had to cut short a deal in Taiwan, fly back here early, and what? You're on holiday!"

"It happens to be your son's birthday tomorrow," she replied icily. "I've come to arrange a party."

"Uh, damn," he faltered as if skewered by a lance. "Okay, so come on, let's get your things and go," he said brusquely.

I heard footsteps move toward the closet.

"Don't tell me what to do. Sammy's expecting a party tomorrow. We're staying."

"I need you."

"Oh."

"I need to use you to interpret."

"Need to use me to interpret?" She spoke the words slowly, her voice getting husky, coming from the back of her throat.

"Come on, let's go."

"Don't touch me!" Her voice cracked into a raw shriek. "*Use me?*—you whoring bastard! You get out of my house and hire a slut from Pat Pong to interpret for you and your goddamn meeting!"

I heard the sound of stumbling footsteps as her rage increased. James was retreating, grunting as if being hit, backing out the door as Tham's screaming continued down the stairs, until I heard the sound of his wheels spinning over gravel.

I sat in the dark, between Tham's picture albums and dresses, not yet ready to come out and face the woman who had probably just saved my life. Was this outburst the end or just a particularly effective technique for managing a business partner? It was easy to tell who wore the fins in the relationship. Forty years in the closet seemed a mighty wise idea. I decided to heed the rest of the spirit's advice and get out of Thailand, quick. Sammy whimpered in the room next door. I heard Tham's gentle footsteps on the stairs. They headed towards Sammy's bed to comfort him. The family below us was settling back to sleep. I imagined them lying on their mats on the linoleum, looking up at the ceiling, Thai smiles covering their faces.

Tim Ward is a Canadian journalist who spent six years in the Orient. He is the author of What the Buddha Never Taught, Arousing the Goddess, *and* The Great Dragon's Fleas, *from which this story was excerpted. He lives in Maryland.*

Miraculous stories about the supernatural powers of amulets grace the pages of half a dozen magazines in Thailand devoted solely to these charms. One story from an amulet magazine shows a pickup truck riddled with bullets, the body of a man riddled with bullets, and an amulet from Wat Paknam in Bangkok. The amulet was a gift from husband to wife: he was killed in an attack with high-powered weapons; she escaped with bruise-marks where she was supposedly hit by bullets which did not pierce the skin. After the attack, she recovered and drove her husband to the hospital, where he died. Different issues of Wat Paknam amulets are said to be very powerful—some commanding prices of 30,000 baht ($1,200).

Amulets are made from a variety of materials—shaped from precious stones, or carved from bone, tigers' teeth, or from lucky trees like the sacred fig. The most common form of amulet, however, is a clay tablet bearing a seated Buddha image in shallow relief, and produced from a mold. These amulets are often designed and stamped out at monasteries. The special power of the amulet comes from the blessing by an important abbot or ruler; amulets are said to be ineffective if the wearer has a malevolent mind or does not believe absolutely in their power. Perhaps for this reason, amulets may demonstrate their powers for some, yet not for others—no matter how long they may have them.

—Michael Buckley, "The Arcane Power of Amulets"

KAREN SWENSON

* * *

Roaches and Redheads

A poet roams the days in a fishing village.

THE TAXI DRIVER WHO HAD BROUGHT ME HERE FROM HAT YAI, the sin city of southern Thailand, carried my bags to my room upstairs in the tiny hotel. He then tried to insinuate his way into the room. This should have told me something, since neither of these are typical Thai taxi driver actions. However, either due to the cold that was causing me to suppurate in my own juices or just the daze one gets into coming to a new town, it wasn't until the next day that I realized I had booked myself into a brothel. It was a little like living in a girls' dormitory, particularly on Friday night, when a number of them came home drunk and threw up in the bathroom across the hall.

There are essentially two attractions to Songkhla, a small fishing town on the east coast of Thailand: 1) there are practically no tourists, and 2) there is a museum created from a renovated governor's mansion. With a wad of tissues in my pocket I left my shoes at the front door of this large house and glided about rooms with floors of hand-hewn teak that have been polished by a hundred years of bare soles. The rooms are large and cool because of deep eaves over the windows. Standing in a shadowy room, where the gleaming floors repeat the forms of museum cases holding

259

Buddhas, one looks out with a sense of indolent elegance through tall windows, closed across the bottom by a Chinese red fence, to brilliant sunshine and startling acid-green trees. The museum collection is eclectic—Khmer statues, Thai Buddhas, Ganesh, the Hindu elephant god, with a sweeping arch of trunk, Ming pottery, the silver G-strings that little Thai girls wore three generations ago, betel boxes, and bronze jewelry from an archeological dig. Outside in the courtyard there is a shadow-puppet theater equipped with its regiment of lacy *dramatis personae*. The stair that leads down is being, literally, eaten by a tree that has already consumed the balustrade into its trunk.

Walking around the town buying oranges in the market, the only other non-Asian I saw was a big-bellied redhaired man who pointedly ignored me. After a nap in my oven-like room—which had two windows looking directly into the rooms of other people's houses and walls decorated with pale geckos—I went downstairs to find the redhaired man sitting in one of the lobby chairs slinging Old Testament quotes at the little whores as they scurried up and down the stairs. His name was Kevin, a born-again Christian; he had come to Thailand from Alaska. He was working for a man he knew only as Jack, a 'Nam vet, who had a boat in the harbor that was used to rescue Vietnamese boat people, or so Kevin believed. He told me about a doctor down the street who spoke English.

I found the office easily since it was the only house with a Mercedes in front of it. Never have I been so totally chastely examined. I removed nothing and he listened to everything through walls of clothing, giggling all the while. Instead of getting formal when embarrassed, Thais giggle. This causes them trouble with Westerners, who are always sure they are being made fun of. He prescribed, giggling some more, a sufficient number of pills to make my luggage overweight if I didn't take them all before returning home. He also directed me to a pharmacy.

Coming into the pharmacy from the bright sunlight it was difficult to see, but I threaded my way between cases filled with Chinese nostrums—boxes of antlers, jars of roots, boxes of fish skeletons, dried fungus—toward the back. There, among more boxes, I found myself to my surprise looking into a pair of blue eyes, belonging to a very pregnant redhead standing next to, as it became apparent later, her wizened Chinese mother-in-law, who looked as though she had been constructed out of the compounds in the Chinese section of the pharmacy.

"Good heavens! How did you get here?"

"I married a Thai my last year at the university," she said with an Irish brogue and a smile.

While my prescriptions were being filled I asked how many children she had while her mother-in-law watched us benignly.

"Oh, this is number three and I think it will happen tomorrow."

I met Kevin for dinner lugging my pills along and swilling them down with Coke. He proudly took me to a stand that he said made wonderful shrimp. The owners certainly knew their customer. The shrimp were

Pregnant women may not go to a cremation and may not go to visit persons seriously ill. This is probably protection against thinking too much, which might cause fear and loss of confidence. They are also forbidden to go and see other women give birth, because it will make delivery impossible, the children in the womb being embarrassed by one another and so refusing to be born.

There is another belief connected with pregnancy. If she would like to rear her child easily, a pregnant woman must seek an opportunity to walk under the belly of an elephant, but is necessary to choose an elephant with a kind disposition. If she has passed under the belly of an elephant, the child that is born will be easy to rear.

—Phya Anuman Rajadhon,
Some Traditions of the Thai

overcooked and saturated with ketchup. I was polite, but on the way back I bought a shrimp pancake. These are made from whole tiny unshelled shrimp lightly held together with batter and deep fried. You dunk the patty, in which you can see little lacquered shrimp heads complete with tiny black eyes and antennae, into a plastic bag of syrupy but viciously hot sauce that clears your sinuses immediately.

The next morning I walked snuffling through the fish market, where Thai women squatted, gossiping as they skinned squid and heaped them up in shimmering ivory piles in the blue-rimmed white enamel basins. Kevin picked me up and took me on a boat around the harbor, where we saw Cat and Mouse Islands. To reciprocate, I asked him to go to a *wat* with me. He said he couldn't go to places of heathen idolatry. His god was a jealous god.

That night, while I was reading a *Newsweek* I'd bought at a stand run by a very pretty Eurasian girl, whom Kevin said had been rescued from a garbage can as a baby by some Thais who then raised her, there was a knock at my door. I asked who it was because there had been a number of knocks over the past few nights by hopeful men. An American female voice answered. I let in a long-legged woman in diminutive shorts. She seemed to just want to talk and get some general advice about places to visit in Malaysia. I started by telling her to wear a skirt. When she left I shut out the light. Again there was a knock. She was back apologizing for waking me but wanted to change some dollars for baht since she was leaving before the banks opened. Then she told me what was really bothering her. She was afraid she had head lice. I couldn't see anything on her head and suggested she wait a few days, inspecting her head each day before she bought a bottle of Kwell.

She left. I turned out the light, but in the middle of the night thought I heard someone at the door and turned it on again. As I was lying there, a monster roach, half the size of the universe, flew up from the floor, toward my head. I jackknifed up, flinging him to the other side of the room. I got up and stomped him with my flip-flops with full crunching sound effects. Feeling I should receive the Congressional Medal of Honor for this act, I calmed my shattered nerves with a *Newsweek* article on Arab terrorism and slept with the light on the rest of the night.

The next day my cold was much improved and I bought a seat on the night bus to Bangkok. Kevin saw me off, but before we left the police came on with a camcorder and photographed each passenger. There had been a number of bandit attacks on buses in the last month that had included a stooge inside the bus. Better a strange bandit than a familiar cockroach.

Karen Swenson, a poet and redhead who travels frequently in Asia, won the 1993 National Poetry Series for her book, Landlady in Bangkok.

✳

On the whole, Thailand is a fairly hassle-free destination for women travellers. Though unpalatable and distressing, the high-profile sex indus-try is relatively unthreatening for Western women, with its energy focused exclusively on *farang* men; it's also quite easily avoided, being contained within certain pockets of the capital and a couple of beach resorts. As for harassment from Thai men, it's hard to generalise, but most Western tourists find it less of a problem in Thailand than they do back home. Outside of the main tourist spots, you're more likely to be of interest as a foreigner rather than a woman and, if travelling alone, as an object of concern rather than of sexual aggression.

—Paul Gray and Lucy Ridout, *The Rough Guide Thailand*

STEVEN M. NEWMAN

✦ ✦ ✦

Flying Kites

*Dispirited and lonely in Bangkok,
the author rediscovers his childhood
through a serendipitous experience.*

IN BANGKOK I DISCOVERED, PARTICULARLY ON THE QUIETER SIDE
streets and in the less hectic hours of the dawn and late night, that
even the modern society was threaded with fantasy.

As beautiful as they were in the sunlight, the graceful and in-
tricately adorned spires and columns of the more elaborate *wats*
took on a true fairy-tale quality in the late hours of night. Their
brightly colored porcelain, ceramic, and gold reflected the lights of
both the city and the moon as if they had been dusted by a magical wand.

In the earliest gray of the dawn, as I stepped noiselessly, almost
furtively, along the empty sidewalks, I saw on every block the or-
ange-robed Buddhist monks performing the ancient custom of
bintabat, the taking around of a bowl in which to collect the day's
food from the faithful.

At one market stall, I saw cockroaches on sale for use in cooking, while another offered monkey brains.

But of all the new experiences that opened up to me, perhaps
the most meaningful occurred in a park by the Grand Palace.
Tired, soaked, and resigned to the idea that I would never get back
on the correct bus, I slumped onto a bench in the shade of a small

tree. Leaning back to rest, I saw right above my head a special bit of exotica—kites!

There were hundreds of them. All fluttering about on the sky's currents like graceful, long-tailed tropical fish struggling on the ends of fishermen's lines.

I wondered if there were any kites to be purchased in the park. There were. So many I could hardly decide what manner of shape and size I wanted my air pet to be. At last I settled on a pink fish.

Timidly, I released my striking little paper fish into the currents, then marveled at how strongly such a delicate creature could struggle for its freedom. Memories of a windy spring I spent as a child on an old farm in upper Pennsylvania came back to me. That had been twenty years ago. Could I really have gone so long without knowing again the thrill of coaxing a kite into the clouds?

Abruptly, I was again in Bangkok. My fish was escaping! My kite's string had snapped.

Frantically, I zigzagged through a maze of fruit and soda-pop vendors in a futile effort to keep up with my fleeing fish. Breathing heavily in the thick air, I dashed onto the grounds of an enormous *wat* where I felt sure the kite had come to rest. I looked high, low—and then I started laughing. Cradled in the lap of a golden meditative Buddha statue was my little kite.

Steven M. Newman is listed in the 1988 Guinness Book of World Records *as the first person to walk alone around the world, an adventure he recounted in* Worldwalk: One Man's Four Year Journey Around the World. *"Flying Kites" and "Walking South" in Part Four were excerpted from this book. He grew up in Bethel, Ohio, where he began his epic trudge.*

✳

The Thai flag, known as the *trai-rong* (three colors), can be seen as a symbol of the forces from which the kingdom derives its strength. Two bands of red, at top and bottom, represent the nation, while two white bands suggest the purity of the Buddhist faith. In the center, a blue band, filling a third of the total area, symbolizes the monarchy, still a vital element after seven centuries.
　　　　　　　　—William Warren, *Thailand, Seven Days in the Kingdom*

✳ ✳ ✳

Farang Correspondent

He's there ahead of you, testing the beds, sampling
the food, finding the bargains, making your
life on the road a whole lot easier.

JOE CUMMINGS FIRST HEARD THE EXPRESSION "WT," SHORT FOR world traveler, in the mid-seventies. Not long out of college, he had just arrived in Thailand for a two-year stint with the Peace Corps when his colleagues took him aside to warn him about WTs, those seekers, searchers, and scruffy nomadic backpackers who were infesting Asia like lice.

"I was told, 'Avoid these people. They'll rip you off, and if they don't they'll ruin your reputation with the Thais,'" Cummings reminisced as our taxi bulled through the gridlock around Bangkok's Khao San Road, one of the most notorious WT ghettos in Asia. Fortunately for all of those who have since pitched up in Thailand without a clue of what to do or where to stay or eat, Cummings ignored the advice. After a year he quit the Peace Corps, hit the road, and went on to become one of the most authoritative writers on shoestring travel in Southeast Asia and, for that matter, anywhere else.

Cummings is an area specialist for Lonely Planet, the guidebook company that publishes guides to more than 70 countries, most of them developing nations. His beat extends from Indonesia to southern China, and since 1981 he has written or contributed to eight of the series handbooks on Asia and has just written a ninth, a Bangkok city guide. His life's work, however, is *Thailand—a travel survival kit*. It's the biggest seller on Lonely Planet's list—more than 350,000 copies since the first edition fifteen years ago—and has been translated into French, German, Italian, Japanese, Hebrew, Spanish, and Swedish. He researched that first edition in ten weeks and wrote it in three. Since then, he's returned to Thailand about every two years to update and expand the book, and the job has become more difficult each time. Last year, five million people visited Thailand, more than twice as many as in 1982, and the tourist infrastructure has expanded accordingly. The first edition of *Thailand* was 136 pages long; the fifth is 620.

Everyone consults Cummings, from businessmen in the sex clubs along Bangkok's Patpong Road to bond traders sunning on the beaches of Phuket to Hilton hippies who fancy themselves to be off the beaten track in Chiang Mai. His core audience, though, is the WTs. During high season on the well-trodden guest-house circuit, there is a copy of his book in every backpack.

"This is one of Asia's three K's," Cummings explained while our cab bore down on the Banglamphu District, designated a Cheap Hotel Area on the Survival Kit's city map. "There's Kathmandu, Kuta Beach in Bali, and Khao San Road." Cummings was about ten weeks into a fourteen-week research blitz for the fifth edition of the Thailand guide and seemed strung-out. Willowy to begin with, he'd dropped to 145 pounds, which looked positively gaunt on his six-foot-one-inch frame. Not only did he have to canvass Thailand from top to bottom; he'd also wedged in a two-week dash through Burma (or Myanmar, as its now called) to update that country's guide and had budgeted ten days in Bangkok to research the new city guide.

Ghettos like Khao San Road take on a life of their own, thriving by word of mouth on the traveler's grapevine. Yet as pied piper in this particular case, Cummings feels a kind of paternal responsibility for Khao San Road. Some years ago, he went searching for alternatives to the usual digs around the Malaysia Hotel (the then-

WT hangout, which possessed a bulletin board displaying the most amazing information and misinformation from all over Asia, Cummings notes) and discovered two Chinese-run hotels on Khao San Road. They were tidy, close to major sightseeing spots, and cheap, and he gave them positive if restrained reviews in fine Lonely Planet style—neither guidebook gushing nor bitchy slagging allowed. After his review appeared, the hotels were soon unable to keep up with demand. Enterprising Thais smelled blood in the water, a frenzy of building ensued, and now more than a hundred guest houses crowd the neighborhood.

Just beyond the Democracy Monument, a Khao San Road landmark and the site of violent pro-democracy demonstrations that would take place some months later, Cummings signaled the driver to let us out. The traffic noise was deafening, and the air was a yellowish broth of humidity and exhaust fumes. Uniformed traffic cops in white plastic filtration masks looked like extras from *Blade Runner,* heightening a sense of post-apocalyptic doom. We fell in behind a *farang* with bleary eyes and bare feet. At the first corner, he turned left and in an instant was swallowed up by the bedlam of trekkers, skinheads, braless women with hair in cornrows, anxious couples clutching rucksacks to their chests, and hippies got up like harlequins in garish native clothing. Khao San Road was like Kathmandu's Thamel district, condensed into a space of 300 yards: pirated cassette tapes, paperback books, t-shirts, counterfeit Levi's jeans, $40 Rolex watches, incendiary vegetable curries, fruit smoothies, ice cream, noodles, you name it. People who had come halfway around the world were packed like rats into some multinational sidewalk sale.

"Now comes the hot, dirty part," said Cummings, plunging into the turmoil. His loping, storklike stride and slight backward lean recalled R. Crumb's Mr. Natural cartoon character, only he moved with the ease of a seasoned walker. Swiftly down the gauntlet we marched—the Hello Restaurant and Guest House, Mama's Guest House, the Ploy, the Dior, the Buddy, and a succession of crash pads identified by initials: NS, PR, VC, PB, and the particularly obscure PR215.

"How does it make you feel to know you created this?" I asked Cummings.

"Good," he replied smoothly, ignoring my bait, "at least for the local people. They were poor when I first came here, but some of them can afford to send their children to school now. There's even some real affluence."

Whatever ambivalence Cummings felt about the *farang* ghetto itself—and the whole WT scene that he has helped create in the last decade—he had put aside. For the moment he was on duty, and these were his people. For all their independent-mindedness, the WTs of Khao San Road were relying on him to scout ahead for the real Thailand, the unspoiled part, to discover the deals and sniff out the scams, to test the mattresses and inspect the bathrooms, to sample the food and drink, and see if the buses ran on time. And when he did, they would be right behind, looking cool and experienced, stealing glances at their guidebooks when no one was watching, having, as Cummings puts it, "their private Asia experience."

"It's almost like a huge package tour," he remarked, "and I'm the leader."

The next morning, we were streaking upcountry in the subarctic chill of a "sprinter" train. Outside, a picturesque landscape whizzed by like a video travelogue without the soundtrack; rice fields dotted with white egrets, ox carts on red-dirt lanes, hamlets of teak shanties on awkward stilts. Now and then an ancient, crumbling *chedi,* a pagoda, would appear through the window, evoking a powerful sense of antiquity.

Our destination was Phitsanulok, 250 miles north of Bangkok, at the head of Thailand's central valley, the country's rice basket. Cummings planned a day in the town, and then we would head west, toward Burma and uncertain intrigue. Government troops there were fighting both secessionist insurgents and mercenaries loyal to various opium warlords. Though we wouldn't enter Burma, stray mortar shells were a remote threat. Desperadoes had also robbed and killed several lone travelers on the Thai side, but

Cummings's latest intelligence suggested no new incidents of violence since the late '80s.

Small upcountry restaurants are sometimes hang-outs for drunken jii-khoh, *an all-purpose Thai term that refers to the teenage playboy-hoodlum-cowboy who gets his kicks by violating Thai cultural norms. These oafs sometimes bother foreign women (and men) who are trying to have a quiet meal ("Are you married?" and "I love you" are common conversation openers). It's best to ignore them rather than try to make snappy comebacks—they won't understand them and will most likely take these responses as encouragement. If the* jii-khohs *persist, find another restaurant.*

Unfortunately restaurant proprietors will rarely do anything about such disturbances.

—Joe Cummings,
Thailand - a travel survival kit

From all appearances, Joe Cummings leads the kind of romantic life most people fantasize about. He spends half the year exploring places like Burma, Indonesia, and Laos, and the other half writing about them. One of Lonely Planet's 70-odd roamer-writers, he is one of its most successful. He owns a home in the San Francisco Bay Area and has been married for fourteen years to a woman who understands his compulsion to travel.

Cummings prefers traveling incognito, but because his photo appears in the travel guide, his cover is sometimes blown. As a rule he avoids WTs, not out of snobbery, but because they tend to treat him like a celebrity. He prefers to travel alone and moves fast, averaging a town a day, carrying only a travel pack, a camera case, and a bright red *yaam,* a hilltribe shoulder bag. It's the only vivid color in his unobtrusive wardrobe, which is mostly baggy and black. For a three-month journey he packs just three pairs of pants, four shirts, two pairs of underwear, socks, two sarongs, and a toilet kit.

Cummings is constantly jotting notes in a meticulous script or murmuring into a pocket tape-recorder if he happens to be driving. After making the rounds of a town's guest houses, he likes to wind up at the night market to eat and gab with the locals over a pint of Mekong rice whiskey. That is where he picks up his best information (although Lonely Planet readers themselves are a vast intelligence-gathering network—in the previous two years he'd received 2,000 letters from them, and perhaps 500 contained solid tips.) Before retiring for the night, he might review reader mail concerning the next town on his itinerary (letters are forwarded to him) or transcribe the day's research into a notebook or a laptop computer.

Ultimately, everything Cummings collects in the field for each of his eleven guidebooks ends up on disk. His database on Thailand alone is enormous. "I'm conscious of the fact that this is the top-selling book among Thailand aficionados," he said, "and I'm always trying to live up to their expectations and find new trails to blaze."

Cummings speaks Thai fluently (along with Lao, Malay-Indonesian, and a smattering of Mandarin Chinese); has a scholar's depth on Thai history, art, and architecture; and possesses a gourmet's taste for Thailand's fabulously varied cuisine, which he calls "my one great joy."

"Some of Lonely Planet's guides tend to do the basic minimum on these subjects and concentrate on the nitty gritty—how to get from point A to point B, where to stay and eat," he explained. "I'm trying to impart a sense of place. I'm hunting for ethnic markers."

Like that of many former Peace Corps volunteers, Cummings's affinity for the developing world dates to the late '60s and in his case grew out of antiwar activism. "All of my papers in college ranted against U.S. policy in Southeast Asia," he says. He read omnivorously about the region but was drawn to Thailand because of its Buddhism and fierce independence. When he signed up for the Peace Corps, he insisted on being posted in Thailand. He became such a keen student that he went on to earn a master's degree in Asian Studies from the University of California at Berkeley. In 1981 he was considering getting a Ph.D. in Thai literature, a choice that would have led him into academia. But having already spent seven years in school, Cummings asked himself, "Do I want to spend five more years at this or parlay my skills into a job?"

He wrote a letter to Tony Wheeler, asking if he needed someone to cover Thailand. By then Lonely Planet had been in business about eight years. It had grown from an operation that "could fit in the boot of a Ford Cortina," as one writer recalls, into an established publishing house. Gone were the days when Wheeler and his co-publisher wife, Maureen, could rely on gonzo contributors; they needed specialists like Cummings. Wheeler agreed to the proposal, and Cummings hit the ground running.

For a person of his scholarly bent and nomadic upbringing—the army-brat variety—Cummings and his job seem a perfect fit. "That's what everyone believed. I'm planning to write a book called *Confessions of a Travel Writer* to give them the reality of it," he says, only half joking. "It's bloody hard work, slogging around for months with your luggage, sleeping every night in a new bed, and walking—a lot of walking. There's also the loneliness, the deadlines, the tropical diseases, bus crashes, drownings at sea…."

Miraculously, he's dodged serious encounters with most tropical diseases, except amoebic dysentery, which he contracted at an ashram in India "doing the *dharma*-bum thing" after the Peace Corps. Before he kicked the bug, his weight fell to less than a hundred pounds. "He looked like a concentration-camp victim," says his wife, Lynne. But he did come perilously close to drowning in 1988, when a fishing boat that he and eleven other WTs had hired to take them from Java to Krakatau conked out in a horrific storm. They spent a terrifying night pitching and rolling in the Sunda Straits. In the morning the gale subsided, and the crew ingeniously dismantled the engine with a hammer and chisel to replace a blown gasket. "Actually," says Cummings, "I wasn't so worried about drowning as about losing my notes from the previous two months. I had an image of myself treading water, keeping my notes over my head."

Fifteen years on, the romance of travel has dulled, but only slightly. "It's not boring," Cummings says, "just ordinary. I've lost the awe of travel. It used to be like going from one world to another. Now it can be like going from room to room in a house." He must also cope with the rote of covering familiar ground over and over. But traveling six months a year jogs him out of a routine, he says, and "refreshes the relationship" with Lynne. "By spending time apart, you appreciate being together more."

"When he returns from a trip," Lynne says, "it's almost like a honeymoon. As long as there is that trust between us, the separations are tolerable."

The bottom line for Cummings is that he is his own master, free to roam. "A Thai monk told me, 'You know why you like to travel? Everywhere you go nothing belongs to you. When you're home surrounded by your possessions, you're weighed down.' I think he was right. It is liberating being stripped down to one suitcase."

The air in Phitsanulok had none of the oppressive heaviness of Bangkok's, but the sun was still broiling. Making the rounds to hotels and guest houses was more than "bloody hard work"; it was drudgery. Cummings verified every listing in person and spent a few moments nosing around or chatting with the manager. Afterward, he recorded the changes in a much-annotated copy of his book.

Much had changed since his last visit, and much remained the same. The town's main attraction, the temple Wat Yai, had been there since the 14th century and wasn't going anywhere. But new hostels had opened, room rates had ratcheted up, and in the city center, mere blocks from the historic riverside temples, a luxury hotel and a bank were under construction. In its sleepy provincial way, Phitsanulok was feeling the effects of tourism and Western culture as much as Bangkok was.

We hailed a pedicab to take us to our next stop, but on arrival the driver demanded double the fare Cummings had negotiated, protesting lamely that the quoted price had been a per-person rate. Cummings scolded the man and turned angrily on his heel, while I paid the agreed-upon ten baht, about 40 cents.

"That is *so* un-Thai," Cummings steamed. "Some sleazy operator started this with the package tourists, who'll pay anything. Pretty soon all the drivers will be pulling it. I feel an obligation to travelers to keep rates at the local level or close to it. I don't mind paying a couple of extra baht, but double is ridiculous." He made a note to himself to warn his readers about the scam. I ventured that people might misinterpret his motives as neocolonial. "Fuck 'em," he shot back.

Later he regretted snapping at the driver. Cummings claims no formal religion, but the outburst had violated the Thai prescription of keeping a "cool heart," which has stood him in good stead while traveling. "Getting angry in Asia is always counterproductive," he said. "Everyone loses face."

By now Cummings was becoming worried about our progress. To meet his deadline—and he had never missed one yet ("It makes me too anxious to be late," he says)—he had to cover the entire northwest, including the immensely popular hill-tribe trekking area, in less than three weeks.

In Mae Sot, on the Burmese border, we found room in a guest house near the city center. It was owned by a handsome young Thai with a bright smile, but his aloof and officious German girl-friend seemed to have usurped the role of manager, check-in clerk, and breakfast cook.

"Among any group of travelers, there's always a little competition as to who has been on the road the longest, who was in Kathmandu first, who got the cheapest airfare," Cummings later explained. "The pecking order is set according to who has been in Asia the longest. The old hands hold court, and the newcomers have to pay deference." Having "gone native," the German woman was one caste above the WTs in guest-house society and lorded it over everyone. When Cummings mentioned our plans to travel by motorbike she looked at us as if we were daft. "Take the *songthaew*," she said, actually managing a smile.

Literally translated, *songthaew* means "two rows," referring to the wooden bench seats bolted lengthwise to the bed of a pick-up truck. They became our primary mode of transportation as we pushed north into the mountains of the Golden Triangle, heading toward Mae Sariang. We shared space with illegal refugees from Burma, hill-tribe families in traditional dress, one carsick infant, many bundles, and five Karen girls and their stern brother. The girls tittered at the sight of two *farang*. They wore cream-colored sarongs fringed in hot pink, and their hands were dripping with pink Burmese rubies. Leaning over, Cummings whispered, "They're virgins. After they sleep with a man, they switch the cream outfits for red." A mile beyond their village we passed a work elephant lumbering along the road. The *mahout* wore a carbine slung across his back.

The views were becoming more exotic, the country more vertical. This part of Thailand was a Lost World landscape of dome-shaped limestone peaks and dense forests of bamboo and teak. There were few settlements, and eventually Cummings and I were the only fares. Careening down one hill we passed through a cloud of butterflies; grinding up the next, I counted their corpses littering the back of the *songthaew.*

In Mae Sariang Cummings pounded the pavement for about an hour, but he'd come down with the flu and turned in right after dinner. I stopped for a beer in the busiest bar and shared a table with two urbane Londoners on holiday, David Bosdte and James Selfe. They'd been on the world-traveler circuit before—this was Bosdte's second trip to Thailand—and in the jaded manner of well-traveled Brits he bemoaned the difficulties of finding the country's undiscovered remnants. When I mentioned I was with Cummings and asked their opinion of the Lonely Planet guides, they rolled their eyes.

"One always picks up a copy," said Bosdte, "although I wonder if the series hasn't contributed to the ethos that the traveler with his backpack is somehow superior to the tourist who stays in a Holiday Inn."

Selfe added, "Personally, I wonder if we aren't sort of turning the Third World into a theme park for our amusement and polluting the culture with our money. Are we enriching people's lives as cultural ambassadors, or just making them feel deprived?"

I related the conversation to Cummings the next morning. "Oh, they should have just stayed home," he said in a huff. "It's hypocritical of them to wonder if they should have come. It all goes back to everyone wanting their own private Asia."

Beyond Mae Sariang, we lumbered through the mountains in a huge bus with air-conditioning and a full entertainment center— TV, VCR, and stereo—above the driver. From the jungled ridges we dropped into valleys beribboned with irrigation channels and rice paddies. It was harvest time, and field hands gathered in circles to thresh the grain, using giant rattan fans to winnow the chaff. Soon we were cruising past the Holiday Inn Mae Hong Son. Downtown, on every corner, travel agencies advertised TREKS LEAVING TODAY. Backpackers roamed the streets, and several groups of package tourists sat in their parked minivans, looking nervous and impatient to leave.

"Welcome to the new Chiang Mai," Cummings said. He had recommended Mae Hong Son to an adoring young traveler we'd met earlier as a less-rutted jump-off point than Chiang Mai, long the departure point for hill-tribe treks. Cummings feels a real ambivalence about trekking the Golden Triangle. On one hand, his book lists 24 trekking outfitters in Chiang Mai alone; on the other, he's uncomfortable with the voyeuristic aspect of "ethnotourism" and the inevitable overcrowding it brings.

By comparison with Chiang Mai's souvenir stands and "trek buses," Mae Hong Son seemed positively authentic, but there were signs of things to come. A woman who had opened the first guest house in Mae Hong Son had recently relocated to a secluded spot away from the carnival atmosphere of town. "Things are getting weird," she said. "The other guest-house owners hire touts to hang around the bus station and say my place is closed. Once someone put black magic on my poster down there. Nobody came for days. I had to hire monks to bless my place. The next day we got some guests."

Cut off by the corrugated country along the border, the town of Pai, our last stop together, had escaped much of the tourist-boon fallout. Unfortunately, its isolation and the availability of cheap heroin had attracted a number of junkies. A $50 a day habit could be supported for less than a dollar, and the junk was pure. Even so, Pai had retained its charm and friendliness and still had a strong sense of community. In spite of having been discovered by WTs and trekkers, it felt like the kind of refuge where one might kick back for a couple of months, years, or longer.

But Cummings, as usual, had no time, not even to nurse his flu, which had grown worse. "Never enough time," he said over our farewell dinner in a hectic *farang* restaurant called Own Home, where nothing but Creedence Clearwater Revival was allowed on the sound system. "There used to be these little explosions of tourist activity here and there. Now…well, I really ought to hire assistants."

In the next week, Cummings intended to cover 500 miles of back roads by motorbike. He brightened at the prospect of exploring the region around Nan, which he predicted would be Thailand's new frontier of tourism. Would he try to steer readers away from the area, to limit the impact? That was not his job, he said, although sometimes he did refrain from writing about a sensitive area. "People complain, 'Oh you're giving away all the secret spots,' but that's not true," he said. "Half the time I hear about a place because travelers have been there. Anyway, it's presumptuous of someone from the West to tell the Thais how to manage their tourism. *That* is neocolonial paternalism. The Thais have resisted colonialism for centuries, and they can handle tourists, too. They'll just absorb it and take the good." Khao San Road and Chiang Mai's trek buses seemed to contradict him.

Tourism is something we all love to hate, but we're better off putting energy into becoming better guests—not bemoaning the loss of the good old days when the road was less crowded.

— JO'R and LH

In the morning I rented a motorbike, which I planned to take as far into the mountains as possible—my private Asia experience. First, though, I went to see Cummings off at the bus depot. He plunged into the jostling crowd but ended up without a seat. Standing in the aisle, still ailing with no headroom, he faced four hours of twisting mountain roads. Another *farang* might not have had such a cool heart. At the last moment, as we said our good-byes, he reached into his *yaam* and pulled out a stack of business cards. "Here," he said, shoving them at me. "Pass these out on your ride. And take good notes for me."

What drives every true WT, Cummings believes, "is to be able to say they were there when"—when the cultures were pristine.

That day I reached a Karen village isolated from Pai by 40 miles of badly rutted road. Initially, my notes to Cummings said that the settlement seemed untouched by Western civilization. But it was a hasty and naïve observation. Inside the hut that served as a community center, every child in the village was glued to a TV set, watching a show about the Statue of Liberty.

Michael McRae is a contributing editor of Outside *magazine, in which this story first appeared. A collection of his stories entitled* Continental Drifter, *which includes "Farang Correspondent," was published by Lyons & Burford. He lives with his wife in southern Oregon.*

★

Upcountry the typical Thai bathroom consists of a tall earthen water jar fed by a spigot and a plastic or metal bowl. You bathe by scooping water out of the water jar and sluicing it over the body. It's very refreshing during the hot and rainy seasons, but it takes a little stamina during the cool season if you're not used to it. If the "bathroom" has no walls, or if you are bathing at a public well or spring in an area where there are no bathrooms, you should bathe while wearing the *phâakhamaa* (sarong for men) or *phâasîn* (sarong for women); bathing nude would offend the Thais.

—Joe Cummings, *Thailand - a travel survival kit*

JOEL SIMON

★ ★ ★

In the Dark

While the power grid has no doubt improved since this
story was written, the question remains: how many
farang *does it take to change a light bulb?*

QUITE UNEXPECTEDLY, TINA AND I ARRIVED IN BANGKOK DURING a waterfight. It was no ordinary skirmish involving the occasional balloon or bright orange plastic pistol, this was an all-out national splash. Fire hoses, garden hoses, in fact every hose in the country was turned on, Thai on Thai. Water from buckets, cups, cans, and leaky vessels was being hurled off fourth-floor balconies, the backs of pickup trucks, ox carts, and from every window facing the street. The avenues, the pedestrians, and whimpering dogs dodging droplets with tails tucked between their legs, were all awash. Everything was wet; everyone was smiling. Laughter and cooling water filled the air.

We had arrived during Songkran, the Thai New Year, and waterfights were the order of the day. In fact, they were the order of five days. Like flags on the fourth of July, the Buddhist spirit covered every available space. Frustrations pent up for a year were released in refreshing and harmless exhilaration and we were in the midst of it. Welcome to Thailand!

Eventually we dried out and made our way to the North. Doesn't everyone? The heat increased, indications of English, spoken or otherwise, decreased. We were, more or less, on our own, separated by that invisible curtain drawn between people as when Babel descended.

The afternoon that Tina and I reached Chiang Rai, we checked into a small outlying guest house. A deal at a few dollars. The room—rustic, small, dark, with hinged shutters across the window—was graced with a single bare 15-watt light bulb hanging by a bent and wiggly wire from the ceiling. Thinking ahead to peaceful moments of turning pages and writing notes before bed, we decided to look for a higher wattage light bulb. There was a shop on the corner, a small room crammed with at least one of everything, floor to ceiling and then some. We entered, approached the counter and communicating with hands and pictures, made our request.

The shopkeeper, a gentle elderly fellow with a quiet smile, proudly brought out a 15 watter. It was time for specifics. When the bulb was carefully laid down on the counter, I responded with a drawing of the same bearing a bold "100" across the rounded top. A small, nearly indiscernible frown replaced the shopkeeper's smile. He disappeared into the back room. We heard a stepladder being jostled from one location to the next. After several minutes he returned with a dubious expression on his face. He slowly placed a 60-watt bulb on the counter. Perhaps he thought that all rooms in Chiang Rai came with 15 watts as standard equipment. Everyone smiled and nodded and the deal was struck.

Pleased, Tina and I continued our afternoon rounds. As dusk settled over the wooden buildings and dirt lanes we sought out dinner. With a finger pointing to my mouth, and a hand on my belly, I asked a newspaper vendor where we might eat. He laughed, and pointed to a small doorway a short way off. We entered the "restaurant," carefully navigating between low wooden tables, lower chairs, numerous men, conversations, smoke, and a single 15-watt bulb suspended jauntily from the ceiling. In the dim light we asked about the menu. The cook pointed to what was on the fire—a rotund black cooking pot with upside down pale-yellow chicken feet along with other less recognizable parts oozing up from the bubbling broth. With a wide grin, and simple hand gesture, he asked if we cared to dine. Tina and I glanced quickly around at the many soup-slurping patrons, and two sleeping dogs in the corner, then at each other. It was, evidently, tonight's special. We nodded our heads, extended our hands, and said with a smile, "Let's Eat!"…while thinking, "Oh, what the heck?!" The cook presented each of us with a huge bowl of broth (gratefully without any feet) to which noodles, eggs, and a few vegetables were then added. Not bad. It tasted much better than it looked…which, well, wasn't so difficult. Beers countered the tongue-sizzling spices and drowned any remaining doubts.

When we returned to our bargain-basement sanctuary, I flipped on the light. As we suspected, 15 watts just wasn't sufficient. The era of 60 watts had arrived. I turned on my small flashlight, turned off the single overhead, and replaced the bulb. A perfect fit. Again, I flipped the switch with a flourish.

After some moments, the bulb began to glow. Brighter. And brighter. I opened my tattered guidebook; Tina took out her journal. And that was it. Our improvement started flickering. After exerting a few final feeble waves of light…darkness. Not just our room, but the entire block had gone pitch black. No light came from the window. No light came from the hall. No light came from the street. The entire block was out.

We began to hear voices. In the dark. Inquiring voices, foreign words. In the dark. They were unintelligible, but we understood. We quickly replaced the bulb and lay quietly. Would they know it was us? What would the shopkeeper say? And to whom? Dogs barked, a few chickens scuffled in their perches. We lay motionless, expecting the owner of our lodging to come pounding at our door. In the dark. Eventually, the voices grew quiet. Sometime later we fell asleep. The next light was that of dawn.

There had not been even one small paragraph in my guidebook warning against bulb replacements. I vowed if I ever got the chance, I would try to spare fellow travelers the fate of having to tell a similar tale. And so the story goes of another not-so-bright idea far from home, this time from Chiang Rai.

Joel Simon's photo assignments have taken him to all seven continents, including the North Pole, the Antarctic, and 95 countries in between. When not traveling, he's at home in Menlo Park, California, with his wife, Kim, cat, Ichiban, and an itinerant possum named Rover.

★

Real Thai food, unlike American versions of it, is one of the wonders of the world. I ate take-out lunch in my kayak under the shade of a foot-bridge. I had roast chicken with a hot dipping sauce and an old favorite, *som tam,* a salad of unripe grated papaya in a marinade of lime juice, chili pepper, tamarind sauce, tiny dried shrimp, and peanuts. But I was no more used to the heat of the spices than I was to the heat of the sun. My mouth burned with a fire that teared my eyes. I remembered reading why this pepper pain became so habit forming. The chili caused pain killers to be released by the brain so eating the marinated shrimps became a sort of luncheon high.

—Peter Aiken, "Thai Waterways"

ALAN RABINOWITZ

* * *

Tapir Tracks

*Impatient to return to the comforts of
Bangkok, the author rediscovers the
meaning of his work in the forest.*

I WAS TIRED. NOT JUST PHYSICALLY TIRED BUT THAT DEEP, BONE-weary tired that comes from having pushed beyond your limits not just once but every day for months. I was finishing up more than twelve weeks of difficult tracking through some of the largest forested areas in Southeast Asia, where I was searching for the clouded leopard, one of the most elusive cats in the world. The hardships of the jungle were beginning to take their toll. Now, fighting fatigue, I was just trying to make it through the last leg of the survey before going home.

This was my first time in Thailand, and my fourth day in the Huai Kha Khaeng Wildlife Sanctuary, one of the few remaining "forest gems" of this country. But after having spent the last few months tracking leopards in the dense, lush vegetation of Borneo's rain forest, this dry semi-barren area seemed anything but gem-like. Efforts to find clouded leopard tracks in the area of a recent sighting had, so far, proven futile, though there were abundant signs of tigers and Asiatic leopards. Normally, this would have excited me, but right now, this hike seemed like just another delay in my quest for a cold drink and a soft bed. As my Thai guides jabbered away in a language that sounded completely non-

283

sensical to me, I calculated the days, hours, and minutes before I might reach Bangkok.

Six hours out from camp, and a little after midday, when the heat was at its most merciless, we reached the Huai Kha Khaeng, the main river which runs through the heart of the sanctuary. (*Huai* means river in Thai.) This watershed is one of the most pristine forest areas remaining in Thailand, and it contains some of the richest wildlife populations in the country.

Racing ahead of my companions, I veered off from the old elephant trail we'd been following to get a drink of cold water from a small feeder stream nearby. As I knelt to scoop the water in my hands, I heard a high-pitched squeal, followed by the sound of something crashing into the water. Looking up, I froze. Twenty-five feet in front of me was a large prehistoric-looking beast. After being scared by my approach, it had leaped into the main river. All my weariness vanished at the sight.

It was a Malayan tapir, a hulking, secretive creature whose starkly contrasting black-and-white coloration helps render it inconspicuous during its travels through the forest. Its six-hundred-pound bulk had been moving quietly through the dense undergrowth parallel to our trail, reaching the riverbank at the same time as I did. I watched its wet hippolike body glisten in the midday sun as it stopped abruptly in midstream and turned its head in my direction. Raising its fleshy snout like an elephant's trunk, it bared large white teeth that could easily have inflicted a severe bite, then emitted a harsh, grating sound. I knew this action was meant to threaten me but I couldn't help but smile. He was brave, this one. He would have presented a tempting target for a hunter.

It was my first sighting of this species in the wild, which

Malayan tapir

is considered rare even by men who have lived in this part of the world. The tapir's preferred habitat of lush lowland rain forest made its presence here, at the drier northern extremity of its range, unusual. Yet even where tapirs are more common they are not often encountered. This strange-looking relative of horses and rhinos, considered one of the most primitive mammals in the world, is now on the list of the most threatened.

Realizing that I posed no immediate threat, the tapir continued to thrash his way across the river, then disappeared into the forest undergrowth with a speed that seemed impossible for such an ungainly animal. The other men, only one of whom had ever seem a tapir before, had caught up and were standing beside me, watching quietly. We were all smiling. Many years earlier, a traveler in Burma had described the tapir as "an enigma," a survivor of a "more gentle and legendary time…wandering in unique isolation in a world not yet mature enough for its wisdom." I suddenly remembered what had brought me to this part of the world. I was seeking a little of what was left of the "wisdom" of the forest. For the remainder of the day, I looked upon the terrain with new eyes, no longer in a rush to be anywhere else.

Alan Rabinowitz is a research zoologist who contributed five other stories to this book.

✳

Thailand is roughly the size of France, California, Kenya, Iraq, Morocco, Botswana, Papua New Guinea, or Sweden.

—JO'R and LH

JANE HAMILTON-MERRITT

✦

A Meditator's Initiation

A Western novice finds her way in the
male world of Buddhist monks.

VERY AFRAID, I APPROACHED THE ABBOT'S *GUTI*. AS I KICKED OFF my sandals at the door of his little house, I could see a monk, the Abbot, sitting Buddha-like in a mound of saffron robes inside on the floor. A flurry of thoughts hurried through my mind. Be sure to prostrate three times. Don't touch him. Always keep the hands in a respectful *wai* position.

As I waited in the doorway for him to acknowledge my presence, I wanted to disappear. What was I doing here? This was a man's world. Foreign women had no place in a Buddhist *wat*. The red and saffron asters which I had brought seemed heavy in my hands. "He's important; he's the Abbot of one of the royal *wats* of Thailand. Kings were ordained here, including the present one. This is one of the most significant *wats* in Bangkok. Do I dare enter this world?"

Finally he looked toward me. Awkwardly, flowers in my hands, I approached him on my knees. Never let my head be higher than his, I told myself again and again. When I had crawled close to him, I laid the flowers aside and prostrated three times, touching my head to the floor with my hands held in prayer-like fashion. This was new and troublesome because I did not know how to do it properly. Each time I raised my head, I noticed that he was watching me, making me even more nervous.

After the prostration, I sat on my knees, immobile, waiting. He seemed to be staring through me. I felt that he could read my mind. Unable to bear the silence, I, with my hands in a *wai* before my face, tried to introduce myself and make my request to study Buddhist meditation with him. He seemed not to hear. He continued to stare at and through me. I wondered what I had done wrong. I was wearing a high-necked, long-sleeved, full-length dress which I had been told was appropriate. Maybe I should not have spoken first? Sweat trickled down my body from fear and heat, but mostly from fear.

He didn't answer, so I gathered up the flowers and extended them to him. Since neither he nor any monk can receive anything directly from a woman, he took a piece of saffron cloth and put it before me. I laid the flowers on the cloth and he pulled the cloth and flowers near him, but he didn't look at them nor say thank you to me.

I sat still, keeping my hands in the respectful *wai* position. I noticed that the right side of his mouth was twitching. Eventually he spoke, very softly and slowly in English. "What do you know about Buddhism?"

I answered in a voice that was undoubtedly too loud and which expressed my fear. "I've read books on Buddhism, but I've come here to study meditation."

More empty minutes. He spoke again. "What is meditation?"

Trying to hold my trembling voice to a softness resembling his, I answered. "I don't really know. I've only read generally about it, but for me it seems impossible to know or to understand meditation by merely reading about it. That's why I want to study with you here at Wat Bovornives."

It seemed as if he were looking inside me. What was he searching for? Sincerity? I did not know. But I knew that I was nervous, uncomfortable, and aware that I was out of the world which I knew. After some empty minutes he spoke. "*Dhamma* class and meditation class meet tonight here in my *guti* at 6:00. You may come."

I prostrated myself three times and backed out of the room on my knees. Outside I could barely stand. I fumbled with my sandals and with heavy heart walked slowly within the *wat* compound along a small *klong* bridged with walk-overs. At one bridge, I sat down to reflect.

The late afternoon heat hung heavy in the air. Barefooted monks, robed in saffron with newly shaven heads, strolled by slowly. Sunspots edging through heavily leafed trees dabbled geometric designs on their robes. Erect, stately, like statues, they moved. An occasional breeze stirred their flowing robes. As I watched I became calm.

Why had I been so afraid? Thailand was not a new place for me. I was familiar with Thai ways. I had visited many *wats* and often found them a retreat from heat and noise. *Wats* had always been a place of contemplation for me. But this was different; I was trying to enter a way of life that demanded seclusion and meditation and was primarily open to men. Monks are not only celibate, but they must not touch a woman. They may speak to a woman, but only if another person is present. So it is easier not to have women living in *wat* compounds, particularly *farang* women.

I did not want to do something stupid or break a rule which would cause a monk to go through a complicated purification ceremony. But was I being overly sensitive?

As I waited for the evening class on *dhamma,* the teachings of Buddha, dusk descended into the compound. An evening breeze brushed the temple bells, which hung from the roof gables, producing a symphony of fragile tinkles. Delicate and yet omnipresent the sound of the temple chimes brought back the serenity that I had always experienced on visits to *wats.*

It was here, in this particular temple, in the early 1800s, that Prince Mongkut spent fourteen years as the Abbot before becoming the King of Siam. It was here that this prince, who was a philosopher, scientist, linguist, and scholar, attempted to purify Buddhist philosophy by going back to the ancient Pali scriptures, to the original teachings of Buddha. As a result of his scholarly research, he founded the strict Dhammayut sect in order to strengthen the rules of Theravada Buddhism which, in turn, greatly influenced the already existing sect known as Mahanikai.

As I reflected about the life of King Mongkut, perhaps one of the best minds among Oriental leaders in his time, I felt a oneness and a bit of rage because the West only knew this small man, who spent a total of 26 years in the monkhood, as a raucous degenerate, sometime tyrant, and often as a buffoon. All of this was dreamed up by one Anna Leonowens in her books, *The English Governess at the Siamese Court,* and *The Romance of the Harem,* which eventually became popularized by Yul Brenner in the play and then the movie, *Anna and the King of Siam.* What a pity!

Here in this *wat,* a-tingle with the music of miniature bells, I soon forgot the contemptuous manner in which Americans thought of King Mongkut, to think of other famous people who had entered this *wat* to study the teachings of Buddha and to practice meditation. It was here that the present King of Thailand, Bhumipol Adulyadej, in 1956 donned the saffron robes of monkhood for several weeks. The King must know and practice the teachings of Buddha since it is he who is the protector of Buddhism.

A few minutes before 6:00, I approached the Abbot's *guti* to watch several meditators take off their shoes at the doorstep and disappear inside. I gathered my courage, and once again tapped off my sandals and, bending low, entered.

Do not speak unless you can improve on silence, said a Buddhist sage.

—Tim Ward, *What the Buddha Never Taught*

The meditators were not gathering in the room where I had earlier met the Abbot, but in an adjoining room which resembled an office with chairs and a big modern desk which dominated the room. The females were sitting on the right and the males on the left. I slipped into the only vacant chair only to find that it was higher than the others, making me stick out like the newcomer I was.

To try to subdue my uneasiness, I took out my little notebook and began to record my impressions.

One shabbily dressed, tall and skinny youthful Western man.
Four monks sitting rigidly with downcast eyes. Three of the
monks are *farangs;* one Oriental. All heads newly shaven.
Farang monks look strange. Noses too big, skin too light,
bodies too hairy.

Great silence. Only the rustle of vegetation tousled by the
evening breeze. Desk overwhelms room. Heaps of artistic
arrangements of roses, orchids, ginger, and jasmine on the
desk. White and purple predominate for flowers given to
the Abbot, not orange and red as I brought. Strong smell
of jasmine.

Oriental monk must be meditating. Hands folded in lap, eyes
half-closed, only the whites of his eyes showing. Incredible
how much his eyes look like the half-open eyes of Buddha
statues. It doesn't appear that he's breathing.

The silence and my attention were broken by the appearance of
two young temple boys dressed in khaki shorts and white shirts.
They brought two trays of yellow Chinese tea cups emblazoned
with dramatic blue Chinese characters. I assumed the cups held
tea, but I could not see because they were topped with lids.

Each meditator took a cup and held it, but no one drank.
Neither did I. The boys departed. Silence returned.

Almost simultaneously, the monks and lay-meditators placed
their tea cups on open window ledges or on the floor while I
continued to hold mine, wishing that I did not have it.

As I struggled with my teacup and notebook, the Abbot walked
in. The monks stood and *waied* as he edged past them. Some of
the lay-meditators stood also and everyone *waied* to the Abbot,
except me, of course, who still held a hot cup of Chinese tea in one
hand and a pen and notebook in the other.

The Abbot sank behind the immense desk and silence ensued.
Everyone seemed to be looking at the Abbot, but he wasn't looking back. It was as if he were not in the room, but somewhere
else. I was afraid to move, but I had to get rid of the tea cup. Finally,
I took courage and carefully leaned and stuck it under my chair.

After what seemed to be ten minutes of silence, I noticed the Abbot's face beginning to twitch—just as it had done earlier in the day. Then he spoke, softly and haltingly in English with long pauses. I sensed that it was difficult for him to speak English. As he talked, I entered the following in my notebook.

> You should learn what the Buddha taught. Buddha taught that life is *dukkha*—suffering or unsatisfactoriness—caused by wanting, desire, craving, clinging, grasping. Birth, illness, old age, and death are *dukkha*.
>
> He taught that *sukkha*—happiness or lack of suffering—is the elimination of all desires, including the desire to cling to life itself.
>
> He taught *anicca*—impermanence—a constant decaying and changing that is common to all things. You, the moon, this desk, all things are changing constantly. Happiness does not come from liking or not liking things which are impermanent.
>
> To see all this, Buddha taught us to meditate—to clear our minds, to abandon the bad and develop the good. To do that we must purify and develop our minds. That can be done through meditation.
>
> For example—sound. Think what the mind is doing. Hear the boys playing outside. Think what the mind is doing; it's hearing.
>
> We must develop mindfulness, *sati*. *Sati* is memory—opposite of forgetting; it is to be awake—opposite of sleep; it is to know, to comprehend—opposite of ignorance.
>
> The truth comes from one's self. One's self is the big book.

When the Abbot looked in the direction of the monks, they responded in unison with a *wai* and bowed their heads until he looked away.

There followed another long pause. Again it was as though he wasn't in the room. His brown skin seemed warm against the subtle saffron of his robes—the man and his robes merged.

Then he began again, so softly.

We must develop mindfulness. To develop mindfulness, or *sati,* we must concentrate on air, our breathing, to get the feeling or knowing of *sati.* In this manner we should have memory— mindfulness.

There are four places to fix the mind: 1) body 2) feeling 3) mind 4) phenomena. Use these to develop the mind, make it mindful.

I wrote it all down, but I had little understanding. I was too shy to ask a question. After another lengthy silence, he spoke again and I recorded:

Breathing—be aware of the air touching your nostrils as it passes in and out. For beginners, it helps to count. One for the in-breath and two on the out-breath. Or count one-in and one-out, then two-in and two-out. Count up to ten breaths and then begin counting again from one.

Be mindful, but don't force your mind. When it wanders gently bring it back to being mindful on your breathing. Be patient.

Body—sit in a half-lotus position or with legs folded. Be certain to have a comfortable position. Use a cushion if neces- sary between the buttocks and heels in Japanese fashion. Keep your back straight. Fold your hands right over left with thumbs touching. Bend the body forward and sideways to make the body comfortable. If you can't sit still for thirty minutes, it's all right, but don't disturb the others.

Another period of silence followed before a bell rang some- where and the two temple boys appeared. The Abbot motioned his hand to the upstairs and they disappeared. It was difficult to believe that an hour had passed since I had entered this small room.

As the Abbot rose, the students *waied* to him as he left the room. This time, I *waied,* but felt uncomfortable because I was not certain just how to do it before this important monk or why. One *farang* girl, who spoke English, whispered, "We go upstairs now to meditate in the Abbot's meditation room."

I tagged along. We dropped our shoes at the dark door and waited until a temple boy opened the screened door and motioned us to enter. Inside it was dull dark. Eventually a pinkness pushed away the dullness as the monks began to light candles and incense at the front of the room. I searched for the girl who had whispered to me, but before I could locate her, a young man handed me a pillow. "You might be more comfortable if you use this," he whispered.

"No," I replied. "I don't need it."

"Then sit on these little rugs," he suggested, pulling one closer.

I suddenly realized that everyone was kneeling on the rugs, I quickly got down on the floor. Everyone seemed to be waiting for something. All eyes were on the Abbot and the monks who were sitting in front of an altar in the front portion of the room. The room seemed to have two distinct sections; one for the religious and one for lay people.

As those in the saffron robes began prostrating themselves three times before the Buddha image, the meditators joined in. I remained rigid in a kneeling position, watching. After prostration, everyone maneuvered himself into a lotus or half-lotus position. I kept my eyes on the girl in front of me—trying to duplicate her every movement.

One temple boy entered and turned on an overhead fan of Somerset Maugham vintage,

Mystic Thomas Merton spent 25 years as a Trappist monk in Kentucky before going to Thailand to study Buddhism. After a short time in Bangkok, he accidentally electrocuted himself with an electric fan.

—JO'R and LH

then plugged in a small electric fan, pointing it so that it blew directly on the lay meditators. As the first breeze passed over me, I was glad, for not only would this gentle breeze relieve some of the evening's oppressive heat, but it might prevent most mosquitoes from sampling my blood.

Prior to departing for the *wat,* not knowing that there would be fans in the *wat,* I had doused myself heavily with Sketolene, a powerful Asian mosquito repellent.

Finally I maneuvered my legs and body into a tolerable half-lotus position. I was glad that my loose dress didn't seem to touch my body anywhere. Its fullness gave me sufficient room to sit cross-legged in a modest fashion. I reminded myself always to wear something too big for me when I came here.

At last I seemed ready to begin. Mind on my breath, I began bringing in large amounts of air. I could tell that my breathing was abnormal, but it was interesting to feel the air, cool and tingling rush along the hair follicles inside my nose. Now to be mindful—to concentrate on nothing but the air coming in and coming out. I started to count—one-in, one-out; two-in. Then my mind was gone. It skipped to the powerful smell of the mosquito repellent, then it jumped to wonder if there would be mosquitoes in my room tonight, and then flitted to review my afternoon meeting with the Abbot. I started to count again—and again—and again. But each time my mind escaped, to rapidly climb a mounting thought only to flit to another, or to touch on a past event, or to stop to rest momentarily on a really stupid, mundane episode like the taxi driver who overcharged me.

This made me nervous. I could not hold my mind still for even a matter of seconds. Then I remembered the Abbot's words of warning, "Don't force it." When your mind wanders, gently bring it back. Maybe I was trying too hard. If I could only relax. But I could not. It was such a new experience for me and for some reason I seemed to be very emotional about beginning this adventure.

Finally I gave up the struggle and opened my eyes. I looked at my watch. About fifteen minutes had passed. The other meditators remained motionless in the dim light. The Abbot was no longer there, but the four younger monks were still meditating, immobile.

As my eyes became accustomed to the soft light, I noticed beautiful Chinese-style porcelain bowls and plates displayed in ornate cabinets along the walls. I wondered about their origins. Monks were not supposed to own anything. Later I discovered that the faithful had donated them to the *wat*—a way to make merit, to do a good deed.

Deep red and maroon colored rugs, with intricate designs, which the monks were sitting on, appeared to be Persian.

I slowly moved my hand to touch the floor; it was cool, hard, and, made of teak. The candles sputtered dramatically in the man-made breeze sending erratic tongues of light over the silent monks and the image of a sitting Buddha atop the altar. No matter where the flickering light fell on the image's face— whether the eyes, nose, or mouth, there was a sense of rest- fulness or tranquillity, or was it peace?

Smoldering incense defied the flopping fan to hang heavy in the air. It smelled good—or was it the jasmine flowers adorning the altar that piqued my senses?

This room was becoming friendly.

*O*rdination is not something that can be performed on a whim. Usually, the applicant is expected to memorize all of the Pali recitations to be used in the ceremony. To prepare, foreign appli- cants can study a copy of the English language Ordination Procedures *(available at the Mahamakut Buddhist bookshop opposite Wat Bowonniwet in Bangkok or at the office of the World Fellowship of Buddhists)*. This book explains ordination in detail and gives both the Pali and the English for the necessary recitations.

—Joe Cummings,
The Meditation Temples of
Thailand: A Guide

After another twenty minutes, meditators began to stir—very slowly at first, maybe only the lifting of a head or the moving of an arm. Then they began shifting their sitting positions. I sat very still, pretending my eyes were closed, mainly because I did not know what was to happen next.

The monks came to life slowly. One by one they prostrated themselves three times in front of the Buddha image. Soon the lay meditators did the same.

Quietly, and without any pomp, the lay meditators arose and tiptoed out to the door to search in the dimness for their shoes. With their shoes on, they walked away silently into the darkness.

No words had been spoken. I followed, but a bit more slowly. My right leg had fallen asleep.

I limped out of the quietness of the *wat* compound into the noise of traffic and the din of a Chinese cloth market, and headed for my room, several blocks away. I wanted to think about the past two hours, but it was too noisy. Later, as I walked down my dimly lit lane, the sweet smells from the flower market oozed out into the tropical night air reminding me of the jasmine smell in the Abbot's *guti* and I began to wonder if I would *ever* be able to hold my mind still past the count of two? I was doubtful.

Besides, in the past I had always found it most exhilarating to allow my mind to roam wildly. Some of my best ideas came when my mind raced like the wind through and over myriads of recollections, images, and fantasies. Did I really want to change all this?

As I walked the final dark yards to my room, I reflected on the evening. Suddenly, I realized that the whole class had been directed to me. The Abbot had obviously gone back to the beginning precepts of meditation—just for me, the newcomer. A rush of warm feeling for this man came over me. "I must try," I whispered to myself as I unlocked the door. "I must practice his instructions again and again."

I sat down on the floor in the darkness of my room and began to try to be mindful of my breathing. I began counting—one-in, one-out; two-in. I began over and over—one-in, one-out; two-in—And thus it went for almost an hour, although I never legitimately went beyond two without my mind rebelling from the task at hand.

Tired and disillusioned, I crawled into bed. Across the floor, moonlight, distorted by the heavy tropical vegetation, danced in fleeting images—as did my mind.

Jane Hamilton-Merritt grew up on a dairy farm in the American midwest, flew as a bush pilot in East Africa, and was a war correspondent in Vietnam. She has published two books for young adults on the peoples and cultures of Southeast Asia, Boonmee and the Lucky White Elephant *and* Lahu Wildlife.

★

The mind is like a monkey, say the Buddhists. It hops from place to place, restless and wild. We have no control over it. Our sensations, perceptions, memories, wills and thoughts chatter erratically in our heads. There is no peace. The aim of meditation is to learn first how to control the monkey mind, then to be free of it. This is not how the West views the mind. The scientific and artistic traditions of the human race are not erratic chatter to us. We exalt our minds. We raise our consciousness. Our sense of self is our most important possession. We cannot comprehend what the Buddha taught....

I sit on my porch and concentrate on the trembling sensation of breath in my nostrils. The ease of absorption begins to come at last. Hey, now I'm getting somewhere! This is meditation! Concepts spring into awareness, shattering the calm. One word, one thought leads to the next. The chattering left brain takes over like a bully. Yes, I'm finally meditating. Well, almost there for a second. Sure is hot now. When's coffee break? Remember coffee break back on the rigs? Fudge brownies. Damn mosquitoes.

—Tim Ward, *What the Buddha Never Taught*

THALIA ZEPATOS

* * *

In the Akha Village

*Living in an unfamiliar culture offers
countless lessons about life. It
can even change your diet.*

WE RODE THE BUS FROM CHIANG MAI THROUGH THE LUSH GREEN hills of northern Thailand into the heart of the Golden Triangle. A couple of hours after leaving town, the Dutch traveler sitting beside me waved the driver to stop at a wide place in the road. We got out beside a small thatched shelter.

"Now what?"

"We wait. "

"For what?"

"A truck that may be going a few miles up toward the village. The road is muddy during monsoon season, so the truck will take us as far as it can go. We'll walk the rest of the way up."

Short, dark people emerged from the shadows and joined us in the little shelter. Some of the women were dressed in Western trousers and t-shirts. Others wore homespun jackets and pants the blue-black color of indigo, trimmed with red and white appliquéed designs. Then a woman walked straight out of the pages of *National Geographic*. I tried not to stare at her magnificent headdress. Rising from her head like a conical tower, it was crafted from row upon row of silver coins and beads, red and white buttons. Tassels fashioned from dyed fur and feathers hung from its sides.

Geert saw me watching the woman. "Wow," I said in a low voice. "Just wait," he responded.

I'd met Geert on the tropical beach of Koh Samui, an island off the southern coast of Thailand. I'd told him that my traveling partner, Mary, would soon be leaving for other adventures and described my dream of traveling alone and visiting remote villages. He offered to take me to the hillside village of the Akha tribe where he'd spent the previous three months.

Geert would help organize my stay in the village and remain available for advice and support the entire time I was there. He was enthusiastic about my goal—to make friends and live as independently as possible.

Two men arrived in a small green pickup truck. They pointed uphill and motioned to the group that had gathered at the thatched bus stop. The Akhas piled into the back. I followed their lead, taking a seat on the open side, placing my pack between my feet on the truckbed. The pickup revved its motor and sprang up a dirt track into the hills.

The truck careened from one edge of the muddy track to the other, swerving wildly as the tires bounced out of deep ruts and spewed mud into the air. Akhas and foreigners crisscrossed arms, holding on to each other to keep from getting bounced out. The rear wheel below me skidded off the road and hung for a breathless eternity in thin air; my gaze was sucked down the steep jungle ravine to the twisted wreckage of a Land Rover 100 feet below. Two silver teeth punctuated an Akha man's smile once we regained solid ground. A red pom-pom atop his wool beret marked time as he sang a low tune.

Truck wheels chewed deeply into mud until they could go no farther. I welcomed the chance to get my feet on the earth. The diminutive Akhas walked gingerly atop the crusted mud; my foot broke through on my first step and I sank to my ankle in the slippery goop. Everyone laughed.

After an hour's climb, we reached the village, perched below the crest of a hill. We stopped at a sort of central square, a flattened piece of earth with benches on three sides. I circumspectly looked around. Three main streets radiated from the square, following the contours of the land. Bamboo houses stood neatly along wide avenues, each house built on a platform jutting out from the hillside with one end propped up on stilts. Children carried wood in baskets and water in large gourds; no one was idle. An Akha man who had come up with us spoke some English and would negotiate my stay with a village family. Geert would remain as interpreter; even though he knew but a dozen words of Akha, it was twelve more than I knew. We walked together down one avenue and entered a fenced compound through a bamboo gate.

I was introduced to Azo and Apu. Azo was the headman's brother, and a respected elder of the tribe. About forty years old, he was lean and strong with a distinguished face. Looking into his calm eyes was like gazing down a well a century deep. Apu, his wife, sized me up with awe. She pantomimed an observation that she was half my height, then motioned me into the house with a high-pitched laugh, displaying her red, betel-nut–stained teeth and lips to full advantage.

The shy and retiring Akha construct their villages at high elevations to escape neighbors and provide privacy for opium cultivation. Primitive wooden figures flanking the village entrance gates are carved with prominent sex organs to ensure fertility and ward off evil spirits. Don't touch these talisman gates or the bamboo spirit houses scattered throughout the village.

—Carl Parkes,
Thailand Handbook

I felt blind when I entered the dark house. The bamboo floor swayed lightly under my feet. I was relieved when Apu motioned for me to sit down. She was preparing rice and vegetables, and when my eyes became accustomed to the slanted rays of light that filtered through slats in the walls, I offered to help. She put a knife and some greens on a chopping block before me. I methodically began to perform my task. Moments later, Apu swept aside my dainty movements and finished it with three well-placed chops of her machete. A fierce squawking outside was silenced by a loud "thwap." Chicken for dinner. Azo brought the gutted carcass inside.

We ate from a low bamboo table on the men's side of the house. Serving bowls in the table's center held cooked greens, bamboo shoots, the chicken dish, and hot chili sauces. We used chopsticks and Chinese flat-bottomed spoons, taking turns to scoop food from the common bowls. Reaching into baskets set on the floor, we grabbed handfuls of steamed rice and molded them into little cakes before taking a bite.

After the meal, the small table was moved aside. Rice and food that had fallen on the floor were swept through a wide crack to the ground below, where pigs and chickens gobbled up the remains. A perfect eco-system, no garbage.

Some neighbors came to meet the *farang*. We sat, staring and smiling at each other until I retrieved a child's toy from my pack. A ball on a string hung below a plastic cup; the proper toss would place the ball in the cup. The toy was passed round and fierce competition ensued. Later, I joined the women on their side of the house while the men lit a small kerosene lamp, lay back against their bedrolls and smoked.

The Swing Festival started the next morning; it was a harvest celebration that marked the beginning of the Akha New Year. Men of the village gathered at a high promontory in early morning fog to build a tall swing from four saplings stripped of bark and branches. After planting the four poles in a square, they shimmied up and lashed the tops together into an arch. They hung a swing from the center of the arch, choosing the heaviest from among them to test it.

We went to the headman's house and drank a bowl of fragrant rice whiskey with breakfast as young people gathered outside. The teenagers rhythmically pounded large sections of bamboo against a flattened tree trunk, making a steady beat to accompany their songs. For three days, the Akha wore their finest traditional clothing and stayed home from the fields. One by one, each villager took their place on the swing, singing a New Year's song as they teetered over the cliff. Teenage girls swung tandem and flirted with young men. On the third day, Apu brought me to the swing. She helped me balance on the narrow seat and pushed me off into the sky. I leaned my head back and sang the swing song, imitating the words I had heard a hundred times in the hours I'd stood watching. When I came back to earth, a toothless old woman wearing heavy silver neck rings nodded and drew me to her side. I'd made a new friend.

Then the festival was over and it was time for work. Apu left her finery hanging on pegs inside the bamboo house, slipped on her oldest homespun jacket and pulled a pair of torn men's trousers underneath her skirt. She placed a fitted hood on her headdress and chose work clothes from my pack for me. Geert rigged large baskets on either side of a child-sized packhorse. Apu gave me a bamboo-and-rattan basket to carry, showing me how to support it with the woven tumpline across my forehead. It was an odd sensation, hanging the basket from my forehead instead of my shoulders.

We followed winding paths away from the village, up a hill and along the top of a tree-covered ridge. Apu stopped along the trail to harvest fresh greens and bamboo shoots for dinner. She darted from side to side, checking traps she had set days before. On one steep hillside, she sang out a triumphant cry. A trap had been triggered, and she ran for the prey. She lifted the log that had smashed the animal, and held it up for us to see. The scaly carcass was about a foot long, covered with crawling white maggots.

It had been dead too long. Geert and I covered our noses against the sickening stench. Apu smiled and patted her stomach, reassuring us that it would be tasty to eat. "No, no!" we responded. We held our noses, pantomimed bad stomachs from eating something so foul. She laughed merrily, lopped off a giant banana leaf with her machete, wrapped the animal in the leaf, and tossed it into the basket behind her back.

She reset the trap, showing us how the log would crash down on the next animal to pick at the bait tied to the Y-shaped trigger. We adopted the sound she used to imitate the falling log as the name of the stinking carcass that had been its victim. We called it the Blap.

We tried to reason with Apu. She should throw the Blap away. It was no good. She laughed and walked on ahead, singing an Akha song in her bell-like voice. Geert and I hung back, muttering.

"She can't cook that thing, it'll kill anyone who takes a bite!" I said.

He smiled, "Shouldn't we try to be good guests and eat it? Apu must know what she is doing."

"Listen," I retorted, "when Ano shot that iridescent jungle beetle out of the tree with his slingshot and roasted it on the fire, I ate it. I ate the chicken feet and the pig and the dog meat during the festival. And I never once complained. But I'm not going to eat that…Blap."

We arrived at a terraced hillside and set to work, hacking corn off stalks with machetes and tossing the ears over our shoulders into the carry-baskets. I got accustomed to swinging the heavy blade and quickened my pace. But the increasing weight of the corn in the basket pulled my head back until I could only stare straight up at the sky. I stumbled along straining my eyes to spy the next ear from the corner of my vision. Apu spotted my predicament and scurried over, relieving me of my burden with a suppressed grin. It was time for lunch.

Apu unfolded our midday meal from banana leaf wrappings and opened a round basket packed with the nutty-flavored mountain rice. She lit a fire, let it burn down, and tossed the Blap onto the smoldering embers. Several minutes later she pushed the blackened thing away from the coals with a stick. Once it cooled, she peeled the scales from the carcass, smiling and nodding, telling us again how delicious it would be. She wrapped it again and returned it to her carry-basket.

I was relieved to avoid eating the Blap. But I feared it was only a matter of time before the beast appeared on our dinner table. As we shucked corn during the afternoon, I repeated to myself, "I am not going to eat that thing no matter what."

When we returned from the day's work, Apu sent me down to the village shower. Bamboo pipes sluiced water from a spring into a narrow gorge. Certain times were reserved for women to wash, others for men. The Akha girls laughed shyly when I arrived; I followed their custom and wore my sarong while showering. Afterwards, we fought mock battles with the children who'd come to fill their containers with drinking water.

I was suspicious about the dinner that simmered on the fire when I returned. Geert leaned across the divider from the men's side of the house and said, "Don't worry, she got rid of that Blap thing. It's fish for dinner tonight." I vowed to ask about the Blap before every meal.

By the light of the kerosene lantern, Apu slapped one rigid arm on top of the other and told the story of the Blap. Then she mimicked my head tipping back under the strain of the carry-basket to another round of laughter.

"How many days' walk to my home village?" I was asked in sign language.

"Not possible to walk," I pantomimed. "You must fly over the ocean." I took out my notebook and drew a picture of an airplane. Everyone seemed perplexed; they had seen planes up in the sky, but they were so small. How had I gotten inside?

Life slipped into a familiar routine. I spent most days working with Apu, harvesting and shucking corn. She sang Akha songs as we walked toward the fields and taught me the names of plants and flowers. One afternoon on the path back to the village we heard a terrible roar. Apu vaulted into the brush and dragged me behind her. The entire jungle seemed to shake as an elephant came charging past, hauling a felled tree that was chained behind it. A "flat-lander" man ran behind the elephant with a whip. We huddled among the leaves, waiting for the spectacle to pass. Apu took me off the path and showed me a logging camp. It was the only time I saw the smile disappear from her face.

For several days, I stayed home from the fields, bouncing our neighbor Abu's baby as she wove cotton cloth. She outfitted me in her extra clothes; the open black jacket, trimmed in white seeds and red beads, was a bit short but fit fine over my t-shirt. The gathered skirt barely covered my thighs. The towering headdress weighed several pounds and swayed each time I moved, its silver coins, buttons, and beads tinkling beside my ears. I joined a group of chattering women trimming headdresses, tying on dyed monkey fur and chicken feathers and making brightly colored pompoms from store-bought yarn.

I lost track of time. Life flowed in an unceasing pattern of work, each day rung in by the sound of the foot-treadle mortar, husking mountain rice for breakfast.

Finally, I had to leave. Everything seemed poignant that last day, even the gray monsoon clouds that rolled in across the valley. We returned from the fields a bit early for my special farewell feast. Once again I marveled at the mysterious array of delicately seasoned forest plants, meats, and fish that had been stir-fried, pickled, or smoked over the men's hearth. I swept the floor after dinner one last time. Later, we played the ball and cup game that had become our favorite.

The next morning I packed to leave. Azo sharpened my knife on his special whetstone, indicating that no journey should be initiated with a dull knife. The two women, Apu and Abu, strung white seed necklaces with tiny dried gourds trimmed in colored yarn. Tears clouded my eyes when they placed the farewell amulets around my neck.

We took some last photos; Apu imitated a *farang* by posing Western-style and mugging for the camera. In gestures and a few Akha words, I thanked her for her hospitality, her friendship, the lessons she had taught me, the delicious meals she'd cooked.

> *I* have watched the hill tribes in their homes, and I am always struck, as I was then, by a sense of the continuousness of their lives. The women particularly seem to live out one long, undifferentiated chore: cooking and washing, sewing and weaving, milling and winnowing, suckling and mothering, and so on. I'm not saying this is good—I'm not like the Dutchman, who wanted his tribespeople picturesque and underdeveloped—but it seems to be a part of the tribal psychology. The farang life is measured into compartments: work, leisure; day, evening; what I am now, what I will be later. The tribespeople just keep on keeping on, slow and practised and implacable, expecting nothing more than the turning of the day, and of the seasons, and of their lives, after which brief turnabout they join the wider omnipresent wheeling of the 'ancestors,' whom time no longer needs.
>
> — Charles Nicholl, *Borderlines: A Journey in Thailand and Burma*

lessons she had taught me, the delicious meals she'd cooked.

Her face cracked an impish grin. She pantomimed a question about the farewell dinner. "Did you like it?"

"Yes, very much," I patted my stomach. "Delicious."

She tipped her head back and chuckled, lips exposing her red teeth. She patted her stomach, showing the sign for delicious again and again. Then, she gave me a devilish smirk. She slapped one arm down on top of the other—Blap!

Thalia Zepatos is a political consultant, traveler, and writer who lives in Portland, Oregon. She is the author of Adventures in Good Company: The Complete Guide to Women's Tours and Outdoor Trips *and* A Journey of One's Own: Uncommon Advice for the Independent Woman Traveler, *from which this was excerpted.*

★

It's up to *farangs* to adapt to the customs of the hill tribes and not to make a nuisance of themselves. Apart from keeping an open mind and not demanding too much of your hosts, a few simple rules should be observed:
- Dress modestly, with long trousers or skirt and a t-shirt or shirt.
- Loud voices and boisterous behaviour are out of place. Smiling and nodding establishes good intent.
- Most hill tribe houses contain a religious shrine. Do not touch or photograph this shrine, or sit underneath it.
- Some villagers like to be photographed, most do not. Point at your camera and nod if you want to take a photograph. Never insist if the answer is an obvious "no." Be particularly careful with pregnant women and babies—most tribes believe cameras affect the soul of the foetus or new-born.
- Taking gifts is dubious practice; writing materials for children are very welcome, but sweets and cigarettes may encourage begging.
- Smoking opium on a trek is a big attraction for many travellers, but there is evidence of increased addiction rates among hill tribe villagers who are regularly visited by trekkers.

—Paul Gray and Lucy Ridout, *The Rough Guide Thailand*

STEVE VAN BEEK

* * *

Sin, The Buffalo Man

On a two-month journey down Thailand's
largest river, the author finds refuge
with an isolated tribesman.

IN THE DUSK LIGHT, THE HALF-NAKED MAN STOOD IN SILHOUETTE, blocking the trail through thick vegetation. The moment I said a tentative *"Sawasdee, Khrap?"* (hello), he pulled a longknife and set his feet in a defensive stance.

It was a logical reaction for an old man deep in the jungle where few strangers set foot, but it caught me by surprise. In the pale evening light, the longknife, freed from its bamboo sheath, glowed with deadly intent as its owner barked in Thai, "What do you want?" I quickly explained that a border patrol soldier up-stream had told me I might find a night's accommodation in the old buffalo herder's hut.

"Why'd he tell you that?" he muttered in an agitated voice. "He had no right saying that. Go away. Get out of here."

The sight of the knife should have compelled me to "get" but I had nowhere to go. High in the hills along the Burmese border, night held many threats, most of them two-legged since hill tribesmen had long ago hunted out the tigers and other beasts that had once stalked the tangled forests. To calm him down, I explained quietly in Thai that I was on my way down the Ping River and had gotten soaked trying to wrestle my way over a five-meter-high weir. I had paddled this far in search of shelter and the herder's hut was the only thing I'd encountered.

His fierceness wavered a moment at the words "paddled." "Paddled? Paddled what?" he demanded.

"A boat. Paddled a boat," I said, repeating the words *pai rua* (paddled).

"Nobody paddles a boat in this jungle," he said, scoffingly. "Where is this boat?"

"Down at the riverbank," I said, pointing down the thickly treed slope.

He peered for a long moment in the direction my finger pointed but obviously could see nothing. His attitude had changed, however. The knife was still up but now he was shifting from leg to leg, his curiosity piqued.

"Let's go see," he said, finally. "You first, I'll follow." The wariness was still there but he sheathed his knife and I breathed a little easier.

We stood on the bank of the rushing river as he ran a gnarled hand over the hull of the teak skiff. Nodding approvingly, he said, "Nice boat. Don't see any this far north." Straightening up, he said, "Stuck, huh? I don't have much out here. This is the jungle. You'll have to sleep in a lean-to. I only have curry and rice, but you can have some of it." Home free.

On the way back up the hill, he said "You startled me. Nobody comes out here except to make trouble. I have nine water buffalo and they are worth a lot of money." He said it, not in apology for his actions, but as a statement of fact about a hard life.

For most of the year, Sin Phoma, a Shan tribesman, lived with his wife and three grown sons in the village of Muang Ngai, two valleys away. While the garlic ripened, he spent the three months in the jungle letting his buffalo fatten on the luxuriant grass that grew amidst underbrush made lush by monsoon rains. His eldest son often stayed with him but had gone out hunting the day before and was not expected back until the next morning.

Like many hillmen, Sin Phoma was short and sinewy, browned by years in the sun and used to taking care of himself. In a small patch he had cleared among the tall trees, he had erected bamboo thatch walls on posts one and a half meters off the ground and capped with a thatch roof. Access to the porch was by a log notched with steps. It was obvious from his exertions in climbing it that he was no longer young.

"Sixty-three," he said with a smile when I asked him. "Old already. That's why I have to be careful of strangers. There are black-hearted people in these hills," he said, sweeping his arm across the silhouettes of the ridges. "They wouldn't hesitate to kill me to steal my water buffalo."

Down in the Central Plains, water buffalo were rapidly disappearing, replaced by small tractors that didn't get sick and could power irrigation pumps and small farm trucks. Here in the north, buffalo were still valuable as draft animals, and sources of milk and meat.

Across the yard from his hut was a wooden platform raised 50 centimeters off the ground, enclosed on three sides by thatched walls and covered, like the house, by a thatched roof. It was just big enough for two people to sleep in cramped comfort. Like a manger, its floor was covered in straw which softened the hard wooden floor and covered the cracks between the planks. It would not keep out the cold but would shelter a sleeper from the dew. It was here that Sin indicated I would sleep for the night.

On the hard dirt yard a small fire was burning. Sin brought more wood to build it up and I began unpacking my gear, hanging the sleeping bag over the front of the shed opening to dry. Tomorrow, it would stink of wood smoke but I didn't care; dry beat smelly. Sin fingered its material and asked what I used it for. He was intrigued by my reply. "That would be useful in the hills," he said. "Wouldn't have to worry about the blanket slipping off in the middle of the night and exposing you." I noticed that he adjudged everything in terms of how it would serve in a jungle situation and concluded that he had spent many years there.

"When we came up here years ago, it was all jungle," he said. "It was a long time before we had enough land cleared to grow enough crops to feed us. In the meantime, we had to forage for everything. In the old days, it was easy; the forests were full of game. Today…" he looked wistfully into the blackness, "…there's not much. You can still find the kinds of fruits we ate when we didn't have anything else, but the animals…I guess most of them have been shot."

A northern January night, even in tropical Thailand, can be bitterly cold. The fire was warm and I huddled close to it to dry myself. Sin squatted by it for a long time. Then, unhinging his legs and sighing, he got up. "I guess we should have some dinner. I don't have much…. Can you eat Thai food?" I'd already told him I'd lived in Thailand for eighteen years so it seemed an odd question but I said, yes. *"Phet?* (spicy)." "Can," I said.

Hidden by the bamboo lattice that enclosed the porch, Sin puttered about with some pans, lighting a cooking fire in a firepit. "Sticky rice?" he shouted from the depths, assuming I bowed to the Central Plains abhorrence of anything—sticky, brown, scented—other than polished, fluffy white rice which the northerners believed was wholly lacking in nutrition or substance. "Can," I answered.

I knew it was going to be a meager meal but I didn't care. It had been a tough day and I was very hungry. While he was making dinner, I recorded the day's events in my journal.

Eventually, Sin invited me inside to eat. It was now dark and the dingy interior was lit only by the glowing embers of the cooking fire and a single wick stuck into half a tin can filled with kerosene, a sooty, smoky lamp that served as the sole form of illumination in the rural areas. In the darkness, two ragged cats prowled, the firelight occasionally illuminating a broken tail or glinting eye.

As I suspected, dinner was an unidentifiable mass of vegetables and something which crunched and from which I had to extract bones. Perhaps the dim lamp had its benefits after all. Uncertain of what to do with the bones, I set them on the floor. Sin put down his spoon, picked up the bones and, without looking, threw them in the general vicinity of the cats who immediately pounced on them, each growling at the other to keep clear. Some of the sticky rice that was left over was also dumped on the floor for the cats to eat. The rest was left in the pan which was set beside the fire.

After dinner, we returned to squat by the outside fire. Sin threw a large *mai daeng* log onto the fire, angling it so it would reflect its heat into my lean-to. The cats, which had been wandering around the fire, jumping nervously each time the burning log popped, curled up on my now-dry sleeping bag and seemed determined to spend the night there.

Over the next hour, in a leisurely manner, Sin questioned me about my journey and my time in Thailand. Listening but seldom looking directly at me, he paused after each question to absorb the answer, like his water buffalo ruminating before digesting a fact. He said nothing for a while. A few hard crickets provided music in the cool night.

Then, as to himself, he said: "*Farang* women," directing his comment at the fire. What? "*Farang* women. They're so big." I'd heard this before; Thai men intimidated by the height and bulk of foreign women. As in much of Asia, there was a fascination with the blondness and the—as perceived from movies—seeming sexual promiscuity of foreign women; their willingness to jump into bed in a flash. The concept was intriguing to Thais but there was a hesitation about what to do with all that mass of flesh. Sin must have shared that same awe and that same curiosity.

"Thai women." Ah, here we go, I thought. Thai women were best, didn't I agree? "Thai women," he repeated. "Too small, too thin," he snorted dismissively. "*Farang* women. That's the size women should be," he said chuckling to himself. Hello? What a switch! Here was a man who knew no bounds, for whom size was a challenge, not a defeat. I had to smile at the intensity and certainty with which he said it. Not obscenely, not lecherously. Just plain fact. We lapsed into silence.

A moment later, Sin spoke to the fire. "*Jai rai* (evil hearts)." He pointed with his chin to the riverbank. "When you get farther down the river, there are black people, especially around Chiang Mai. Plains people. You'll have to be on your guard."

As in most countries, there is a natural antipathy between hill and plains people. As a foreigner, I fit into a third category. These hill people didn't know exactly how to deal with me but assumed that I posed no real danger, even if they couldn't figure out what would compel someone to paddle down a river, and alone, for God's sake. That I was traveling alone made me even less of a threat. Almost. I noted as we prepared for bed, that unlike the Lahu tribesman who had invited me to sleep in his house, Sin had placed me outside. He climbed the notched log, bade me good night, closed the door firmly behind him, and shot the bolt. He wasn't taking any chances.

My journey down the Ping River had started years before on the banks of the Chao Phraya river which the Ping feeds. A chance encounter with friends had given me possession of a house in Bangkok past whose door the Chao Phraya flowed. Indeed, because the house was perched on stilts, the river flowed under it and, during two years of particularly bad floods, through it as well.

It sat on the river bank opposite the Grand Palace and the Temple of the Emerald Buddha and just upriver from *Wat Arun*, the Temple of Dawn, and for eleven years afforded me some of the best moments of my life. There are few pleasures greater than sitting on a porch in a wicker

Along some sections of the river [in Ayuthaya], the tree growth to the bank was almost jungle-like in thickness. I could rest from the sun under canopies of brush and liana-covered tree limbs, listening to birds and rocking in wakes left by longtail boats racing up and down the river. Even from the low vantage point of my kayak, I could see chedi towers, broad-based and tapering to great heights, wats and temple walls through surrounding foliage. At the river's edge, grandmothers with short-cropped white hair led children to the water to bathe. Students in white and blue uniforms waited on a dock for a river taxi. I reached the Dutch cathedral of St. Joseph's—out of place beside the gleaming orange, white, and green of Wat Buddaisawan— and was reminded of the Dutch colonial empire it symbolized that stretched from India across the Indonesian archipelago, harvesting spices for European tables.

—Peter Aiken, "Thai Waterways"

rocking chair, rocking in rhythm with the earth and watching the world roll by.

It was a simple four-room wooden house covered by a tile roof, under which the rats scampered and fought, all with great din, the few periods of silence indicating that a green pit-viper had slithered down from the mango or bottle-brush trees and was dining among them.

When I moved in, the bedroom facing the river had a small window in a high wall. I tore out the entire wall and replaced it with glass panels. Then, I cut a hole in the floor and put in a window so I could watch the waves wash back and forth under the house. Finally, I built a small bay window with a glass floor. When it rained, I could pull up the floor and drop in a fishing line without getting a drop of rain on me.

When one rocks back and forth for so many years, one begins to get curious about where all that flowing water is coming from. I asked many Thai friends about the river but got only rudimentary answers about a river system that was so vital to their lives. The Chao Phraya drained the northern and central regions of Thailand and was fed by four tributaries, the Ping, Wang, Yom, and Nan that began at the Burmese and Laotian borders and flowed south to the sea, a journey of about 1,200 kilometers. More than that, few people could tell me and books were even less helpful. It began to dawn on me that no one had ever run the river for its complete length. One day, my curiosity got the better of me and I decided to find out. I picked the Ping because it was the westernmost. It begins on the border with Burma about 150 kilometers above Chiang Mai and runs south along the Tenasserim Range that forms the border with Burma, flowing through Chiang Mai and Tak where it is joined by the Wang. It then heads southwest to combine with the Nan-Yom at Nakhon Sawan and drops south again as the Chao Phraya through Ayutthaya and Bangkok to the Gulf of Thailand.

After exploring the headwaters with Lahu hunters, I had a small teak boat built in a village near Tak and set off on a journey that would end 58 days later in the sea. Eventually, I would paddle the other three tributaries, spending five months in all, sleeping in villages, Buddhist monasteries, the jungles, and occasionally in the boat when no other alternatives were available. It was after several days in the jungles, and bamboo forests that I had reached Sin's hut.

Like most tribals, Lahus are animists who believe their village priest can exorcise evil spirits with black magic and heal the sick with sacred amulets. And, like the Karens, they anticipate a messianic movement lead by Guisha, the supreme Lahu god who created the heavens. Their most famous post-war messiah was Maw Naw, the gibbon god who failed in his attempts to restore true Lahu religion and lead his people back into Burma.

—Carl Parkes,
Thailand Handbook

The difference between Sin's initial reception and his greeting the next morning was markedly different. It had been a cold, crisp night and a beautiful dawn with a clear yellowish sky. When I awoke, I could hear the water buffalo stamping their feet and someone making clucking sounds as he fed them.

When he saw I was awake, he came up to squat and warm his hands by the embers of the *mai daeng* log. Barefoot, he wore short pants and a flimsy cotton shirt yet, aside from his hands, did not seem to feel the cold. With straw beneath me, I had slept quite warmly, awakening only once in the night when I had difficulty breathing. In my half-coma I was aware of fur covering my face and slowly realized that both cats had snuggled up next to my head. They were probably covered in vermin and I groggily tried to push them away. Half asleep yet alert, they responded by growling menacingly, a deep-throated warning that I thought it best to defer to. When I awoke in the morning, however, they were gone, stalking something in the darkness under the house.

We talked for a few minutes and then he went inside to prepare breakfast. Finding it too cold for a shower, I shaved and began packing my gear. It was a beautiful morning and I wanted to get an early start.

Sin had other ideas, however. "I want you to meet my son when he gets here. He should be here soon," he said, peering into the jungle hopefully.

In Thailand, "soon" can mean anything up to half a day. As Sin had not had a very clear idea the evening before of his son's expected arrival time, I could see myself sitting impatiently for a long while.

It was apparent that Sin had been living as a bachelor for some time because his idea of fixing breakfast was to warm up the sticky rice of the night before. The cold air had congealed it to a hard mass, the grains nearly as firm as they had been before they had been boiled. To give it some flavor, he stacked a few slabs of salted fish the thickness of crepes on the plate along with two fresh young bananas, and handed it to me. I had only sipped the water he had given me the night before because I was not sure of its purity but with this mass, it was going to take a great deal of liquid just to get the food to chewing consistency let alone to swallow it. As usual, I smiled as I accepted the glass which looked as though it had last held a paint brush and thinner.

During breakfast, he kept telling me of his son's imminent arrival as if his words might lure the phantom to quicken his pace. By the end of the meal, the sun was just beginning to clear the hill and we were still alone. It was apparent that this man who couldn't wait to get rid of me the night before, had decided I was O.K. and now could not bear to have me leave. I'm sure that he didn't get many visitors and certainly none as exotic as a foreigner, paddling a boat.

"Come look at my garden," he said. In the clearing, he had planted papaya and a half-dozen other fruit trees, as well as a small garden which fed him. Most of the area was given over to a pen made of bamboo poles set horizontally in rough-hewn wooden-slab fence posts. Behind it, nine black, bulky water buffalo with scimitar horns sweeping back over their broad backs sniffled and shot blasts of steam from their nostrils as they stamped to keep warm. Beside the pen, the garden began.

I trudged behind him as he gave me a botany test. "What's that?" he asked, walking by a tree, not even stopping to look at it. "Jackfruit," I dutifully answered. "Um, um," he said, pleased. "And that?" "Teak." "Um, um. *Geng* (clever)." We must have gone through 15 plants and still had not exhausted the possibilities. In a Thai jungle there can be 300 varieties of plants, creepers, trees, bushes, vines, in addition to everything he'd planted in his garden and I could see my legs being walked off before we'd catalogued even half of them. Where in the hell *was* that son?

After a moment, however, we'd completed a circuit and he seemed pleased with my knowledge. I'd failed on only one, probably the simplest plant in the world, one I'd seen at least a million times. He pointed at a knee-high plant with two stems reaching up from the ground, each stem fanning out with a broad, pleated leaf. "Uh," I ventured, baffled. "Is it a kind of banana?"

He seemed surprised by my ignorance and almost scoffed in giving the answer: "Coconut." My goodness, I really was slipping.

Finally, we arrived at his buffalo pen when he immediately began introducing me to each of the placid beasts. I repeated each of the names as he spoke them, like a good schoolboy.

Sin seemed to have run out of steam. We went back to the shed where my pack lay and he seemed bereft of ideas for conversation. "Where is he?" he said, looking into the pathless jungle. He was so eager to have me stay that I decided, to heck with an early start, I'll sit and talk with him. He obviously had a lot he could tell me about the jungle and would be a valuable source.

I had slipped the pack onto my shoulder but now laid it down again. When Sin saw that I intended to stay a while longer, he perked up. He left to get me another glass of water and as he came out of the house, we heard sticks crackling among the trees.

A younger version of Sin with a shotgun barrel sticking above his shoulder and shod in rubber boots strode into the yard. In his belt was a hatchet and had I met him in the jungle I might have run. He did not seem in the least bit surprised to see me, even after Sin had explained who I was and what I was doing. The son set the gun down and squatted by the fire. His had been a fruitless hunt; no game to be found, not even edible birds.

He and Sin talked for a few moments. As they conversed, the son walked to the house wall and began looking along it. He stopped at one of the rough teak pillars which had a number of bird feathers stuck into it. Still talking quietly, he selected one, pulled the hatchet from his belt and with one swift blow, chopped the long end from the feather. I was puzzled. Was he about to perform a rite to call game to him? No. He used it to clean his ears, all the while talking with his father.

Sin, in the meantime, pulled out a dried leaf that had been cut into a square. He flattened it with his thumb against the wooden boards of the shed. He saw me watching him and, breaking off his conversation abruptly, held it up for me to see and said, "*bai thong gloy*," a leaf I'd seen growing near his garden. From a small tin can he pulled out a few chopped tobacco leaves, also grown in his garden. From a piece of folded paper, he pinched a small amount of lighter-colored tobacco, "It's called *chaiyo* (victory) Makes the jungle tobacco burn better."

Mixing the tobaccos, he spread them along the wrapper and then began rolling, tightening as he went. As the finishing touch, he extracted from his pocket a small pair of rusty scissors and neatly snipped off both ends of the tube. He then made a diagonal cut along one edge of the wrapper and from yet another paper, pulled out a bamboo sliver stuck with a bit of gum which appeared to be wetted with sticky rice. Applying it to the underside of the wrapper, he completed a cheroot. He offered it to me, reaching into the fire for a glowing brand to light it. The *chaiyo* had done little to refine the taste of what was a very rough tobacco. Down the valley, the Thai farmers grew a fine tobacco that was prized in the U.S. and elsewhere for its mildness. Up here, a straw fire would have produced a smoother smoke. The son borrowed his father's scissors to complete the same operation, taking a glowing stick from the fire, touching it to the end of the green wrapper and inhaling contentedly. These men obviously had asbestos lungs.

We had no sooner begun smoking than the son stood up, reshouldered the gun and strode off towards the river as unceremoniously as he'd arrived. Even Sin seemed surprised, looking down the trail after him as the underbrush swallowed him up.

"He wanted to get back to Muang Ngai," he said, almost apologetically. Now, I felt almost duty-bound to stay around for a while longer. But he surprised me by saying "Well, I guess you want to get on your way as well."

I had planned to pay each of my hosts for the food they had provided. Sin's eyes lit up when I handed him a 50-baht ($2) bill. He seemed exceptionally pleased, hoisting my heavy pack to his thin shoulders and almost running down the slope to the river with it. As I lashed the pack to the deck, Sin said: "We met by accident and accidents are usually painful. This was a good accident," he chuckled. I waved goodbye and pushed off.

Steve Van Beek is a long-time resident of Bangkok who has written several books and films about Thailand, including The Arts of Thailand, APA's Cityguide Bangkok, *and the current edition of* Insight Guide: Thailand. *He writes regularly for the* International Herald Tribune.

✳

The hunters also saw no contradiction between their Buddhist beliefs and the taking of animals' lives. There was a clear understanding by all the hunters that what they did was not in strict accordance with the Buddha's teachings, but being merely men, not monks, they had to live as best they could. The villagers also drew a distinction between killing in general and the killing of forest animals which were viewed as having been created for man's use. Buddhism allowed for these kinds of discrepancies, the men said, by neither condoning nor condemning an individual's actions. Still, the hunters observed special rules in the forest to indicate their respect for the Buddha.

—Alan Rabinowitz, *Chasing the Dragon's Tail:*
The Struggle to Save Thailand's Wild Cats

BARBARA SAVAGE

* * *

Could This Really
Be the End?

The risks of travel are manifold,
but so are the laughs.

WE HAD RETURNED TO THE TWENTIETH CENTURY. AFTER EGYPT,
India, and Nepal, the shocking sight of freeway overpasses,
Mercedes and BMWs, modern buildings, computerized gas stations, swank hotels and restaurants, stores jammed with consumer
items, and people dressed in the latest western fashions hit us
like a sledgehammer. We spent our first few days in Bangkok
feeling bewildered and disoriented. There were no warm, familiar manure piles sitting on the sidewalks, and the streets were free
of cows, water buffalo, rickshaws, and men and boys urinating.
Even Sally's house, located in one of the classier districts of
Bangkok, was modern and roomy. The air-conditioned master
bedroom contained a queen-sized bed with pillows, a mattress,
and box springs. And off it was a bathroom with a bathtub and
a sit toilet.

Doing anything more than sit or take short walks those first
days in Bangkok proved to be a real chore. The humidity, which
was 90 percent or more each day, seemed unbearable. Breathing
felt uncomfortable, because the stagnant air was saturated. The
temperature stayed in the nineties throughout the day, and
swarms of unmerciful mosquitoes gathered in any unscreened

rooms. I had no idea how we'd survive bicycling in the heat and humidity of Southeast Asia, since they sapped our energy even while we were sitting still. I figured we'd probably sweat to death pedaling south.

That afternoon, on our way back to Sally's, the curse of the Himalaya grabbed me, and I made a mad dash for the nearest restroom. After I'd finished, I gave the toilet bowl a quick glance before I flushed it. By then I'd learned to always check my bowel movements for blood or mucus, the telltale signs of dysentery.

Oh My God! I thought, as I stared into the toilet bowl, I *am* going to die, and it won't be from sweating to death or being riddled by bullets. What I saw in the toilet made my whole body feel weak. I flushed it and hurried outside.

At first I didn't say anything to Larry, because I couldn't bring myself to accept what I'd just seen. But the mental picture of it kept flashing in my head. If my days were limited, and that seemed to be the obvious though dreaded conclusion, I should tell him right away. I knew he probably wouldn't believe me right off; but later, when it happened again, he'd see for himself, and then we would rush to the hospital. But from what I'd just seen in the toilet, it was already too late.

"Barb, how come you're so quiet?" Larry asked as we continued walking back to Sally's. "You looked kind of pale when you came out of the restroom. Everything O.K.?"

"Well no…No, not really," I stammered.

"What's the problem?"

"Well, see…I went to the bathroom and…"

"Yes?"

"And I think I'm going to die!" I shouted.

"So what's new? You always think you're going to die," Larry answered calmly.

"Yeah, well this time it's the real thing!"

"Why *this* time?"

"Because I looked after I went to the toilet and there were these giant worms in it! Giant, huge, clear worms! Do you understand what that means?"

"Yeah, you're seein' things."

"To hell with that. I am *not* seeing things! They were there. Big, giant worms. I saw them as clear as day. And that means my intestines are full of them, and as big as they are, that means I'm doomed with a capital D!"

Larry didn't respond right away. He kept walking, staring at me with an I-can't-believe-you're-really-that-dumb expression on his face.

"Barb, it's impossible for a bunch of giant worms to live inside a person's intestines," he said matter-of-factly.

"But I saw them," I shot back.

Neither of us said much after that, and the subject didn't come up again until we were back at Sally's. We fixed a spaghetti dinner that evening, and just as the first bites hit bottom, the urge struck me again. I ran for the bathroom and prayed that Larry was right—that I hadn't actually seen the worms this afternoon, that this time everything would look normal.

I looked into the bowl after I'd finished, and again my body fell limp. There they were, just like before—the worms. Larry came into the bathroom and I stood back and waited for him to take a look. He seemed unconcerned when he walked in, and that calmed me. Larry will have a logical explanation for this, I said to myself, and everything's going to be all right.

"O.K., let's have a look at those so-called giant worms," he muttered. There was a hint of exasperation in his voice.

I pointed into the bowl, and for a long, uncomfortable moment, Larry said nothing.

"Can't be," he finally whispered.

My hopes took a nose dive.

"This just can't be! Those worms are huge! An inch long and a quarter-inch thick, each one. Man, you should be dead by now! Nobody can live with things like that in their stomach. I can't believe what I'm seeing. But look, there they are and lots of 'em. Get your passport quick! We're going to the hospital *right now!*"

The idea of entering a hospital in a strange country terrified me as much as the worms did. I thought about how the Australian fellow staying in the hotel room next to ours in Kathmandu had gone into the city hospital to be checked for dysentery and had come away with severely damaged intestines. The doctors had given him the wrong medicine. After that episode, I swore I'd never set foot in a foreign hospital.

"Barb?"

"Yeah?" I answered hesitantly.

"Barb, come here for a minute."

I walked back into the bathroom. Larry had scooped a worm and stool sample into a jar to take with us to the hospital. He stood holding the jar up to the light, studying the worms.

"Tell me what you had for breakfast this morning," he said.

"Tea, toast, and that weird grapefruit Ubon gave me."

"What was weird about it?"

"Well, it's hard to describe. Each section was made up of a bunch of these long, clear strands and—"

"And I bet they looked a lot like these worms," Larry sighed, and both of us burst out laughing.

"You're saved kiddo!" Larry chuckled in relief. "Hey, imagine if we'd gone to the hospital with this stuff. They'd be laughing for months about the weirdo Yank with the grapefruit worms in her turds!"

After biking around the world and writing Miles from Nowhere: A Round-the-World Bicycle Adventure, *from which this piece was excerpted, Barbara Savage died in a cycling accident in California. Her husband, Larry, and The Mountaineers, her publisher, established the "Barbara Savage/Miles from* Nowhere *Memorial Award" for the best unpublished adventure travel manuscript.*

★

If you have the urge to pat a child's head, don't—it is considered the abode of the soul.

—JO'R and LH

ALAN RABINOWITZ

✷ ✷ ✷

A German Monk

The unlikely appearance of an English-speaking
German monk at a forest camp opens
the door to understanding.

OVER DINNER I WAS TOLD THAT AN ENGLISH-SPEAKING GERMAN monk and a novice Thai monk had arrived that day at camp. At least a dozen monks had come and gone since I first encountered them that day with Noparat [the camp manager], but I had done no more than jog or walk by their huts and observe them from a distance. By now I had finished reading two books on Thai Buddhism and I thought I had found answers to some of the technical questions that had puzzled me. I understood now how the forest monks who came through the sanctuary differed from the monks I had seen in the towns and cities. The town or village monks, characterized by a practice known as *bariyat,* or "thorough learning," usually have their temples in more urban areas. Their daily routines include chanting, lessons in Pali, ceremonies, festivals, and counseling members of the local community. Forest monks, characterized by *batibat,* or "practice," stay in temples on the outskirts of towns or in the forest. These monks lead more highly disciplined lives, with fewer interruptions. They place a larger emphasis on individual meditation. In the evenings, these monks often force themselves to meditate until sleep overtakes them.

Although my readings clarified some things, they didn't explain the contradictions I sensed. Attempts to discuss Buddhism with Noparat usually left me unsatisfied. His English wasn't proficient enough to allow him to explain some of the finer points, and he often felt, like many Thais, that my questions stemmed from my Western mind's inability to comprehend Buddhism within the Asian framework from which it was born. I, in turn, was surprised by the unquestioning acceptance by many Thais of the basic rules and assumptions of Buddhism. Buddha himself had felt that his teachings should be questioned, that they were not dogma, but basic truths, to be tested and discovered for oneself. There were many things I wanted to ask this new *farang* forest monk who had somehow merged his Western upbringing with traditional Buddhist philosophy.

I was surprised when I encountered a Thai novice dressed in white, not the usual orange robes. I later learned that he was not a novice at all, but a *khon teu sin,* or a man who follows the eight precepts. He was trying out monkhood, so to speak, rigidly adhering to the more basic rules but not yet on the path to becoming ordained. Without questioning why I was there, he directed me to the hut of the German monk, which sat furthest back in the forest. No one was around, so I sat in the open doorway and waited.

The belongings of the German monk were laid out neatly in a space that was no more than seven feet square. A little thatch sleeping mat was rolled up against one wall below a small opening that looked out into the forest. His *baht,* or bowl in which he accepts and carries food, was sitting in a dark corner, its orange lid blending in with the shadows. A toothbrush and tube of toothpaste lay next to a little portable alarm clock to the right of the doorway, placed in a

> *The monk should not solicit robes from a layman except under certain stipulated conditions; he should not accept robes in excess of his needs; without being invited to do so, he should not instruct the giver how the robe should be made or what quality of robe should be purchased on his behalf.*
>
> —S. J. Tambiah, *Buddhism and the Spirit Cults in North-East Thailand*

groove between two bamboo slats making up part of the floor. That was it. His only other belongings, as I soon learned, were his robes, a small sewing kit to repair robes, a razor, a strainer to exclude small creatures from his drinking water, and a bar of soap that was currently with him at the river.

I was daydreaming when I first heard his gentle chanting coming along the path that led to the hut. Then a tall, thin, pale-looking character came into view. When he saw me, his chanting stopped and his already large smile spread out into a huge tooth-filled grin.

"Ahhh, so good to see you," he said in clear Germanic English, as if we had long been friends.

I couldn't help but smile back, feeling the kind of immediate bond that I so rarely experience with people. His English was music to my ears.

After that first visit, it became part of my daily routine to join him for coffee in the late afternoon. If I happened to come by earlier, he was usually away from the hut, meditating or exploring new areas of the forest. He encouraged me to visit whenever I could, and if he wasn't there, to beat on the *graw* that was hanging by his hut. The *graw,* one of the oldest Thai instruments, is made from a piece of hollow bamboo with a small vertical slit cut between the joints at each end. When a wooden beater is tapped against the bamboo, its deep, hollow sound carries easily through the forest.

This monk had been given the Thai name Supanyo, meaning "good thinking." At first, we spent most of our time together discussing Buddhism, and he seemed to get great pleasure when I challenged him, voicing doubts or criticisms. I told him of my early encounters with the monks and how I had felt that some of them were just going through the motions, making them seem like little more than beggars. They were supposed to be humble, righteous men, I said. They were supposed to follow Buddha's teachings, but many of their actions seemed hypocritical to me. And what about the rules that Thai monks allegedly lived by? I asked him. A set of 10 basic precepts was understandable, but why the additional 217 rules that told the monks how to hang their robes after washing, specified when a crack was big enough to justify replacing your food bowl, or said you couldn't open your mouth until the rice reached your lips?

Even when I did little else but berate Thai Buddhism, Supanyo just listened and gently explained.

"Monks are not beggars. You must understand this first," he said. He told me that when monks go on morning food rounds, they walk silently, often concentrating on meditation. Anything that is given is accepted. A monk doesn't thank those who give him food or show either pleasure or disappointment at what is given, because the food itself is of no concern other than for nourishment. It is the act of giving and allowing to give that is important.

"But if monks are just regular people, then why do Thais kneel and bow their heads to them?" I asked. "What is this 'merit' that is gained by giving to the monks? Does merit wipe out bad deeds?" To me it sounded suspiciously like the sins and absolution of Christianity.

"A monk is thought to be elevated, set apart from the normal world. The title 'Pra' that a monk is given means holy and exalted. When people bow before a monk, it is simply a show of respect. It doesn't have to be done. You thank the monk for allowing you to gain merit, which, though often misunderstood, means teaching you to be giving and compassionate. You are thanking the monk for helping to carry on the teachings of the Buddha. Such teachings can make the world better, even if some people choose not to be involved in them. And bad deeds are not wiped out so easily. They are a burden for you alone to carry."

"What about all those rules?" I pressed on. "Why should it matter if a monk's cheeks bulge while he eats or where he goes to the bathroom?" Supanyo grinned broadly. "It doesn't matter. The rules can be cast aside once you rise above them. But remember again, my friend, monks are simply men trying to do better with their lives. Most men need rules, they need something which defines their world and helps set patterns of behavior and good habits. Though you may think monks are above worrying about such mundane behavior, this kind of understanding can come only after much striving and meditation.

"Buddhism is faith combined with wisdom. At first you accept certain practice on faith alone, and then when you come to understand the truth inside yourself, you attain wisdom. Many people get stuck on the rules and practices alone and do not attain wisdom. Not many monks are truly 'noble' and you cannot take 'refuge' from all monks. You should seek the real refuge within yourself."

He made himself another cup of coffee with the mandatory four heaping teaspoons of "medicinal" sugar.

"Be careful of trying to think through everything or gaining understanding just from books," Supanyo said, offering me the pot of hot water so that I could make my own coffee. (A monk doesn't serve a layperson.) "Of course, it is good to question as you do. Buddha wanted people to question. But don't expect understanding to come so easily."

"Will it come to me in this lifetime?" I laughed.

"Ahhh, you wish much," he said, smiling. "I am only a little older than you. I have worn the robes for eight years now, and have been seeking much longer than that. I am far from wisdom yet."

"I'm not greedy," I said. "I only want a little wisdom."

"Me too, my friend, me too. Maybe you have more than you think."

Alan Rabinowitz is a research zoologist who contributed five other stories to this book.

✳

From the outset of his ministry the Buddha emphasized a Middle Way of conduct lying between self-indulgence on one hand and extremes of asceticism on the other. His doctrine was based on the incontrovertible, undeniable truth about humanity's suffering, a truth that he embodied in a formula of four parts to which he gave the adjective "noble." These Four Noble Truths, constituting what might be termed the Buddha's diagnosis of humanity's sickness, took a simple form: 1) No one can deny that existence involves a great deal of suffering for all human creatures.

2) This suffering and general dissatisfaction come to human beings because they are possessive, greedy, and, above all, self-centered. 3) Egocentrism, possessiveness, and greed can, however, be understood, overcome, and rooted out. 4) This rooting out can be brought about by following a rational Eightfold Path of behavior in thought, word, and deed that will create a salutary change in viewpoint.

This Eightfold Path is the Buddha's basic formula for deliverance from the kind of crippling invalidism that comes with having a "body-identified mind," as Gerald Heard has described mankind's general state. The eight requirements that will eliminate suffering by correcting false values and giving true knowledge of life's meaning have been summed up as follows: "(I) First, you must see clearly what is wrong. (II) Next decide to be cured. (III) You must act and (IV) speak so as to aim at being cured. (V) Your livelihood must not conflict with your therapy. (VI) That therapy must go forward at the 'staying speed,' the critical velocity that can be sustained. (VII) You must think about it incessantly, and (VIII) learn how to contemplate *with the deep mind*."

—Nancy Wilson Ross, *Three Ways of Asian Wisdom*

GAYLE DETWEILER

✦ ✦ ✦

Thai and Dry

*If you want to develop a deep
appreciation of water, try
running in Thailand.*

I RUN ON DIRT ROADS BAKED A DEEP ORANGE BY THE SUN. THEY
snake around rice paddies and through villages of houses on
stilts whose wood has been smoothed by the rigors of the monsoon rains.

As I run, children suspend their play and yell, "*Allo farang!*"
Elders, just returning from the fields, stop and stare, balancing
loads of rice stalk on a bamboo pole. Some smile broadly, showing
betel-stained teeth, and yell, "*Lawn mai*" (Hot, isn't it?). Others
shake their heads and mutter something that I can't hear—but I
imagine it's a prediction similar to the one my father made when I
started running fourteen years ago: "You're going to kill yourself
with all that running!"

Currently still alive, I'm living in Thailand, training for the
Bangkok Marathon. If there are those (and there are) who think
that running is silly, then I suppose they would proclaim racing in
Bangkok inane, what with all the heat and exhaust fumes. But I'm
going to do it anyway. Mostly because I hear they're giving out
free water every two kilometers.

My exaggerated appreciation of water began seven months ago
when I and twelve other volunteers arrived in Bangkok to teach

English. That was our long-range goal. The more immediate goal was to survive the heat of the first night with just a cot, a fan, and one bottle of water.

One month later and settled in my little village, I decided to take a short run around the block, a mere 2.1 miles. Hello heat! It sat on my shoulders, inflamed my face, and clung to my chest. Once home, my body demanded water—every cell cried in unison: Water! Water! Water! I grabbed a water bottle and sucked it down.

There are three seasons in Thailand—hot, hotter, and hottest. (They brag of a so-called winter—three months of sunshine with temperatures in the 80s and a cool breeze.) Two of these seasons, hot and hottest, from November to May, are dry—no rain for six or seven months. Then, mercifully, the god of Rain, "Phra Purin," indulges. The earth gratefully takes in the rainwater, drinking…like a marathon runner.

The Bangkok Marathon is held one month into "winter." Race officials optimistically predict that the mean temperature on race day will be 75 degrees with 70 to 80 percent humidity. I don't know how many gallons of water the 5,000-odd entrants will soak up on race day, but I know I'll be drinking my limit. I'm sure it'll be the best damn water I've ever tasted.

Why do I run? So I can drink more water. Of course, I use this sort of complicated justification only for the benefit of non-runners. *Real* runners know why they run. The reason originates in the soul and needs no explanation. In fact, it defies any.

So, I don't mind when the villagers I pass laugh, clap, point, or scold me. If my running entertains the Thais (who are generous to a fault) then that's a bonus.

Besides, if one girl, today sitting astride her water buffalo, feels the urge to run on those same dirt paths someday because she remembers that crazy *farang* doing it, then I'll be thrice blessed by the sport I love so well.

Meanwhile, there's water.

Gayle Detweiler runs and drinks water in Baltimore, Maryland.

★

The average daily temperatures in Bangkok in December range from 68°F (20°C) to 87°F (31°C), with the highest recorded temperature 100°F (38°C). The range of temperatures in April, the peak of the hot season, averages from 77°F (25°C) to 95°F (35°C), with the highest recorded temperature 106°F (41°C).

—JO'R and LH

JOHN SPIES

* * *

Under the Golden Triangle

*Better known for poppy fields and drug
lords, the Golden Triangle harbors
another kind of underworld.*

A Lahu hill tribesman lights some resinous pine-wood and places it under the edge of an enormous stack of felled trees and bamboo, parched dry by a hot summer sun.

The flames spread rapidly and the bamboo begins exploding, the blasts booming like cannon fire off massive orange and white limestone cliffs circling the field clearing. Thick smoke rises in huge whirls, turning the late April sun a deep ruby red.

Half a kilometer beneath this searing heat, a group of four Australian spelunkers—cave explorers—huddles together around flickering carbide lights: cold, wet, and exhausted.

We are deep under the Golden Triangle in Thailand's rugged and remote Mae Hong Son province, twelve hours' tough subterranean walking and swimming from the nearest natural light, and, in a place no humans have ever been before. We are lost.

Dorothy has suffered a short fall and her ribs are aching—bruised, possibly broken. I have smashed my shin into a jagged underwater rock and movement is painfully slow. Dorothy's husband John, and Atilla, a hardy Tasmanian, are both unhurt but have little energy left.

The roof of the monstrous river tunnel we have been exploring has collapsed in gigantic house-sized blocks of limestone.

Some of the collapse looks menacingly fresh, as recent as the last wet season.

A quick tally of our survey readings measured against a topographical map tells us that we are within a kilometer of where the river, the Nam Lang, sinks in an impenetrable hole on the eastern side of the mountain.

We clamber up into the loose jumble of broken roof, squeezing through small gaps between boulders, hoping to discover an unknown exit, an easier passage into daylight, forest greenery, and some cold beers in a local village.

Across the collapse, a more treacherous rock pile stretches ahead of us, covering the entire tunnel. A few hundred meters more and the passage becomes totally jammed with rock.

Disappointed, we start heading back to find our only exit blocked by the awesome maze of a collapsed cave roof, bigger than a football field. None of it looks familiar and we cannot remember which of the many holes between rocks we had come through.

To save time we break up our search. Dorothy and I begin working along the southern wall while Atilla squeezes down precipitous slots towards the river level. The constant roar of the Nam Lang, deep below us, echoes ominously in the huge chamber. We have been underground more than 30 hours and have limited batteries and carbide, and virtually no food. Nobody talks about the unthinkable.

It is close to an hour before John finds a recognizable rock in the pile and the way back to the main river passage. It takes us another four hours of hard caving over slippery rocks and through deep water to reach our supplies and campsite from the previous night, a "dry," higher cavern, away from the river, more than five kilometers inside the cave.

Despite our fatigue we cook dinner on a kerosene stove and tally up our survey measurements. We had extended Tham Nam Lang ("Tham" is the Thai word for cave) to 8.3 kilometers, making it the longest known cave on mainland Southeast Asia, and, with an enormous main passage rarely less than 10 meters wide and 20 meters high, one of the biggest river tunnels anywhere in the world. In places the cave roof is well over 100 meters above the river level—black holes beyond the reach of powerful flash-light beams.

The campsite is quiet, the stillness broken only by the distant rumble of the Nam Lang and perpetual cave drips.

After twelve hours of fighting our way along what seemed like Mother Nature's alimentary canal, sleep comes deeply and securely, as if we are now safely inside the womb of the earth.

Next "morning" we wake early, our clothing damp from drip-ping stalactites and heavy cave mist. Our plan is to explore a higher cavern, an ancient tunnel of the Nam Lang, on our way out. John and Dorothy had discovered this cave on an expedition a year earlier and claimed that it was so stunningly beautiful that it was their main reason for returning to Thailand.

With heavy backpacks we climb down to the river level where we had left an inflatable boat two days earlier. For the next kilo-meter we are able to enjoy a pleasant drift down the Nam Lang until rapids and rocks block our way.

The climb up to the higher-level cavern looks dangerous. From the river the rubble slope looms over us, almost vertical. I cannot imagine how John had been enticed to risk climbing this rockfall for the first time, not even knowing whether there was a cave up there.

John and Atilla ascend one at a time to avoid the risk of loose rocks in the clay matrix starting a new slide. After much procrasti-nation I follow, while Dorothy, her ribs still aching, waits by the river. As I climb, her carbide light diminishes to a hazy speck in the cave mist. I hear John and Atilla on top, then nothing but the incessant roar of the river. I feel very alone and vulnerable climb-ing in such a huge and forbidding place.

I finally reach the top ledge and hurry to join the others in an enormous cavern, several hundred meters long. The cave is mag-nificently decorated with columns and stalagmites towering to more than 30 meters high. The passage ends in a precipitous drop back down to the river level.

We sit in silent awe in this chamber, listening to the cave grow, the drips sounding eerily loud as they splatter on stalagmites. We are dwarfed by the massive formations and my mind boggles at the aeons that have passed since this limestone was formed under the ocean, lifted and twisted into mountains, then carved and sculptured by so many millennia of flowing water and drips.

At one side of the chamber we find a small stream with scores of small white cave fish, without eyes. It ends in a sump and Atilla, an experienced cave diver, peers underwater into a deep and distant blue.

Safely back in the main river passage, we move on slowly towards the light. We stop only once, at an immense set of of rimstone pools, to eat the last of our food. The glittering formation is 50 meters long and 15 meters high: terrace upon terrace of white crystalline rimpools, brimming with aqua-clear cave water. In the intense blackness I find it almost impossible to photograph. Firing off over a dozen flashes, I can illuminate only a small part of the sparkling terraces.

The first faint glow of daylight in the tunnel appears as a mystical gray haze, intensifying with each painful step. We round a bend and, after 54 hours of immersion in the most complete blackness known to man, our eyes feast on the breathtakingly beautiful sight of rich beams of late afternoon sunlight streaming into the cave's exit.

The blue sky and the lush greenery of the forest have never looked so intense. The smell of the forest air and the rotting leaves is refreshingly strong.

We almost limp the last kilometer back to our campsite where the rest of our expedition greets us with blasts from bamboo tubes filled with carbide and water, and a bottle of Thai rum.

It felt great to be out.

Virtually unknown except by a handful of cavers and a few local hunters, the great cave systems under the rugged limestone hills in Thailand's far northwest corner are truly world class.

In the region there are some ten caves more than a kilometer long. Two of these, Tham Nam Lang and Tham Mae La Na, have over eight kilometers of mainstream passage with more upper-level caverns yet to be discovered.

Fortunately one doesn't have to be a spelunker (spelcologist, if you are British) to enjoy the enchanting subterranean world under the Golden Triangle. Even the totally inexperienced, equipped with a good flashlight or rented lantern, and a sense of adventure, can safely explore several large caves in the area. ·

The adventure starts when you board the morning bus in Chiang Mai, headed northwest for the small Shan town of Pai. The road through to Mae Hong Son was originally built by the Japanese Army during the Second World War—one of several invasion routes into Burma. The road is currently being improved but sections of the original track still exists—as rough as ever.

Daily several buses ply the 110 kilometer mountain stretch between Pai and Mae Hong Son, and passengers are treated to some of the finest scenery in Southeast Asia. Sheer limestone pinnacles and knobs—craggy peaks exquisitely sculptured by nature—jut from dense sub-tropical forest. In the distance, range after range of rugged mountains, foothills of the mighty Himalayas, stretch northward into Burma's Shan State.

Near the market village of Sobpong, a little less than halfway from Pai to Mae Hong Son, are several easily accessible tribal villages where the way of life has changed little for centuries.

The best place to start caving is at Tham Lod—"Through Cave"—near Ban Tham, a Shan village, seven kilometers, walk or rented pick-up ride north of Sobpong.

Tham Lod is a huge river tunnel carved through a limestone hill by the Nam Lang. The cave is about 20 kilometers upstream from Tham Nam Lang, and its main passage, though much shorter and easier to negotiate, is similar in scale.

It is possible to walk from the enormous entrance chamber of Tham Lod through to the even larger exit, fording the Nam Lang six times. Lanterns can be rented at the nearby forestry camp but it is advisable to take along a flashlight also as a back-up.

There are three upper-level caverns in the cave, the largest one well decorated with an immense column over 20 meters high dominating the chamber. The other side passages can be reached only by ladders.

Deep inside a cavern, high up in the wall of the gaping exit chamber, are the remains of several ancient wooden coffins. Carved from teak logs, the coffins are about four or five meters long and resemble dugout canoes. The locals believe they were built by "*pi man*," unfriendly spirits that lurk in the caves.

Archaeological excavations in a few of the dozens of *"Tham pi man"* in the area tell a different story. During the mid-1960s, Chester Gorman, an American archaeologist, excavated a small coffin cave near the Burmese border and found evidence of human habitation stretching back 14,000 years.

Digging through successive layers of earth to the bedrock floor of the cave, Gorman discovered carbonized plant and animal remains, pottery shards and stone tools. Subsequent radio-carbon dating enabled Gorman to reconstruct the primitive cave dwellers' steady advance from basic hunting and gathering to the beginnings of agriculture, ceramics, and advanced stone tool production.

What makes Spirit Cave such an important archaeological site is the antiquity of the plant and seed remains, which Gorman believed were almost certainly cultivated. If they were, what is now north Thailand may well have been home to the earliest agriculturalists in Asia, more than 10,000 years ago.

The coffins are much more recent, the oldest being around 2,000 years ago. Most likely they were made by Lawa tribesman who lived extensively over the northern hills well before the Thais arrived from the north. The Lawa were animists and in their coffins they left clothing, food, pottery, and jewelry for the deceased's use in the spirit world. Some of the coffins are huge, up to ten meters long, perched high up inside caves, twenty meters up a cliff-face. One assumes such burials were reserved for the old and important.

Every evening at dusk hundreds of thousands of Himalayan swiftlets swirl into the exit chamber of Tham Lod, while thousands of bats leave for the night—changing shifts, sharing space. Just before nightfall the twilight sky is thick with spiralling birds while large bat-eating hawks soar high above. The sounds of the jungle combine with the incessant whistles of the birds. A pterodactyl or some other weird prehistoric creature, winging out of

the cave gloom, would hardly seem out of place in this eerily
primeval setting.

Mae Hong Son's most well known cave is Tham Pia (Fish
Cave), 17 kilometers before town on the Pai Road. The surrounds
have been developed into an attractive picnic area, popular with
the locals. The cave itself is an impenetrable stream rising—a pool
teeming with hundreds of large carp, believed to be sacred.

Across the road from Tham Pia and 100 meters back toward
town is a dry cave, well over a kilometer long. The entrance is
30 meters off the road, above a small stream rising.

Virtually inaccessible but certainly worth a mention is the cave
in the "Spirit Well," the biggest natural hole in Thailand. Hidden
among rugged peaks about 50
kilometers before Mae Hong
Son and an hour and a half walk
from the road, few people know
of its existence.

Named after its shape and unnatural dimensions, the Spirit Well
is an awesome pit, 90 to 140 meters deep and more than 100 meters across, with sheer rock sides.

The cave opening is 100 meters high, set in the highest cliff
face of the Well. In May, 1985,
two Australian cavers used ropes
and climbing equipment to be
the first people to descend into
the Spirit Well. They explored

> *A* "bad death," greatly
> *feared by the Lahu,*
> is one resulting from a tragedy,
> generally involving bloodshed.
> Death caused by stabbing,
> shooting, wild animals, childbirth,
> drowning, and lightning are all
> considered bad death. They believe
> that if the victim was calling out at
> the time of dying the "bad death"
> spirit will repeatedly call out in the
> same manner at that site. Conse-
> quently before the body can be
> buried a religious specialist must be
> called to drive away the evil spirits.
>
> —Paul and Elaine Lewis,
> *Peoples of the Golden Triangle*

the forest and cave but could find no way leading into the mountain. Later that night, back at camp, one of them, the fittest caver
on the trip, suffered a stroke, partially paralyzing half of his body.

Sometimes it is more than just fear of malicious spirits that
keeps the local hill tribes out of the caves. When a Lahu hunter
first showed me the small hole leading into the extensive Tham
Mae La Na, he claimed that no one had dared enter the cave as

several years earlier he and his friends had shot and wounded a large "buffalo bear" and it had escaped into the hole.

We went in anyway and were about 200 meters inside when we noticed a deep impression in the sand that looked just like a bear's paw print, claws and all! Then suddenly, up around the next bend we heard a loud splashing noise. We froze—it sounded like a large animal walking along the stream. Gingerly we crept forward and shone a light around the corner. Thankfully the large "bear" turned out to be large fish swimming in shallow rapids against the current.

And as if the caves aren't already laden with enough archaeological and natural treasures, there has long been a rumor around Mae Hong Son that the retreating Japanese armies left a huge amount of gold—looted from Burma during the war—inside a cave. The cave entrance was reportedly sealed with dynamite and the gold is yet to be found.

Rumor has it that the cave is close to the road, on a hill, about halfway from Pai to Mae Hong Son.

John Spies is a spelunker who spends so much time in caves we couldn't find him—until his mother wrote from Lilli Pilli, New South Wales, Australia, to tell us that her son has two trekking and caving lodges in northwest Thailand.

*

The blessings which the Lahu so avidly seek are expressed in couplets, called *taw pa taw ma* (male word, female word), and may be stated either positively or negatively.

Positive

Give us easy minds and hearts.
Give us sufficient food and drink.
Give us health and strength.
Fulfill in us the hopes and longings of our hearts.
Purify and cleanse us so we will have good health.
Unite us in the same purpose and thoughts.
Separate us from evil and deliver us from misfortune.
Protect and care for us.
Give us enough from our toil and labour to live on.

Negative

Don't make us worried or sad.

Don't make us suffer hunger and starvation.

Don't let us fall sick and die.

Don't let evil spirits and people deter us.

Don't let us get the 33 kinds of sickness.

Don't let there be fighting and quarreling.

Don't cause us suffering or tragedy.

Don't let farming tools, wood, and bamboo wound us.

Don't cause us to have to stretch out our hands as beggars and supplicants.

—Paul and Elaine Lewis, *Peoples of the Golden Triangle*

CHARLES NICHOLL

* * *

Mekong Days

In the Mekong River, near the Laotian border,
a young woman's spirit flees. The only way
to get it back is to call on a spirit-man.

HARRY WAS DUE THAT NIGHT BUT HE DIDN'T SHOW. WE SAT OUT
on the verandah, burning *joss* to keep the mosquitoes at bay. I got
hungry and suggested we go down to Porn's noodle shop on
Main Street. This had become our regular eating place. Katai had
no desire to "experiment" in the *farang* way. We had happened into
Porn's on the first evening: the
atmosphere was friendly, the
bean-curd soup delicious, and
from then on we took just about
every meal there.

Katai said she'd wait, in case
Harry came. "We can leave a
note," I said.

"I'll wait anyway."

She sat on the floor of the ve-
randah with her chin on her knees. She had put on that same t-
shirt again, freshly laundered, the one that reads: "Hurts So Good."
Harry had given it to her.

When I got back from Porn's, the light was on in her room. I
tiptoed past, but the verandah creaked. Her door opened.

Harry is a French trader; Katai is his young Thai girlfriend, who works as a chambermaid in a Bangkok hotel. At this point in his narrative, the author and Katai are in Chiang Saen.

—JO'R and LH

"Oh, hello Charlie." She tried not to sound disappointed, but I knew she was, and I knew that was why I had tiptoed.

"Harry's not here, then."

She shook her head.

"He'll be here tomorrow. You'll see."

She leant in the doorway. The cicadas trilled, the dark smell of the river came up at us: the unseen so close around us all the time. She had a dreamy look. I thought she might cry, and I might have to take her in my arms.

Instead she grinned, put on her cynical Bangkok drawl, "Yeah. Mad dog come tomorrow. Mad dog say he sorry. I should kick him away, but…"

I nearly said, "Maybe you should," but I stopped myself. The room behind her, half-seen through the doorway, exuded an indefinable softness, and her voice was soft again as she said, "Goodnight, Charlie."

"Goodnight, Katai."

Her door closed and I went to my room, where old tobacco smoke hung in the air, and my clothes lay where I had left them.

Waking in the little wooden room, chinks of brilliant light in the shutters, strange birdcalls, a rattle of pots and pans in the cooking area, another hot day on the way. A gecko cackled above the door as I walked out onto the verandah.

Katai was down in the yard talking to Suree. She had got the morning organized. We were borrowing a couple of bicycles and going for a picnic.

At the market we bought fruit and beer and Coca-Cola, and a bagful of cooked rice and vegetables, and some quids of *miang* (fermented tea and spices wrapped in a leaf: you hold it inside your cheek, refreshing and faintly stimulant). We set off south, into the sun, past the tobacco factory, across small bridges, the river on our left and the promise of the hills in front of us. Katai wore a wide-brimmed straw hat she had borrowed from Suree. It was a bit too big, and blew off her head as she cycled. She chattered and joked, talking back over her shoulder. I could only hear half of it. She had lost the melancholy of the previous evening. Harry wouldn't come till tonight, she said, so we might as well enjoy the day.

Watching her pedal down the hot dirt road, hat on her back, baggy black trousers and black singlet, she seemed to me the quintessence of Southeast Asia. I thought of a phrase of Harry's: *Indochine, mon amour.*

The heat shimmered in the trees, mostly low and scrubby, occasional giant shade-givers. Passing vehicles set up a cloud of dust which left us choking by the roadside. After a while we stopped to rest and wash the dust out of our throats. Katai grimaced at the taste of the sterilizing tablets I had put in the water. On we went, past Chiang Saen Noi, with its old temple on the hill. The road curved east. We crossed the Kok River, which here joins the Mekong, and at a village called Ban Sae we left the road and followed a bumpy riverside track, skirting an alluvial plain filled with rice stubble.

By early afternoon we were ready for our picnic. We found a track leading down to the river's edge, past scorched plots of tobacco and maize. There was a palm-thatch shed, too small to live in, perhaps a crop-store or a fisherman's shelter. It was shaded by a stand of banana trees, the unripe green fruit clustered, the mauve tendril hanging down like a tasseled bell-pull in a Victorian drawing-room. Here we left our bikes. I took a swim. The river was very low: I was still in my depth several metres out. A long pale sandbar basked in the middle of the river. The water was surprisingly cold. Despite the appearance of slowness, the current was powerful as soon as you left the shallows.

> *The Mekong River flows 2,600 miles from its remote source in Tibet into China, Burma, Laos, Thailand, Cambodia, and Vietnam, emptying into the Gulf of Thailand.*
>
> —JO'R and LH

We ate and drank. The Singha beer was sweet and warm. I lay back in the grass, drowsy and content, content in a way I hadn't felt for years. Bangkok seemed like another world. Even Harry seemed distant and vague, someone I had known long ago. I wondered if he was really going to turn up at all: part of me wanted him to come, and part of me didn't, and I was too sleepy to work out which part was right.

Then Katai said, "I want to go across."

I said sleepily, "Across where?"

"Across there." I looked up, squinting in the glare. She was sitting cross-legged beside me, looking across to the hazed, scruffy tree line of Laos on the far bank.

"You're crazy," I said. "No one goes to Laos. They lock you up in a re-education camp if they catch you, and then they throw away the key." This is the basic lore about communist Laos.

"There's no one there to see us." She was on her knees now, scanning the horizon. "Look, there's nothing there."

"So why—"

"Because I never been to another country before, that's why. Because I got no passport, no money, no way to travel in the world like the *farang*. I want you to take me to Laos, Charlie."

"And back," I muttered, still thinking of the warnings I had heard about Laos, but the way she looked at me right then, I would have taken her to the moon.

"Look," she said, "We can get to that sandbank there, and then we're almost there."

"It's deceptive," I said. "How well do you swim?"

She didn't answer. Instead she told me to turn my back. When she was ready—a sarong knotted above her breasts and tucked between her legs, the traditional bathing gear for a Thai woman—she put out her hand to me, and we walked together into the Mekong.

We got across to the sandbank without too much difficulty. We could wade until we were about fifty yards from it. Then we had to swim. The current was strong, but the sandbank stretched for a good half mile, and there seemed no danger of getting swept out past it. We let the river take us, swimming diagonally. Katai swam like a child, doggy-paddle.

Our feet touched ground again and we waded ashore. The sand was speckled with fool's gold. It was strangely elastic: our feet sank in, but didn't break the crust. We left no footprints behind us. We walked back along to the upstream apex of the sandbank, and contemplated the second leg of the crossing. It was not much wider than the stretch we had come across, but it looked faster and deeper. This was the business side of the river: the stretch we had crossed was a meander in comparison.

"I don't like the look of it." I said.

"What does the *farang* fear?"

"Salt, sugar, and getting drowned in the Mekong, that's what."

She looked disappointed. "Well, I'm sorry, Charlie, but I must go over alone then."

"You're crazy," I said again.

She stood resolutely on the shoreline. I saw birds rising and wheeling above the trees on the far bank. Then I heard a voice behind us, away down the far end of the sandbank. A man had come across on a bamboo raft. He was waving at us.

We walked on down. He was an old man with a wizened monkey face and close-cropped hair the colour of tarnished metal. He was from a village called Ban Suan Dok a few miles further up the riverside track. He had a plot of vegetables here: tomatoes, cucumbers, and a small root-plant that looks like a refined type of potato, and has a sweetish crispy taste. He must have carried earth over to mix with the sand.

Katai asked if he thought we could swim across to the Lao bank. He laughed and wagged his forefinger at her. "*Ra wang,*" he said. "Take care. The river is very strong."

"Will you take us across in your *sampan*?" I asked. "We will pay for the crossing."

He looked at me suspiciously. He said to Katai. "Why does the *farang* want to go over?"

"We just want to go to Laos," she said.

He shook his head, grinning. "But little girl, you are in Laos now."

We stared at him. I said, "You mean this is Laos, right here?" He nodded. He took up his bamboo punt-pole, and ran it along the shoreline of the sandbank.

"*Chai daen,*" he said. The border.

He ambled off to his plot, watered it with scoopfuls of river water. The opportunism of the peasant farmer: this stretch of land would be covered when the Mekong was in spate, but meanwhile he wasn't going to waste it. After a while he started pulling the raft back down into the water. He asked if we wanted a lift back.

I said, "It's O.K., we'll swim."

"*Ra wang,*" he said again, and punted off downriver towards the Thai bank.

"So how does it feel to be in another country?" I asked.

She shrugged. "Same same," she said.

We should have taken up the old farmer's offer. On the way back to the Thai bank we were careless. We set off from the sand-bank further downriver than where we had arrived. We soon found the channel was deeper and the current stronger than before. We tried to push back upstream, but the water was up to our chins, and every step was an effort.

Katai started to get frightened. "Charlie, I don't like this." Her voice was shrill.

I said, "It's O.K., if it gets too strong we can go back to the sandbank, try further down."

"Yes, let's go back, please."

But somehow we couldn't. The river seemed to have closed in around us. Whichever way we turned the water deepened. Just to stand still was getting an effort: the current wrapping around our legs, the silt squeezing between our toes, pulling us off towards the China Sea.

"We'll have to swim for it," I said, trying to sound calm. I wasn't at all sure about this—there seemed a real danger of getting swept out past the sandbank, and then we'd really be in trouble—but there didn't seem any choice.

"Charlie, I'm frightened."

"Swim!" I shouted. We struck off together, towards the Thai bank. The current beat against us, and for a while we were swimming furiously without seeming to move forward at all. I heard her choking, belching. I knew that once someone starts to take in water they get weaker by the second. I treaded water, ready to help her, and as I did so my feet touched bottom.

"Look, I can stand!" I shouted. She was looking pretty wild, breathing heavily. I held her in my arms, keeping her chin up, letting us both rest. "It's O.K.," I said. "We've crossed the deep part. We can walk now."

Or could we? The topography of the river was strange and treacherous. We were just a hundred yards downstream from where we had set off—I could see our clothes piled on the bank there—but everything was different. As soon as we started towards the bank I felt the river-bed shelve away beneath us. I noticed too that the bank was steep here, red earth and roots showing, a good four or five feet between the water and the level ground.

We were swimming again now, caught in a whipping eddy, Katai spluttering and squawking. I tried to help her, but I'm no life-saver and things only got worse. She flailed, rapped me in the face with her elbow. She was taking in water again.

"Oh no, oh no," she cried.

Then suddenly the current changed again, and we were bobbing off towards the bank. I saw the farmer's raft in a little inlet. When we were close enough I let go of Katai. The current threw her against the stern of the raft. She grabbed hold of it. I was swept on for a bit, out of sight of her, but soon managed to grab the loop of a root in the bank.

I would find [the Mekong] called by many names: River of Stone, Dragon Running River, Turbulent River, Mother River Khong, Big Water, the Nine Dragons. Along it empires, kingdoms, and colonial realms have risen and fallen; successor states have been plunged into war and bloodshed. Death and hardship are its legacy.

—Thomas O'Neill, "The Mekong" *National Geographic*

I hung there gasping and grateful. I realized we had nearly drowned. I heard Katai call my name, whether for help or out of concern for me I didn't know. I called back, "You O.K.?"

"No."

She was sitting in the mud, coughing and choking. The old man was kneeling beside her, holding her head down between her knees. She had taken in a lot of water. As she coughed it out, she was crying.

"Oh God, I thought we both gonna die," she said when she saw me.

"We were O.K., Katai, *no pompen*," I said unconvincingly.

"Oh God," she said again. She would never have sworn by the Buddha, but she had heard *farang* saying "Oh God" and "Oh Jesus" all the time.

The old man was talking to her quietly. I couldn't understand what he was saying to her, and she wasn't about to translate for me. Later she told me: "The old man say to me I am very lucky girl. He say the river is hungry. That was the word: *hungry*. He say that every year, before the rains come, someone drowns in the Mekong. Last year it was a boy from Chiang Mai: he was a very strong swimmer but the river take him. The people here say that if the river does not take someone, the rains will not come, the crops will die."

"Like a sacrifice," I said.

"Yes. It is the *naga* of the Mekong. He must take someone. In return he will bring rain."

We cycled back down the sandy track to Chiang Saen. The sun was bleached out with a heavy haze. It hung over the river, over our heads. It made it seem like we were pedaling uphill. Katai was quiet and pale. The water had left a greyness on her skin. She cycled very slowly, always keeping behind me.

We stopped to rest. Mosquitoes mustered round my sweating shoulders. Katai stared out at the river and she began to cry again. She said, "I wish Harry was here. You take no care of me. You nearly let the river take me. Harry take good care of me."

Back at the guest house, she ran up the steps and went into her room without a word. The door slammed shut behind her.

"You're *farang*," Katai said sulkily. "You couldn't understand."

"Try me."

A couple of hours had passed since our return to Tang Guest House. I had knocked on her door, said I was sorry, refrained from pointing out that it was her crazy idea to cross the river in the first place. She admitted me to her neat little room. She had hung a *puang malai* garland above her bed, and a red sarong over the window, which mingled the greenish river light with a rich pink, gave the room the air of a shady summer bower.

"O.K., I tell you. But you won't laugh?"

"Of course."

"It's what we call *khwan hai,* Charlie. It is the losing of my spirit. It happen today in the river. The spirit inside us we call *khwan.* It is not our life spirit: this we call *winjan.* When the *winjan* goes we die. The *khwan* is something we might lose many times in our life. When you are sick, or when you have the big shock: when this happens we say *khwan khwaen,* which means that your khwan is hanging above you." Her fingers made dangling movements above her head. "You might lose your *khwan* at some great change in your life, like you get married, or have a baby, or when someone dies who you love very much. The *khwan* is what flies away from us. We call it the butterfly soul, it flies from us so easy."

"Where does it go when it flies away?"

"That depends. You remember the old man we met?"

"The man we met…in Laos?"

When a baby is fast asleep or scared, if it gives a sharp cry or abnormally continues crying or weeping, the mother will pacify it by patting its breast gently with her hand and say such sweet words as, "Oh dear khwan, *please stay with the body." This is the manifestation of an old belief that the* khwan *is leaving the body, and that, by such persuasion, the* khwan *will come back and the baby will come to itself again and stop crying.*

—Phya Anuman Rajadhon, *Some Traditions of the Thai*

She smiled in a way that seemed to say yes, of course it was a crazy idea to cross the river to Laos. "Well, he tell me the river has taken my *khwan* away. It did not take all of me, I was lucky, but it has taken my *khwan,* and now I am sad and empty."

It wasn't just the river accident either. Her *khwan* had been in a volatile state for a while—ever since grandfather's death, in fact. "You remember at Chiang Rai? The fortune stick which told me I had no fortune. And today, when we walk in the sand in Laos, did you see?"

"See what?"

"When we walked we left no footprints."

"Yes, I did, but—"

"So all these things are telling me I have lost something, that I'm in a bad way, I'm empty. *Tai bau dee*: mind not good, *na*?"

"But you've seemed so happy," I protested. "This is your holiday, Katai."

"Not holiday," she said firmly. "It is bigger than holiday. This is the first time I travel out of Bangkok alone. And there's Harry. We got plans, Charlie. This is big change in my life."

"Plans?"

She didn't answer. She sat down on the bed. "He won't come tonight," she said in a matter-of-fact way. "So we must think about my *khwan*."

"Right." I cast around for something to say, some tone to say it in. "Well. We've got to think of a way—"

She laughed, laid her hand on my shoulder. Her laugh had an edge to it. "The poor *farang*," she said, shaking her head in mock sympathy. "He don't like anything on the inside of people. He always like to stay on the outside, where he can feel big and strong. So. What does the *farang* fear?"

"Salt, sugar, and chili?" (dutifully).

"No. The *farang* fears what is inside him."

"Oh, for Christ's sake."

She put her finger to my lips, stopping my anger, cooling my hot heart. "It's O.K., Charlie. I'm sorry. This is not your fault. It is my bad mind talking like this. It is because my *khwan* has gone." She rubbed her eyes. Her face still had that greyish pallor: the shock of the river still on it. "Anyway," she said, "I know what we must do."

"What must we do?"

"We must find someone here in Chiang Saen who will perform the ceremony for us. We call it the *bai see soo khwan*. The ceremony to call back my *khwan*."

We went to Porn's noodle shop. Porn would know what to do. She sat attentively as Katai explained how we had swum across to Laos, how we had nearly drowned, how the old farmer had said that the river was "hungry" and had tried to "eat" her, how she felt so strange and thought the *naga* of the river had taken away her spirit.

Porn nodded and murmured sympathy. Yes, of course, the classic symptoms of *khwan hai* were there. Yes, she knew of a *mau khwan*, a specialist in *khwan* ceremonies. Porn's daughter, a pleasant, tubby girl of about fifteen, was despatched in search of this man. She went off into the darkness on her bicycle.

The ceremony would be expensive, Porn warned. The *mau khwan* would have to be paid; the offerings needed would have to be bought and prepared. It seemed that Porn was taking on a managerial role here: she would organize the whole thing. The cost all-in would be 700 baht (around $30).

"That's a lot of money, Katai," I said. She was careful with money, used to making it stretch.

She said it was worth it. It would be worth it at twice the price. "It's like paying for an operation when you're sick. Whatever it costs it has to be done."

"I'd like to watch the ceremony," I said. "It would be very interesting to me. Perhaps I could help out with the money. You know: *farang leech...*" I mimicked her Bangkok drawl. She always pronounced "rich" with a sneer, so it came out like "leech."

"No, Charlie, thank you. I know you mean it well, but the *soo khwan* ceremony, well, you don't buy the ticket to watch like it was a pussy show in Patpong."

I started to protest, but she stopped me. "Of course you can watch. You were in the Mekong with me." A fleeting warm note in her voice, a sense of something shared, even if it was just a fear— the fear when we felt the primal power of the river, the *naga* force, pulling us away to kill us. She was quickly sardonic again, looking at me through half-closed eyes. "You think you are the strong *farang* swimmer, but I know you were frightened for a bit there. Perhaps the *mau khwan* will say a few words for your spirit, Charlie. Maybe your spirit is not so good too. But I will pay. This is Katai's ceremony."

"You're the boss," I said, and we both laughed.

Porn's daughter came back in, wheeling her bike through the eating area to the kitchen out back. The *mau khwan* was out of town, she said. He had gone to assist at an important ceremony down at Ban Son That: a blessing on a new school house. He wouldn't be back until next week.

Porn wasn't put out. She knew another man, perhaps not quite so expert, but a very competent *prahm*. This word Katai translated as "spirit-man." The *prahm* is an all-purpose local ritualist, versed in various ceremonies: the word actually derives from "brahman."

The spirit-man lived not far away. Our meal now finished, it was decided that we should visit him without further ado. The four of us walked off down Main Street, leaving the sleepy-eyed servant girl in charge of the noodle shop. We cut down a couple of shady *soi*, dense foliage overhead, and came round the far side of the town park, to a cluster of wooden houses. In one of these, seated on a verandah, was a small, frail old woman, doing embroidery by the light of an oil lamp. Formalities were exchanged. This was the spirit-man's mother. She sat there serenely as we trooped on up to the *jaan*. I bumped my head on the roof of the verandah. Porn's daughter giggled.

Her son was not there at present. We waited a bit. The old woman sewed: an undulant motif, it might have been a *naga*, aquamarine thread on peach-pink silk. There was talk and there was silence, the Muang women smiling as they spoke, the Bangkok girl sharp and making them laugh, the *farang* on the edge of the circle, nodding like a mascot.

The man didn't come. Was he out doing a ceremony? I asked. No, he was out having *sanuk*, his mother said.

"We all like a good time," I said. Everyone smiled at my bad Thai, nodded at my profound insight.

Katai said, "Sure. The good times you have had, it's the one thing they can't take away from you. That's what Harry says."

A message was left for the spirit-man. The old lady said she was sure he would be able to perform tomorrow morning, unless...

"Unless what?" said Katai.

"Unless he's had too much *sanuk* tonight."

We walked back to the *guess how* [guest house], the streets dark and quiet, the moon over the river crooked with haze. I don't know how she knew, but she was right that Harry wasn't coming tonight. Having got over her disappointment the night before, she seemed to have fallen back on the general Thai view that it's no big deal if someone's a few days late. I saw her eye flicker over the verandah as we climbed the steps, looking for some sign that Harry was here, but everything was dark and still, just a dog barking down the street and our rooms waiting as we had left them, with the untenanted room like a borderline between them.

"It's been quite a day," I said.

"Oh yes, and tonight we will sleep very well."

She kissed me on the cheek, so quick it might have been the touch of a moth. She was right too. I lay down on my bed and when I woke up next morning I was still dressed.

It was Katai knocking that woke me. The sound of her knocking joined in with the clucking of the hens in the yard, like the segue into the reprise of "Sergeant Pepper." She put her head round the door, face fresh again, saying in sing-song *farang*-speak— as she did countless times up on the fourteenth floor—"Good morning, sir."

She had already been down to Porn's. Everything was set up for the *soo khwan* ceremony: it would take place, in the room above the noodle shop, at ten o'clock. "I'm going to get my *khwan* back today," she said, like it was her birthday or something.

She watched me, arms folded, as I sat up. "Just like Harry," she said. "Look *real* bad in the morning."

I showered with the bucket and scoop. There was coffee and "scramble-egg" waiting for me. Katai was taking Chinese tea, nothing else. Was she nervous? "*Nid noi.*"

We walked up to Main Street. It was a glorious morning, the sun low and clear, sucking up mist off the river, the sky blue between the old *chedi* and the dark mangoes, blue between the thin grey trunks of the teak grove at Wat Pa Sak.

At the noodle shop four women were preparing the offerings and decorations for the *soo khwan*. They sat cross-legged on a low wooden dais in the back of the restaurant. Cartons, tools, bicycle parts, pots and pans had been pushed to the back, and the area where they were working had been swept clean. The scene was fragrant with flowers, bright like the morning. They worked with a quiet cheery expertise: the pleasure of preparing for it seemed a part of the ritual's tonic effect. There was music on the radio, a lilting piece with some string instrument. Katai said it was music from Issan, her father's homeland. She looked as if this was significant.

The women arranged the flowers in bunches, wrapped around with a freshly cut banana leaf. They carefully polished each leaf with a damp cloth, giving it a bright sheen. The mass of flowers—chrysanthemums, frangipani, sugar-cane flowers, a red flower called *sathaan,* and many others—reminded me of the Flower Festival the day I arrived in Chiang Mai, less than two weeks ago, but so far away in the slow elastic time of these Mekong days. There were white lotus blooms too, for the Buddha, though it was explained to me that the *soo khwan* was not a ceremony involving the Buddha. The ceremony was to be addressed to a tutelary spirit, in this case the local *naga*, the river-spirit into whose domain her *khwan* had strayed. We were in the realms of the old village spirit cults now.

The flowers were to grace the *pha khwan,* a kind of tiered conical structure set on a silver-gilt dish. This is the central item of the ceremony. Its framework was decorated with a serrated ridge of folded leaves. These, Porn said, were called *nom maew,* the teats of the cat. The little coils of leaf around the candles were called *hang nag,* the tail of the *naga.*

The *pha khwan* is a holder for the offerings that are made to entice the errant *khwan* back. As well as flowers, the objects arranged on it were two boiled chickens; a half-bottle of Mekong whisky; sweetmeats of sticky rice, sugar-cane and candied marrow; quids of *miang,* betel leaves and areca nuts; pink birthday-cake candles; and a range of small token gifts, cunningly fashioned out of leaf-cuttings: a bracelet, a wrist watch, a cup suitable for an elfin-sized dram of Mekong.

There is something very charming about this characterization of the *khwan* as a flighty, childish creature, won back by these baubles and bonbons laid out for it.

The spirit-man arrived on time. He was a thin, neat man, per-haps about fifty, balding and bespectacled. He was half-Burmese, and had the distinctive Burmese skin, smooth and pale-brown like varnished wood. His short-sleeved white shirt was crisply ironed, frayed at the collar. He carried a couple of exercise books. In his breast pocket was a sheaf of folded papers, a spectacles case, a cou-ple of *biros*. He might have been a village headmaster, or a moder-ately prosperous trader, or a minor *fonctionnaire* like Katai's father.

Not—one would have thought, wrong as usual—a caller of spir-its, our special envoy to the *naga* of the Mekong.

We went upstairs. There was a thin kind of parlour with cush-ions on the floor, and a couple of aged armchairs. We were directly above the cook shop. High on the walls were cobwebbed old monochrome photos in gilt frames. The prints had emulsified, faded to a pale tweedy brown. The King and Queen were there, circa 1960, hung with withered garlands. Down near the street-side window was a big dusty TV set that one knew didn't work. It served as a little family altar: on it were Buddhist statuettes and medallions, jars of spent joss, and also a small collection of dolls: cutesy dolls in synthetic lace, jovial pudgy baby dolls, a Snoopy with a smile badge. Pride of place was given to an ornate pen-holder: two plastic *biros* shaped like old text-pens, and between them a nickel-plate model of a vintage car which served artfully as a universal calendar. On the base of this object, bearing strange news of another old spirit-cult, was the legend, "Season's Greetings From Don and Tammy, Tulsa County Autos, Your Caring Car-Mart".

We settled ourselves, Katai kneeling, the spirit-man sitting cross-legged, me off to one side fiddling with my tape recorder, the women in the background on cushions, ready to enjoy a morning's entertainment. Porn's husband, who I had not seen before, turned up. He greeted us all courteously, and hovered at the back of the group. He looked like he had recently woken up. I saw the old wedding photo of them on the wall, he with his hair slicked across from a dead-straight parting, Porn with her veily little hat on, the signature of the photographer almost faded out in the bottom corner.

The *pha khwan,* laden with offerings, stood between Katai and the spirit-man. Everything looked neat and succulent and glossy on the silver tray. The bottle of rice whisky had been opened. All was ready for the calling of the *khwan.*

The ceremony began quietly at first. The spirit-man asked Katai to say her name, though he knew it already. He asked her about herself, her place and date of birth. He noted she was born in the *pee katai,* the Year of the Hare. He ran through the circumstances in which her *khwan* was lost. When he spoke it was partly to her, partly to the rest of us. The tone was one of exposition, very matter-of-fact. He might have been opening a meeting of the local PTA.

He touched all the offerings on the *pha khwan:* gentle, fussy movements. A silence fell. Dust moved through the sunlight. He opened one of his exercise books. The pages were filled with neat handwriting, Thai script, on alternate lines. He began to chant. The chant had no tune, just a couple of tones, up and down, a soporific slow-motion sirening. His voice was catarrhal. He stopped to clear his throat. He had the look of someone pausing after effort. When he settled back into the chant there was no sign of that effort, but you felt it was there.

I didn't understand any of it, and a lot of it was unintelligible to Katai when we played the tape back a few hours later. She said that some of it was in Pali, the old ritual language of Buddhism:

she recognized a common Pali formula, *Namo tassa sammasam buddhassa,* which means, "I worship the enlightened Buddha." Some of it was Burmese, and some a language she didn't recognize at all. Some of it was obscured by the noise of trucks and motorcycles on the street below, so much louder on tape than they had seemed at the time.

The preamble went as follows: "Glory and greatest prosperity. Today is a day of great auspiciousness and purity. On this day the *garuda* will roar. On this day parted families will see one another again. On this day we will recall how King Asoka bestowed the seven blessings upon the people. On this day little children will learn to speak the tongue of their forebears."

He spoke of the 32 *khwan,* which are really 32 *mini-khwan,* each a part of the *khwan,* residing in different parts of the body. He spoke of creatures called *ngueak.* These are apparently river-spirits, in serpent-form like the *naga,* but lacking any of the latter's beneficent aspect. They are wicked, predatory creatures, and were doubtless involved in the incident in the river. Any appeal to them would be useless—a different and more difficult rite must be performed to reverse their influence—so the spirit-man was appealing to the higher authority of the *naga* to get the fled spirit back. He spoke of "Lady Coconut Flower," a kind of wood-nymph, to whom Katai was likened. It was for Lady Coconut Flower that the first *soo khwan* ceremony of all was performed, by Grandfather Tanha and Grandmother Maya, when she was sick and her *khwan* hung outside her.

Then he invoked the *khwan* itself. "Come, O *khwan.* Let not the *khwan* of the head be discouraged, nor any of the thirty-two *khwan* of the young girl's body. You may return here safely. Be content. Look, we have prepared a feast for you. We have laid out pretty robes for you to wear, a mirror for you to see yourself, though we cannot see you." (These items were represented in banana leaf: a rich man's *soo khwan* would have real little clothes and mirrors for the *khwan.*) "We have prepared a splendid feast for you." He enumerated the tempting goodies on the dish: chicken and whisky, white rice and sugar-cane, betel and frangipani....

This went on for about a quarter of an hour. All the while Katai knelt, head bowed, her right hand touching the *pha khwan*. The spirit-man cleared his throat one last time, concluded the chant, and we all sat in silence, a deep silence, for maybe two minutes, like Remembrance Day. I didn't seem to hear the trucks and motorcycles rolling down the street below. They're on the tape, together with a bird that sounds like it was singing straight into the mike, but I didn't hear them then at all.

The spirit-man sat looking thoughtful. Then he gave a little nod, signifying completion of some sort, and everyone shifted and relaxed, and the normality of the room closed in over the silence, like water over sand. The spirit-man was cheerful, as if the difficult bit was now done with. Katai explained to me later that it was at that point during that silence, that her *khwan* returned, enticed by the spirit-man's chant and by the knick-knacks of the offering. "It came into the *pha khwan* then," she said, "though not yet into me." When we played the tape, it was the silence that she wanted to hear again, and the singing of the bird that sounded like it was inside the room.

Next came a very elegant bit of the ceremony. The spirit-man took one of the flowers from the *pha khwan,* dipped it in a bowl of water, and dabbed Katai's hands with it. He repeated the motion several times, sprinkling a bit of water on each of the principal offerings. Then he took a few choice morsels—a bit of chicken skin, some boiled rice, some sugared marrow, a quid of *miang*—and put them in her hand.

This was food for Katai to give to her *khwan* to encourage it on the last leg of its return. Here the spirit-man recited three brief verses. These are called *kham jam,* "feeding words." They are spoken while the *khwan* "feeds" on the morsels in the supplicant's hand. The word *jam* is used in Thai to refer to the old-fashioned pre-utensil way of eating, by dipping balls of rice into a central bowl of food. Earlier in the ceremony, the spirit-man had invoked *Khao Jam,* a minor spirit with special responsibility for "feeding" *khwan*.

One of the *kham jam* went: "Come, O *khwan,* feed at her hand. Let her be strong and daring, let her be free of illness, let her open her palms and gain what she wishes. Come feed."

Finally, to seal in the returned *khwan,* the spirit-man tied the "auspicious thread." He used a Muang term for this, *faay mongkon,* but the Thai generally call it *sai sin.* The auspicious thread is simply a length of string tied, with appropriate blessing, around the wrist. Its most important use is in rituals like this, but the *sai sin* can be done in a casual way by anyone with the wisdom or status to do it—a parent, an older person, a monk. The tying of the auspicious thread around the wrist is a tying in of luck, health, and happiness, and in this case a sealing in of the *khwan,* without which these attainments are impossible anyway.

This wound up the ceremony, but, good to her word, Katai asked the spirit-man to do the *sai sin* for me too, because I had been in the Mekong as well. I knelt before the bespectacled shaman, trying not to dwell on his headmasterly aspect. He spoke a couple of brief formulae, dabbed my hands with petal-water, and tied on the white threads. One of them fell off a couple of weeks later, but the one on my left wrist remained for months, yellowed and tattered, and one night in Bangkok I actually patched it up with sellotape for fear of what might happen to my luck, health, and happiness if it broke.

Katai was congratulated, the spirit-man was thanked, Porn was paid, and we went on our way. The day had hazed over. If felt like we had been at Porn's for a long time, though it was little more than an hour. Katai was full of energy, greeting strangers. By chance or design we passed the gates of Wat Pa Sak, and there was Moonsong, sweeping the path to the *sala* with a besom broom, near enough to the road to talk with passers-by.

He greeted me with the words, "Who will rid me of this turbulent priest?"

We talked about the morning's ceremony. I asked him if, as a monk, he disapproved of the old cults like the *soo khwan.* He said no, on the contrary: at certain times, for instance during ordination, a kind of *soo khwan* was performed by and for monks.

He asked me what the English word for *khwan* was. I said I supposed it was "spirit."

"And do you believe in your spirit?"

I burbled a bit about "life force" and "psychic energy." I observed that the state of *khwan hai,* spirit loss, is probably what we in the West would call "depression."

Moonsong is a monk and former tuk-tuk *driver who makes an appearance in Charles Nicholl's "Moonsong and Martin Luther" in Part One.*

— JO'R and LH

He leant on the broom handle, nodding sagely. "Hmmm, depression." He sounded dissatisfied by the word. It seemed like a narrow, stingy sort of word the way he said it. He composed himself, a scholar settling into his subject. "The word *khwan,* I believe, is from the Chinese word *kwun,* which expresses much the same meaning." He turned the broom upside-down and traced some lines in the dust with the handle. "This is the character for *kwun,*" he explained. "It is composed of two characters: that one means 'demon' or 'spirit,' and this one means something like your breath, or the mist on the river, I do not know the right word. Also when water boils." His hand trembled in imitation of something light and floating: we settled on the word "vapour."

"So, these are the first meanings of *khwan.* It is a spirit, it is a breath or a vapour, it is something inside us that is always ready to fly away. There are also some Thai words that belong with the word *khwan.* One is *ghwan,* which means 'smoke'. Another is *phan.*"

Here he turned to Katai, as if she could better explain. "The *phan* is a dream, Charlie."

"Sometimes when you dream," said Moonsong, "you go off into the world of the *khwan.*"

Katai said, "Also *phan* is the word for our sweetheart. When we are in love with someone we say *khwan ta:* you are the *khwan* of my eyes."

Moonsong stared monkishly into the middle distance, into some space where the meanings and memories of the sensual world lose their awesome power, then he continued, "When the *khwan* is gone, yes, you feel…depression. But look where it goes. It crosses a border, into the spirit-world. And when it comes back, when it is called back in to *soo khwan,* it brings back the air and the touch of the spirit-world. We cannot go across that border yet, but our *khwan* can. To lose your *khwan* is very difficult, very dangerous even, but you must lose it. You must let it go, and pray that it will return."

His hands motioned the freeing of a bird into the air, and his eyes seemed to follow it into the tall canopy of the teak grove.

Charles Nicholl also contributed "Moonsong and Martin Luther" and "Poppy Fields" to this book.

*

It has been said that ignorance is to Buddhism what original sin is to Christianity. By ignorance, the Buddha did not mean merely absence of knowledge, but an erroneous point of view. He particularly urged a new approach to the question of the nature of the self. To the Buddha the idea of a separate self was a mere intellectual invention, corresponding to no reality at all. The self, he argued, was plainly "a process in time," not a single solid "thing" or "fact."

—Nancy Wilson Ross, *Three Ways of Asian Wisdom*

PART FOUR

IN THE SHADOWS

ALAN RABINOWITZ

✦ ✦ ✦

Wildlife Abuse

Few places are more fascinating than a good market,
but if you're in doubt about the origin of a
wildlife product, don't buy.

THE MORNING AFTER I REACHED BANGKOK, I WENT TO VISIT THE famous Chatuchak Weekend Market, an intricate maze of over five thousand vendors which spreads over twenty-eight acres. It's like a massive flea market and Thai-style county fair rolled into one. There were stalls selling everything from wild boar meat to human skulls. If shopping became tiresome, you could go watch a cockfight in progress.

I'd seen some of these Thai oddities before. There were scores of open-air shops in Bangkok selling stuffed cobras, or caiman and crocodile handbags and wallets by the hundreds. On all the major streets, stalls hawked up-country jewelry alongside cases upon cases of beautifully mounted butterflies, scorpions, and bats. Many of these species, which are so abundant on the street, are rare in the wild.

Anyone looking for something more exotic can visit the numerous leather shops selling boots and handbags made from the skins of snakes, turtles, sharks, lizards, crocodiles, and elephants. On one pair of cobra-skin boots, I saw the snake's heads were still attached hissing at me from the toes. Or there were numerous stores with bear, tiger, and leopard teeth and claws, all beautifully mounted in gold and silver settings. Twice, I was offered the skins and heads of the animals that went with these accoutrements.

When I got to the wildlife section of the Weekend Market, I was stunned at the variety of animals that could be bought openly and cheaply. There were hundreds of cages filled with wild jungle fowl, beautiful little pittas, hill mynas, pheasants, hawks, eagles, falcons, macaws, and parrots. The harder-to-obtain or illegal species were sold in darker, more hidden areas of this part of the market. One cage housed both a baby gibbon and a baby langur, the animals clinging to the wire of their cage. Their mothers were most likely killed to get them. Another cage held a python, and still another contained two leopard cats.

But the most pitiful sight was the squirrels—one of the more popular "pet" items at the market. Burmese striped tree squirrels, Indochinese ground squirrels, grey squirrels, and white-bellied flying squirrels were all tied by little strings around their necks to the top of a table, with no food or water nearby. The sun found its way through rents in the awning and beat down on the more unfortunate ones. Nails were clipped, sharp teeth were filed, tails were fluffed, all in order to make them cuter playthings.

In April 1991 the Worldwide Fund for Nature (WWF) denounced Thailand as "probably the worst country in the world for the illegal trade in endangered wildlife," and branded Chatuchak Weekend Market "the wildlife supermarket of the world."

—Paul Gray and Lucy Ridout,
The Rough Guide Thailand

I watched Thai children pass by with their parents, poking here and there, trying to play with the cute furry balls. When one young boy went to pet a white-bellied flying squirrel, its stiff body simply shifted space. A look of puzzlement flashed across the child's face, and the vendor quickly replaced the dead animal with a young golden-colored ground squirrel. The boy smiled and giggled as the new little squirrel snuggled against his finger. The sale was made.

What struck me most was that there was no conscious maliciousness on the part of the vendors. These animals were commodities to be bought and sold like anything else. I looked at the body of the dead squirrel that had dropped to the floor. How many in a day? I wondered.

The next morning, while jogging in Lumpini Park in the middle of Bangkok, I was attracted to an area on the perimeter of the park where groups of people were milling about. As I approached, I saw cages of snakes, and then a curtained off area where a live king cobra hanging from a hook was being split open for its warm blood and gallbladder. At a table nearby, joggers, the majority of whom were Chinese, finished up their runs with a cocktail made of cognac, cobra or Russell's viper blood and gall. There were several of these stands open six days a week, except Monday, when the streets were cleaned.

At this point, I was thoroughly disgusted by all I had seen and I decided to spend the next few days in Bangkok talking with people, following leads, and looking through old newspaper files. I wanted to try to understand how extensive the illegal wildlife trade situation here was because it directly reflected on the government's true attitude toward protecting what wilderness was left in Thailand....

...After a few days of research I knew I had only scratched the surface of this enormous problem, so I decided to talk with some of the officials whose job it was to protect Thailand's wildlife.

"You have only been here a short time; things have gotten better," was a common response from Forestry Department officials.

"Our hands are tied," one man told me. "We patrol these areas, but wildlife officials don't even know what is protected and what is not."

"There are too many ways around the law," another said. "People can legally possess two of any protected species as long as they don't capture or sell them."

"The police are corrupt and don't care. They hinder all our efforts."

All these statements were, to some degree, true. But I was bothered by a feeling that had been plaguing me at Dancing Woman Mountain [Huai Kha Khaeng Wildlife Sanctuary in western

Thailand]. It seemed that much of the sentiment expressed in Thailand, the constant assurance that "things have gotten better," was all just a façade to keep up appearances both for the international community and for Thais themselves. The reality was that the wildlife was being exploited more than ever before. I was starting to believe that the poorest villager cared more about conservation than the highest-ranking officials.

Symbolically the forests and wildlife represent many things to the Thai people: life forces to be protected and nurtured, the spirit world, fear and power, beauty and strength. However, in day-to-day practices, animals and trees represent resources to be tapped and land to be utilized. Wildlife is to be used: strong animals are put to work, and anything can be caged or chained for man's entertainment. Three hundred years ago there was a thriving trade in rhino parts between Thailand and its neighbors. Now that the rhino is extinct, other species have taken its place.

Even Buddhist practices in Thailand have been severely corrupted. I was especially offended by the Thai tradition of buying little containers or cages containing birds, fish, and turtles, then setting them free during special occasions such as festivals or birthdays. Through this beneficent act the buyer gains "merit" for his next life. Yet it is obvious that the sale of such animals, captured for just this purpose, is a thriving business in death and torture which contradicts the most fundamental Buddhist beliefs. Most of these animals soon die or are quickly recaptured after their release. One vendor told me that she addicted her birds to opium so they'd return to her. Now, she bemoaned, opium was too expensive.

I stopped counting the gibbons and macaques I saw chained by the neck at Buddhist temples. Monks accepted such gifts freely from the people, sometimes believing they were doing the animal a service by caring for it. Often, however, the monks knew the value of such animals to their temple. Sometimes the abbot of a temple requested certain species of animals because they brought in tourists and increased the temple's donations. Many temples had little zoos. One temple compound in Uthai Thani kept a leopard cat, a civet, a Javan mongoose, and numerous forest birds in pitifully cramped little cages to attract the townspeople. The monks fed them what little remained from their own meals. The water dishes in most of the cages were bone dry.

Then there were the buckets of frogs in the marketplace. I watched as women skinned them alive, then severed the legs from their bodies to sell. With eyes bulging, the still living naked torso was thrown into a separate pail to be discarded.

"Why don't you kill the frogs before you dismember them?" I asked repeatedly.

"It is not right for Buddhists to kill," I was told.

Alan Rabinowitz contributed five other stories to this book, all excerpts from his book, Chasing the Dragon's Tail: The Struggle to Save Thailand's Wild Cats.

✳

It is obvious that only with strong popular participation can Thailand effect a reasonable enforcement of protective laws—which are already plentiful but often ignored. Current examples of "people power" include the hundreds of forest monasteries that voluntarily protect chunks of forest throughout Thailand. When one such *wat* was forcibly removed by the military in Buriram Province, thousands of Thais around the country rallied behind the abbot, Phra Prachak, and the *wat's* protectorship was re-established. On the other side of the coin, *wats* with less ecologically minded trustees have sold off virgin lands to developers.

—Joe Cummings, Thailand - a travel survival kit

DIANE SUMMERS

✦ ✦ ✦

Dark World of
Gourmet Soup

*They climb bamboo poles 300 feet into total darkness
to look for bird nests. But now the birds and a way
of life are threatened by poaching and habitat loss.*

I LOOK UP INTO THE DARKNESS. THE CAVE ECHOES WITH THE
twittering of birds. It's damp and reeks of guano. Cockroaches and
beetles crawl in a seething carpet over the cave floor. A scorpion
scuttles up the rock wall into blackness. It's my worst nightmare
come true. Even my husband, Eric, who has climbed in the
Himalayas, looks nervous about tackling this place.

Ip, a 45-year-old Thai who climbs here daily, points upward to
a flimsy tower of bamboo that reaches hundreds of feet into the
blackness. With a boyish grin, Ip says to Eric, "*Ma* [come with
me]." It is a challenge.

We are in a vast cavern called Rimau, the Tiger Cave, on an
island in the Andaman Sea off Thailand. Here erosion has sculpted
caverns as large as cathedrals and labyrinths of winding tunnels. In
these protected spots, edible-nest and black-nest swiftlets, about
the size of sparrows, weave the nests that have been sought after
for centuries to make bird's nest soup. In Hong Kong, the world
market for birds' nests, one kilo sells for up to $2,000.

Nest collectors report that swiftlet colonies are shrinking, perhaps the fault of poaching, perhaps of cutting the forests where the
swiftlets feed. Dwindling bird populations may lessen the demand

for the ancient skills of nest collection and extinguish a way of life along this coast. Before the birds and traditions disappear, Eric and I want to document the lives of the men who spend ten hours a day in caverns working by torchlight, scaling cliff faces hundreds of feet high and trusting their lives to a slender scaffolding of aged bamboo poles.

No one before us has scaled the cliffs and photographed the Thai climbers from the heights, and the men are not accustomed to Westerners. They are a proud and independent people, descendants of Malay Muslim fishermen from the south. Their craft has been passed down from father to son for generations. If we are to win their respect, Eric cannot refuse to go up the bamboos in Rimau.

Ip leads the way with two companions: a 55-year-old climber named Sahat and his 22-year-old son, Em. Eric follows, climbing barefoot like the Thais, without the security of ropes. Yet he weighs 30 pounds more. Bamboos that scarcely move under the nesters' feline motions shudder and groan under Eric. Quickly, shadows en-

Most fishermen of the Phuket Islands are either descended from Muslim wanderers who drifted north from Malaya and Indonesia over the ages, or are one of four distinct races, each with its own language, who are collectively (and I think wrongly) known as the "Sea Gypsies." This appellation stems from their habit, before the tourist boom, of shifting their abodes from island to island, from beach to beach, with the change of monsoon seasons and with the movement of the fish. They would be better termed the "sea nomads," for even today the sea people of Rawai herd the fish into nets on the bottom of the sea by walking along the sea bed at depths of 60 feet or more wearing only a mask and supplied with air by a decrepit compressor on board their longtail craft.

—Tristan Jones, "An Island Between Two Worlds"

velop all four men, and only the red flames of their torches mark their progress. I stand below, wondering if I will see my husband again.

For the nest collectors, the darkness and danger are just part of a day's work. But in the climbers' own way they do not take chances. In the cave they never speak words for fall, death, blood, or fear, in case such powerful words incite demons to cause an accident. Workers use a special vocabulary inside the cave. If a flashlight falls, it has "gone down." A "slippery" bamboo is "wet." If a vine breaks, it is "torn."

At one time the wives of the collectors did not oil their hair or sweep out their houses while their husbands were at work for fear the men would slip or be swept off the bamboo. Now many of the old beliefs have been replaced by pragmatism. Ip says, "You can judge the length of a man's life by the way he maintains his bamboos."

Good bamboos are critical. The collectors' determination to find nests takes them into many dangerous situations. In one cave, the birds enter through passages high in a cliff inaccessible to humans. Nest gatherers swim into the cave through a passage completely submerged in the sea. Another cave is accessible only to the slimmest of the collectors. Holding their breath, they slide through a narrow shaft that opens into the top of a chamber 600 feet high. No wonder the passage is called *Rapo,* "Born a Second Time."

The nests that drive men to such risks come from two species of swiftlets, distinguished from other swifts by their ability to form nests from strands of saliva. The birds regurgitate a long, thin, glutinous noodle from a pair of salivary glands under their tongues, winding it into an opaque, half-cup nest. The nest-building substance bonds quickly to the cave wall. Occasionally nest gatherers find a swiftlet that has died a prisoner of its own saliva, its claws or feathers caught by a strand that hardened like quick-drying cement.

Swiftlets build their nests on a vertical face close to an overhang, or sometimes as far as two miles into underground tunnels. The birds navigate through the blackness of the caves by uttering a rapid clicking call. Scientists have found only one other group of birds, the unrelated oilbirds of the American tropics, with this echolocation ability.

The climbers of Rimau swear by the revitalizing power of these birds' nests. During harvest season, from February to July, the men work ten hours a day on the bamboos without carrying food or water. The collectors' sole nourishment while climbing comes from the one or two nests a day they pry off the walls and eat raw.

In a fine restaurant, preparing nests for soup is a lengthy process. First, they are soaked, developing the consistency of fine noodles. Workers pick impurities form the swollen mass with tweezers and then cook the nests in chicken broth or blend them with coconut milk as a dessert. For a more elegant dish, chefs concoct "Phoenix Swallowing the Swallow," a whole chicken stuffed with birds' nests.

Asians have eaten swiftlet nests since the Ming Dynasty as a treatment for lung disease or fed them to children, the elderly, and convalescents. In Hong Kong, wealthy old ladies come to hotels once a week for a bowl of the soup, believing that it clears the skin and strengthens the body. The treatment certainly lightens the wallet—sometimes $50 per bowl.

To see if medicinal uses have a scientific basis, biochemist Yun-Cheng Kong at the Chinese University of Hong Kong analyzed birds' nests. He found a water-soluble glyco-protein that promotes cell division within the immune system. Ironically, making soup is not a good thing to do to this substance. "The water-soluble protein is destroyed during the cleaning process, and the therapeutic properties are lost," says Kong.

Nevertheless, harvesting birds' nests has been big business for centuries. Kong believes swiftlets' nests have been eaten in China for 1,500 years. In southern Thailand, collecting for export began about 1770, when an astute Chinese settler, Hao Yieng, recognized the value of the nests he had seen on two nearby islands. He presented the king with a list of offerings including 50 cases of tobacco and his land, wife, children, and slaves, begging the king to grant him the right to collect nests. The king accepted the tobacco, returned the list of people and property, and granted Hao Yieng a lease in return for an annual payment.

China remained the biggest importer of birds' nests until the Communist revolution. The new government frowned on the nests as a bourgeois extravagance. Today Hong Kong is the biggest consumer, importing about 100 tons, or 25 million dollars' worth, annually. The Chinese communities of North America rank second.

To feed this worldwide market, collectors gather nests from cliffs throughout Southeast Asia, including Vietnam, Singapore, Burma, and Malaysia. Indonesia is the biggest supplier, Thailand ranks second.

In most nest-producing countries, swiftlet colonies are diminishing. The birds need forests—where they feed—as well as caves, and the demand for timber has depleted the region's forests. Another danger is the booming nest market itself. (Prices doubled in the past two years.) Kong says, "If harvesting continues on this scale, the species may die out within five to ten years."

The leaseholder at Rimau, Apichat, is concerned about the swiftlets' survival and instructs the crews to take nests only three times during each breeding season. (Swiftlets rebuild the nests after every harvest.) Apichat employs Ip, Sahat, and about 100 other men to collect nests from caves and cliffs scattered over 70 islands. In the mid-1980s, he paid $1.5 million to the Thai government in exchange for exclusive rights to collect the nests for five years. Yields vary, but in a week at Rimau, Ip and Sahat gathered about 55 pounds of top quality white nests worth about $50,000 in Hong Kong.

When the season ends, crews leave the caves to return to their other jobs. Ip is a boat carpenter; Sahat and Em are fishermen.

Now, in the black cavern of Rimau, a sickening crunch of a breaking bamboo makes me look up. A torch plummets in a shower of sparks. I hold my breath until I see a replacement torch light up, and four glints of light waver some 200 feet above.

Eric is following Em, who rubs dry guano on his hands to improve his grip, then disappears upward, climbing with his feet flat. At Eric's turn, bamboo joints groan. His bare feet slip. But he regains his grip. In places the rock bulges over the bamboos like a paunch, forcing him to swing farther out over the abyss. He comes to a niche in the rock and climbs in it to rest, curling himself to fit. By then, even Em has pearls of sweat running down his chest. The climb is not easy.

The bamboo leads up to a dark chamber. Here Eric's feet sink into a thick carpet of guano rustling with roaches and smelling overwhelmingly of ammonia. From here another bamboo leads even higher. The bamboos creak when Eric takes hold. Finally, after more nerve-wracking steps on the straining scaffold, he reaches Sahat and Ip.

From a rickety perch, they can look down into blackness. Almost 300 feet below them a pool of daylight illuminates the cave floor. People, Lilliputians from this height, move about in the world Eric left only 30 minutes before. There is nothing between the climbers' bare feet and the abyss but a few bamboo poles.

In the gloom, the young climber, Em, bangs his head against a stalactite. A long, low booming sound reverberates, echoing through the silence of the cave below.

A light flashes briefly between the stalactites—one of the older climbers is checking the walls. A hand, invisible in the darkness, reaches out to lead Eric across a narrow bridge to the inner cave.

Silently they move through a honeycomb of cave passages. Without warning, Ip shines his flashlight on the ceiling and shouts. Startled swiftlets brush against the men, the beating of wings and clicking calls the only sounds in the stillness. Ip searches the intricate rock folds above for more nests.

The men climb higher still, holding lighted torches between their teeth. The smell of burning resin fills the air. Bats' eyes gleam. Shadows of the creeping climbers dance over the rippled stalactites.

Nest collectors concentrate on each step. The strength of the next bamboo is the key to survival. Some poles are so old that they crumble to dust. Men have died trusting their weight to a rotten bamboo. "Tap the bamboo," one collector has said. "If it answers like cardboard, leave it."

"My friends tell me, 'You have a dangerous job,'" says Sahat. "But that's not true; otherwise we would all be dead. My father fell three times before he died. It was not his time."

Below, I pace around the cave floor and explore passages, returning to check for any sign of the climbers' return. After several hours, they descend from the bamboos, covered in grime and guano, black as the shadows.

Dinner that night is at the nest collectors' camp, a loosely woven platform of bamboo hanging from stalactites at the cave entrance and jutting out over the sea. A fish stew simmers in a communal pot. Ip soon has all of us in fits of laughter with his impersonation of Eric's heavy-footedness as he struggled on the bamboos. We are beginning to be accepted. We have passed the test.

Diane Summers is an Australian lawyer who met Eric Valli while on a bus in Nepal. Living in the Himalaya with their two daughters, they are regularly featured in National Geographic *and* Geo *magazines and have written numerous books, including* Honey Hunters of Nepal, Caravans of the Himalaya, *and* Shadow Hunters: Nest Gatherers of Tiger Cave, *a book about Rimau.*

★

The king cobra greets me as I walk down his path one morning. He looks at me lazily, not bothering to arch his black hood. I squat less than two metres away, watching him smell me with his tongue. I am glad to be in his presence again. He has more compassion than us all. He could rise and kill, but he chooses to let me work out my *kamma* for myself. I wish I had his peace. Slowly the long muscular body surges across the trail, gliding like a flowing stream. I wait until the tail is swallowed up in jungle, then raise my hands high up to my forehead in a respectful *wai*.

—Tim Ward, *What the Buddha Never Taught*

IAN BURUMA

* * *

Fooling Yourself
for Fun

Has Thailand lost its cultural sense of self?
Or have the Thais maintained their
indestructible self-respect?

ARRIVING IN THAILAND FROM MORE OPPRESSIVE NEIGHBORING
countries is always a relief. The taxis smell of flowers. The people
are gracious. Hedonism comes without guilt. So what if people
want your money. And if the city is a little crass. After the air of
slow death of Rangoon, I felt like kissing the ground of the newest
Bangkok shopping mall. Here the king plays jazz.

But soon, once blind enchantment has worn off, one begins to
wonder about modern Thailand, or at least Bangkok. There is
something a little over-the-top about the obtrusive desire to please.
Delight is replaced with a no doubt puritanical skepticism, which
can, it must be said, swing back to delight at great speed. How, one
wonders, do Thais preserve their dignity in a world of coarse
commercialism? How have decades of tourism, American GIs on
Rest and Recreation, and a deluge of dollars and yen affected the
urban Thais? Has capitalism indeed corrupted their souls, as some
people like to think? Have they lost themselves in greed?

The glossy posters, the orchids in the airplane, indeed all the
grace of Thailand cannot disguise the basic truth about tourism:
Many more foreign men visit Thailand than women. You hardly
see any Japanese women, let alone women from the Middle East

or Malaysia. Most visitors come from Malaysia, mainly to a city called Hadyai, a kind of Thai Tijuana on the Malaysian border,

Economically, young Thai country women are just another kind of crop. By the standard of their poverty, what they earn as sex workers in the city is phenomenal—more in a couple of years than their parents earn in a lifetime. For men in the city, on the other hand, where the average income is four times what it is in the country, sex comes cheap.

"The fact that [prostitution] has become an integral part of the Thai economy," stated an International Labor Office Study, "…undermines any realistic possibility of short-term cures…No amount of agitation is likely to change things while the cost incentives remain the same, and the opportunities for alternative employment are so limited…"

—Richard Rhodes, "Death in the Candy Store," *Rolling Stone*

where the prevalent business is sex. Paid sex is one of the main tourist attractions in Thailand. If isolation has turned Rangoon into a stagnant backwater, Bangkok is beginning to resemble a sexual supermarket, a capital of discos, go-go bars, massage parlors, VD clinics, German beer halls, Japanese nightclubs, and brothels for Arabs. Bangkok is the playground for the world's frustrated men. All this means big business—indeed, tourism is the largest foreign exchange earner for Thailand. But while the government, businessmen, pimps, girls, and policemen rake in the cash, Thais are deeply concerned about their image, about national Face. In a newspaper article about poor Thais selling the services of their young children to foreign pornographers, a police colonel concluded that the parents "should not be too greedy for money…and moreover, the image of the country will be tarnished because of their ignorance."

As an antidote to this bad image, a good image is presented to the world, that of ancient Thai culture. I was given some examples by the editor of a cultural magazine in Bangkok, an intellectual worried about the damage that tourism was doing to his country. Ordinations of monks, an important event in most Thai lives, are sometimes organized around special fairs for tourists, complete with folk performances and parades. When traditions are no longer practiced, they are revived, drained of all the original significance, or invented especially for foreign or even Thai visitors. Ceremonies are designed by the Fine Arts Department in Bangkok and local schoolteachers are put in charge to teach their students how to perform them. The old city walls of Chiang Mai appeared to attract tourists. Consequently all towns with walls were encouraged to build tourist facilities. A deep cave, a picturesque waterfall, a ruin, anything would do as an excuse to build a hotel, a disco, a coffee shop, waiting for the tourists. "I think people live in a fake world today. They fool themselves for fun," said the editor's wife. The editor smiled and said Thais think foreigners are gods.

I had heard this said before, in Japan. This does not always mean foreigners are liked. Gods are outsiders with great and unpredictable powers. They are to be appeased, by all means, lest they mean harm and do damage. It is better still if their powers can be exploited. Therein lies the key to your own survival.

The wish to impress visitors with traditional culture and then to exploit it for money seems inconsistent. It smacks of preachers on the take. "No," said a good friend of mine, a prominent Thai journalist, "I don't think so at all. It is pragmatic. The essence of those traditions is still valid. Making money won't affect that."

It is easy for the visitor to Bangkok to feel that he is in a fake world, a world of images, of empty forms, foreign styles divorced from any meaning. It is easy to condemn Thailand, or at least Bangkok, for being so hopelessly corrupted by "Westernization," "cultural imperialism," "Coca-Colonization," or whatever one wants to call it, that it has lost its identity altogether; indeed a place where people fool themselves for fun.

Every night in Patpong, on three neon-lit streets in the midst of airline offices and international hotels, the pimps wait for the tourists to arrive. "You want fuck? You want live pussy show? Sucky sucky?" Before the 1960s, when Patpong became a major entertainment area for GIs on leave from Vietnam, it was a rather swank district of nightclubs and dance halls frequented by well-to-do Thais. Now it is a cluster of go-go bars, massage parlors, and live sex show joints. Patpong really is a bit like Disneyland, a jumble of displaced images, of erotic kitsch, Oriental decadence for package tours. Dark-skinned girls fresh from the rural northeast dance naked on long bars to deafening rock 'n' roll, while overweight foreigners watch American movies or boxing on video screens. I was taken to such a place, called the Bunny House. Naked girls were carefully drawing the names of customers by swiveling their hips with long ink brushes sticking out of their private parts. Ah, I thought, giving in for a moment to the romantic fantasy of a provincial European, Berlin '29, and in came a guided tour of white-haired ladies seeing Bangkok by night. They spoke German.

IDS came late to Thailand. It surfaced one day in 1984, slipping in as stealthily as Death slipped into the Masque of the Red Death in Poe's story, inside a walled castle where "the prince had provided all the appliances of pleasure." The first reported case in Thailand that year was a gay Thai who'd returned home from living in the United States.

—Richard Rhodes, "Death in the Candy Store," *Rolling Stone*

"You buy me Coke." "You my darling all night." "You want body massage?" Sexuality in Patpong is so divorced from daily life, so utterly absurd, that it ceases to be obscene. It is more like a charade, a show for the benefit of foreigners, a fake world set up to make money.

There appears to be an almost insulting contradiction between the image of the delicate Land of Smiles, of exquisite manners and "unique hospitality," and the world of live pussy shows. Yet, to see these images as contradictory is perhaps to misunderstand Thailand. Patpong kitsch and Thai traditions coexist—they are images from different worlds, forms manipulated according to opportunity. The same girl who dances to rock 'n' roll on a bar top, wearing nothing but cowboy boots, seemingly a vision of corrupted innocence, will donate part of her earnings to a Buddhist monk the next morning, to earn religious merit. The essence of her culture, her moral universe outside the bar, is symbolized not by the cowboy boots, but by the amulets she wears around her neck, with images of Thai kings, of revered monks, or of the Lord Buddha. The apparent ease with which Thais appear able to adopt different forms, to swim in and out of seemingly contradictory worlds, is not proof of a lack of cultural identity, nor is the kitsch of Patpong proof of Thai corruption—on the contrary, it reflects the corrupted taste of Westerners, for whom it is specifically designed. Under the evanescent surface, Thais remain in control of themselves.

Perhaps because of this shimmering, ever-changing, ever-so-thin surface, Thailand, to me, is one of the most elusive countries in Asia. Thais clearly don't suffer from the colonial hang-ups of neighboring peoples; they know who they are. And yet trying to grasp or even touch the essence of Thailand seems impossible, like pinning down water. But if I did not succeed in pinning down Thailand I did spend a lot of time talking to Thais who claimed that they could.

One such person was the architect Sumet Jumsai. "We seem to take over only the veneer of other cultures," he said, "but our essence is still there, like the wooden houses behind the modern department stores. Opposites always coexist in Thailand. At one point we were basically Chinese. Then, about seven hundred years ago, our literary culture was Indianized. A basically Sinicized people became Indianized. Quite contradictory, really. Funny thing is that civilizations seem to disappear without a trace here. No continuity, you see. People just start again. Sukhothai, in the 13th century, was a great civilization. Nothing much was left. Only two hundred years ago Ayuthaya was destroyed. Hardly had any influence at all on Bangkok. We had to begin all over again. Of course, the unwritten part of our culture, the reflexes, the ceremonies remained. But they may be disappearing now too. Would you care for some more tea?"

Bob Halliday, a genial American who has lived in Thailand for decades, calls it a state of mind. "Everything comes and goes in waves here. High-rise buildings, now there's an example. Suddenly everyone with money wanted one. Tourism is the thing now. But underneath all that, the state of mind does not change at all." Quite what that state of mind, those reflexes are is impossible to define. Halliday, an expatriate who shuns Patpong, speaks fluent Thai, and appears to be content to live the rest of his life in

Thailand, describes it as a natural empathy for friends, a certain delicacy of feeling.

Around 1912, King Rama VI devised a slogan to sum up what he saw as the essence of Thailand: Nation, Religion, Monarch. The religion is, of course, Buddhism. "Buddhism," I was told by a Thai writer, "fits Thai ways well. Because we believe that material surroundings are an illusion, and only the internal world is real, to be Thai can be anything we want." It would explain both the lack of resistance against foreign forms, "Westernization" if you like, and the ease with which they are discarded.

The Thais have been both clever and lucky in their relations with foreigners. The Thais were lucky that the British and the French, the two major colonial powers, neutralized each other, so that Siam became a kind of buffer zone between Burma, Malaya, and Indochina. They were clever in the same way as the Japanese, the only other Asian nation to escape colonialism: they—that is, the elites—"Westernized" themselves to counter the might of the West; they modernized themselves to avoid having modernity imposed on them by others. The phrase used for this by the British pioneer of Japanese studies, Basil Hall Chamberlain, was "protection by mimicry."

The emphasis on monarchy and religion, which seems so atavistic today, was an essential part of this process. The Japanese turned their emperor into what nationalists like to call a "priest-king," a European-style monarch in military uniform, who was at the same time the center of a religious cult. The Thai monarchy turned itself into something similar. King Chulalongkorn (Rama V), visited Europe in 1897. He toured the slums of London— quite a remarkable thing to do for a visiting monarch—and saw the problems of European modernity, but was impressed by modern science, by the legal systems, and the bureaucratic institutions. Back in Siam, he stated that "there exists no incompatibility between such acquisition [of European science] and the maintenance of our individuality as an independent Asiatic nation." This enlightened thought, which could not have occurred in a colonized mind, is crucial to the development of modern Thailand. In fact, the king was ahead of the great modernizers of early Meiji Japan, who believed that total Westernization was the only road to modernity.

During his reign, lasting from 1868 to 1910, a collection of regions ruled by aristocratic families was transformed into a state. Buddhism was reformed and institutionalized as a national religion, taught in schools and monasteries all over the country. The supreme patriarch was a Siamese prince. Buddhist monks taught a new standard Thai, as well as science and mathematics, something their counterparts in Burma absolutely refused to do. The chief ingredient in the attitude of the Burmese Buddhist hierarchy was, as the historian D.G.E. Hall put it, "its opposition to what may be termed modernity." Thai monks, in contrast, became the first modern teachers. One thing Burma and Thailand had in common, however, was that a generation later Thai government propagandists and young Burmese anti-colonialists were convinced that true patriotism was inseparable from Buddhism. But Buddhism, unlike the state Shinto of prewar Japan, was always a universalist faith, far removed from the Shinto myths of racial purity. This has contributed greatly to the relative openness of Thai society.

While the Thai elite was educated for government service, Chinese merchants were encouraged to build a modern urban economy, which they still dominate. Chinese businessmen enriched the Thai elite in exchange for status in Thai society, a situation which also still persists. A Sino-Thai journalist in Bangkok told me that "one hundred years ago the Thais knew nothing. The Chinese taught them how to weigh, how to buy, how to sell." To be sure, my friend, who does not speak any Chinese, is a bit of a Chinese chauvinist. But he was not entirely wrong. When I asked him how Thais and Sino-Thais got on today, he smiled as though the answer was self-evident: "No problem. We mix now because of Westernization. TV, discos, Walkmans—we all move to the same point." He was not wrong about this either. But when I asked him whether he would mind if his daughter married an ethnic Thai, he did not hesitate: "That I would not allow."

Chulalongkorn's successor, King Vajiravudh (Rama VI), who ruled from 1910 to 1925, was educated at Sandhurst and Oxford, where he read history and law. There is a picture of him, taken in 1914, on the bridge of the royal yacht, splendidly dressed in white ducks, double-breasted blazer, the cap, holding a brass telescope. It was typical of his chosen image—just as typical as the photograph of the present king playing jazz is of his—the priest-king as a modern naval officer. King Vajiravudh was fond of the theater and he wrote plays exhorting his subjects to become modern nationalists, more like Europeans. His hectoring prose could have been written by the moralists of Meiji Japan:

> Let us unite our state, unite our hearts, into a great whole.
> Thai—do not do harm or destroy Thai,
> But combine your spirit and your strength to preserve the state
> So that all foreign peoples
> Will give us increasing respect.

Respect from foreign people. There it is again. Siam not only should be modern, but it should look modern, or, rather, if it looked modern, it was modern. Through the king's encouragement, women began to adopt European dress and hairstyles. He introduced the Gregorian calendar, designed a new national flag, and encouraged team sports and Boy Scouts. The king himself was Chief Scout-General and his youngest schoolboy followers were Tiger's Whelps.

Modernity, however, creates its own monsters. The students sent abroad by the modern monarch returned and were no longer satisfied with the rule of the priest-king. In 1932, during the reign of Vajiravudh's successor, King Prajadhipok, absolute monarchy came to an end, pushed aside in a coup staged by 49 military and naval officers, and 65 civilians, led by 2 modern men, both educated in France, one a soldier, the other a civilian: Plaek Khittasangkha and Pridi Phanomyong.

Pridi and Plaek (better known as Phibunsongkhram or Phibun) represented two faces of modern Thailand, which are still at odds. Pridi, the son of a Chinese immigrant, was a civilian intellectual attracted to "progressive" politics. He hoped to establish a more democratic system in Thailand. Phibun was a modern military man, inspired by right-wing populist nationalism, like that of King Vajiravudh. The military being a more powerful and efficient modern institution than anything the budding civilian intelligentsia could muster, Phibun's power grew, while Pridi's declined. In 1938 Phibun became Prime Minister, with Pridi as his Minister of Finance. He belonged to the same school of thinking as Dr. Ba Maw in Burma and the ultra-nationalists in Japan. He wrote approvingly of Hitler and Mussolini and believed in the *Fuhrerprinzip*. He changed his country's name from Siam to Thailand, as though to emphasize that Thailand belonged to the Thai-speaking peoples and not to outsiders like the Chinese.

This is why many "progressive" nationalists today still insist on using the name Siam. One of the most prominent social critics, Sulak Sivaraksa, believes that the name Thailand "signifies the crisis of traditional Siamese Buddhist values. Removing from the nation the name it had carried all its history is in fact the first step in the psychic dehumanization of its citizens, especially when its original name was replaced by a hybrid, Anglicized word. This new name also implies chauvinism and irredentism." Phibun's most powerful intellectual ally was a writer called Luang Wichit, who liked to compare the Chinese in Thailand to the Jews in Germany; both, in his view, were a noxious and polluting presence.

Like Rama VI, Phibun was eager to impress the world with a progressive, modern Thai image. This meant more Western forms: trousers, gloves, shoes, a national anthem, saluting the flag, and so forth. This was hardly a case of blind adulation for things European. On the contrary, it was a re-creation of Western forms to strengthen Thai nationalism. Western clothes, yes, but made in Thailand.

The full force of modernity, however, only came in the 1950s and 1960s. As usual, it was mixed with tradition, or pseudo-tradition. In 1958, Field Marshall Sarit Thanarat staged the second coup in two years and formed a "Revolutionary Party." "The fundamental cause of our political instability in the past," wrote Sarit's adviser and later Foreign Minister, Thanat Khoman, "lies in the sudden transplantation of alien institutions onto our soil without proper regard to the circumstances which prevail in our homeland, the nature and characteristics of our own people, in a word the genius of our race, with the result that their functioning has been haphazard and even chaotic. If we look at our national history, we can see very well that this country works better and prospers under an authority, not a tyrannical authority, but a unifying authority, around which all elements of the nation can rally." (Quoted by David K. Wyett in his *Thailand: A Short History*.) The unifying authority was the priest-king, reinstated as a real force once again. The monarch lent legitimacy to the new regime, just as the Meiji emperor had done for the Japanese modernizers since 1868.

It is a common theme in Southeast and East Asia, the use of tradition to bolster modern authoritarianism. Ferdinand Marcos saw himself as a tribal chieftain in the Philippines and Park Chung Hee as a Confucian patriarch in South Korea. And as was the case with the other Asian strongmen, Sarit's modern authoritarianism was financed by massive American aid, meant, in the buzzword of the time, to "develop" Thailand. The constitution was abolished, martial law declared, the streets cleaned, crime reduced, and critics arrested. The Vietnam War escalated and U.S. bases grew in size. At the same time there was high economic growth, rapidly spreading education (from five university-level institutions with 1,800 students in 1961 to seventeen with over 100,000 in 1972), the beginning of tourism, and a communist insurgency. Sons and daughters of peasants moved to the cities, the middle class grew, students read Marx and listened to the Rolling Stones—in short, Disneyland came to Bangkok. Intellectuals reacted as they usually do under these circumstances: they wrote about spiritual dislocation and moral drift.

Does civilization kill? Has modernity wiped out traditional values to the extent that nothing but empty forms and pragmatism remain? I turned, once again, to cultural interpretation. One of the most interesting theories, by Dutch anthropologist Niels Mulder, is that traditional values, far from being eroded by anonymous modern amorality, have actually been enhanced. Mulder begins by pointing out that Thai Buddhists are still animists at heart. The world is divided into a private sphere of pure moral goodness, exemplified by a mother's love for her children, a teacher's for his pupils, by the Buddha himself, and by the land that provides our food, and a public sphere of amoral powers, called *saksit*. "Basically, *saksit* power is amoral, because it does not ask for intentions and protects the good and the wicked alike. It is unprincipled and reacts to mechanical manipulation and the outward show of respect. It is not concerned with right or wrong, or with the development of moral goodness. Contracts with *saksit* power are guided by their own businesslike logic, and there is no higher moral principle that guides these."

It is good to avoid conflict

hailand has a reputation for being open to homosexuality…Although excessively physical displays of affection are frowned upon for both heterosexuals and homosexuals, Western gay couples should get no hassle about being seen together in public. The Thai tolerance extends to cross-dressers and you'll even find transvestites doing ordinary jobs even in upcountry towns.

Possibly because of the overall lack of homophobia in the country, there's no gay movement to speak of in Thailand—the nearest equivalent to an organized gay political force is the Fraternity for AIDS Cessation in Thailand (FACT), which runs AIDS awareness campaigns, staffs a telephone counseling service and publishes a bilingual monthly newsletter.

—Paul Gray and Lucy Ridout,
The Rough Guide Thailand

with outside powers, by polite manners, by hiding one's true feelings, and so forth, and it is also good to manipulate those powers to your own advantage. It is the basic approach to all foreigners. The huckster and the stickler for etiquette are two faces of the same man. But he can also have a third face, that of the devoted friend, an example of the empathy and delicate feelings that Bob Halliday called "the Thai state of mind." In Mulder's words: "The world of modernity is a world of increasingly rapid change filled with self-seeking, impersonal power, and the experience of powerlessness for most. No wonder that the old animist perceptions of power are strongly revitalized, not only in Thailand but worldwide, in the losing battle between the temple and the bank."

He applies the same idea to prostitution: "To sell one's body is an outside phenomenon and so it is to buy and does not imply any feelings of loyalty or even moral respect for oneself. It is a monetary transaction, and money is widely admired and the preeminent embodiment of power…. As long as [the prostitute] cares for her relatives and recognizes the *bunkhun* [moral goodness] of her parents in terms of gifts and money, she can still present herself as a good person. When she has accumulated enough, or when her fortunes turn, she may resettle in her village of origin, marry, and be accepted."

The City is the world of outsiders, the Village the moral home. The trouble is that for more and more people there is no more Village; the City is the only reality they know. Crime and prostitution are but extreme forms of manipulating amoral powers. Impulsive violence is usually a sign of long-suppressed feelings; the behavior of people having to present Face in a pragmatic and increasingly anonymous world. It is often when Face is insulted that sudden violence occurs; a bump of the shoulders in the street, a stranger's glance at the girlfriend in a nightclub.

How to moralize the amoral new world? Boy Scouts, racial pride, and military discipline? Marxist dialectics and learning from the Village? The most common answer in Thailand is none of these; instead people point to the personal example of the king and Buddhism. This is where Thai morality and politics continue to connect.

One of the heroes of the October 14 generation was Sulak Sivaraksa, a genial dandy who goes around in traditional Thai clothes, a cloth bag over his shoulders, and a cane in the hand. His ancestors were Chinese, something he does not hide. He calls himself a Buddhist activist. He is a popular speaker on the international lecture circuit as a leading Southeast Asian intellectual. Sulak was raised as an Anglican and studied classics in Britain.

To Sulak the resurgence of Siam is a moral issue. The modern world is amoral, because it is capitalist, which fills man with greed. What's worse, this greedy new world is foreign. Sulak's very modern response to modernity is profoundly anti-modern. "The present single worst enemy of Buddhism in Siam is of course new technology which comes hand in hand with industrialization and progress...."

Society "pollutes," for it makes us crave power and riches. Western powers "took away a lot from our Buddhist way of life. They provided hospitals for us in the Western way, they provided everything Western for us, and so the temple lost all its functions." The Buddhist precepts are undermined—for example, the precept that you should not kill. "But now you have all the machinery of killing, you have the multinational corporations dealing with killing, and they are linked to banks, and the first precept on killing relates to the second precept on stealing, and so on."

> "*The October 14 generation*" *refers to the demonstrations in October, 1973, that brought down a military dictatorship and established an elected, constitutional government. This change lasted only three years, until October, 1976, when another coup re-established a right-wing military government.*
>
> —JO'R and LH

The answer to these modern challenges is to return "to the essence of our Buddhist culture, with its spiritual and moral base, in order to wipe out the danger from modern cultural imperialism." Gandhi's concept of the "Village Republic should be studied more seriously in order to find alternative models to capitalist development ideology...." Traditional medicine, administered by monks, should be revived. Bangkok must be developed "Buddhistically—against satanic development models which are now prevailing everywhere, by trying to be big, to be rich and powerful..." It is a utopian response resembling Luddite movements in Victorian England. Sulak does not even wish to keep the ruby which "spun a web of greed"; he wants to throw it back into the sea. This seems curiously un-Thai, the response, perhaps, more typical of a lapsed Anglican classics scholar.

More and more Thais seek to strengthen the legal and political institutions which hold personal excesses—"power and greed in our hearts"—in check. Buddhist fundamentalism, with its distrust of capitalism and secular institutions, would seem to be taking Thailand in the opposite direction. The enormous importance attached to the personal benevolence of the monarch is part of the same world view. It might work if the monarch is believed to be truly benevolent, as appears to be the case with the present king. There is little reason to believe that the people in cinemas, or other public places, who jump up instantly as the portrait of the king appears, do so reluctantly. But if these were ever to change, the country could become dangerously unstable.

King Bhumibol spends much of his benevolent energy in rural areas, bolstering the Village. When communist rebels installed themselves in large parts of the northeast, the king encouraged the government to make those areas more prosperous to undercut the communist cause. Khao Ya, a mountain near the northeastern town of Petchabun, not far from the Laotian border, was a communist stronghold until 1982. Now it is the site of a royal mountain lodge. A visit there seemed a fitting way to end my trip to Thailand. I had been told it was now a prosperous place, where farmers lived happily after the guerrillas were defeated by the Thai army in 1982. I also heard it had become a popular tourist destination.

Khao Ya, and Khao Kor, the former rebel headquarters, must have been beautiful once. And in a strange way they still are. What was once a jungle has been transformed into a red desert, with the occasional tree stump scorched by fire. Great gashes of erosion, like nasty red flesh wounds, mark the bare mountains. On top of Khao Kor is an army museum and a memorial to the 1,300 soldiers who died in the battle against the communists. In the museum an officer explained to a group of Thai tourists how the guerrillas were flushed out of their camps. There were exhibits of guns, a few rusty AK-47s and M-16s. There were some tattered red flags, a few Chinese embroidered portraits of Marx, Lenin, and Stalin, and a book on Kim Il Sung's thoughts, in French.

We drove past the royal mountain lodge, perched in isolation on the denuded hill. We drove past the newly built villages along the excellent roads. There were signs in English welcoming tourists. But there were no people. The villages seemed completely deserted. In the valley we finally saw some trees. There were signs warning us not to "make noise to alarm the animals." We saw no animals. There were a few souvenir stalls, where Hmong hill tribesmen in their native dress sold trinkets made by different hill tribes near Chiengrai, hundreds of miles farther north. The souvenir business was subsidized by the government, they said. But there were not many tourists around to buy anything.

A group of Hmong men were having soft drinks in a wooden shack where snacks were served. "There were once ten thousand communists here," said one of the men, before getting up to leave. "Look at the color of that river," said the woman who ran the restaurant. She pointed at a river which looked like fluid caramel. "It was not like that before they came and chopped the trees down." According to her story, the army had let loggers in from all over the northeast to take away the trees. The villagers were paid to grow corn. That way, it was hoped, guerrillas could no longer hide in the hills. The villages along the road were deserted because nothing would grow anymore. The government kept on busing new villagers into the area, so that tourists could be welcomed. "Still," said the woman, "we feel safe here now that the troops protect us."

She fell silent and I looked at the rather sad-looking souvenir stalls, the signs about not making noise, the caramel river, the bald mountains, the empty Pepsi-Cola bottles. "Everything they try to preserve," the woman said suddenly, "has already gone—the animals, the trees, everything."

It would be the perfect literary metaphor: the loss of traditional values, the destruction of the Village, the emptiness of capitalist development, and so on and so forth. Yet the metaphor would be too easy, too neat. For every image of loss can be countered with an example of gain. The mountains of Khao Kor have no trees, but the political destiny of Thailand is no longer decided by gunfire in the mountains. More and more, it is decided by debate, choice, politics. The Hmong drink Pepsi-Cola, as do most Thais, as do most people. It is sad, perhaps, that popular consumption is often in bad taste and wasteful, but a poor choice is better than no choice at all. Modernity in Thailand is sometimes ugly, and perhaps Thais have lost something in their quest for material well-being. But they have managed to retain the thing that is most precious to them, their self-respect. This is their most attractive quality and it seems indestructible, in the villages, but also in the cities, among students, merchants, politicians, and peasants, and, yes, even among "the chicks of Fun City," the dancing girls in Patpong.

Ian Buruma lives with his wife and daughter in London. He is the author of Behind the Mask: On the Sexual Demons, Sacred Mothers, Transvestites, Gangsters, Drifters, and Other Japanese Cultural Heroes, *and* God's Dust, A Modern Asian Journey, *from which this was excerpted. He is also a regular contributor to* The New York Times.

★

At five in the morning, the boys and girls who have found no clients still walk the streets. There are still a few sex tourists looking for business. "The nice thing about Bangkok," says Greg, "is that you need never feel lonely. You only have to go out, any time of the day or night, and you can find someone to go with you. Of course," he says wistfully, "it isn't a relationship, but beggars can't be choosers. And we're all beggars aren't we? Economic beggars, emotional and sexual beggars. That's the way of the world, my dear."

—Jeremy Seabrook, "Cheap Thrills,"
New Statesman

PRATYA SAWETVIMON

★ ★ ★

After the Night of
the Generals

*In May, 1992, pro-democracy demonstrators were gunned down
in Thailand's worst political violence in two decades. The
king interceded, military leaders were shamed.*

I STROLL DOWN RACHADAMNOEN AVENUE ONE LAZY SUNDAY
afternoon in the middle of June. The rainy season has begun at
last and the raging heat of May has been tempered by winds of
moderation. Laid out in the 1880s by order of King
Chulalongkorn, Bangkok's most elegant boulevard—the name
means "Royal Progress"—is lined with fine cassia trees. The bronze
streetlamps are in the shape of Kinaree, the half-bird, half-woman
angel of Thai epics.

I was here one month earlier. Rachadamnoen then was a scene
of horror—the unspeakable sadness of Thai soldiers gunning down
Thai civilians. During the tense days before the May bloodbath, the
avenue was packed curb to curb all the way up to the barbed-wire
barricades of the police and army. Facing them were demonstrators
demanding the resignation of the prime minister, General
Suchinda Kraprayoon. Here Major-General Chamlong Srimuang,
governor of Bangkok until four months earlier, had galvanised the
immense throng by vowing to starve himself to death unless the
military police gave in to the crowd's demand to get out of politics.

Here a peaceful protest turned ugly as troops and civilians con-
fronted each other in nervous tension. Bottles of gasoline were

393

thrown by youths whose love of peace was less defined than their love of democracy. Volleys of rifle shots punctured the tense night standoff. Here fell the dead and wounded. Along this elegant avenue marched soldiers firing M-16 automatic rifles into the air. On these sidewalks three thousand people were brutally shoved into army trucks. And here was destroyed the image of Thailand as a sophisticated modern nation where things like this do not happen.

Pratya Sawetvimon is a staff correspondent for Asiaweek *magazine.*

★

General elections were held four months after the massacre in Bangkok, with five parties that opposed the military's political meddling coming to power in a coalition government. While it's unlikely that the military will intervene again because the people wouldn't accept such a move, Thailand's modern history is riddled with coups—eighteen since the absolute monarchy was eased aside in 1932—and there's no telling what will happen in the future.

—JO'R and LH

STEVEN M. NEWMAN

* * *

Walking South

On a solo walk around the world,
Steve Newman encounters his worst
nightmare in southern Thailand.

IT WAS THE HEIGHT OF THE THAI SUMMER, AND EVERY STEP I HAD taken south from Bangkok seemed to be edging me closer to the fires of hell. Beneath the large striped golfing umbrella I held over my head, I felt as if I were inside a sauna. By each midmorning, my clothes were soaked; by midday, I barely had enough energy left to find some tepid shade to collapse into.

By the time I had reached the city of Phet Buri on April 6, I was so sapped of strength by the unyielding humidity that I had no choice but to spend four days recovering beneath a cheap hotel room's wobbly ceiling fan. I had gone only 60 miles, but my poor body felt it had suffered through 60,000. My worst fears about the effects of tropical heat on my Ohio-raised body were being realized, I thought uneasily. And, worse, since every step took me closer to the equator, I knew the battle to keep my strength would get tougher each day. I had never taken well to heat and humidity, and here I was trying to plod my way through the worst of it with fifty pounds of dead weight on my back and the monsoon season coming. The chance of my reaching Singapore, the end of the 1,300-mile-long walk through Southeast Asia, seemed remote.

I decided that I was going to have to do more of my walking at night, when it was cooler. Yet I knew that if I did, I was brazenly inviting death. Ever since I had left Bangkok, cars or trucks had pulled over to the side of the road to tell me that bandits were everywhere. As the drivers drew their forefingers across their throats and let their eyes grow larger with their warnings of sure death ahead, it was all I could do not to laugh at their animations. But there had been frequent news articles about packed buses being held up in broad daylight by bands of armed robbers along the same highway I'd be following. If they were reckless enough to rob an entire busload of people in the daylight, then what chance did *I* stand, alone and totally exposed? Behind my seeming calmness there took root a nervousness that I hadn't known since North Africa.

Violent crime against tourists is not common, but it does occur, usually to people making an ostentatious display of their belongings. Be wary of accepting food and drink from strangers, expecially on long overnight bus or train journeys; it may be drugged so as to knock you out while your bags get nicked. This might sound paranoid, but there have been enough drug-muggings for Tourism Authority of Thailand to publish a specific warning about the problem. Finally, be sensible about traveling alone at night in a taxi or tuk-tuk *and on no account risk jumping into an unlicensed taxi at Bangkok's Don Muang Airport at any time of the day: there have been some very violent robberies in these, so take the well-marked authorised vehicles instead. In the north you should be wary of motorbiking alone in uninhabited and politically sensitive border regions.*

—Paul Gray and Lucy Ridout,
The Rough Guide Thailand

Still, I hated the heat so much, I was willing to risk walking at night. Even a police officer who rode up to me on his little motorcycle the evening I left Phet Buri and forbade me to go any farther on foot was not enough to make me change my mind. I tried to justify my foolishness by reminding myself of all the hundreds of times on the walk I had heard people cry wolf before.

And so, deeper into the dusk and then into the night of that mid-April day I pushed myself, hoping that the same guardian angel who had helped me make it unscathed through so many of the world's other danger spots would not abandon me for at least one more night.

It was around 11:30 on a moonless stretch of empty road thirteen miles south of Phet Buri when I found out just how far I could go on insulting common sense. This time it *was* the wolf—or rather, the wolves. And, worse, there was no one to hear my screams. Nothing but empty pineapple fields, jungle, and the thickly muscled men behind the machetes.

Then I looked down the tall bank on which the road had been built to keep it out of the quicksand and soggy peat of the jungle, and saw two men crouching in the tall weeds between me and a fire-blackened pineapple field. Quickly, deftly, they came at me with their long, thick machetes poised.

I stood frozen with fear and shock that my life was to end in some snake-infested jungle. Why or how I even thought to do it I will never know, but at the last split-second something caused me to raise my folded umbrella to my right shoulder, take aim at the bandits' faces, and yell through my mouth in a ferocious voice:

"HALT! OR I'LL SHOOT"

It was the craziest, most insane deception I'd ever tried, but it worked. It brought me that extra second I needed to think about how I might escape. For the slightest of moments, the men paused in their advance and looked confusedly at the long, metal-tipped object in my arms. Meanwhile, in my own head the voices of reason were running amok.

Steve! What are you doing?! They're going to see it's only an umbrella. No rifle has red, blue, and yellow stripes running up and down it, for crying out loud! scolded one side of my brain.

Well, what'll I do! I don't have any tanks or bazookas! pleaded a higher-pitched voice from the other side.

Run! came the chorus.

If I'd waited just a second more, I would never have made it away. The bigger and uglier of the bandits had already decided he was being made a fool of. Even as my body was turning to run, the machete in his thick right arm was swooshing past my face close enough to guarantee I would not blink again the rest of the night.

Running for all my long, skinny legs and flailing arms were worth, I struck back out in the direction of Bangkok as though the entire Russian Army were on my heels. Desperately, I willed any car, truck, scooter, or policeman in Asia to come roaring down the road just then. But the long, dark ribbon of asphalt ahead of me stretched emptily on and on.

Since my legs were probably nearly as long as the bandits were tall, I was able to get quite a jump at first. But that was soon dissipated by the awkward weight of my backpack causing my rubbery limbs to go everywhere, it seemed, but straight ahead. As the patter of the bandits' own shoes drew nearer and nearer to my back, I was like a marathon runner at the halfway mark of the race, before he has caught his second wind. Yet the big bandit passing me on my left looked strangely serene and refreshed, as if he were out for a casual jog. He was carrying his machete in his raised right hand, as though he were a torchbearer in an Olympiad.

"Hey! Stay away with that! I'm a nice guy, I never hurt anyone! You don't want to rob me!" I said over and over, as he passed me as effortlessly as if I were standing still.

But he stopped before me and waited. He knew he had me, that I was dead. And I had to agree, when I heard his partner's shoes pounding closer from somewhere just behind.

Then, with a howl, I did the only thing I could think of: I charged madly at the bandit in front, trying my very best to get him to eat my umbrella. He slashed away at the heavy umbrella stabbing and pounding at his face. Crying, screaming, cursing, spitting, yelling, barking, pleading a thousand words, a minute, I whirled and jumped and dived and dodged like a man who has half a dozen cobras and a couple hundred fire ants down his pants. And so it might have continued until one of us dropped from exhaustion, or my umbrella fell apart.

But then the other bandit caught up with our strange sword fight. Grabbing my pack, he pulled me backward, away from his hapless partner, and let fly with his own machete. From the corner of my right eye, I could see his machete's blade sweep toward my neck. My mind went blank, as if refusing to feel the blade slice through my skull and neck, but was jarred back when the blade hit my pack's exterior frame, an inch from my jugular vein.

Not for a second did my wild gyrations stop. If only to stay alive for another few seconds, I fought on with a new surge of fury. And suddenly the bandit in front looked as if he were seeing a ghost and ran off into the jungle.

I whirled to confront the other—only to see headlights bearing down on me like two runaway comets.

Waving my arms frantically, I charged the lights and screamed at the Datsun pickup truck as it passed me.

The truck's brake lights flashed on.

I rushed to its back end, but it was piled so high with loose pineapples that I doubted even a monkey could have found a handhold. Wasting not a second, for I knew the bandits would come as soon as they saw the driver was not the police, I scrambled to the passenger door's window. The front seat was crowded with a farmer, his wife, and two young girls. Even without my pack, I couldn't have fitted a leg in alongside them. But I had to make the truck's passengers realize I was inches from literally losing my head.

With the ragged umbrella flailing in my right hand, my left one demonstrating my plight by slicing and stabbing me silly with an invisible knife, I ranted and raved outside the door, as the eyes in the truck expanded in terror.

When I saw the shaking farmer's hand fly to the gearshift on the floor, my skin leaped a mile. If they drove off without me, I was a dead man. Throwing all caution to the stars, I tore open the door and jammed my arms, shoulders, head, and what I could of my pack inside. Onto and across the girls' legs I wriggled madly, my hands groping blindly for anything to hold onto.

Over the next several minutes, as the truck sped down the road with my legs flopping out the side, it was a scene even a nightmare would have had difficulty matching for sheer confusion: everyone was screaming; my heart was pounding against my eardrums; and in my mind I saw the bandits sprinting alongside the truck trying to grab my legs so they could chop them off.

Though I had no ideas what it was I had grabbed to keep myself in the truck, I was aware that it was soft, and screaming something frightful.

Only when the truck eased to a stop in what was a tiny police shack's dirt yard did I finally loosen my eagle grip. Then I found to my embarrassment that for two miles I had been hanging entirely by the poor farmer's wife's breasts. Though I had grabbed her in her stomach area, I had latched onto her bra-less breasts because they hung low.

And it seemed I wasn't finished tormenting her yet. While trying to act out for the two policemen at the post that I had just been attacked by bandits, I kept pointing frantically down the road, putting an imaginary rifle to my shoulder, and shouting, "Bandits! Go kill! SHOOT!"

Only instead of putting some clothes on—they were in their underwear—and hopping onto their little Honda scooter to go after the bandits, they kept giving me the meanest looks. Because standing in the direction I was pointing was the bent-over old woman beside the truck, still trying to coax her chest back into shape. The policemen thought I was telling them to blast the poor innocent woman.

Eventually, everyone came to understand what I was jabbering about. The policemen put on some pants and boots and puttered away with a rifle in the direction of the ambush. But of course they were too late. All they found was a silent road, and my crippled umbrella.

Later that night, as I was lying on the floor in the back room of the wooden post, listening uneasily to splashing sounds in the swamp outside and watching the gecko lizards chase each other across the dingy ceiling, a familiar voice I'd struggled with so often the past years spoke to me again:

There is nothing to be ashamed of in quitting, Steve. You have gone far enough. Everyone will understand. Why risk your life anymore? You can't expect to continue to be so lucky in escaping from death.

But I knew that quitting anything because of fear somehow did not seem "right." To give up now would have been proof of how terrible the world is to those so eager to condemn it.

I had to keep going, if only to show there were not as many bandits as some were trying to make us believe.

Some things in life couldn't be explained in words. And certainly one of those was fear, that mysterious cloud on the human spirit. Why some were so willing to be its slaves, while others chose to challenge it to the last round would probably be something I could spend a lifetime seeking an answer to....

Respectfully, I eased myself onto the cold earth behind the five men, just outside the globe of the candles' glows. And with much inner groaning, I tried to coerce my stiff legs into the lotus position favored by the monks.

From atop a low altar in front of them, a golden Buddha with feline eyes, long ears, and a benign smile gazed down upon the disciples. Mountains of candle wax lay at its feet, a yellowing stratum of ancient prayers and long sultry nights spent in silent meditation.

While the monks' attention retreated inside themselves, my own flitted about the temple, darting from shadow to shadow to see what surprises their holy grotto held. There were many: a pair of long deer antlers protruding from a skull like gnarled stalagmites; enormous hand-sized spiders resting on their webs; a dozen moldy and stained paintings of the Buddha's mortal life in India over 2,500 years ago; short blank paper prayer slips, and squares of gold-colored foil stuck onto the statues like freckles run amok; portraits of the present-day king and queen dressed in the costumes of their ancestors.

A rustle of rough cloth brought my eyes back to the monks. They were bowing low, as if in response to an unspoken command. I bowed, too, lest some misfortune fall upon my head for not being attentive. Deep chanting filled the cave:

"Araham samma sambuddho bhagava. Buddham bhagavatam abivademi...The Lord Buddha, the perfectly enlightened and blessed one. I bow before the Buddha, the exalted one...."

I had not expected to have any close contact with the religious community of this nearly totally Buddhist society. But because of the attack by the two bandits near Phet Buri, and the stories I heard of thieves who liked to slit their victims' throats while they were sleeping, I knew I could no longer walk at night. And so I had decided to seek refuge in the *wats* whenever I did not have a family to take me into a home.

While a few of the *wats* I had stayed in since that frightful night were large and centerpieced with a tall and glittering temple, most were a tiny cluster of stilt-legged plank huts deep inside a forest or at the base of some half-wild mountain. Gardens of tranquility, those little *wats* were normally occupied by a handful of elderly monks who wanted a place to spend their final years undisturbed. Occasionally, there might also be a lone *maichee* (nun), humbly dressed, her head also shaved. Always there were the stray animals and chickens, dashing about in search of food scraps.

Though rarely visited by anyone other than the village children and the farm wives bringing food and idle conversation, the monks did not shy away from my unexpected appearance. They always showed me the bathing well or stream, then waved me up rickety steps to their one-room bungalows for some hot Ovaltine and a meal of rice, fish, and boiled bamboo. Furnished with little more than a straw sleeping mat, a mosquito net, a kerosene lamp, a small altar, and perhaps shelves crowded with old prayer books and a few chipped teacups, their dwellings reflected their humble views of man's existence.

The south of Thailand is a distinct part of the country—there are more Thai Muslims, as opposed to the central and northern Buddhists, the closer one gets to the Malaysian border.

—Peter Aiken, "Thai Waterways"

At most of the *wats,* my stay was no longer than one night. I stayed at one, though—Wat Suan Moke—near the city of Surat Thani, for over two weeks. Its head monk, the Venerable Buddhadasa, was said to be one of the world's greatest living masters of the Buddha's teachings, but it was from the monk just under him, the Venerable Poh, that I received an invitation to pause and rest my body and soul.

I decided to try the life of a monk while I was there, both the mental and the physical aspects. To do so meant I had to dissociate myself from all my normal habits and, most important, from my own ego. Like the monks, I was to live a life filled with inner meditation and learning to achieve harmony with the forces of nature. It was a demanding and—contrary to popular image—a very grueling life-style. I had to learn to go every day without doing anything that might distract me from concentrating on my inner "light" or peace. I could not speak to anyone other than my teacher (Poh), could not make eye contact, write, read, listen to the radio, make music, eat meat, leave the *wat's* secluded compound, or kill any living creatures, including ants and mosquitoes.

In the end, my mind proved too restless. Nor were all the scorpions and snakes that surprised me on the paths of that forest monastery helpful to my concentration.

The monsoon rains had caught up with me at Wat Suan Moke, and with them had come hordes of what I hated more than snakes—mosquitoes. It was bad enough trying to take a bath in a creek where I had to dance around leeches and scoop up the water in a droopy plastic pail. But to have to fight off a million frenzied bloodsuckers at the same time was more than I thought even Buddha could have endured...

"You must see that this 'I' and 'mine' is the main cause of all forms of pain and unhappiness," Poh said in a very low voice the last night I was there, as the glow from a ring of kerosene lamps played off his impassive eyes. "Whenever there is a clinging to anything, then there is the darkness of ignorance. There is no clarity, because the mind is not empty."

"And what of my dread of another attack by bandits?" I asked.

"One does not look on anything as ever having been, as currently being, or as having the potential to be self or belong to self. There is no self in the present and no basis for anxiety regarding self in the past or future," he replied in his usual serious, indecipherable way.

One thing of Poh's I did decipher, though, was *his* worry for me, on the morning he came to see me off. It was at the same huge front gate where we'd met two weeks ago that he said, "I wish you would consider taking a bus. Otherwise, I will worry so much."

"But I am walking. You know that," I replied.

"I know...I know," was all he said, letting his eyes say the rest.

When I walked through the monastery's tall front gate to continue on my way to Malaysia, I told myself I was unquestionably a much calmer person...even if poor Poh was still fretting.

Steven M. Newman also contributed "Flying Kites" in Part Three of this book.

★

The railway network in Thailand, run by the Thai government, is surprisingly good. After traveling several thousand kilometers by train and bus, I have to say that the train wins hands down as the best form of public transport in the kingdom. It is not possible to take the train everywhere in Thailand, but if it were that's how I'd go. If you travel third class, it is often the cheapest way to cover a long distance; by second class it's about the same as a "tour bus" but much safer and more comfortable. The trains take a bit longer than a chartered bus but, on overnight trips especially, it is worth the extra time it takes.

The trains offer many advantages; there is more space, more room to breathe and stretch out—even in third class—than there is on the best buses. The windows are big and usually open, so that there is no glass between you and the scenery—good for taking photos—and more to see. The scenery itself is always better along the rail routes compared to the scenery along Thai highways—the trains regularly pass small villages, farmland, old temples, etc. Decent, reasonably priced food is available and served at your seat or in the dining car. The pitch-and-roll of the railway cars is much easier on the bones, muscles, and nervous system than the quick stops and starts, the harrowing turns, and the pot-hole jolts endured on buses. The train is safer in terms of both accidents en route and robberies. Last, but certainly not least, you meet a lot more interesting people on the trains, or so it seems to me.

—Joe Cummings, *Thailand - a travel survival kit*

CHARLES NICHOLL

✦ ✦ ✦

Poppy Fields

*On the opium trail, the author comes face to face
with "Old Longhead"—and himself.*

INSIDE THE HAW'S GLOOMY STOREROOM APPA WAS PURCHASING
opium. I watched through the bead curtain. The trader had a fat
black wedge of the stuff, two or three kilos, wrapped in banana
leaves and polythene. I guessed it was produce the Shan men had
sold him. He tore off a small piece, showed it to Appa, said something which sounded like a price. Appa nodded.

Harry was at my shoulder. "Let's go in. He won't mind. This
is just a casual deal."

They looked up when we walked in but didn't say anything.
Harry asked to look at the opium Appa was still holding. He said
to the Haw, "*Chandu, mai?*" The Haw nodded. He asked how
much for this piece. The Haw said, "One hundred baht." Harry
said he would buy some too.

"Is that a good idea, Harry?"

"You wouldn't want to leave without tasting some of the local
produce would you?" He said it lightly, but I saw the skulking
look in his eye. There are some battles you never win.

Chandu, Harry explained, is proper smoking opium. The raw
opium, the stuff we saw on the poppy pods, is dissolved in hot
water, strained through a cotton cloth, then the water is boiled off.

405

It is one stage purer than raw opium. From *chandu* they then make morphine base, and from that heroin, but neither the hill-tribe grower nor the Haw trader would have anything to do with those later stages.

The trader took down a wooden case, teak, shaped like a small violin case. Inside was a set of iron balances, and, each nesting in a separate compartment, half a dozen weights sculpted in the plump shape of the Chinese Buddha. He chose the second small-est. It squatted in the shallow iron bowl of the weights. I remem-bered the shrine at the Gipsee Rose strip club: you meet the Buddha in the strangest company, and I suppose that is one of the beauties of Buddhism.

Actually—as Katai soon pointed out—Buddhism is not at all in favour of intoxicants. Monks, of course, may take no drugs or alcohol, though they can and frequently do smoke to-bacco. She told of the legend that the Buddha, when he was strug-gling towards the light of *dharma,* cut off his eyelids to stop himself from falling asleep. Where his eyelids fell there grew the first opium poppy, a symbol of the falsehoods—false rest, false vi-sions—that the *bodhisattva* must cast aside on his quest for the true light.

O pium, and its medicinal derivative morphine, was introduced to the West in 1815 after a German pharmacist isolated the principal alkaloid and named it for Morpheus, the Greek god of dreams. Public usage became com-monplace in the early 20th century after Bayer, the pharmaceutical company, promoted diacetyl morphine (heroin) as a miracle cure and packaged the pills in small boxes marked with lions and globes. The Bayer trademark was later used by Laotian traffickers who sold their product under the Double-Globe brand.

—Carl Parkes,
Thailand Handbook

We walked to another village, an hour's walk, then a steep climb. This was a Lahu village: less colourful than the Akha—in none of the Lahu villages I visited did I see people wearing traditional costume—but very friendly. Here we were invited to drink and eat. A huge *burri* of local tobacco was tamped into a bamboo pipe and passed around.

One of the Lahu boys got out a musical instrument. It was a kind of banjo, wood and hide, with three wire strings fastened to pegs at the neck. He played a mournful, striding sort of tune, three chords, hill-tribe blues.

Inside, the women were preparing us a meal. Strips of pork fat were torn from a row of meat hanging from the rafters. These were fried in a wok on the fire. In another rice cakes sizzled. I passed round the tea wine that Katai had given—"a present for my two *farang*"—when she came back all breathless across the bridge at Mae Sai.

The hut was filled with lumber and rags, broken farm tools, cobwebs and shed dust. Appa was quiet, aloof. Perhaps he was just relaxing. Perhaps, though I couldn't really believe this, he was tired. We ate our meal. The Lahu squatted on the balcony opposite, watching each mouthful with pleasure.

One of them told a mischievous story about the Akha, how in the "early time," the Great Creator's sons and daughters all paired up, and out of their unions came the various hill tribes: the Lahu and the Lisu, the Meo and Yao, and so on. But the Akha boy had no partner, so he was forced to marry a monkey in the jungle in order to found his dynasty.

Appa laughed, showing his betel-blackened teeth. In his village, he said, they told the same story about the Lahu.

Harry and I sat side by side on a low bed in Appa's house at Pa Kha. He had invited us back to smoke the opium we had acquired from the Haw. Katai had declined and returned to the *guess how* [guest house].

Appa's wife brewed Chinese tea in a kettle. She squatted by the smouldering fire, muttering at it as she fanned the embers. She was a small, quiet, amiable woman. She wore no headdress, just a scarf of cloth on her head, but she wore the embroidered leggings, and the short indigo skirt with the long sash hanging down, for modesty's sake, when she sits or squats.

Their son was there too, a stocky boy in his teens. He wore a t-shirt that said, for no particular reason, "Block Bust." He was shy at first, though later he talked with us.

The house was dark and low and redolent of woodsmoke. Chinks of light glowed through the bamboo walls. Apart from the low doorway, curtained off with blankets, these were the only source of light in the hut. It was a "ground house," built on a floor of packed earth, rather than up on piles with air underneath. We were up at about 5,000 feet here, the higher altitude range for hill tribes. The mornings can be misty and chilly, and these low-built houses retain the warmth better. In terms of tribal status, elevated houses are more up-market, because they're harder to build. There were some of these at Pa Kha but not Appa's.

There was a raised area to the right of the doorway as you came in. There were two mattresses here, covered with blankets, and between them lay the blackened clutter of Appa's opium kit: bamboo-stem pipes with small metal bowls, a wick lamp, dibbers and needles, and a small rusty knife.

Also among the impedimenta were several sachets, one or two revealing white powder inside. For a moment I thought it was heroin but I knew this was unlikely. The hill tribes have nothing to do with heroin as such. I saw more of the white powder scattered around, mixed with the black ashy detritus of previous sessions.

I asked Harry what the powder was. He looked down at the sachets. Something seemed to surprise him. He reached out to pick one of them up. "I don't believe it," he murmured.

"What is it?"

"It's Old Longhead!"

"What do you mean, Old Longhead?"

He laughed, "It's just aspirin. Chinese headache powder. They mix it with opium." I asked him what for. "It's mostly to bind the opium. When its fresh, it's a bit too wet, unstable. They put the aspirin in, like straw into the mud to make a brick. Some people say the aspirin also stops you getting a bad head after you've smoked."

He handed me the sachet: it had smudgy Chinese characters on it, black on green, and a line drawing—done in the timeless, tacky, joke-shop style—of a man with a hugely elongated forehead.

"The strange thing is," Harry said, "I haven't seen Old Longhead for maybe twenty years. When I was a smoker, in Vientiane, the rickshaw boys used to mix it in. It was always this brand: the guy with the great long headache. So after a while we—not the Lao boys: I mean the French—we used to make it our word for opium. Monsieur Tête Longue. *Allons visiter Monsieur Tête Longue…*"

He tossed the sachet back onto the tray, laughed dryly. "Well, here I am back again, *mon vieux.*"

Appa lay on one bed, propped up on his elbow. We sat on the other, drank the tea his wife gave us—muddy and luke warm, nothing of the pungency of the Haw lady's brew—and watched him preparing the first bowl of opium.

First he scraped out the bowl of the pipe, made a small pile of black residue: ash and oxidized opium from the previous session, the "tailings" as Harry called it. He explained that they often mix this with the opium, to make an inferior but cheaper smoke. Tonight we would be smoking pure *chandu*.

Appa gently tore a small piece off the wedge of opium. In the lamplight I saw the rich colour of the opium, where it was stretched and pulled. It was a deep reddish-brown, the colour of a young conker, the colour of plum jam. He kneaded the piece between his fingers, mixed in some of the powdered aspirin. He

> "*Ngan*" has two diametrically opposed meanings: "work" and "party." Thais approach each with the other's attributes. On the one hand, they take a relaxed approach to work, seldom burning the midnight oil. Conversely, they may stay up until dawn several nights running to prepare a floral float for a festival.
>
> —Steve Van Beek,
> "Thailand Notes"

now had a rounded pellet the size of a large pea. He impaled it on the end of a dibber, a thin metal spike about six inches long, and heated it over the meager flame of the wick-lamp. He held it so that the ball was just at the fringes of the flame, never quite touching. He kneaded some more, his fingers grimed with opium and carbon. It was now ready for smoking. He pushed it into the shallow bowl of the pipe, held the bowl at an angle over the flame, and wrapped his lips around the bamboo mouthpiece. Still the opium must not touch the flame. It sizzles and sweats but never quite burns. He used the dibber to prod and tease the melting pellet, to keep the airway open, to keep the smoke coming. He took the smoke in, slow and level, in one long grateful draught. The mellow, sickly smell spread through the dark hut.

The light faded unnoticed. After a few bowls everything takes on a loose, underwater feel. If you close your eyes you can easily imagine that you're floating, that these ripples of sensation are carrying you off through the darkness, and when you open your eyes again you'll be somewhere else: but where?

Harry quotes Rimbaud, of course: "*Comme je descendais les fleuves impassibles….*"

Everything is now done in the horizontal position that opium exacts. Appa is propped on one elbow, smoking, preparing, face close over the lamp, restful and intent. When your turn comes round, you crawl into the smoking position, lying on your side, head resting on a pillow of old clothes. You are like a child in your posture. Someone could come and cover you with a blanket, and you'd smile and say "Thank you" without looking up. Your eyes are on the pipemaker, his grimed hands nudging the gear into the bowl, his face lit up from the wick lamp, his Chinese eyes with the pin-prick pupils. He swings the long stem towards you, the opium sputters, you suck the woody smoke down as slow as you can (though taking three or four draughts where Appa only took one). You can taste the smoke but hardly feel it, it's so mild. The taste is sweet. The taste is bitter. Your eyes are still on the pipemaker. You fear that if you look too long into his eyes you will disappear into them, tumble slowly down long black tunnels, like Alice down the rabbit hole. But nothing matters, least of all your fears.

Harry said this was high-quality opium, this was stuff the tourist trekker would never get. I said benevolently, "You get it right, don't you, Harry? You get the best out of things."

He said, "Code of the road," and we laughed.

Harry told me I would probably be sick for some time. This was natural, because I didn't "have the habitude" for opium. I had already felt twinges of nausea, but found that as long as I didn't move too much, as long as I lay still, with my eyes shut, the sickness remained somehow apart from me. It was happening in some distant region: my body. Most of all you don't want to stand up. Your two-legged self, upright and uptight, has gone off somewhere, and left this smiling cadaver with enough motor energy to talk, to light cigarettes, and to crawl into place for the next bowl.

We lay side by side on the bed. We talked up to the ceiling. Harry drifted into reminiscence: his "smoking days" in Vientiane, back in the '60s.

The Laotian capital in those days probably had a heavier concentration of opium dens than any other city in the world, he said. "The spooks at the U.S. embassy had done a survey, you could say, considering the stakes the Yanks had in the opium business in those days. They found there were a thousand *fumeries* in Vientiane, give or take. That's about one for every fifty men, women, and children in the city.

"There were *fumeries* in the centre of town, and all around The Strip, but the best opium I ever smoked was out on the edge of town. You'd get a rickshaw boy to take you there, to the places where they smoked themselves. These were rough places. I mean, these were the shanties, nothing fancy. But the opium was so sweet, man, so strong. You could spend a night and a day in there, never realize the time.

"In the next shack there's the rickshaw boy's coffee shop. Here they sell you *café électrique*. That's strong black coffee with amphetamine laced in. Speed coffee. So the boys would come in, have a few bowls, then a shot of *café électrique,* and then they go out to work again. The rickshaw boys, they never slept.

"The *fumeries* in the residential quarter were something else. They were high-class dens. Like Madam Chang's. That's where you went if you wanted to discuss a little something, some *beez-ness clandestin,* perhaps. It was a very cosmopolitan clientele. You'd meet the *colons* there, the good old trading boys. I remember one old man, his name was Mazarin, so of course we called him the Cardinal. He was a teak merchant, had a Lao wife or two, knew the country back home. He was what we call *un vrai Indochinois.* He'd be there every night at Madam Chang's, had his own pipe, his special pipemaker: she was a lot prettier than this guy here, I can promise you!

"I remember he said to me once: the first time you smoke the opium, he said, it is like the first time you look into the eyes of a beautiful woman, and you *know* you're going to regret you ever met her.

"Sometimes I'd smoke it up in the hills, with the *montagnards.* The Hmong tribe: they call them Meo in Thailand. They had a kind of legend about the opium poppy. There was once a Hmong who fell in love with a fair-skinned *farang* girl. The girl died and out of her corpse there bloomed an opium poppy. The *montagnard* says: the sap of the poppy is sweet, as she was; the sap of the poppy relieves my sorrow, as she did.

"There is another opium legend too, but perhaps you do not know. It is the story of Narcissus. The flower *Narcissus* is not the daffodil, as we have it. It is the opium poppy. It is from the Greek word *narke,* numbness. My friend the Cardinal told me about this: he was a scholar of such things. Narcissus is the opium smoker. He stares into the black pool of the opium reverie. He sees there his own face, his own self. He finds it beautiful. When you smoke the opium you look inside you. Some people, they don't ever want to look outside any more. They fall in love with the dream. They die beside the pool, like Narcissus.

After eight or ten pipes we were no more disposed to talk. We lay sprawled on the bed, like Narcissus beside the pool. When I shut my eyes I started to get the visions.

I see faces, but not my own. I see the faces of Appa, and of Harry and Katai, and of the Shan man who grew the poppies and the Haw trader who sold the opium. Then the portrait gallery takes on a random life of its own. I see my mother and father as I knew them when I was small. They are sitting in the Old Hillman brake that got stuck on the one-in-three at Lydford Gorge. Faces come up of people I haven't seen for twenty years, the mathematicians and carpenter's wives of my life, and now here is L'Italienne, the beautiful woman you regret you ever met, seen exactly, in a certain garden, wearing my check shirt, laughing as I tell her in my teenage poetic frenzy that she's like the Hyacinth Girl in *The Waste Land*. But now the faces are beginning to speed up. They are taking on elasticity and movement. Some of these people I definitely don't know. They are twisting and deforming. They are growing pustules and carbuncles. They are doing Les Dawson faces. They are entering cycles of decay and putrefaction before my eyes.

Then I start to think I might be dying. This is the movie, the roll-call, passing before the drowning man. It strikes me that, of course, it *has* to speed up like this, to get it all in before you go. Drowning is what this death would be like, drowning in the black pool. This is for a moment a real fear, but so distant, like a voice calling far enough away to be ignored. The fear passes, as everything passes, serenely across and out of mind. Perhaps when you die you are silently inwardly laughing at these visions, as I am now: laughing at this Keystone Cops caper, laughing scared through these crummy ghost-train tunnels, laughing so hard your lips don't even move.

I know I can snap out of it if I want to. All I need to do is flick open my eyes. I look up into the rafters, try to make out the shapes up there, things stored, rags and bones and corn-cobs. I close my eyes again, and now there's nothing there, just these ripples spreading through my body when my hand moves to scratch an insect-bite, or when Harry shifts beside me, or even when there is a murmur from Appa or his wife; the tiniest disturbance registering on the quiet black waters.

We slept where we lay, like drunken peasants in a Bruegel painting. Once in the night, as Harry had warned, I had to get up and be sick. There was a convenient spot not far from the hut. It was hardly like being sick at all: it came easily, copiously, painlessly.

Out there in the midnight I knelt and covered my vomit with dust
and leaves, and in the morning there was no trace of it at all.

*Charles Nicholl also contributed "Moonsong and Martin Luther" and
"Mekong Days" to this book, excerpted from his book,* Borderlines: A
Journey in Thailand and Burma.

★

> Breathe in, calming the mind.
> Breathe out, calming the mind.
> So taught the Buddha.
> —Tim Ward, *What the Buddha Never Taught*

PART FIVE

THE LAST WORD

VATCHARIN BHUMICHITR

* * *

By the Sea

*A Thai man reflects on subtle changes
near his childhood holiday home.*

HOLIDAYS AT THE SEASIDE HOLD THE SAME ATTRACTIONS FOR THAI children as for those of any other land: swimming, building sand castles, beach football. I, however, always found greatest pleasure in walking alone for hours down an endless strand of white beach. I liked to stop and stare into a rock pool, watching a creature tentatively peep out of its shell, and I was always amused by the near transparent ghost-crabs scuttling sideways, as if turning cartwheels, before diving into their impossibly tiny holes in the sand. The only things which ever worried me were the giant jelly fish, washed into the shallows during the rainy season. These monsters could be found on the beach when the tide went out and I would sometimes pick them up with two sticks to throw them out of reach of the sea, so that there would be one less danger for swimmers.

As a child I would stay at my great-aunt's house at Hua Hin, a beach resort a half-day's drive from Bangkok, on the western shore of the Gulf of Thailand. As the daughter of a prince, it was almost obligatory that my great-aunt should have her holiday house in Hua Hin which, since the '20s, had been a second home for the Thai nobility. The region around Hua Hin had known royal visitors since the last century, but it was the construction of the railway link

417

between the capital and Malaya, after the First World War, that put the sleepy seaside town within a four-hour train journey of Bangkok. In 1926 King Rama VII began work on his villa, Klai Kangwan, "Far from worries," and this brought in its wake beach bungalows built by princes, princesses, and other court officials in the then fashionable style of English suburban bungalows. Visitors could stay at the Railway Hotel, a fairy tale construction of wooden verandas with Victorian-style fretwork awnings, with topiary hedges carved into the shapes of animals apparently grazing on the well-watered lawns.

The king was to discover that "Far from worries" was hardly the most appropriate name for his new residence for, in 1932, word came that there had been a revolution in Bangkok. Overnight His Majesty had been transformed from an absolute to a constitutional monarch. None of this affected Hua Hin, which spent the next thirty years as a pleasant place for the well-to-do, away from any unrest in the capital. The town remained the country's principal resort until the Thai government started actively to promote tourism about twenty years ago. This led to the booming growth of Pattaya as the Miami Beach of Southeast Asia, a gaudy promenade of skyscraper hotels, discos, massage parlours, and international restaurants on the opposite side of the Gulf from sleepy old Hua Hin. The tourists have flocked to Pattaya. European ladies bare their breasts by the swimming pools, Arabs from the more puritan parts of Islam come to enjoy the sins of the flesh, and every nationality can be found along its garish neon-lit main street, out for the evening stroll.

The more discriminating visitor has had to go further round the Gulf to enjoy the real pleasures of Thailand's coast, its wide deserted beaches and its simple fisher-folk life. Until ten years ago, those in the know made the journey to the island of Phuket, off the western side of the narrow isthmus that divides Thailand from Malaysia. Set in the Andaman Sea, the island offered simple accommodations in beach-side huts and the pleasures of freshly caught fish and lobster grilled on an open fire. Nearby was Phangnga Bay, one of the world's most extraordinary natural beauty spots, a seascape dotted with surreal limestone outcrops; thin yet dizzyingly tall, rising dramatically out of the placid green waters. Built out into the bay on stilts, a fishing village offered wonderful food in a setting of breathtaking beauty. Too good to last, for in 1979 an international airport was opened and the hotels began to spring up. However, there is no need to despair, Thailand has many islands, and the adventurous can always keep one jump ahead of the builders. Today, young travellers backpack their way to the island of Koh Samui or continue down the coast from Pattaya to Koh Samet, a journey which takes them to the town of Rayong—famous as the main centre for the most essential ingredient in Thai food, fish sauce. There's no mistaking it, the whole place smells of drying fish. To offset the odour is the intriguing sight of thousands of pinkly translucent squid hung on lines to dry in the sun, like hosts of strange butterflies caught in gossamer nets.

While new resorts like Pattaya were springing up, Hua Hin still remained largely unchanged. There was the addition of one or two more modern beach houses built by successful companies to provide weekend rest for their tired executives, but overall it was felt that the brasher aspects of the tourist trade should not infringe on the Royal Family's holiday home. A few miles to the north, at Cha'am, a modern hotel was built, but it is so neatly secluded from the old town that most of the tourists who stay there do not know that a short distance from where they are staying is a piece of fantasy well worth finding—near the local army barracks, right on the beach is a pleasure house built by King Rama VI, a series of airy wooden rooms on stilts, linked by walkways and verandas, one of which goes on out into the sea like an English pier. This was a place for parties and dalliance. Until recently, no one seemed to be responsible for looking after it and it was slowly crumbling away. It had the look of a haunted palace, a place of dreams, the only visitors an occasional group of young people who had ignored the warnings and clambered out onto the pavillion above the water to eat a picnic, play music, and laze an afternoon away. Happily, a decision has now been made to try to restore this magical place.

Today, Hua Hin's atmosphere of gentle decay may be ending. Faded scions of the older aristocracy still come for their holidays but the place has acquired a new smartness among the sophisticated young, who are drawn to its old world charms. Change has been modest. The old Railway Hotel was spruced up with a coat of paint for its role as the Phnom Penh Hotel in the film *The Killing Fields,* and in 1986 the French Sofitel chain with their Thai partners undertook a sensitive restoration, keeping all the '30s fittings, so that the pleasures of the past have been improved by only the barest touches of modernity. My only complaint is that they have not kept the old name "The Railway Hotel," with its nostalgic image of pre-war travel. However, as we Thais believe that your luck is improved if you walk under an elephant, so for me the best way to savor Hua Hin is still to enter the hotel by its gardens, passing under an enormous bush shaped like an elephant. In the foyer of the hotel one can admire a photograph of Miss Thailand 1940, and look into cabinets displaying the porcelain and silverware once used by the old Siamese Railways—worth more than a glance. After an apertif you can ride in a *samloh* (a bicycle rickshaw) to the jetty, brightly flood-lit, where the larger motorized fishing boats have anchored. These are manned by tough deep-sea sailors, their arms blue with protective tatoos depicting religious or magical symbols. These wiry men live dangerously, often staying out for at least three days and nights at a time. The haul they bring in is huge, a tumbling avalanche of silvery fish destined for the shops and restaurants of Bangkok. At night, the scene is almost overdramatic: weird figures wear cloth hoods with eye-holes, like Halloween ghosts, to protect their skin from the sharp fish scales; ships about to depart are loaded with crushed ice which steams in the hot air, adding to the aura of mystery. After the best of the catch has been tossed from hand to hand, from boat to truck, the tiny sprats and the sweepings are loaded into baskets destined for the duck farms that supply Bangkok's insatiable appetite for that delicious bird.

Having admired the haul, it is time to sample it. There is a fish market at the entrance to the jetty and beside that, a row of restaurants. It is to one of these wooden rooms, jutting out on stilts over the water, that the visitor must go for an evening meal. At the entrance is a brightly lit stall groaning under the results of the owner's bargaining session with the fishermen: a cascade of glistening clams, white and purple squid, a tank crowded with so many fish only the fisher-folk know their names. But the diners will have no problem choosing their meal, a young helper will offer a book of photographs illustrating the cook's specialties. She can be seen just behind the stall waiting near her wok for the choice of ingredients to be made. A fish is pointed out, the net dips into the tank; mussels are selected, a handful are scooped up—all go into the wok so fast you can barely follow her movements. It is all as easy and as abundant as the seas and rivers of Thailand itself which teem with fish so that the smallest child can be sure of a catch. If Bangkok floods in the rainy season, shoals of fish migrate up the city's highways, darting and weaving about the half-submerged cars as if they were so many rocks.

After the main meal, diners can stroll from the restaurant to the Hua Hin market in the center of town where nighttime food stalls are set out with tropical fruit, sweetmeats and puddings, ice creams and cold drinks to finish off the evening's dining. If you are lucky enough to be staying in a beach bungalow you can return via the moonlit sands where the final pleasure is to watch the lights flickering on the boats of the in-shore fisherman waiting for the night's catch to enter their long line of nets. In the morning these shallow-bottomed boats will be dragged as near shore as possible offering the haul to the occupants of holiday homes. Crabs will be bought by the bucketful for a great steamed feast. There will be lobsters and prawns, floundering and scrabbing about in the bottom of the vessel. But at night these boats are merely dark shapes gently tossed on the returning tide while on the nearby headland a giant statue of the Buddha silently watches over the waters, offering protection to all those who live by the sea.

Vatcharin Bhumichitr is a Thai chef and restaurateur who has lived in England for many years. He is the author of A Taste of Thailand, *from which this was excerpted.*

WHAT YOU NEED TO KNOW

WHEN TO GO/WEATHER

Thailand's tropical climate is hot and humid year-round. The year is divided into three seasons: hot, cool, and rainy. The cool season, between mid-November and February, is the best time to visit. Temperatures are in the 80s and the air is dry; in the North, nighttime temperatures can drop to the low 40s so take a sweater. In the hot season, (March to May), temperatures average 93°F and commonly reach 105°F. With humidity hovering at 90 percent, it is a good time to head for the beaches, and Thailand has some of the most beautiful in Asia.

In the rainy season, temperatures range between 80°F and 90°F between June and mid-November. While September experiences the heaviest rainfalls, even it has bright sunny patches. Many travelers avoid this season but it offers the freshest air and the greenest scenery. After heavy storms in June, rains taper off from mid-July through August, prelude to the deluges of September. Rain falls heaviest in the south; lightest in the Northeast. From mid-September through mid-November, monsoon-swollen tides combine with storms to flood Bangkok's streets, bringing life to a standstill. It is a messy time but a great one for seeing how Thais cope in a carefree manner with adversity. If traveling upcountry, however, be prepared for washed out roads and railways.

CUSTOMS AND ARRIVAL

All visitors must have a passport valid for at least six months longer than their intended stay in Thailand.

Transit Visas

Those entering the country with an onward airline ticket and who plan to stay no more than 30 days can obtain a Tourist/Transit Visa on arrival. These visas cannot be extended. Stays up to 60 days require a Tourist Visa obtainable from a Thai diplomatic mission. They may be extended by 30 days at Immigration Department offices in Bangkok and major cities for 500 baht. Visitors overstaying their limit are fined 100B for each day upon departure.

Up to 200 cigarettes, 250 grams of cigars, and one liter of wine or spirits, can be imported duty free. Officially, one still camera, video camera, or movie camera, five rolls of still camera film, or three rolls of 8 to 16mm movie camera film may be brought into the country, but officials generally ignore camera-laden tourists, feeling that the photos they take will attract more visitors. Nonetheless, reasonably-priced major brands of film are available in Bangkok and tourist destinations, as is processing. Narcotics, obscene materials, firearms, and explosives are prohibited.

𝒢ETTING INTO THE CITY

Thai Airways International (thai) and several private companies offer air-conditioned limousine service to and from Bangkok's Don Muang International Airport; there is also direct service between the airport and the beach resort at Pattaya. Ordinary taxis can be hired at a desk on the south end of the airport. There are two types—metered and unmetered—and you are advised to use the unmetered. Air-conditioned airport buses make the 18-mile journey into the city along three routes and are a safe, economical means of reaching many destinations; luggage space is provided at no extra cost.

ℋEALTH

The only vaccinations required before entry are those for Yellow Fever from anyone who has visited an African nation in the preceding seven days. You are advised, however, to consider several vaccinations at least six weeks before you leave home. Opinions vary on what is necessary, but it's a good idea to have current immunizations for tetanus, typhoid, polio, Hepatitis A and B, Japanese B encephalitis, and rabies. See a tropical medicine specialist for the best advice.

Some Helpful Tips:

+ Get a checkup before you leave home. In the case of a medical emergency, Bangkok hospitals and doctors are first-rate.
+ Don't drink the tap water. Drink bottled water or purify tap water. Ice in large restaurants can be trusted.
+ Peel or boil vegetables and peel fruit before eating.
+ If you wear prescription glasses, bring an extra pair.
+ Rehydrate, rehydrate, rehydrate.
+ Take the proper precautions against mosquitoes: wear a good repellent and sleep under a net when possible. If there is no net or screen where you are sleeping, burn mosquito coils or use the inexpensive electric type that burn odorless pads.

Pack a medical kit which includes: aspirin or acetaminophen, antihistamine, antibiotics, Lomotil or Imodium for diarrhea, rehydration mixture, antiseptic such as iodine or Betadine, Calamine lotion, bandages, bandaids, tweezers, scissors, thermometer, cold and flu tablets, insect repellent, sunscreen, chapstick, water purification tablets, and possibly even sterile syringes with needles, dressings, and gloves. All, however, are available in pharmacies in Bangkok and major cities.

Also consider taking a travel kit of basic homeopathic remedies and a homeopathic first aid book. Such remedies can provide rapid relief from common travel ailments including gastrointestinal problems, fevers, and many acute conditions. Books and travel kits are available through your local health food store. If you come home with any serious tropical diseases, including malaria, effective treatment is available from homeopathic medical practitioners.

Emergency Assistance

If you have an unexpected health problem and don't know where to turn, the following hospitals in Bangkok tend to have a better understanding of the English language:

THE NEXT STEP

Bangkok General Hospital
2 Soi Soonvichai 7
Tel: 318-0066, 318-1549-52

Bumrungrad Hospital
33 Sukhumvit 3
Tel: 253-0250-69

Samitivej Hospital
Soi 49, Sukhumvit Road
Tel: 392-0061-5.

Travel Insurance and Assistance

It's a good idea to get a travel insurance policy to cover theft, loss, and medical problems. Your travel agent can recommend a good insurer. Be sure to read the fine print to see if the policy includes "dangerous activities," a.k.a. "all the fun stuff you want to do," (scuba diving, trekking, motorcycling). Also, check to see if the policy covers ambulances or emergency evacuation. If treated by a doctor in Thailand, keep all bills and receipts for processing claims back home.

Several U.S. and European companies provide emergency medical assistance for travelers worldwide, including 24-hour help lines, English-speaking doctors, and air evacuation in extreme cases. Travel agents and tour companies can recommend reliable companies.

TIME

Thailand is seven hours ahead of Greenwich Mean Time. Thus, when it's noon in Thailand, it is:
9 p.m. yesterday in San Francisco (10 p.m. during Daylight Savings months)
7 a.m. today in London
midnight today in New York (1 a.m. during Daylight Savings months)
1 p.m. today in Hong Kong
2 p.m. today in Tokyo
3 p.m. today in Sydney

Thais tell time both by the military system (1430 hours, etc.) and an ancient system based on six-hour segments. For all practical purposes you won't need to know this system, but its worthwhile being famliar with it. From 6 a.m. to noon, the classifier is "*chow*" (morning) as in "*nung* [1] *mong* [hour] *chow* [morning] (7 a.m.), *song* [2] *mong chow* (8 a.m.) etc. up to noon (*Tieng*). The six hours from noon to 6 p.m. are designated by the word "*bai*" as in "*bai song* [two] *mong*" (2 p.m.) although from 4 p.m. to 6 p.m., the hour is called "*yen*" [evening] as in "*ha* [five] *mong yen*" [5 p.m.]. From 6 p.m. to midnight, Thais use "*thum*" [the sound of a drumbeat], as in "*song thum*" (8 p.m.) etc. up to midnight (*song yaam*). From then to 6 a.m., the word "*thi*" [the sound of a gong being struck] precedes each hour designation i.e. "*thi song*" [2 a.m].

ℬUSINESS HOURS

Businesses are open Monday through Friday from 8:00 or 8:30 a.m. to 5:00 or 5:30 p.m. Large department stores are open from 10 a.m. to 9 p.m., seven days a week. Other stores generally open at 10, close at 6. Government offices are open 8:30 a.m. to noon, 1 p.m. to 4:30 p.m, Monday through Friday. Banks open at 8.30 a.m., close at 3.30 p.m., Mondays through Fridays. Foreign exchange kiosks operated by banks open at 9 a.m., close at 8 p.m.

ℳONEY

In Thailand, the unit of currency is the baht. It is divided into 100 satang. Paper money comes in denominations of 10B (brown), 20B (green), 50B (blue), 100B (red), 500B (purple), and 1,000B (gray). Brass coins are valued at 25 and 50 satang while silver coins are in denominations of 1, 2 and 5B. A 10B coin is composed of both silver and brass. There is no currency black market.

Credit cards (American Express, Visa, Master Card, and Diner's Club), debit cards, ATM cards and traveler's checks can all be used to obtain baht at ATM machines; there are over 2500 ATMs nationwide, but a minimum 1.5% surcharge is usually attached. Traveler's checks can be cashed at banks throughout the country, (even small towns have foreign exchange services); exchange rates are better than those for cash. The *Bangkok Post* and *The Nation* newspapers post the current exchange rates.

Visitors are allowed to bring up to 2,000B per person and unlimited foreign currency, although amounts exceeding US$10,000 must be declared. A maximum amount of 500B per person is allowed to be taken out of the country.

ELECTRICITY

Electric current is 220V, 50 cycles. Most electrical wall outlets accept the round, two pole plugs. You will find some that take the flat, two bladed terminals. Voltage converters and international plug adapters can be bought at any electrical supply shop.

MEDIA: NEWSPAPERS, RADIO, AND TELEVISION

Thailand's English-language press has recently been ranked the best in Asia, by a survey conducted by the Political and Economic Risk Consultancy. The group comprises 180 expatriate managers in 10 Asian countries, and cites the *Bangkok Post* and *The Nation* as their main source of regional and global news. The *Bangkok Post*, delivered in the morning, is better known for its international coverage, while *The Nation*, also a morning paper, is reputed to have better national and regional coverage. The *International Herald Tribune*, *Asian Wall Street Journal*, *Time*, *Newsweek* and other popular US and UK magazines can be found in bookstores in Bangkok, Chiang Mai, Phuket, and Pattaya. Metropolitan newspapers from major world cities are also sold, although the price is often high.

Radio Thailand, Bangkok's national public radio station, broadcasts English-language programs on 97 FM from 7 a.m. to 11 p.m. This is the station to listen to for up-to-date news reports, local, national, international news, sports, business, and special features. A similar station is 107 FM. BBC World Service, The Voice of America, Radio Canada, Radio New Zealand, Singapore Broadcasting Company, and Radio Australia all have English and Thai-language broadcasts over short-wave radio. The frequencies and schedules change regularly and can be found in the *Post* and *The Nation*.

ABC, CNN International and English-subtitled Thai programs can be found between 6 and 10 a.m. on Channel 5; English language news is aired at noon and 7 p.m.; CNN headlines are on again at 11:00 p.m. For other English-language programming turn to Channels 3, 7, 9, and 11. Most hotels offer cable and/or satellite service.

$\mathscr{T}$OUCHING BASE: PHONE CALLS, FAXES, POSTAGE, EMAIL

The postal and telecommunications system in Thailand is efficient. International calls, faxes, and telexes can be made from GPO telephone offices throughout the country. In most provincial capitals they are open daily from 7 a.m. to 11 p.m.; shorter hours prevail in smaller towns. Bangkok's international phone office in the GPO and at the Telephone Organization of Thailand (TOT) on Ploenchit Road next to the Le Meridian President Hotel, is open 24 hours. Large hotels offer DDD service from the room.

Air-mail letters and packages can be sent from any post office; the post office can sell you the packing boxes for small items. Travelers with American Express cards can receive mail at SEA Tourist Company Limited (2) 216-5934, 128 Rajthevee Road, Suite 88-92, 8-F Phayathai Plaza. Their hours are 8:30 to noon and 1 to 4:30 p.m. during the week, and 8:30 to 11:30 a.m. on Saturday.

Email can be quite costly in Thailand. Modem access can be found through the telephone lines in most of the larger hotels. To be on the safe side, bring a transformer to plug in your laptop in case your hotel is not equipped with the proper current converters. While

$\mathcal{T}$HE NEXT STEP

Internet Service Providers continue to grow in numbers and outreach, it is best to check with your provider about their international rates, policies, and access numbers before traveling.

CULTURAL CONSIDERATIONS

$\mathcal{L}$OCAL CUSTOMS: DOS AND DON'TS

* Disrespect for the monarchy is considered a serious offense in Thailand. Thais have a deep reverence for their royal family and visitors should show respect for the king, the queen, and the royal children. This includes standing when the royal anthem is played in a cinema or when they see others standing at attention when the national anthem is played at 8 a.m. and 6 p.m. daily.
* *Wai* is what the Thais do instead of shaking hands. You press your palms together as if praying, and raise them before your face.
* Maintain "*jai yen*," or a "cool heart." To the Thais, getting angry means a loss of face for everyone present. Hold your temper under all circumstances. Talking loudly is considered rude.
* Thais believe that the head is the most sacred part of the body. Do not touch anyone's head except very small children.
* Never stand over someone, especially monks and those older or wiser as it implies social superiority. To be courteous, lower your head when you pass a group of people.
* The feet are considered the lowest part of the body. Don't point them at people or objects and when seated, make sure the soles of your feet are not facing anyone. Do not step over anyone reclining on the ground.
* Don't sit on pillows or on books, both associated with the head.
* Shorts, sleeveless shirts, and tank tops are gaining popularity among young Thais but only in informal situations. Otherwise, dress casually but neatly. When visiting a Buddhist temple or Muslim mosque, dress conservatively and remember to take your shoes off when you enter.
* Nudity on beaches and public displays of affection is offensive to most Thais.

- You can stand next to or below a Buddha image while having your photo taken but not atop it or in its lap; tourists who overlooked this rule have been jailed. Buddhist monks must be treated with respect at all times; women are not allowed to touch them, nor can monks accept anything from a woman's hand. The back seats and front window seats on buses are reserved for the monks; passengers must vacate when necessary.
- Thais are sociable and often mix business with pleasure. The person who has extended the invitation pays for the meals or drinks. If it isn't clear who extended the invitation, the senior-most person at the table has the honor of paying. If you are the only foreigner present, it is polite to offer to pay but will generally not be accepted.
- Avoid scheduling a meeting after 3.30 p.m., because Thais like to get an early start on the evening rush-hour trip home.

*E*VENTS & HOLIDAYS

These days are observed as official public holidays:

- New Year's Day: January 1
- Magha Puja: February full moon
- Chakri Day: April 6
- Songkran: April 13
- Labor Day: May 1
- Coronation Day: May 5
- Visakha Puja: May full moon
- Asalaha Puja: July full moon
- H.M. the Queen's Birthday: August 12
- Chulalongkorn Day: October 23
- H.M. the King's Birthday: December 5
- Constitution Day: December 10
- New Year's Eve: December 31

Chinese New Year in January (date determined by lunar calendar) is not officially recognized as a holiday, but many shops close for four days.

THE NEXT STEP

Plan your visit to coincide with a Thai festival. Thais celebrate even their religious holidays with verve and invite the visitor to join in; do so, and enhance the enjoyment of a stay. Dates change from year to year; check with the Tourism Authority of Thailand (TAT) before finalizing your plans.

January–February

Borsang Umbrella Fair (North only). This colorful festival honors the craftsmen of one of the oldest Chiang Mai arts. Competitions and exhibitions are highlighted by the selection of Miss Borsang.

Flower Festival (North only). Held when Chiang Mai's flowers are abloom, it offers flower exhibitions and a grand floral procession through the city streets, with floats, marching bands and beautiful Chiang Mai women.

Magha Puja celebrates the spontaneous gathering of 1,200 disciples to hear Buddha preach. In the evening when the full moon is rising, Buddhists gather at *wats* to honor him. Arrive about 7 p.m. to buy incense sticks, a candle, and flowers from a vendor. After the sermon, follow the monk-led procession around the temple. After completing three circuits, place your candle, incense sticks and flowers in the sand-filled trays as others are doing, *wai* and depart.

March–April

Poy Sang Long (Mae Hong Son only). Young Shan hilltribe men ride elephants to the temples be initiated into the Buddhist monkhood.

Songkran, the traditional Thai new year, finds the Thais at their boisterous best. In Bangkok, on the first day Thailand's second most famous Buddha image, the Phra Buddha Sihing, is carried in solemn ceremony through the streets to Sanam Luang where it is anointed by the Buddhist faithful. On the second day, one is supposed to bless his friends by sprinkling water on them but it soon gets out of hand and water flies everywhere. Expect to get drenched and dress accordingly.

Phra Padaeng down the Thonburi side of the river celebrates in rowdier fashion.

May–June

The *Plowing Ceremony* marks the official beginning of the rice planting season. Presided over by His Majesty the King, this beautiful, semi-mystical rite predicts the amount of rainfall that will fall during the coming monsoon season. Sacred bulls are offered a variety of grains and seers note which ones they eat. Obtain free tickets beforehand at the Tourism Authority of Thailand office.

In the *Rocket Festival,* one of Thailand's most exciting festivals, villagers in northeastern towns, including Yasothon, build rockets of bamboo and pack them with homemade gunpowder. By so doing, the villagers hope to induce the sky to pour down rain in the coming rice season. The village whose rocket remains in the sky the longest, wins.

Chiang Rai's lychee harvest is sufficient reason for a celebration. The *Lychee Fair* features displays of agricultural products and handicrafts and a beauty contest to select Miss Lychee.

During the *Phi Taa Khon Festival* in Loei, townspeople dress as ghosts in remembrance of Buddha's last incarnation when spirits welcomed him back from exile. The costumes and masks are quite imaginative.

July–August

Candle Festival (Ubon). Beeswax is beautifully crafted into scenes from Buddhism and mythology and paraded through the streets to mark the beginning of the annual Rain's Retreat when monks meditate for three months.

Asalaha Puja commemorates Buddha's first sermon to his first five disciples. It is celebrated in the same manner as Magha Puja.

September–October

The Vegetarian Festival is the most unusual of Phuket's festivals. this Chinese celebration runs from the first to the ninth day of the ninth lunar month. There are daily processions through the streets of Phuket but its highlights are demanding tests of devotion. While in trances and thus oblivious to pain, devotees run skewers, hoses, spears, even Chiang Mai umbrellas through their cheeks and tongues. Among the most daring feats is walking barefoot across fiery coals. Other devotees, called "Soldiers of the Gods," climb ladders with rungs made of knives.

November–December

Buy tickets to sit on the terrace at the Sheraton Royal Orchid Hotel to watch, or join the thousands of others on the banks of the Chao Phya River between the Harbor Department and the hotel to watch the *Long-boat Regatta*. It begins at 8 a.m. and ends at 6 p.m.

Loy Krathong (in the North, called *Yi Peng Loy Krathong*) is the most beautiful of Thai celebrations. As the full moon is rising, Thais fill tiny floral boats with candles and incense and launch them into the rivers, canals, ponds, and the sea to wash away sins and bless love affairs. It is a romantic night for lovers of all ages. Buy a "krathong" from a vendor, light the taper and incense, place in it a small coin and a few hairs plucked from your head, say a prayer and send it on its way down a river, into a pond, or even on to a hotel swimming pool. In Chiang Mai, a procession through the streets begins about 6 p.m. The celebration begins about 7:30 p.m.

Sunflower Fair (Mae Hong Son only). When the Mexican Sunflowers bloom in the hills near Doi Mae U-Khor, Mae Hong Son organizes a three-day festival of oxcarts decorated with the beautiful flowers. Cultural exhibitions, a beauty contest, film shows, music and a Thai Yai Folk Drama are also presented.

River Kwai Bridge Week celebrates the bridge made famous by the movie. Events include a light-and-sound show at the bridge in Kanchanaburi.

Phuket King's Cup Regatta features long-distance yacht racing from Nai Harn Bay with entrants from around the world.

IMPORTANT CONTACTS

*F*OREIGN EMBASSIES AND THEIR PHONE NUMBERS

- ◆ Australia   212-5853-4
- ◆ Burma/Myanmar   234-4698
- ◆ Canada   238-4452
- ◆ China   245-7032
- ◆ France   285-6104-7
- ◆ Germany   2132331-6
- ◆ India   2580300-6
- ◆ Israel   260-4854-9
- ◆ Italy   85-4090-3
- ◆ Japan   252-6151-9
- ◆ Laos   539-6667-8
- ◆ Malaysia   254-1700-5
- ◆ Nepal   391-7240
- ◆ UK   253-0191-9
- ◆ USA   252-5040-9

*T*OURISM AUTHORITY OF THAILAND OFFICES

Tourism Authority of Thailand (TAT)
Tourist Assistance Center
4 Ratchadamnoen Nok Avenue
Bangkok 10100

Tel: 281-5051 or 282-8129
Fax: 280-1998

TAT Airport Office
Arrival Lounge
Bangkok International Airport
Tel: 523-8972 or 523-8973

Other TAT offices:

- Cha-am: (032) 471502
- Chiang Mai: (053) 248604
- Chiang Rai: (053) 717433
- Hat Yai: (074) 243747
- Kanchanaburi: (034) 511200
- Khon Kaen: (043) 244498
- Nakhon Ratchasima: (044) 243751
- Nakhon Si Thammarat: (075) 356356
- Pattaya: (038) 42870
- Phitsanulok: (055) 252742
- Phuket: (076) 211036
- Surat Thani: (077) 281828
- Ubon Ratchathani: (045) 243770

ACTIVITIES

𝒻IFTEEN FUN THINGS TO DO ─────────────────

Bangkok

- Sit at an outdoor cafe in Patpong and watch the parade of humanity, everything from fat, over-dressed tourists to slinky, skinny, skimpily-clad "bar" girls; when tired, turn your attention to the mounted TV usually showing badly-acted but action-filled Hollywood films starring macho men (weighed down with even more macho machinery) such as Bruce Willis, Sylvester Stallone, and Steven Segal.

- Morning or afternoon, Lumpini Park is a window on Bangkokians enjoying themselves in unguarded moments. In the morning, watch swordsmen practicing an ancient Chinese art, boaters in the lake, and tai chi practitioners. In the evening, watch kite flyers, picnickers, and soccer players.

- Take an express boat to the market town of Nonthaburi on the northern edge of Bangkok. A bargain ride that takes you past city landmarks and into the countryside to observe life along the river.

- The train to Samut Songkhram leaves the Wongwian Yai station in Thonburi and heads through farmlands to Samut Sakhon. Disembark, cross the river on a ferry boat, and pick up the train for the remainder of the journey to the fishing port of Samut Songkhram. When you've had your fill, take the same route back.

- At the Bird Market behind the city wall at the intersection of Ratchadamnoen and Mahachai Roads, you'll see the warblers that fetch prices up to $4,000, plus their gilded cages.

- Chatuchak Park, Bangkok's weekend market, is so varied, and everchanging that, like many Bangkok residents, you could go there weekend after weekend and still find something new. Antiques, pets, art pieces, exotic foods, jungle plants, and dozens of other types of items sell for bargain prices.

- To learn the future, consult the astrologers on Ratchadamnoen Road opposite the open field called Sanam Luang and in front of the Justice Ministry. Astrologers will use numerology to predict your future or will rely on a small bird to pick a card on which your destiny is written.

- Snakes give most people the frights but few visitors to the Snake Farm leave without having learned a great deal about a fascinating animal. On Rama IV, the Farm—the second oldest in the world—prepares anti-venom serum by milking cobras and other deadly serpents. You get to watch.

- Buy a funeral shirt. Walk Soi Issaranuphap from the river to Wat Hong Kong through the heart of Chinatown. You'll pass spice stores, artisans making Chinese lanterns, and shops selling incense sticks eight-feet tall and shirts made of paper which are burned to be sent to departed ancestors.

THE NEXT STEP

- Master the art of Thai cooking at the Oriental Cooking School operated by the Oriental Hotel. Take the complete five-day course or choose the types of dishes you want to prepare and take one-day courses devoted to them. Tel: 236-0420, 236-0400.
- Soothe tired muscles with a traditional Thai massage at the herbal medicine school of Wat Po, located behind the Grand Palace.

Chiang Mai

- Ride an elephant and take a raft down the Ping River. At the Chiang Dao Elephant Camp, 58 km. north of Chiang Mai, watch elephants demonstrate how they move gigantic teak logs in the forests, then take a ride on one. Finally, float down the Ping River on a bamboo raft.
- Wander the Night Market. The Chang Klan Night Market offers a wealth of interesting shopping but it is for its ambience that visitors flock to it. Watch while an artist paints flowers and your name on your camera or beltbag.

Phuket

- Safari to the interior. Most people go to Phuket for the beaches. Tour companies take the traveler to discover tropical splendor in its jungles.
- Tap a tree. Awaken early for this one; a chance to watch how farmers tap rubber trees for the latex that may someday become the tires on your car.

National Parks/Conservation Areas

Thirteen percent of Thailand's land and sea area is covered by national and marine parks, making it one of the highest ratios of protected to unprotected areas of any nation in the world. There are 80 national parks in Thailand and that number is expected to grow to over 100 by the turn of the century. Here are some of the top parks and estuaries:

- Kaeng Krajarn National Park, located in Phetchaburi Province along the Burmese border, is the largest and least explored park in Thailand.
- Doi Inthanon National Park near Chiang Mai holds the country's highest peak. The surrounding area is one of the top destinations in Southeast Asia for naturalists and bird watchers.

- Thung Salaeng Luang Wildlife Sanctuary is home to the Siamese fireback pheasant. It is located on Highway 12 between Phitsanuloke and Lomsak, also known as the scenic "gateway" to Northeastern Thailand.
- Khao Yai National Park, Thailand's oldest and most diverse national park, is located in Nakhon Ratchasima Province.
- Nam Nao National Park, adjacent to the Phu Khiew Wildlife Sanctuary, is in Loei Province.
- Phu Kradung National Park, a Thai favorite, is located atop a plateau in Loei Province.
- Khao Sok National Park, connected to the Khlong Sean Wildlife Sanctuary, is in the western part of Surat Thani Province between Takua Pa and Surat Thani. It is home to the bua phut, or wild lotus.
- Similan Islands National Marine Park, off Phuket in the Andaman Sea, is a world-renowned diving destination.

ADDITIONAL RESOURCES

*T*HAILAND ONLINE

There are numerous Thailand resources on the Internet. Point your browser to the following sites:

- Asia One: http://www.asia1.com.sg/travel/thailand/thai.html
- Asia Times: http://www.asiaaccess.net.th/mgrnet/mgr/asiatime
- Asia Web: http://www.pixad.com/directory
- Active Lifestyle: http://www.activelifestyle.com/thailand/bangkok.travel.html
- Bangkok Net: http://www.bangkoknet.com/index.html
- Bangkok Post: http://www.bangkokpost.net/
- CityNet: http://www.city.net/countries/thailand
- Geo Cities: http://www.geocities.com/RainForest/4225/index.html
- Hmpge. Collctns: http://www.rpi.edu/~bholsw/collection.html
- Info Hub: http://www.infohub.com/TRAVEL/TRAVELLER/ASIA/thailand.html

THE NEXT STEP

- Lonely Planet: http://www.lonelyplanet.com.au/dest/sea/thai.htm
- Mahidol University: http://www.mahidol.ac.th/Thailand/Thailand-main.html
- Mnstry of Frgn. Affrs: http://www.mfa.go.th
- The Nation newspaper: http://www.nationmultimedia.com/
- Siam Guide: http://www.siam.net/guide/index.html
- State Department: http://travel.state.gov/thailand.html
- Sunsite Thailand: http://sunsite.au.ac.th/ThaiInfo/TourismInThailand/index.html
- TAT: http://www.tat.or.th/
- Thai Airways Intl.: http://www.thaiair.com/
- Thailand: http://www.cs.rochester.edu/users/grads/edyamp/thai.html
- Thailand Connection: http://www.cris.com/~chuwait/thai/shtml
- Thailand Online: http://www.thailine.com/
- Thailand: http://www.nectec.or.th/bureaux/index.html
- Thailand: http://www.nectec.or.th/WWW-VL-Thailand.html
- Travel Guide: http://www.sawadee.com/
- Welcome to Phuket: http://www.phuket.com/index.html

GIVING BACK

There is a lot to be gained by traveling in Thailand, and many people are moved to support good causes once they've returned home. A few organizations that do good work and could use contributions are:

CARE. The Thailand office originally opened in 1979 to provide emergency relief in the form of food, clothing and medical assistance to Cambodian refugees in camps along the Thai-Cambodian border. Now, CARE-Thailand supports projects in agro–forestry and conservation, children's education, small enterprise development and HIV/AIDS prevention education. To make a donation, write or call: CARE 151 Ellis Street NE Atlanta, Georgia 30303-2439; 1-800-521-CARE ext. 999, Outside the US., call 404 681-2552. CARE also accepts donated Delta Skymiles, call 1-800-422-7385, for more information.

The Human Development Center (HDC) began as a single Kindergarten in the Bangkok slum Klong Toey. Twenty five years and 55,000 kids later, HDC has grown into a model program for grassroots community development. Programs have expanded to include 32 schools, an adult vocational program, an AIDS hospice, social work outreach, shelter for homeless boys and girls, soccer league, credit union, and plans for a legal aid clinic. For more information and to make donations, contact: The Human Development Center 3757/15 Sukhumvit Soi 40, Phrakanong, Bangkok 10110, Thailand http://www.inet.co.th/org/hdc/

The Nature Shop, 220/15 Soi Phadipat 18, Paholyothin Rd., Bangkok 10400. Tel: 279-6533, 270-0478. Operated by the Friends of Women Foundation, the shop sells clothing, jewelry, herbal lotions, and other items made by homeless and former victims of domestic violence. Also herbal saunas and massages. Ask about their other activities in which you can become involved.

The Wild Animal Rescue Foundation of Thailand runs several sanctuaries which care for injured, ill, maltreated, and orphaned wildlife. They work with the international wildlife charity "Care for the Wild," and accept donations. For more information, contact 29/2 Soi 33, Sukhumvit Rd., Bangkok 10110, Thailand. Tel: 258-5560, Fax: 261-0952.

To minimize the impact of tourism on Thailand, visitors should avoid restaurants serving "exotic" (i.e. endangered) wildlife species. If you encounter these restaurants, please write a letter of complaint to the Tourism Authority of Thailand, the Wildlife Fund Thailand, and the Forestry Department at these addresses:

Tourism Authority of Thailand
372 Bamrung Muang Rd.
Bangkok 10100

Wildlife Fund Thailand
251/88-90 Phaholyothin Rd, Bang Khen,
Bangkok 10220

*C*HE NEXT STEP

Royal Forestry Department
61 Phaholyothin Rd, Bang Khen
Bangkok 10330

RECOMMENDED READING

We hope *Travelers' Tales Thailand* has inspired you to read on. A good place to start is the books from which we've made selections, and we have listed them below.

Bhumichitr, Vatcharin. *A Taste of Thailand*. London: Pavilion Books, New York: Macmillan Publishing Company, 1988.

Buckley, Michael. *Bangkok Handbook*. Chico, California: Moon Publications, 1995.

Buruma, Ian. *God's Dust*. New York: Farrar, Strauss & Giroux, Inc. 1989, London: Jonathan Cape, 1989.

Cummings, Joe. *The Meditation Temples of Thailand: A Guide*. Concord, California: Wayfarer Books, 1990.

Cummings, Joe. *Thailand - a travel survival kit*. Victoria, Australia: Lonely Planet, 1997.

Devine, Elizabeth and Nancy L. Braganti. *The Travelers' Guide to Asian Customs and Manners*. New York: St. Martin's Press, 1986.

Fodor's Exploring Thailand. New York: Fodor's Travel Publications, 1993.

Frommer's Thailand. New York: Macmillan, 1997.

Gault Millau: The Best of Thailand. New York: Prentice Hall Press, 1991.

Gray, Paul. *Thailand: The Rough Guide*. London: Rough Guides, 1995.

Great Journeys. New York: Simon and Schuster, 1990, London: BBC Books, 1990.

Hamilton-Merritt, Jane. *A Meditator's Diary*. New York: Harper Collins, 1976.

Harris, Marvin. *The Sacred Cow and the Abominable Pig*. New York: Simon & Schuster, 1985.

Hollinger, Carol. *Mai Pen Rai Means Never Mind*. Boston: Houghton Mifflin, 1965.

Iyer, Pico. *Video Night in Kathmandu*. New York: Random House, 1988.

Kelly, Brian and Mark London. *The Four Little Dragons*. New York: Simon & Schuster, 1989.

Kusy, Frank. *Cadogan Guides: Thailand*. London: Cadogan Books, Connecticut: Globe Pequot Press, 1991.

Let's Go. The Budget Guide to Thailand. New York: St. Martin's Press, 1994.

Lewis, Paul and Elaine. *Peoples of the Golden Triangle*. London: Thames and Hudson, 1984.

McNeely, Jeffrey A. and Paul Spencer Wachtel. *Soul of the Tiger*. New York: Paragon House, 1988.

Mills, James. *The Underground Empire: Where Crime and Governments Embrace*. New York: Doubleday, 1986.

Newman, Steven M. *Worldwalk: One Man's Four-Year Journey Around the World*. New York: Avon, 1989.

Nicholl, Charles. *Borderlines: A Journey in Thailand and Burma*. London and New York: Viking Penguin, 1989, London, Pan, 1989.

Osborne, Christine. *Essential Thailand*. Lincolnwood, Illinois: Passport Books, 1994.

Parkes, Carl. *Thailand Handbook*. Chico, California: Moon Publications, 1997.

Rabinowtiz, Alan. *Chasing the Dragon's Tail: The Struggle to Save Thailand's Wild Cats*. New York: Doubleday, 1991.

Rajadhon, Phya Anuman. *Some Traditions of The Thai*. Bangkok: Thai Inter-Religious Committee for Development and Sathirakoses Nagapradipi Foundation, 1987.

Ross, Nancy Wilson. *Three Ways of Asian Wisdom: Hinduism, Buddhism, Zen and Their Significance for the West*. New York: Simon & Schuster, 1966.

Rutledge, Len. *Maverick Guide to Thailand*. Gretna, Louisiana: Pelican Publishing, 1993.

Savage, Barbara. *Miles From Nowhere: A Round-the-World Bicycle Adventure.* Seattle: The Mountaineers, 1983.

Segaller, Denis. *Thai Ways.* Bangkok: Post Books, 1989 and 1993.

Steves, Rick and Bob Effertz. *Asia Through the Back Door.* Santa Fe, New Mexico: John Muir Publications, 1993.

Stier, Wayne and Mars Cavers. *Wide Eyes in Burma and Thailand: Finding Your Way.* Captain Cook, Hawaii: Meru Publishing, 1983.

Tambiah, S. J. *Buddhism and the Spirit Cults of North-East Asia.* London: Cambridge University Press, 1970.

Valli, Eric and Diane Summers. *Shadow Hunters: Nest Gatherers of Tiger Cave.* Charlottesville, Virginia: Thomasson-Grant, 1990.

Van Beek, Steve. *Insight Guides: Thailand.* Boston: APA, Houghton Mifflin, 1991.

Van Beek, Steve and Vilas Manivat. *Kukrit Pramoj: His Wit and Wisdom.* Bangkok: Editions Duang Kamol, 1983.

Ward, Tim. *The Great Dragon's Fleas.* Berkeley: Celestial Arts, 1993.

Ward, Tim. *What the Buddha Never Taught.* Berkeley: Celestial Arts, 1993.

Warren, William. *Thailand, Seven Days in the Kingdom.* Singapore: Times Editions, 1987.

Wilde, Henry, M.D., Supwawat Chutivongse, M.D. and Burnett Q. Pixley, M.D. *Guide to Healthy Living in Thailand.* Bangkok: Science Division of the Thai Red Cross Society and Faculty of Medicine, Chulakklongkorn University, 1990.

Winchester, Simon. *Pacific Rising.* New York: Simon & Schuster, 1991.

Zepatos, Thalia. *A Journey of One's Own: Uncommon Advice for the Independent Woman Traveler.* Portland, Oregon: Eighth Mountain Press, 1992.

Glossary

ajahn	teacher, guru
alms	donation of food or money, in the name of Buddha, to gain merit
arahant	a monk who has gained enlightenment
baht	Thai unit of currency
bhikkhu	a devotee (male), a monk
bhikkhuni	female monk
bindabhat	monks' daily alms round for food
buri	town
cha yen	sweet Thai iced tea served with milk
chandu	pure opium used for smoking
chedi	pagoda-like ornamental spire on a Buddhist temple
chiang	town or city
dhamma, dharma	truth of Buddha, law and teachings of Buddha
farang	foreigner
guti, kuti	small one-room hut where a forest monk lives
han nam	pitcher of water found outside of a Thai house
huai	river
jaan	entrance platform/veranda of a house
khwan	the spirit inside us
klong	canal
ko, koh	island

Loi Kratong	Festival of Lights
mahout	elephant trainer
maichee	Buddhist nun
mai pen rai	never mind
mee grob	Thai national dish of fried noodles
muang	town or city
muay Thai	Thai boxing
naga	mythical serpent with dragon's head
Pali	Sanskrit-derived language of Theravada Buddhist texts
pacomah, phakhamaa	short all-purpose cotton wraparound; type of clothing
puang malai	garland of flowers
rai	traditional Thai unit of land, about ⅖ of an acre
sala	main temple of a monastery
samlor	pedicab
sangha	the community of Buddhist monks
sanuk	fun
sate, satay	skewered, grilled meat
sawatdi khrap	traditional Thai greeting
soi	lane or alley
song	spirit medium
Songkran	Thai new year
songthaew	small, covered pickup truck that is used for passengers in rural Thailand
takraw	volleyball played with the feet
tham	cave

Theravada	the old school of Buddhism, practiced in Thailand
tuk-tuk	motorized three-wheeled taxi
Vinaya	2000-year-old rulebook of the Theravada doctrine; code of conduct for Buddhists
wai	gesture of respect and greeting
wat	Buddhist temple and grounds`
yaam	hill tribe shoulder bag

Index

Index of Contributors

452

Acknowledgements

Heartfelt thanks to Tim O'Reilly for having the idea and making it happen, Wenda Brewster O'Reilly and Paula Mc Cabe for life-support systems, Susan Brady for so many things we can't even remember them all, Raj Khadka for his early work and enthusiasm, Serm Phenjati and Kathy Baumgartner of Thai Airways in San Francisco for their help with research, Peter Mui for his criticism, Joe Cummings for his discerning manuscript commentary and contribution of Thai proverbs, Edie Freedman and Jennifer Niederst for their spirited artistic involvement, Anna, Noelle and Mary O'Reilly for their patience and good humor, Maureen Sullivan Kravitz for being a true friend, Bob Geldof for his interest and courtesy, and Rich Paoli for helping us hit the road. Thanks also to Michael Buckley, Jeff Greenwald, Susan Fulop Kepner, Carl Parkes, and Steve Van Beek for help towards the end. Finally, a special thank you to all the storytellers whose words are this book. Long may you wander.

"Sixth Sense" by Robert Sam Anson reprinted from *Condé Nast Traveler*, June 1988. Reprinted by permission of Condé Nast Publications, Inc. and the author. Copyright © 1988 by Robert Sam Anson.

"Monk for a Month" by Timothy Fall reprinted from *Great Expeditions*, May/June 1991. Reprinted by permission of *Great Expeditions* and the author. Copyright © 1991 by Timothy Fall.

"Love in a Duty-free Zone" by Pico Iyer reprinted from *Video Night in Kathmandu* by Pico Iyer. Copyright © 1988 by Pico Iyer. Reprinted by permission of Alfred A. Knopf, Inc.

"The Secrets of Tham Krabok" by Michael Buckley reprinted from *Great Expeditions*, Winter 1991/1992. Reprinted by permission of *Great Expeditions* and the author. Copyright © 1991 by Michael Buckley.

"Moonsong and Martin Luther," "Mekong Days" and "Poppy Fields" by Charles Nicholl reprinted from *Borderlines: A Journey in Thailand and Burma* by Charles Nicholl. Copyright © 1988 by Charles Nicholl. Used by permission of Viking Penguin, a division of Penguin Books USA Inc., and Pan (U.K).

"To Eat Means To Eat Rice," "Elephant Scream," "Echo of the Forest," "Tapir Tracks," "A German Monk" and "Wildlife Abuse" by Alan Rabinowitz excerpted from *Chasing the Dragon's Tail: The Struggle to Save Thailand's Wild Cats* by Alan Rabinowitz. Copyright © 1991 by Alan Rabinowitz. Used by permission of Doubleday, a division of Bantam Doubleday Dell Publishing Group, Inc., and the William Morris Agency.

"The Reverend Goes to Dinner" by Kukrit Pramoj excerpted from *Kukrit Pramoj: His Wit and Wisdom*, compiled by Vilas Manivat, edited by Steve Van Beek. Reprinted by permission of Steve Van Beek and Editions Duang Kamol, Bangkok. Copyright © 1983 by Kukrit Pramoj.

"Ghosts of Siam" by Norman Lewis was first published as "Siam" in *Granta*, Edition #26, Spring 1989, and subsequently appeared in *To Run Across the Sea* by Norman Lewis, published by Jonathan Cape Ltd. Copyright © 1989 by Norman Lewis. Reprinted by permission of Rogers, Coleridge & White Ltd.

"Meditation in a Thai Forest" by John Calderazzo reprinted from *Audubon*, January 1991. Reprinted by permission of *Audubon* and the author. Copyright © 1991 by John Calderazzo.

"Island Entrepreneur" by Joe Cummings published with permission from the author. Copyright © 1993 by Joe Cummings.

"Who Was Anna Leonowens?" by William Warren reprinted from *Sawasdee*, the inflight magazine of Thai Airways International, February 1992. Reprinted by permission of *Sawasdee* and the author. Copyright © 1992 by William Warren.

"Where the Footnotes Went" by Carol Hollinger reprinted from *Mai Pen Rai Means Never Mind* by Carol Hollinger. Copyright © 1965 by Houghton Mifflin Company and Carol Hollinger. Reprinted by permission of Houghton Mifflin Company and Curtis Brown, Ltd. All rights reserved.

"Lure of the Chao Phraya" by Thurston Clarke reprinted from *Travel Holiday*, November 1991. Reprinted by permission of *Travel Holiday* and the author. Copyright © 1991 by Thurston Clarke.

"Siriraj Hospital Museum" by Gena Reisner reprinted from *Relax*, November 1990. Reprinted by permission of *Relax* and the author. Copyright © 1990 by Gena Reisner.

"Bite-sized Buddhas" by Jeff Greenwald published with permission from the author. Copyright © 1993 by Jeff Greenwald.

"A Cooking School in Bangkok" by Kemp M. Minifie reprinted from *Gourmet Magazine*, November 1988. Reprinted by permission of *Gourmet Magazine* and the author. Copyright © 1988 by *Gourmet Magazine*.

"*Wat* Massage" by Anthony Weller reprinted from the September 1991 issue of *GQ*, Reprinted by permission of Condé Nast Publications, Inc. and the author. Copyright © 1991 by Anthony Weller.

"Paradise Found, Paradise Lost" by Pico Iyer was originally published as "Indian Summer of Love" in *Islands*, January/February 1991. Reprinted by permission of *Islands*. Copyright © 1991 by *Islands*.

"The Alms Bowl Village" by John Hoskin reprinted from *Sawasdee*, the inflight magazine of Thai Airways International, March 1989. Reprinted by permission of *Sawasdee* and the author. Copyright © 1989 by John Hoskin.

"In the Dark" by Joel Simon reprinted by permission of the author. Copyright © 1993 by Joel Simon.

"A Meditator's Initiation" by Jane Hamilton-Merritt reprinted from *A Meditator's Diary* by Jane Hamilton-Merritt. Reprinted by permission of Souvenir Press Ltd., London. Copyright © 1976 by Souvenir Press Ltd., London, £8.95.

"In the Akha Village" by Thalia Zepatos reprinted from *A Journey of One's Own: Uncommon Advice for the Independent Woman Traveler* by Thalia Zepatos. Reprinted by permission of Eighth Mountain Press, Portland, Oregon. Copyright © 1992 by Thalia Zepatos.

"Sin, the Buffalo Man" by Steve Van Beek reprinted by permission of the author. Copyright © 1993 by Steve Van Beek.

"Could This Really Be the End?" by Barbara Savage excerpted from *Miles From Nowhere: A Round-the-World Bicycle Adventure,* by Barbara Savage, published by The Mountaineers, Seattle. Copyright © 1983.

"Thai and Dry" by Gayle Detweiler reprinted from *Runner's World*, August 1992. Reprinted by permission of *Runner's World*. Copyright © 1992, Rodale Press, Inc., all rights reserved.

"Under the Golden Triangle" by John Spies reprinted from *Sawasdee*, the inflight magazine of Thai Airways International, March 1987. Copyright © 1987 by John Spies. Reprinted by permission of *Sawasdee* and the author.

"Dark World Of Gourmet Soup" by Diane Summers reprinted from *International Wildlife*, January/February 1992. Reprinted by permission of the National Wildlife Federation. Copyright © 1992 by the National Wildlife Federation.

"Fooling Yourself for Fun" by Ian Buruma excerpted from *God's Dust* by Ian Buruma. Reprinted by permission of Farrar, Straus, & Giroux, Inc., and Jonathan Cape. Copyright © 1989 by Ian Buruma.

"After the Night of the Generals" by Pratya Sawetvimon reprinted from *Asiaweek*, July 31, 1992. Reprinted by permission of Asiaweek Ltd. Copyright © 1992 by Asiaweek Ltd.

"By the Sea" by Vatcharin Bhumichitr reprinted with the permission of Atheneum Publishers, an imprint of Macmillan Publishing Company, from *A Taste of Thailand* by Vatcharin Bhumichitr. Copyright © 1988 by Vatcharin Bhumichitr. Reprinted by permission of Vatcharin Bhumichitr and Pavilion Books.

Additional Credits (arranged alphabetically by title)

Selection from "An Island Between Two Worlds" by Tristan Jones reprinted from *Cruising World*, July 1988. Copyright © 1988 by Tristan Jones.

Selections from "The Arcane Power of Amulets" by Michael Buckley reprinted by permission of the author. Copyright © 1993 by Michael Buckley.

Selections from *Bangkok Handbook* by Michael Buckley reprinted by permission of Moon Publications and the author. Copyright © 1992 by Michael Buckley.

Selections reprinted from *Borderlines: A Journey in Thailand and Burma* by Charles Nicholl. Copyright © 1988 by Charles Nicholl. Used by permission of Viking Penguin, a division of Penguin Books USA Inc., and Pan (U.K.).

permission of Souvenir Press Ltd., London. Copyright © 1976 by Souvenir Press Ltd., London, £8.95.

Selections from "The Mekong" by Thomas O'Neill reprinted from *National Geographic*, February 1993, by permission of the National Geographic Society. Copyright © 1993 by the National Geographic Society.

Selections from *Peoples of the Golden Triangle* by Paul and Elaine Lewis reprinted by permission of the publisher, Thames and Hudson. Copyright © 1984 by Paul and Elaine Lewis.

Selections from *The Rough Guide Thailand* (formerly *The Real Guide Thailand* in the U.S.A.) by Paul Gray and Lucy Ridout used by permission of Prentice Hall Travel/a Division of Simon & Schuster. Copyright © 1992 by Paul Gray and Lucy Ridout.

Selections from "Royal Family Thais" by Richard West reprinted with permission from *The New York Review of Books*. Copyright © 1992 Nyrev, Inc.

Selection reprinted with the permission of Simon & Schuster, Inc. from *The Sacred Cow and the Abominable Pig* by Marvin Harris. Copyright © 1985 by Marvin Harris.

Selections from *Sawasdee*, the inflight magazine of Thai Airways International, reprinted with permission. Copyright © 1987 by *Sawasdee*.

Selections reprinted from *Some Traditions of the Thai* by Phya Anuman Rajadhon. Copyright © 1987 by the Thai Inter-Religious Commission for Development and Sathirakoses Nagapradipa Foundation.

Selections from the book *Soul of the Tiger* by Jeffrey A. McNeely and Paul Spencer Wachtel. Copyright © 1990 by Paragon House Publishers. Reprinted with permission of Paragon House Publishers.

Selections from *Thailand - a travel survival kit* by Joe Cummings reprinted by permission of Lonely Planet Publications and the author. Copyright © 1992 by Lonely Planet.

Selections from *Thailand Handbook* by Carl Parkes reprinted by permission of Moon Publications and the author. Copyright © 1992 by Carl Parkes.

Selections from *Thailand - Seven Days in the Kingdom* by William Warren reprinted by permission of the author. Copyright © 1987 by William Warren.

Selection from "Thai Spirit Houses" by Sheila Tefft reprinted by permission from *The Christian Science Monitor*, June 28, 1991. Copyright © 1991 The Christian Science Publishing Society. All rights reserved.

Selections from "Thai Waterways" by Peter Aiken reprinted by permission of the author. Copyright © 1993 by Peter Aiken.

Selections from *Thai Ways* by Denis Segaller reprinted by permission of Post Books. Copyright © 1989, 1993 by The Post Publishing Co., Ltd.

Selections reprinted with the permission of Simon & Schuster, Inc. from *Three Ways of Asian Wisdom* by Nancy Wilson Ross. Copyright © 1966 by Nancy Wilson Ross.

Selections from *The Travelers' Guide to Asian Customs and Manners* by Elizabeth Devine and Nancy L. Braganti reprinted by permission of St. Martin's Press.

About the Editors

James O'Reilly and Larry Habegger first worked together as late night disc jockeys at Dartmouth College in New Hampshire. They wrote mystery serials for the San Francisco Examiner in the early 1980s before turning to travel writing. Since 1983, their travel features and self-syndicated column, "World Travel Watch," have appeared in magazines and newspapers in the United States and other countries. James was born in Oxford, England, raised in San Francisco, and lives with his family in Leavenworth, Washington and France; Larry was born and raised in Minnesota and lives on Telegraph Hill in San Francisco.

TRAVELERS' TALES GUIDES

LOOK FOR THESE TITLES IN THE SERIES

FOOTSTEPS: THE SOUL OF TRAVEL
A NEW IMPRINT FROM TRAVELERS' TALES GUIDES

An imprint of Travelers' Tales Guides, the Footsteps series unveils new works by first-time authors, established writers, and reprints of works whose time has come…again. Each book will fire your imagination, disturb your sleep, and feed your soul.

KITE STRINGS OF THE SOUTHERN CROSS
A Woman's Travel Odyssey
By Laurie Gough
ISBN 1-885211-30-9, 400 pages, $24.00, hardcover
A TRAVELERS' TALES FOOTSTEPS BOOK

✐PECIAL INTEREST

THE PENNY PINCHER'S PASSPORT TO LUXURY TRAVEL
The Art of Cultivating Preferred Customer Status
By Joel L. Widzer
ISBN 1-885211-31-7, 253 pages, $12.95

DANGER!
Ttue Stories of Trouble and Survival
Edited by James O'Reilly, Larry Habegger, & Sean O'Reilly
ISBN 1-885211-32-5, 336 pages, $17.95

Check with your local bookstore for these titles
or call O'Reilly to order:
800-998-9938 (credit cards only—weekdays 6AM–5PM PST)
707-829-0515, or email: order@oreilly.com

$\mathscr{S}$PECIAL INTEREST

FAMILY TRAVEL:
The Farther You Go, the Closer You Get
Edited by Laura Manske
ISBN 1-885211-33-3, 375 pages, $17.95

THE GIFT OF TRAVEL:
The Best of Travelers' Tales
Edited by Larry Habegger, James O'Reilly & Sean O'Reilly
ISBN 1-885211-25-2, 240 pages, $14.95

THERE'S NO TOILET PAPER ON THE ROAD LESS TRAVELED:
The Best of Travel Humor and Misadventure
Edited by Doug Lansky
ISBN 1-885211-27-9, 207 pages, $12.95

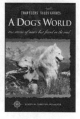

A DOG'S WORLD:
True Stories of Man's Best Friend on the Road
Edited by Christine Hunsicker
ISBN 1-885211-23-6, 257 pages, $12.95

$\mathscr{W}$OMEN'S TRAVEL

SAFETY AND SECURITY FOR WOMEN WHO TRAVEL
By Sheila Swan & Peter Laufer
ISBN 1-885211-29-5, 159 pages, $12.95

*W*OMEN'S TRAVEL

WOMEN IN THE WILD:
True Stories of Adventure and Connection
Edited by Lucy McCauley
ISBN 1-885211-21-X, 307 pages, $17.95

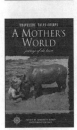

A MOTHER'S WORLD:
Journeys of the Heart
Edited by Marybeth Bond & Pamela Michael
ISBN 1-885211-26-0, 233 pages, $14.95

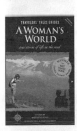

———— ★ ★ ★ ————
*Winner of the Lowell
Thomas Award for Best
Travel Book – Society of
American Travel Writers*

A WOMAN'S WORLD:
True Stories of Life on the Road
Edited by Marybeth Bond
Introduction by Dervla Murphy
ISBN 1-885211-06-6
475 pages, $17.95

GUTSY WOMEN:
Travel Tips and Wisdom for the Road
By Marybeth Bond
ISBN 1-885211-15-5, 123 pages, $7.95

GUTSY MAMAS:
Travel Tips and Wisdom for
Mothers on the Road
By Marybeth Bond
ISBN 1-885211-20-1, 139 pages, $7.95

ℬODY & SOUL

THE ROAD WITHIN:
True Stories of Transformation and the Soul
Edited by Sean O'Reilly, James O'Reilly & Tim O'Reilly
ISBN 1-885211-19-8, 459 pages, $17.95

—★ ★ ★—
Small Press Book Award Winner and Benjamin Franklin Award Finalist

LOVE & ROMANCE:
True Stories of Passion on the Road
Edited by Judith Babcock Wylie
ISBN 1-885211-18-X, 319 pages, $17.95

FOOD:
A Taste of the Road
Edited by Richard Sterling
Introduction by Margo True
ISBN 1-885211-09-0
467 pages, $17.95

—★ ★ ★—
Silver Medal Winner of the Lowell Thomas Award for Best Travel Book – Society of American Travel Writers

THE FEARLESS DINER:
Travel Tips and Wisdom for Eating around the World
By Richard Sterling
ISBN 1-885211-22-8, 139 pages, $7.95

$\mathscr{C}$OUNTRY GUIDES

AMERICA
Edited by Fred Setterberg
ISBN 1-885211-28-7, 550 pages, $19.95

JAPAN
Edited by Donald W. George
& Amy Greimann Carlson
ISBN 1-885211-04-X, 437 pages, $17.95

ITALY
Edited by Anne Calcagno
Introduction by Jan Morris
ISBN 1-885211-16-3, 463 pages, $17.95

INDIA
Edited by James O'Reilly & Larry Habegger
ISBN 1-885211-01-5, 538 pages, $17.95

FRANCE
Edited by James O'Reilly, Larry Habegger
& Sean O'Reilly
ISBN 1-885211-02-3, 517 pages, $17.95

COUNTRY GUIDES

MEXICO
Edited by James O'Reilly & Larry Habegger
ISBN 1-885211-00-7, 463 pages, $17.95

THAILAND
Edited by James O'Reilly
& Larry Habegger
ISBN 1-885211-05-8
483 pages, $17.95

———⋆ ✶ ⋆———
Winner of the Lowell
Thomas Award for Best
Travel Book – Society of
American Travel Writers

SPAIN
Edited by Lucy McCauley
ISBN 1-885211-07-4, 495 pages, $17.95

NEPAL
Edited by Rajendra S. Khadka
ISBN 1-885211-14-7, 423 pages, $17.95

BRAZIL
Edited by Annette Haddad & Scott Doggett
Introduction by Alex Shoumatoff
ISBN 1-885211-11-2
452 pages, $17.95

——⋆ ✶ ⋆——
Benjamin Franklin
Award Winner

ℛEGIONAL GUIDES

HAWAII
True Stories of the Island Spirit
Edited by Rick & Marcie Carroll
ISBN 1-885211-35-X, 375 pages, $17.95

GRAND CANYON
True Stories of Life Below the Rim
Edited by Sean O'Reilly & James O'Reilly
ISBN 1-885211-34-1, 375 pages, $17.95

ℭITY GUIDES

HONG KONG
Edited by James O'Reilly, Larry Habegger & Sean O'Reilly
ISBN 1-885211-03-1, 439 pages, $17.95

PARIS
Edited by James O'Reilly, Larry Habegger & Sean O'Reilly
ISBN 1-885211-10-4, 417 pages, $17.95

SAN FRANCISCO
Edited by James O'Reilly, Larry Habegger & Sean O'Reilly
ISBN 1-885211-08-2, 491 pages, $17.95

Submit Your Own Travel Tale

Do you have a tale of your own that you would like to submit to Travelers' Tales? We highly recommend that you first read one or more of our books to get a feel for the kind of story we're looking for. For submission guidelines and a list of titles in the works, send a SASE to:

Travelers' Tales Submission Guidelines
330 Townsend Street, Suite 208, San Francisco, CA 94107

or send email to *guidelines@travelerstales.com*
or visit our Web site at **www.travelerstales.com**

You can send your story to the address above or via email to *submit@travelerstales.com*. On the outside of the envelope, *please indicate what country/topic your story is about*. If your story is selected for one of our titles, we will contact you about rights and payment.

We hope to hear from you. In the meantime, enjoy the stories!